This Crazy Little Thing Called

LIFE

This Crazy Little Thing Called LIFE

Carolyn Joyce Dodds

Published by Byron Hot Springs www.byronhotsprings.com

ISBN: 979-8-218-00484-2

Library of Congress Control Number: 2022939397

Book cover and interior design: Leigh McLellan Design
Composition: Maureen Forys, Happenstance Type-O-Rama

About the Type: *Text type:* Minion Pro, designed by Robert Slimbach, is
inspired by classical, oldstyle typefaces of the late Renaissance, a period of
elegant, beautiful, and highly readable type designs.
Heads: Hiroshige, designed in 1986 by Cynthia Hollandsworth (now Batty),
was originally commissioned for a book of woodblock prints by the great
nineteenth-century Japanese artist Ando Hiroshige.
Titles and numerals: Chilada is an outrageous display type by designer Patricia
Lillie. The decorative treatment inside Chilada's letters exude an energy of their
own. Big and chunky, Chilada's forms are made up of straight lines only.

This is a work of creative nonfiction. The events are portrayed to the best of
Carolyn Joyce Dodd's memory. While all the stories in this book are true, some
names and identifying details have been changed to protect the privacy of the
people involved.

Printed in the United States of America in compliance with the Lacey Act
by Ingram® Lightning Source®

10 9 8 7 6 5 4 3 2

For general information and reviews, please contact historian@byrohotsprings.com

Disclaimer: All errors and omissions are the responsibility of the publisher

Dedication

This book is dedicated, with so much love, to my sons, Joshua and Benjamin. Without their antics, their perspectives, their triumphs and their losses, none of these stories would be possible. Better than a baby book, I offer each of them this—a collection of memories, as told through the lens of their young mother who held them in her arms, in her mind, and forever in her heart as the two greatest contributions she's ever made to this glorious world. You both have made me who I am, and I love you endlessly.

CONTENTS

Acknowledgments

Thank you to my editor, Carol Jensen, for taking a chance on me, again, and always sprinkling her wisdom and wit into every conversation and instruction. In addition to being astute, she is also pretty amusing. And to June Gomez, my lifelong friend and fellow "wolfie," fellow "goddess," and the best artist I have ever known. Not only has she shared her artistic talent in both of my books, she once altered a beautiful mural of an unknown woman on my patio wall and creatively turned it into a smiling version of myself—something that keeps us in hysterics every time we look at it. Rick Lemyre, the original editor of all of these columns, who after reading the first one, told me in no uncertain terms that I was now considered a syndicated columnist and he expected to see weekly contributions for all 11 of his newspapers. And he held me to that, for eight straight years. His belief in my writing fueled my own. Greg Robinson, the owner of *The Press* newspapers, who, 12 years after my retirement, supported this book and opened a door for more columns to be written in the future. My parents and sister, who generously and unknowingly supplied me with every memory I documented on the pages within. Mom and Dad taught me not only how to use my moral compass, but to find the humor in situations whenever possible. My sister taught me about co-conspirators, sibling rivalry, sharing, keeping secrets and sisterhood in all forms. And to Jim and Lauren Carlson, who came into my life at the perfect time. Jim helped me redefine "family" so many years after these columns were written, and Lauren embraced me as a mom and gave me the opportunity to raise a daughter.

INTRODUCTION

In 2003 my son, Ben, was two years old and diagnosed with myriad medical conditions: cerebral palsy, global developmental delay, and sensory integration dysfunction to name a few. He wasn't walking, he wasn't talking, he wasn't rolling over and his mama was extremely worried. Months spent between UCSF Benioff Children's Hospital, UCSF Medical Center, and Stanford University Medical Center amounted to a laundry list of diagnoses and a robust commitment on my part to learn about each one.

Months of research lead to countless binders of notes. Compiling so much information stoked my inner fire to inform and educate the masses. On a whim, I wrote an article on sensory integration dysfunction and marched into the local newspaper, *The Press*, firmly requesting to see it in print. Whether or not it was my passion, my approach, my quick wit or my fluency in sarcasm which convinced the editor to actually run the piece, we can never be certain. Regardless of reasoning, it went to print and because of the feedback it received, I was asked to submit more. And submit I did. One informative piece after another informative piece was published until the day I accidentally submitted my notes along with the article. My editor perused them just out of pure curiosity.

I was then called in for a meeting. The editor offered me an opportunity to write a weekly column. The request was simple. Write nothing informative, just casual and fun, "like your notes." Panic set in. No more educating? No more advising? No more sharing of resources?

"Be yourself," I was told.

"I trust you," he grinned.

"Go home, and write about life." He patted my back and shooed me out the door.

So, I wrote. Without censorship, without boundaries, without parameters on subjects and topics, I wrote and I wrote and I wrote. And nervously, I submitted.

"You are now a columnist," was his response. "Write more and think of a title."

Instantly, "This Crazy Little Thing Called Life" came to mind. It enveloped the chaos which was my home life, plus it was a nod to Queen and their notorious music. I was a fan. Both of their music and of my tribute to it. The editor approved of my effort to pay homage to a band he admired too. The weekly column was born.

As *The Press* grew in size, the column grew in readership. One newspaper soon became three newspapers, which eventually grew into eight newspapers. Finally, the syndicate included 11 newspapers. This column appeared in every single one.

"You're a syndicated columnist!" my editor bellowed over the phone one sunny Tuesday and soon after, a card of congratulations appeared in my mailbox. As a writer, I had arrived.

Between 2003 and 2011, hundreds of columns appeared in up to 11 newspapers in the San Francisco East Bay Area. I became recognized as a recipient of a coveted award by the National Newspaper Association for "The Best Humorous Column in a Non-daily Newspaper, 12,000 or more" (Chapter 6: Piece of Cake, "Thinking Pink", page 103). All this happened while balancing motherhood, marriage, a social life and writing. I had quite a run.

This book is a collection of more than 200 columns. It is a look into the mind and heart of a young mother raising two sons, one with special needs, long before blogging was a thing. This is a peek into a diary of sorts. *This Crazy Little Thing Called Life* is an uncensored version of perspective, emotion, and a trip down my own memory lane. I am deeply humbled and forever grateful that *The Press* believed that these columns were worth sharing with a growing community.

1

A Barrel of Laughs

Unexpected Dialogue

"**Mom, why do** people shave their bushes?" I almost come to a skidding halt in the car when this question flies forth from the backseat.

"WHAT?"

Josh asks again, "Why does anyone shave their bush? I mean, look at that one," he taps on his window as we round the bend, "That one is shaved like a bird."

"You mean shaped," I correct him. Knowing full well he cannot stand to be laughed at, I clench my jaw in an effort to keep in a flood of giggles and snorts that want desperately to be let out.

"No, I mean SHAVED. Someone did that to them, right?" True. I am at a loss on how to correctly field this question. While I'm thinking of how to answer without hooting, he throws another at me. "Have you ever shaved a bush?"

"Um…noooo," I say slowly, pretending to have to think long and hard about that one, "Not that I can remember." I am thoroughly disappointed that I'm in the car alone with him and no one has heard this line of questioning.

"Well, you should," he tells me, "I bet it's fun and everyone would want to see it when you're done."

I have no answer for him at this point. At least not one in which he would fully grasp the sarcasm. I try to steer the conversation around bush shaving and hope he doesn't see another one shaped more provocatively.

Josh is like this. His spontaneous conversation skills are heightened normally in public, but every once in a while, he will surprise me with humorous inquiries and/or a running commentary on the random bits of trivia that float around in his noggin.

During the holidays he announced to my mother that her pot roast dinner was, "What did you call it, Daddy? Crap?" We skirted the question easily enough, but I later reminded Brad that little rabbits have big ears. He will sometimes repeat what he hears verbatim, other times missing an important detail or two. Usually, he'll just ask the wrong question to the wrong person.

My mother wasn't insulted. In fact, she asked if I recalled asking my godfather during one of his visits if he ever used a douche. I was mortified at the reminder. He was a big burly truck driver, and I was probably seven or so. Having just seen an ad on TV for one, I asked him what specifically a douche was for. After picking up on his discomfort, I was even more curious. "What? Tell me…" I prompted. He muttered they were used for cleaning "things."

"Like what kind of things?"

"Oh," he chuckled nervously, "Just girl stuff."

"Like dishes and clothes?" I really had no idea and found the topic fascinating. My dad sat nearby, fisting a Bud Light, and slapping his knee. Their reaction spurred me on. "Have you ever washed girly things with them too?"

"Enough of this," my mom cut in, "You'll figure it out when you're older." Another age-related topic of discussion I felt I was prematurely excused from.

Josh is silent until we are almost to our destination point. We park next to a tall thin tree, which sits in between two perfectly round hedges at its base. I already know what's about to happen.

"Mom!" Josh sits forward in his car seat, "Those trees look like a…"

"I know!" I cut in sharply. "A rocket ship, right?"

He is quiet. Then says, "Yeah, okay. But I was gonna say a sword."
You just never know.

A Fight, a Lie
and Almost Goodbye

"She's not having it," my friend tells me, "And it's already the third
week." Her daughter has started a new school in a new town and at age
6, the little girl isn't feeling the love from her classmates.

"Oh, give it some time," I tell her, biting into a carrot. "You know
being the new kid is never fun." She's quiet for a second and then says,
"Actually, I don't know. I went to school with all the same kids from the
time I started kindergarten." I struggle to not choke on my carrot. Information like that is unprecedented in this day and age. I kind of figured
that changing schools was about as common as changing underwear for
some people.

"I was the new kid once," I tell her, "And trust me, it was no picnic.
Plus, I almost got suspended for fighting right after I arrived." I hear her
sharp intake of breath and she says, "I didn't know you moved during
high school!"

"High school? No, I was seven! And pretty tough too, if I do say so
myself."

We both start cracking up, only because we know how untrue that
statement is. When my family moved from South San Francisco to Pleasanton in the 1970s, I felt stripped of my friends, my school, and everything I thought comfortable. Rather than have one teacher for all my
subjects, I was tossed into what was termed "The Pod" and made to
partake in the hourly rotation of children and classrooms throughout
the day. It was much like the human version of a cattle herd. During this
rotation one day, I stepped on the back of a shoe of a fellow classmate,
causing her to stumble a bit before regaining her balance. She whipped
around and glared at me. It was an accident. I knew it was an accident,
anyone who saw the situation unfold could easily see I didn't do it on
purpose. The step-ee probably realized my mistake too, in all actuality.

But actuality doesn't carry any weight in third grade. So, after her piercing scowl, she shoved me. Knocked my books out of my arms.

Pride overcame logic. I shoved her back. Hard. Before you could say "Girl fight in Pod 3!" she had me on my back with a pigtail in her fist. I writhed and kicked, howling all the while. I scratched whatever skin I could grasp. I wouldn't go so far as to bite her, but I have an older sister, older cousins. They taught me how to protect myself. I was attempting to roll her over so I could spit on her when strong arms pulled her away from me. Aghast, a teacher escorted us both to the office, lecturing all the way. In third grade, I normally strove be on the good side of authority. I wanted to think of the principal as my 'pal' as the word indicated by its spelling. I was wrong, and being new—I now had the stigma of 'delinquent' hanging above me. I was issued a detention.

Having no priors, I was clueless as to what a detention was so I didn't attend. A phone call home to Mom confirmed my missed punishment and when later questioned, I added "liar" to "delinquent." Fearful of the wrath of Mom, I invented a scenario that had excused me from detention. I was issued a second detention. I missed that one too but another phone call home suggesting my suspension brought my world of illusion to a halt. I knew what suspension was. I fessed up in a hurry.

"Are you kidding me?" my friend is laughing as I regale her with the event.

"I wish I was. Being the new kid is scary, so give Jamie some time."

"I will," she assures me. "And I'll make sure she doesn't step on anyone's shoes."

Nothing wrong with being too careful.

Miss Bee-having

Sadly, I come from one of those families that find humor in one another's suffering. We live by the adage, "It's only funny until someone gets hurt—then it's hilarious." That's not to say we don't empathize, we do—just as a secondary emotion. Initially, we laugh, chortle, giggle, point and then basically make fun of each other before saying anything like, "Are you okay?"

So, when I got a message on my answering machine last week from my dad, I had no plan to call him back that instant until he said, "And well…your mom and I had a run-in with a few bees this weekend, so… uh…call us back if you want to hear how your mom stripped down to nothing on the back deck at the cabin."

Well, who would pass up the opportunity to make that call? Mom, who has a tough enough time saying the word *underpants* without getting embarrassed, would be the last of us to remove her clothing out in public. Not that the back deck at the cabin offers any neighbors a good enough view to take a second glance, but still…the thought of my mom whooping and hollering while tearing off her duds was enough of a visual for me to pick up the phone and get the scoop.

Dad: (snickering) "Ah…you should have seen your mom tearing ass down the side of the cabin. Ha, ha, ha. I can still hear her yelling for help." (He laughs again.)

Mom, who has now picked up the extension to make sure my dad tells the story accurately, interrupts: "I stepped on a *beehive*, Carolyn! Did your father tell you that? Did he tell you I was in a sea of black and yellow?" (Mom tends to favor the dramatic as much as I do.)

Dad: "Whooo boy, she was screaming and carrying on, 'Bill, help me! Help me! I've got a bee in my hair!' She was dancing up and down while the bees were all over her! Heh heh…I told her to RUN for the deck and get her clothes off…" (He sniffs, and I know he's wiping a tear from his eye.)I can actually picture this scene quite well. I don't know if I'm happy or sad that I missed it. "So, then what happened?"

Dad: "Well, your mom had a few bees caught up in her web…"

Mom: "My hair wasn't hair sprayed THAT much, Bill. Just the norm."

I envision Mom's shellacked upsweep alive with activity.

Dad: "Anyway, we got her clothes off and I'll be damned if I could get her boots off without her yelling at me the whole time. I think that's when I got stung all those times."

Mom: (clearly annoyed) "I stepped on a *hive* for Pete's sake! I had bees in my…my…*underwear*. In my *bra*!"

After all was said and done, Mom was stung a whopping 14 times and Dad 4. I can hardly believe this story. The agony of one bee sting is enough to keep me whimpering for hours. They interrupt one another, each giving me details of the story they find humorous, painful, and incredible. My ears perk up when Mom mentions taking a double dose of Children's Benadryl, how it knocked her out.

Mom: "It's true, Carolyn. I was so tired after that. I could hardly walk or talk. I couldn't even..."

"Lift a can of hairspray?" I offer. Dad and I hoot and snort.

Mom: "Oh, you two are really hilarious. For your information I stepped..."

Dad and I: "ON A HIVE...we know!"

This is the kind of sympathy we offer one another in a case like this. Kind of a tough love sort of thing. But hey, like we always say, it's only funny until someone gets hurt, then it's hilarious.

A Picture Says a 1,000 Words

If a picture really says a 1,000 words, then anyone can tell by my childhood school photos that the camera was saying "frightening" 1,000 different ways. When my son brought home his school picture this year, my first thought was, "Adorable." My husband's differed. Later that evening he nudged me and asked, "What's with that look on his face? Didn't they tell him to smile?"

"He *is* smiling," I replied, "See? You can make out his teeth on his bottom lip." We both leaned in closer to have a better look.

"I don't know," said Brad, shaking his head. "I just don't know." Though that was the extent of our conversation, I gave it more thought. My kindergarten and first grade pictures were relatively typical. Big toothless grins, crooked bows in my hair, shoulders held back and chin jutted out with the standard pride of a 6-year-old. Even second grade looked pretty much okay, given the outfit I was wearing. Granted, it was the 70s, so everyone else had collars that enormous too. Third grade is when things started to slide downhill for me, photo wise. It rained on class picture day that year, which explained my soggy blouse. What most people with naturally curly hair already know, I learned that morning: a rainy day is no day for a photo op. My damp mossy curls frizzed around my face, until I patted them down, giving myself a 'do comparable to cotton candy.

Fourth grade was the year of the Gunne Sax Dress. I coveted one of those babies. A friend came through and loaned me a hand-me-down from an older cousin of hers. No matter. I wore it with pride. The front gaped and sagged where I didn't fill it out as well as the cousin, but the smile I am sporting is filled with pleasure for having something name brand, especially on picture day.

Fifth grade marked the beginning of personal expression through fashion for me. Unfortunately, that picture didn't even get framed, let alone displayed, my mother was so embarrassed. The Dorothy Hamill haircut was the fashion in 1982. I had no desire to take part in that rage. I was blond with ringlets, and knew my place among the other fair-haired curly-Q's. The Dorothy Hamill had no business on my head. Mom disagreed, having just gotten the look herself, and was enjoying it so. Ahead of her time, the woman insisted on having a mini-me. It was a sad attempt at beautification on her part; one that ended in me sobbing uncontrollably and her apologizing profusely. She swore never to cut my hair again.

Either way, on picture day I pilfered out a couple barrettes and rushed to clip them in right before my shot was taken. It wasn't until our teacher distributed my big white envelope with the cellophane window that I learned what I had done. Horrified, I saw that a few clumps of excess hair had sprung free from my clips and ballooned out like a crown on top of my head. The photographer had said nothing.

Mom gasped when she saw it and then got angry. She shook the envelope at me. "I can't even send these out Carolyn! What were you thinking?" Perhaps that I could repair the wreckage of a hairdo you inflicted upon me? It was the end of an era for her and I.

Poor mom. If only she knew that the pictures to come in later years would have me smirking through layers of Dusty Rose Blush and Electric Blue Mascara, perhaps she would have been a bit more forgiving of two badly placed hairclips. I'm still unsure why I felt the need to spackle on makeup in the teen years, but I obviously was in a fierce competition with my female peers for both the highest bangs and most colorfully painted face.

Josh's picture is pure beauty, compared to any of mine. In case his dad needs further convincing, I hung Brad's "permed mullet" shot on our fridge to remind him.

A Sign of the Times

Does anybody read posted signs anymore? And when they do, how often are those warnings (Keep Out/Danger) or requests (Please watch children at all times, No Shoes No Shirt No Service) taken note of? I saw a barefoot guy open a door to a downtown shop the other day and traipse on inside. On the door was an enormous board that read 'Shoes Must Be Worn at ALL Times!' Perhaps he missed it, but I doubt it. I felt more as if he ignored it. Especially after he took the time to peruse it, then shrugged and went on inside anyway.

This nonchalance may have spread to reading menus too—possibly only in some crowds though. Unfortunately, the ones I circulate in. I have a friend who, when we go out to eat, doesn't even open the menu—just asks the waitress, "Do you have (insert anything)?" And not just once either, she'll repeatedly ask for varying items, portion sizes, substitutions and special orders. It kills me every time.

"Read your menu!" I flame at her. She'll flick her wrist at me and say, "It's fine, it's fine. They don't mind at all." I'm not entirely convinced of that, but okay. I try to be a low-maintenance customer just in case. Appear as if my friend is new to restaurant dining, look at the waitress with wide, apologetic eyes and then make my order as simple as possible to make up for my friend's lack of forethought.

The night Brad became part of this crowd was almost too much to bear. I always thought of us as a team: a pair of easy order-ers. There's probably not too much more humiliating than getting in a rift and being overheard by the interior staff at a fast-food chain.

We pull up. Brad says to me, "Do you think they have clear drinks?"

Me: "Like Sprite or something?"

The Black Box Voice ("BBV"): "Hi! Welcome to (unnamed famous chain). Can I help you?"

Brad (leans his head out the window): "Do you have clear drinks? Something that isn't soda?"

Me (snorting): "Like what?"

BBV: "Ummm…like Sprite or 7-up?"

Brad: "That's soda. Do you have flavored water?"

I cover my face, mumble: "Oh my God."

Brad waves me off, rather aggressively, and continues, "I like flavored water. Do you have any?"

Me: "Did you see any on the menu?"

BBV: "Um…no. No ma'am, there's none on the menu."

Me: "I know! I was telling him that!"

Brad to me: "I don't need to read the menu; I can just ask her. (Then to BBV) I can just ask you, right?"

Me: "Can we just order?"

Brad: "I'm trying to!"

And then it just escalated from there. Not our proudest moment, and we haven't been back. I'm afraid they'll recognize my truck, gather round the intercom and laugh while they listen to me and Brad start to bicker, place bets or something.

While I'm not sure what to do about the menu issue, I have seen a ray of hope when it comes to the disregard of posted signs. Hooray—I'm not alone! It seems people are turning in their blasé, predictable posted messages and opting for something a little flashier:

I'm not 40, I'm 39.95 plus shipping and handling.

Dear IRS, I would like to cancel my subscription. Please remove my name from your mailing list.

I don't have hot flashes. I have short, private vacations in the tropics.

And my personal favorite for those unconcerned parents who allow their wee ones to wander aimlessly through stores:

Unattended children will be given an espresso and a free puppy.

And Venus Was Her Name...

"Owww!" I threw my razor down in the tub and leaned to slap my ankle where the blade had just nicked me. Gritting my teeth, I lifted my palm to inspect the damage. Not bad, but it still hurt like the dickens. And what with the shower rinsing pink foam into my open wound, I was practically panting in agony.

Shaving is such a pain. Honestly, I cannot stand having to take the time to drag a razor blade against my shins, let alone my armpits. It seems such a sadistic practice. The alternative is just as unappealing to me, so it appears I have no choice but to pay attention when I am shaving and learn how to maneuver the blades around those troublesome anklebones.

You'd think by now I'd have mastered this ritual. I have not. For someone who thought of nothing else when she was 12 years old, this shaving thing certainly hasn't gotten any easier. Oh, I'm not alone though…I spied a small Band-Aid on a girlfriend's knee the other day. I'm sure it was due to a razor mishap. And a neighbor of mine always wears those cutesy little ankle socks…another attempt at disguising nicks and scratches, I'm sure. Why just last week, my own husband came to the dinner table with four or five little flecks of TP stuck to his face, pin sized red dots of blood like targets in the center. It seems I have hooked up with another amateur shaver.

For such a dangerous custom, shaving has certainly been marketed as an act of the Gods, or Goddesses, whatever the case may be. I bought into it, heck—I joyfully purchased a Venus razor not too long ago. I, too, want to be a Goddess. Mine even came complete with a purse-sized Goddess lip-gloss. The very same type I used in 7th grade. How could I lose? Pink razor, pink gloss, I had no choice but to buy the pink raspberry shaving gel in order to make the transformation complete.

I've been had. If anything, I am less of a Goddess today than I was before buying my Venus paraphernalia. The shaving foam actually gets so thick, my razor clogs up before getting dragged halfway up one shin. This, of course, forces me to press the razor harder down onto my leg so as to actually remove hair in the process. Thus, I lose a lot of skin this way too. I'm not very impressed with this triple headed blade. I can't imagine the average Goddess had this problem.

"Ow, ow, ow…" I whined as I shut off the shower and limped out of the tub. With one foot awkwardly on my bathroom counter, I attempted to strategically place a Band-Aid on my wound. During my application of first aid, in waltzes Brad, donning the familiar red dots of toilet paper on his face.

"Don't give me that look," he says, "I know how to shave! It's that stupid pink foam of yours that caused the problem!" Well, what do you know? Neither one of us are Goddesses.

And Yew Thought Yew Knew Everything

I'm leaned up against Pam's countertop in her kitchen last week watching her kids (3) and mine (2) ransack her beautiful home. We're eating fruit salad, drinking our tea and doing exactly what we thought we'd do once we were grownups. A little chit chat, cleaning sticky fingers, wiping gooey faces, and repeatedly telling our children to calm down. It's quite nice. Our only missing link is that neither of us has joined the PTA, which is fine. We overestimated the awe factor of that before we'd actually had our own children.

So, after talk of husbands, ex-husbands, boyfriends, ex-boyfriends, children, work, friends, clothes, and reality TV, there is a short pause in conversation until Pam blurts out, "Oh my gosh—I forgot to tell you, I learned the origin of the middle finger."

"Do tell." Because, seriously, I thought I knew. "Doesn't everyone know what it means?"

She is exasperated. "We all know what it means, Carolyn. I learned its origin…where it came from."

She has my attention, so I lean in and get cozy because this ought to be good.

Pam is great. She tells a story like I do. Broken up, back tracking, waving her hands around constantly interrupting herself with, "Oh wait…hold on…no that's not right…it's something like this…anyway… you know what I mean…" Like I said, she's great and I completely relate to her storytelling abilities. I did get some mention of a war, amputated fingers, and a neener-neener-esque post battle attitude.

Intrigue. I went right home, gathered a few facts, and felt the need to enlighten Brentwood and its surrounding area.

According to legends posted on the internet:

> Before the Battle of Agincourt in 1415, the French, anticipating victory over the English, proposed to cut off the middle finger of all captured English soldiers. Without the middle finger it would be impossible to draw the renowned English longbow and therefore [soldiers would] be incapable of fighting in the future. This famous weapon was made of the native English yew tree, and the act of drawing the longbow was known as "plucking the yew." Much to the bewilderment of the French, the English won a major upset and began mocking the French by waving their middle fingers at the defeated French, saying, "See, we can still pluck yew!"
>
> Over the years some "folk etymologies" have grown up around this symbolic gesture. Since "pluck yew" is rather difficult to say, like "pheasant mother plucker," which is who you had to go to for the feathers used on the arrows for the longbow, the difficult consonant cluster at the beginning has gradually changed to a labiodental fricative "f," and thus the words often used in conjunction with the one-finger salute are mistakenly thought to have something to do with an intimate encounter. It is also because of the pheasant feathers on the arrows that the gesture is known as "giving the bird."

Interesting, yet is it true? It's hard to say for certain since I found disputing evidence on www.straightdope.com, my online source for investigating such mystery. For example:

> The "one-finger salute," is thousands of years old. In *Gestures: Their Origins and Distribution,* Desmond Morris and colleagues note that the digitus infamis or digitus impudicus (infamous or indecent finger) is mentioned several times in the literature of ancient Rome. Turning to our vast classical library, we quickly turn up three references. Two are from the epigrammatist Martial: "Laugh loudly, Sextillus, when someone calls you a queen and put your middle finger out."

In the other reference Martial writes that a certain party "points a finger, an indecent one, at" some other people. The historian Suetonius, writing about Augustus Caesar, says the emperor "expelled [the entertainer] Pylades...because when a spectator started to hiss, he called the attention of the whole audience to him with an obscene movement of his middle finger." Morris also claims that the mad emperor Caligula, as an insult, would extend his middle finger for supplicants to kiss.

Well, well, well. This certainly puts to rest any controversy surrounding the gesture Rose made to Lovejoy in the film version of the Titanic. Critics have scowled at the gesture saying it hadn't been dreamed up yet in the early 1900s. Either way, it seems yew learn something new every day.

Annoying or Interactive?

There are probably a few good names for people like me, you know, those of us who like to talk through movies. I prefer to be called an "interactive movie goer," rather than the standard "annoying person sitting in front of me."

It's a nasty habit, this I admit, but I just cannot help myself. Perhaps it's the dimming of the lights, or the sudden hush of the audience, either way the anticipation of what's to come bubbles up and spills right out of me. Directly into my date's ears.

So far, I've been pretty fortunate. I married another interactive movie go-er. We adore this about one another and enjoy our in-theater philosophizing, predicting, and the ever-popular rehashing of recent scenes. We are just horrible and we know it. We have learned to tune out the exasperated sighs around us and we always have our quick escape plotted out beforehand. Kind of old pros, if you want to go that far.

Now don't get me wrong, I have been told to "zip it" before but since it was a girlfriend I was with, I let it go because she was from England. I figured she wasn't hip on the American ways of movie watching or something. We had gone to see Titanic back in '98. Both of us having seen it previously, we came stocked with small packages of tissue and smuggled cans of Diet Coke. I settled in for a good cry and some stimulating conversation.

The lights dimmed, the music started and, "Oh my gosh," I began, "Isn't it just so tragic that…?"

"Shhh…"

I sat shaking my head, "I mean, it's just so awful, all these people losing their lives…"

"Shut UP!" she hissed.

I must not have heard correctly. So, I started again, "The water is so cold and…"

"Just what exactly are you doing? Why are you talking to me? We are here to WATCH a movie, not discuss it." She nudged me, "So try to say nothing unless you are sobbing, okay?"

Say nothing? Like for three hours, say nothing at all? I was silent for a bit, but only because I was stunned. I tried to respect her wishes but was hard pressed to believe she didn't want to talk about Jack, Rose, the ice, and that detestable Cal Hockley. Apparently though, she did not. While she stared at the screen, quietly wiping stray tears from her cheeks, I wept openly and obnoxiously, bawling loud and hard and sharing my grief with everyone. I offered tissues to those around me, shamelessly blubbering and fighting off the urge to bear hug these perfect strangers. She slunk down in her seat and waved off my attempt to share my Kleenex. Had she no clue on how to watch a sad movie with a crowd?

For now, I stick to moviegoing with my main man. We laugh, confer, debate, predict, and generally guarantee empty seats around us. No bother, this way we are free to talk uninterrupted!

Appointment Gone Right

A little clipping is taped to a cupboard located in the exam room of my obstetrician/gynecologist. It reads:

Why Men Make Lousy Secretaries

A wife finds the following note left for her from her husband.

"Someone from the Gyna College called. They said Pabst beer is normal."

I smiled after reading this little item. My medical visit was turning out better than expected.

For starters, my nifty paper vest wasn't chafing this time around, and it did seem to fit better than I remember. And after mummifying my lower body with the paper skirt I was given, I made myself quite content perched on the edge of the table looking through *People* magazine. Quality reading material is hard to come by in any doctor's office. Usually, I have to rifle through torn up copies of *Hunter's Digest* or well-thumbed issues of *Fishing and Loving It, The Happy Gunman* or *Monster Truck Mania*. Apparently, the number of women who read these magazines is much higher than I would have thought.

But even better than that, was the medical assistant who weighed and measured me. She introduced herself and explained she was in training and to please be patient (ha ha), that she'd try to make it as painless as possible. A comedian. This might be fun. She then weighed me in 10 pounds underweight. Since it is just plain rude to tell a person how to do their job, I, of course, said nothing. I was half hoping she'd add a few inches to my height as well and make me look really skinny in the process, but she measured me accurately.

When the doctor did finally see me, it wasn't after an hour of waiting and readjusting my paper outfit, only a few minutes had passed. I was almost disappointed because I couldn't finish the article on Gwyneth and her new baby Banana. Or was it Plum? See—I needed to finish that piece! And did it say that Brad and Jen are splitting up or was that Ryan and Trista? Marc and J-Lo? Uh oh. How was I supposed to focus on the task at hand without knowing the following answers to some of life's most important questions?

Small talk, a few mysteries solved, the main event, and then I was getting dressed again. It was the shortest time I spent in an office in years. I half wanted to stay and chat some more since I rarely get stimulating adult conversation being at home with two preschoolers.

It seemed a pity to throw away a perfectly good paper vest and skirt. Or was that a sarong? Had I been wearing it incorrectly this entire time? How embarrassing, if I was. What is the protocol on something like that anyway? I contemplated asking at the front desk on my way out, but then realizing it was just an unconscious attempt at initiating conversation, I decided against it. I could just imagine the red mark they'd put on my chart and the side note in the margin that read PATHETIC, if I did such a thing.

They even gave me a goody bag on the way out. Like a birthday party, only no hats. No cake and ice cream either. Come to think of it, I didn't bring a gift, unless you count my co-pay. I did get to wear paper clothing though, and if that isn't a sure sign of an appointment gone right, then I don't know what is.

Are You Down?

I'm all about being informed. I like to know what's going on, what's new, what the latest and greatest is. The problem is I'm kind of *old school*, or so I'm learning. My lingo is sort of *10 minutes ago*. I just found this out and thank God I did or else I would have never even known how out of the loop I am. Or by today's verbiage, I'm so *A Flock of Seagulls*.

You know, I always thought money was just called *money*. It's not. I can go onto any high school campus and ask to borrow some *ducats* or *scrilla,* maybe even some *cheddar* or *snaps*, and although I'd be denied (cold dissed), at least these kids would know what I was soliciting. Some cash: a couple of bills, a few greenbacks, some cabbage, maybe even a c-note or two. But no worries, I'd never even ask. These kids are *toppin' some G's* to spend on themselves, not to finance their *peeps, yo.*

See, I just got the 4-1-1 on urban slang and I'm starting to school myself on how to communicate. In my day, awesome meant just that: pretty impressive. I think we stretched it with 'tubular' and 'righteous', 'that rocks", and 'right on!" but the meaning was still there, even if the tone implied variation. For example, *bounce* today means to leave, and a *crib* is actually a house. All right has been shortened to *'aiight'* and if all this makes sense, then for me to say, "Yo, little dawg, mama has got to bounce this crib, aiight?" I should have no trouble being understood as having told my child, "Sweetheart, Mommy has to leave now, okay?"

One I love the best (I'm down with the most) is the term *tool*. When I hear the word, I naturally think hammer or saw, not a complete meathead. No, a *tool* today can be defined as a person, not a thing, but a noun, nevertheless. A *tool* is someone who can't think for himself, an idiot, what us old-schoolers would deem a poser. Taken to the extreme, you get a *toolbox*. Grab a *tool* who likes to accessorize (sport bling) by wearing phone-wear and you have a *Blue Tool*, the cad who wears his Bluetooth just to look fly (hip, cool, snazzy). Which is of course, straight whack. (Incidentally, a group of tools is defined as 'sheeple', which I think provides a great visual.)

Having recently armed myself with a few choice phrases, I decided to try them out at home.

"Clean up your room, yo."

"Finish that broccoli, aiight?"

And when I got the look from my husband (my baby daddy), I replied with, "Don't trip on me," to which he replied dryly, "I won't if you don't lay down on the floor where I can't see you."

Needless to say, I won't do that again. Not only was I uncomfortable, I completely lack the panache to pull it off.

I can't *front* like I know what I'm talking about. Anyone can easily *dime me out* for trying. And then someone may *go all 5150* on me and *jack me up outside my crib.* That would not be *dope,* I can tell you that much. Can you imagine if the *po-po* or the *bacon* didn't get there in time? I may be all *toe up* on my lawn in my *hood*, none of my *crew* having the D.L. on what *went down.*

Personally, I prefer simplicity. I'd rather say, "That's easy" than stretch it out to "That ain't no thang..." I can always substitute 'bee's knees' for easy, I'm adaptable like that. And if I want to push my creative limits, there is the ever favorite "easy breezy mac and cheesy." But I don't know if I've actually ever heard anyone say that except me. I might have made that up. But who knows, it could catch on...wouldn't that be da bomb?

Bearly Funny

A crowd of people loitering in a parking lot is rarely a good thing. Especially if the crowd is standing around your truck inspecting the damage as you approach.

"Here comes the owner!" I heard someone call out as I began to trot over to the cluster. Alarm must have been written all over my face. They parted like the Red Sea as I entered the scene.

Yosemite. Curry Village. Broad daylight. Apparently, I just missed the bear attack on my truck. I couldn't help it, I started laughing. This was exactly the sort of thing one needs a friend to 'bear' witness to. Paw prints all over the windows, claw marks shredded portions of my bumper and one rear 'wing' window was pulled from the frame and bent out at a 45-degree angle. Bolts and all sorts of previously hidden interior framing paraphernalia were splayed out for all to see. Impressive. And yet, I was alone, had no friend in sight to shove and say, "Look! Look!" to.

"I don't like the idea of you going alone." Brad had said a day earlier, "Find someone to go to Yosemite with!"

"Aw…come on…" I had replied, "What could happen?" Besides, I had wanted to be alone. Hike alone, sleep alone, eat alone. Especially after our last trip there when I came home needing a vacation from my vacation. This was my one shot.

At the scene of the 'attack', each of the spectators had something to say, especially since mine was only one of six vehicles damaged. Broken glass, bent antennas, and one aisle over, I saw a truck with the door mangled into such odd positioning, I wondered how the driver was even going to get into his seat.

While I poked around my truck, I barely heard the Ranger say, "…some fruit bearing trees…blah blah blah…number one place for bear attacks in the entire valley…blah blah blah…become inebriated and come into the village at all times of day on rampages, destroying everything in sight." Wait. What? A drunk bear did all of this?

"Say that again," I requested. He did. Told the crowd how the fruit on the trees in Curry Village falls to the ground and ferments. Bears eat it at night, then lose their 'bearings' and come out in the daytime to wreak some serious havoc. I pictured party hats and baseball bats. High fives, touchdown dances, and bear fraternity hazing stunts.

"Ma'am, this is far from funny." The Ranger was confused by my chuckles.

I couldn't help myself. I always get the giggles at the most inopportune times. I pictured having to tell Brad that a bear busted out the back window, but don't worry honey—he was drunk and just on a bit of a rampage.

When I peeked inside my open window, I saw that the bear hadn't touched a thing. Whew. But what to do about that window? I deliberated between solving the dilemma myself or playing the helpless female card, when a nice young gentleman came to my rescue. Sparkling blue eyes, Orbit gum smile, he had just inspected the damage on his own truck and came over to offer assistance. What a hero. I tried not to grin too widely as he secured my window in place. Again, I needed a friend to shove.

The Golden Rule

Being Full of It

Malarkey, crap, B.S., garbage—call it what you will, but there comes a time in every kid's life when they realize that their parents are full of it. I had my suspicions for years before I actually figured it out, but I don't seem to recall the actual age I was when I realized my parent's stories were just that—stories. Fabrications, exaggerations, colorful illustrations…I could go on and on. That knowledge alone is a powerful thing but combine it with the understanding of threats being empty, justifications being excuses, and fibbing being downright lying. It's enough to put a kid on edge.

Until I was 19 or so, I fancied my mom as a dominating power monger. Oh, I had all sorts of names for her: control freak, orderly, life duty (my not so clever play on yard duty), security guard, and dominatrix. She was never amused. I called my dad "Dad" and tried not to make him mad. He had different boundaries than her and I learned early on not to cross his line.

Take for example the extreme hatred of green beans I have today. Most folks in the psychiatric field would probably tap my chart and nod knowingly if they heard this tale, but truthfully, I think I would still hate green beans even if this had never happened. One night at dinner when I was around six or seven years old, my sister and I were horsing around at the table. Making faces, spitting milk, twirling our chairs around, and doing the old, "See food?" trick and exposing our entire open mouths for the family to enjoy. Dad was less than thrilled. In fact, he slammed his fist on the table and pointing his fork at me, said, "Eat those green beans." I made a face and moved them around on my plate. "Eat them NOW," he threatened, "or I will shove them down your throat." I scoffed. Even at this tender age, I doubted my dad would do this. Now before anyone starts dialing up Child Protective Services, try to remember this was a different time, and a different set of expectations were in line when it came to children. I knew better than to mock my father, yet I did, and I got a lesson in How to Make Dad Furious by Being a Smartass at The Dinner Table 101.

In one swift movement I found myself with a mouthful of green beans and my dad's hand clamped over my lips. I did what any kid in that position would do—I barfed. After that, dinner was over, and I don't recall ever having to eat green beans again.

As I grew older, I realized Mom would always threaten, warn and pour on the pressure. Dad would tell me once to do something and I did it. I just never expected her to employ Dad as her assistant and see the two of them collaborate their efforts.

"Put your bike away," Mom said 20 times a week, "Before someone steals it. You'd be a very sorry little girl with no bicycle to ride around on." True, but I highly doubted anyone in Pleasanton was going to want a neon yellow bike complete with banana seat, checkered basket and fender that read, "Cactus Flower." And besides, I reasoned, I would know who did steal it because nobody else had a bike like that.

And so, I left it out, tipped on its side on the walkway up to the front of our house. Night after night I was told to put it away, and night after night I did so grudgingly, only after my dad hollered, "Do as your mother tells you!" Until that one fateful evening I exited the front door in a sulk and to my surprise, my bike was gone. In shock, I stood there with my jaw open. Fear crept in, not because I was less one bicycle, but because I was going to have to tell my parents my bike had actually been stolen. They were right and I would never hear the end of it. Plus, I was still out a bike. This was awful! I did what I thought was the reasonable thing.

I invented a new reality. (Also called lying in some circles.) I went through the motions of putting my bike away and came inside as if nothing was amiss. My plan was to tell them the following day that my bike had been stolen out of the garage. And maybe if DAD didn't always leave the garage door open, I would still have my bike. Boo hoo. Sob, sob.

I entered the house and declared, "All done. Good night!" Then made a quick path to the upstairs. My parents eyed each other suspiciously.

"You put your bike away?" Mom asked carefully, "And where exactly did you put it?"

I was getting nervous. "In the garage," I stuttered, "You know, over there, where the cars and tools are." Then I shifted to sarcasm, "You know Mom, you might want to check it out sometime. It's a very neat part of the house." Coolly, I tried again to make my exit. But not before Dad said, "All righty then, I'm up for some ice cream. I'll get a carton from the garage freezer." He flashed Mom a look that clearly said, *'Do not be concerned. I have this all under control.'*

I hightailed it out of there and didn't come back down until Dad yelled for me. With my tail between my legs, I descended the stairs and entered the kitchen only to see my bike parked in the middle of it.

"You are grounded for not following directions. You are grounded for lying. And you are grounded for thinking your father and I are complete idiots. Now go upstairs." I got off easy, if I think back on it. And we all won…they never again had to hide my bike in the shed, and I always put it away after that.

Malarkey, crap, B.S., garbage—call it what you will, but there comes a time in every kid's life when they realize their parents are not so full of it after all.

Breaking Up is Hard to Do

I once punched a man. Pretty hard too. But it was because I loved him. And while I don't expect that to make much sense, perhaps it will after a little explanation.

It's true that friends come and go throughout your life but it's also true that some friends just come. They stay. You know them forever. We have a friend like that. I'll call him "Scott."

I first met Scott 10 years ago at a neighborhood gathering. He handed me a red cup and said, "Soooo, you're the girl who lives with her two brothers. Nothing personal, but didn't I see you kissing one of them the other day out in broad daylight?" Pause for a smile, and then, "Where are you from anyway?"

I was horrified. "What? NO!" I laughed nervously, making me appear even more guilty. He later explained that he had recently met our friend Dean, who was staying with us for a short stint when we first bought our home back in 1996. Dean—bless his heart—said he was living with his brother and sister. Though Dean has no blood relation, we consider him family. Thus, the introduction. It made for quite an interesting opinion of us to those who hadn't yet been told the truth.

The meeting solidified a friendship that grew into a closeness usually seen within the ties of family. Vacations, parties, the births of children, the passing of parents—sometimes arguments. The occasional spiff. The even less common, but still present 'fist to cuff' fight.

Scott came to work with Brad years ago, so I talked with him daily. I saw no need to fancy myself up for him and he greeted me with such one-liners as, "Lookin' good baby," or "Nice hair," when I'd open my front door after just rolling out of bed in the morning. Sometimes the guys would make breakfast before hitting the road, sometimes just hang around in the kitchen and talk. It was a comfortable, comfortable time.

Five years ago, when Scott and his wife Michelle split up, I didn't take it well. I decked him. Then cried. He cried too. Then we both cried harder, then we got over it. Kind of.

Just recently he told us he was moving to Virginia—taking the new wife and child, gonna work there for a bit, see what happens. I was presented with the opportunity to be honest with how I felt about his decision, or to be a supportive friend and allow him to leave without ever knowing the truth. I chose the former. Forget tact when you're feeling abandoned.

"It's like we're breaking up!" I sobbed into his chest. "Are you breaking up with me?" I joked through my tears, "Am I being dumped?"

The day before the move Scott and his family stopped over to say goodbye. I was tough. On him. On her. On the situation at large. It wasn't until I realized that a part of me was envious at their freedom to go and not look back that I let go of my anger. Who hasn't wanted to move across the country and start a new life at some point? I dreaded saying goodbye.

Because other folks were witnessing this farewell, I tried to make light of it and held back any real emotion. When he hugged me and said, "I'm coming back—you'll see," I just shook my head and bit my lip. I waited until they drove off before falling apart.

But a short time later he reappeared at our door, looking for his daughter's shoes. I directed Brad out back to hunt around then turned to Scott and said, "That's a BS excuse, coming back for shoes and all."

"Huh?"

"Yeah—you just wanted to have a tearful goodbye." Then I started sobbing hard. "You say you'll be back, but you won't." I was bawling into his chest again.

Poor guy—having to console this emotional basket case, and I'm not even his wife. But he was crying too and trying to reassure me that yes, he'd for sure come back to California. "I will, you'll see…" But I knew better. I had talked to his wife. It'd be a long time before we ever saw Scott again.

I was still sniveling when Brad reappeared, caught off guard at my red eyes and tousled hair. I pointed at Scott. "He hit me." I smiled weakly.

"Yeah," he chimed in, "She didn't see it coming. I got her with a left and right."

In truth, I felt hit. I think we all did at that moment—smacked with the finality of our situation. Saying goodbye is never fun, but breaking up is hard to do.

Bringing Rotary Back

I have a new desk and because I have a new desk it only makes sense that I should have a new phone to go on it. My old phone is the standard Costco cordless. Boring in ten different ways, except for perhaps the banner on it. I love changing banner messages on my phones. I do it all the time and right now the one in my bedroom reads "1COOLMOM" because, well, I am. In the kitchen the phone banner says "OWWBABY" and

I recently programmed the one in Brad's office to display "GOHELPWIFE." The messages have become pretty tame over the years since Josh learned to read. I like to program my friend's phones too when they're not looking. There are a few houses here in Brentwood with banners reading things such as "DODDSROCK" and "CALLDODDS." In fact, I once programmed my friend's phone banner to read "DODDSRCOOL" and she never changed it after moving out of state. "I think of you every time I hold my phone," she told me. And I like that.

But since I have a new desk, I thought a new phone with a different style would be a nice decorative touch. My train of thought left the station and went like this: new black desk, need fancy phone, old-fashioned equals retro, retro sounds like rotary, voila! I looked everywhere for a rotary phone. And I found a couple—for a few hundred bucks. Good Lord, I had no idea. Of course, rotary-esque phones are available at any Pottery Barn, but I wanted something that actually dialed and did its job. Made calls, rang alarmingly loud, and would become a conversation piece to everyone who entered my home office. (Who that would ever be other than myself or Brad, I don't know—but still, I dug the idea.)

I called my dad and complained about the expense of a real rotary phone. "Four hundred dollars," I said, "People on eBAY want four hundred dollars for a rotary phone." He laughed and said I could have all three of the phones he and my mom had stored in the garage. I could hardly wait.

Two of the telephones they delivered needed some wiring to work correctly, but one that didn't was a mustard yellow wall phone, circa 1972. I know this because it was the very first phone I ever used. I cradled that yellow handset between my shoulder and my ear while stretching its mile long cord across our kitchen during the 1970s until it was removed from the wall and banished to the garage sometime during the 1980s. My dad proudly hung it in the garage (and used it) until my mother replaced it with a push button phone on a whim. "Rotary is *out...*" she said coolly, "Everyone has push button phones these days." And we never saw it again.

I thanked them profusely and because I did, my mom became a little anxious about giving me such a treasure. No matter that it had long ago been exiled to storage due to its 'horrific color' and tedious dialing requirement, she now gazed at it with a new appreciation. I could see an internal struggle blooming.

"Thank you," I told her pointedly, hugging the phone to my chest.

"That's an antique," she hesitated, "I don't know, Bill. Shouldn't we keep it for nostalgia's sake?"

"You've had this boxed up for years, and I'm going to actually use this...for nostalgia's sake." I tried hard to not panic.

She pursed her lips together. "Well...(pause)...okay...for now."

I breathed a sigh of relief and went happily about hanging it on the wall.

And while my kitchen is up one mustard yellow wall rotary wall phone, my office remains phone free for the time being. But I don't care; nobody ever comes in it anyway.

Brutal Honesty Unwelcome

When people tell you to be brutally honest, they're lying. I have yet to meet someone who really wants to hear it like it is. Children will be brutally honest and when they are, we laugh it off and say things such as, 'kids will be kids' pretending to be shocked at their candor, when in fact we are secretly wishing we could pull off saying how we really feel.

I have a friend who has absolutely no tact. I love her. She's funny and classy and smart, yet fires questions and commentary at people without fear of offense. I admire this. Though I don't strive to be like her, I do love to be with her. Especially in a crowd, extra especially if she's been drinking. We'll throw her into any situation with the particulars of what we'd like to learn, and she always delivers the goods.

"Why are you dating that girl? She seems shallow and mean. And is she missing a tooth? Doesn't she have a job with benefits?" She'll stand her ground and actually get an answer. Impressive. I think most folks are too taken aback by her frankness to do much more than give her an answer. "How much did you pay for your house? In this market? Are you serious? Boy, you got screwed..." I'm sure she's been a topic around many dinner tables. She's the closest I have come to being in the company of someone who is brutally honest and doesn't apologize for it one bit.

I grew up hearing my mother ask my father to be brutally honest, then watching him defend himself.

"Bill, does this dress make me look heavy? Be brutally honest, I can take it."

"Heavy as in Mack Truck, or heavy as in Brick House?" then he'd throw his hands up to protect his face.

If memory serves, the last time I was brutally honest was in the late 1970s. My sister and I sat at the dinner table with our parents, silent but for the clinking and scraping of our forks meeting plates.

"Bill, (dramatic pause) how do you like my new recipe for meatloaf?" A tablespoon was held in midair, as my mother preened using the backside of it as a mirror. A knowing smirk on her face, Mom patted her shellacked upsweep, blotted her lips, examined her eyelashes and then in a high falsetto, sang, "I mean, be brutally honest…" her voice lifting with each word as she flashed a bright smile to Dad. In the long stretch of silence that followed, my sister and I watched intently the back-and-forth as we awaited the reply. Though the spoon remained in midair, Mom was no longer gazing at her reflection in it. She was eyeballing my father, who sat staring at his fork, chewing slowly while he worked hard to find the right words.

The lull in conversation was answer enough. The spoon slowly descended. "Would anyone else like to tell me what they think of dinner?" She glared at my father. Young as I was, I understood by her tone that no, she was not interested in my opinion, nor that of my older sister. And yet, "I think it tastes like s**t on a shingle!" I blurted, having recently overheard the phrase my father used to describe a meal he left unfinished at a restaurant. Her reaction told me two things: a request to be brutally honest merely means 'tell me what I want to hear and nothing more', and that little girls who try shock value in an attempt at an early dismissal from the dinner table can usually expect to have their request granted, though they may not be emerging from their bedrooms anytime that evening.

Normally I can avoid being brutally honest by using a little discretion and a big smile. It's pretty obvious if people want your truthful opinion, or a sugar-coated version thereof. For example, Brad biannually re-designs the mailer for his company. Our conversation might go some-thing like this:

> Him: Okay—tell me what you think of this. But don't edit it, don't correct my spelling or punctuation, ignore the color scheme and graphics but be honest—tell me what you think.

> Me: I think you need some big-boy positive feedback!

> Him: No, no, seriously, I want to talk about this mailer. (He shakes it at me.)

I know what he really wants to discuss is what's good about the mailer. His vision of our tête-à-tête probably has me fawning over the glossy paper, blinking rapidly and shaking my head in awe. I am left speechless, lost in a haze of wonder that his knack for font selection, word alignment and graphic design has gone undiscovered for so long. "Tell me what you think of this" is code for "tell me how impressed you are with the time and energy I spent creating it." I'm no dope.

He holds it up and I shut my eyes tightly. No peeking, so I haven't got a clue what I'm commenting on. Deep breath in and then, "It's astound-ing, really. The descriptive adjectives, the breathtaking photos, the way you sell yourself combined with the specs on the company…it all comes together beautifully. A complete package, if I do say so myself." I open my eyes, smile, and pat his arm. "Good choice of color too."

"Yes, well…thanks. I appreciate your brutal honesty." Exchange of nods and grins and we both win.

I stick by my original thought: if you think you can handle the truth, then ask a kid. They're the only ones who can pull off being brutally hon-est and even then, we're more likely to laugh after we hear it.

Cricket House of Horrors

It's happening again. Just when I think it's safe to walk down the hall, I have a chance encounter with a handicapped cricket. I thought this was all behind me. I thought the cat had gotten over her sick fetish with dismembering harmless crickets. Apparently, I thought wrong.

See, having a cricket or two in the house doesn't bother me. Even four of five won't send me into panic induced frenzy the way a beetle or spider will. Thanks to *Cricket Magazine* for publishing a poem I submitted at the tender age of 7, I have always had a special spot in my heart for the little guys. And after seeing Disney's *Mulan* for the umpteenth time, how can I think of crickets as anything less than lucky?

It's just the ones I happen to stumble upon who are missing limbs that make me uneasy. Hobbling down the hall…hoping I won't see them… trying desperately to get out of harm's way. I imagine them hunkering down a little as I approach and then squeaking, "Please noooooo," as I scoop them up and deliver them, pleasantly surprised, to safety.

Living in the Ag belt that we do, it's difficult to get through the day without having a run in with a bug, spider, beetle, roach, or other entomological specimen. Tooter (the sick and twisted feline we call our cat) has no interest in toying with anything other than crickets. We have yet to figure this one out. She doesn't kill them and eat them. Oh, no. It's the removal of one leg and then she's done. Moves on to find her next victim.

This cricket horror show hasn't happened in a while. I rarely see a one-legged cricket making its way through the corridors of my home these days. So, picture this, my 4-year-old approaches me at my desk the other day and beaming, tells me, "I saved them."

Clackety clack on the keyboard (Me): "Hmmm…ok. Saved who, hon?"

Ear to ear grin, all teeth (Josh): "The crickets, Mama. I let them go. They went *boing, boing* all over the kitchen! They're happy now! Come see, come see!"

Uh oh. We have a container of feeder crickets for our frog, high on a shelf next to the tank. Correction: *had.*

By the time we enter the kitchen, two or three stragglers are left, the rest have joyfully hopped off to higher ground, having no clue of the fate that awaits them should their paths converge with Tooter's. I am torn. Do I laugh or cry? Doing neither, I opt to just keep a sharp eye out for survivors. I tell Josh to do the same.

After a few days this is where we stand: three rescued in my closet, two more in my bathroom behind the wastebasket. One unfortunate little guy who didn't make it through the night under the covers with Josh, four more inside his closet who did. Two living in our sofa, two more of their relatives living underneath it. All successful rescues, only one missing a limb perhaps by a mistake of its own and not due to Tooter. Sigh, and six one-legged crickets still living, rescued and released into the grass out front by special request of Josh.

Lastly, one extremely long lecture on the dangers of shelf climbing, combined with a large dose of positive reinforcement for respecting the lives of all creatures—even crickets.

Dedication to Fitness

"Today's the day!" I happily announced to my family, "I am dedicating my life to health and fitness and whoo-hoo…it's gonna be great!"

I clapped my hands together, did a stretch, shook my booty and then embarrassed myself further by breaking into *The Running Man.*

Brad barely looked up from his cereal bowl. "Is this a dedication, or a re-dedication? I'm just curious, since you have dedicated your life to fitness about 12 times in the past 9 months."

I stared at him. Gradually, my Running Man became the Walking Man, then the Standing Still Man and then I wasn't dancing anymore at all. "What do you mean?"

"Oh gee, I don't know. Maybe I'm referring to having to exchange the Treadmill for a Healthrider just so you have a place to hang your dirty laundry now."

My mouth is hanging open rather unattractively as I listen to him catalog the equipment I sought after and then purchased, much to his chagrin.

"…and the Ab Roller, which Josh disassembles every chance he gets. Do you know I found the screws for that piece of crap in my shoe the other day? And what about the Portable Stair Stepper you bought off Joanne? Do you actually take it anywhere to stair step on the go? And *puleeeze* tell me why we have that mammoth Yoga Ball rolling randomly around our home? It stalks me, that ball. Follows me from room to room and Babe, it is starting to freak me out."

He does have a point. The Yoga Ball does seem to materialize in every room of the house. While cooking dinner, bump—it taps me on the rear. While putting laundry in the dryer, there it is…suddenly looking over the open door. I once exited the bathroom expecting to trip over a playful kitty who had been tapping on the door while I conducted my business. Imagine my surprise, then alarm, only to discover my Yoga Ball. It tags along while I put the children to bed, while I work in the office, and strangely enough, I sometimes see it peering through the glass as I shower. I'm not sure if I should feel extra safe, or especially apprehensive. "Use me…use me…" it silently expresses its need.

"And should I even begin to list the videos you have in the cupboard?" Brad is getting worked up, "Tony Little, Billy Blanks, Buns of Steel, Pilates and Yoga. I have never seen you meditate a day in your life!" That's not true. I stand silently stretching and concentrating all the time as I bend into my fridge and scrutinize the selection in the rear. And I keep the videos for special occasions. I can always whip out Tony Little if only to get a laugh out of him sneering, "You can DO IT!" while sporting that ridiculous mullet. As for Billy Blanks- that guy is my hero. And as far as I'm concerned, it took Pilates to second the motion that Yoga and all Yoga-like activities are not meant for people who need loud music and flashing lights in order to get a good workout. I like to think of those tapes as my primary education on fitness. In order to succeed at what you like; one must learn and surpass what he does not. I'm sure the sages say that somewhere.

"Okay fine then—to you, it's a re-dedication. All I know is that for the first time ever, I am starting a New Way of Living." I smugly stuck out my tongue.

He scoffed and muttered, "Another one?"

Destined for Greatness

"**I was destined** for better than this!" Instead of saying 'hello,' like a normal person would, my girlfriend answers the phone this way. It makes me laugh.

"Oh no you weren't," I reply. "You're a woman—destined to do laundry, chauffer children, scrub toilets, and still…make a difference in the world. But go unnoticed until something goes wrong. Then you graciously accept the blame and move forward, all while grinning broadly and carrying a tray of muffins."

"Damn straight. I'm the whole kit-n-caboodle babe. And how is the world treating YOU these days?"

I contemplate sharing with her the tale of Ben's new car seat, then decide to go for it. "Well, Ben's new car seat was delivered today," I begin.

It's a seat that's designed for children with motor coordination issues, among other special needs. At five years of age and living with cerebral palsy, Ben has long outgrown his five-point harness, yet isn't ready for a typical booster seat. I special ordered this particular car seat and have been anxiously awaiting its arrival since last June. When the gentleman from the company brought it in, I almost fell over. Partly because the thing was gigantic, but mostly because hefting this enormous piece of equipment was Antonio Banderas.

"Um…can you please show me how this works?" I stuttered. But then I became easily distracted by his accent.

"Ah Madam…I am…how you say…no good weeth theens like-a thees. For you though? I shall try…" I watched him as he buckled, strapped, and snapped pieces together incorrectly.

"That's okay," I wiped drool from my chin, "I can figure this out." When the Antonio impersonator left, I peered down and knew within seconds there was no way I could assemble it to Ben's proportions, let alone get it into my truck. Easily, it will take up a seat and a half. I pity the kid who must ride next to him, crowded by fluff and padding.

"Not much to say except I think Antonio Banderas delivered it." I tell my friend, then add at the last minute, "I'm coming over."

When I arrive at her place, she has conveniently set up two barstools at a high table in her backyard. She ushers me over to take a seat. "Sit down, sit down. Let's play Dr. Phil."

"Noooo," I whine. "Be someone else, like a real journalist. Diane Sawyer or Babba Wawa."

"No Carolyn," her voice is now baritone as she assumes the role, "I'm Dr. Phil and we're going to talk about you here today." She smiles out at the yard, seeing an audience I presume.

"Well fine. You look exactly like him anyway."

After a brief pause to glare at me, she begins. "I sense you have a great deal on your mind. You are confused and high anxiety. I can help. Why don't you tell me why you are such a troubled young lady?"

I feign surprise. "What? I thought I was here for a makeover!" I address the same invisible audience.

She tries again, "Do you think hiding behind jokes and sarcasm is your way of protec…"

"Knock-knock," I cut in, then start snickering.

"You are quite obviously in the 'rebellious teen' stage," she concludes between hoots. "You need help!"

"Good. Send me to boot camp, or I'll TP your Dr. Phil House."

After a few more laughs I have to leave to pick up the kids from school. I cart them home, fix the troops a snack, then start another load of laundry. I go through the mail, tidy up the office and then load the dishwasher. Strangely, I feel content and happy. I think about my good friends, my good family, and my good life in general, despite all the chaos and havoc. When the phone rings next, I pick up and say, "I wasn't destined for better than this!" And I mean it.

Do You Know the Muffin Woman?

"**Are those new** jeans?" my friend asked me the other day.

"Um…no. They're the same pair I've been wearing all week, they're just tighter now." It's true too, dang it. From Thanksgiving until Christmas, every time I bend my elbow my mouth opens and food falls in it. By the time the 25th of December rolls around, I feel like I've been crowned the Grand Prize Winner of a gluttony contest. On December 26th I declare myself done with the holidays and then try to starve myself through to January 1, so when I do finally step on the scale, it won't read some catastrophic digit. I resolve every year not to do this…and yet, the day after Christmas is rapidly approaching and I have yet to put down my fork.

It wasn't always like this. I used to make dinky little resolutions such as "shave legs before necessary" and "read compelling literature, watch a classic movie" or "discover a new poet." Yawn, I'd be lucky to shave my legs before my children comment on the hair length ("Yo legs ah howie…") and these days, a classic movie is something along the lines of *Elf* or *Christmas Vacation*. I haven't discovered what that smell in my laundry room is, let alone a new poet. I'm doing good if I make it to my weekly boxing class once a month.

I should probably resolve to eat a meal that doesn't require me to unbutton my pants when I'm done. One that isn't accompanied by a stretch, a groan and an ever-present twinge of guilt for not exhibiting one iota of self-control. My girlfriend and I were in an ice cream parlor up in Washington a few weeks back and as we sat licking our cones she sighed and told me, "I've got the full-on 'muffin syndrome' happening here." For those of you who are unfamiliar with the 'muffin syndrome', as I was until she so kindly explained it to me, it's this: if you go to put on a pair of pants and find yourself squeezing, jumping, and shimmying yourself into them, you are preparing to be a muffin. Once you zip them up and any excess flesh hangs out over the top of your waistband, spilling over and rising up like the cap of a cooked muffin, you are, by definition, experiencing 'muffin syndrome.' To think I've had a syndrome for quite some time and didn't even realize it. Amazing. Alert Stanford Genetics Department.

"So, what's it called when your bra strap gets lost in back fat?" I'm curious with my inquiry. Surely, there must be a term for this too. And since we're on the topic, "What do you call it when your undies disappear into the fat on your hips?" I'm dying to know. She is a friend that would be privy to this kind of information, and I've actually seen this on a couple young girls wearing low-rise jeans. I've noticed it and wondered what to call it, other than unbelievable.

I'm hoping the idioms for such incident will be charming too, such as "muffin". Though I can't imagine how or what they could be. I love cute terminology for the undesirable. I recently told my family over Thanksgiving that I thought I may be getting a little "fluffy" only to have my mother dispute it by calling me "healthy." My husband cackled and replied, "Then I've never seen her healthier in all the years we've been married." He had to duck and weave to avoid getting pummeled.

He drops hints though, such as, "Let's try to eat healthy together," and "It's only a decision…to eat right and exercise. We're only one decision away from living good lifestyles." Ugh. He may be right, but I still hate hearing it.

Just last night he told me, "I'm hungry. What've you got for dinner around here?"

Other than this muffin, I have no idea.

Dressing Room 3

Dressing Room 3 at the Slatten Ranch Mervyns' is a good dressing room. It's a nice dressing room. It's kind and friendly and supportive. I know this because I walked into it the other day with an armload of swimwear and was feeling a little "I am appalled that I'm even going to attempt this" about myself when I saw it: a loopy scribble on the wall that read "*YOU ARE BEAUTIFUL.*" And while I may normally wrinkle my nose at graffiti, I couldn't help smiling. I contemplated exiting to go scrawl it on the walls of every other dressing room there.

When I squeezed myself into the first suit, I made sure to look at the quote. I began to have my doubts though during the "shove this, squash that, grip, clutch and jiggle" dance that I didn't intentionally begin. I had to wrestle with the second suit to get it off and by the time I had twisted into the third one, I was shimmying around trying to fight back tears. I held off arguing with the ink on the wall, just gathered up my swimwear and decided to go shop for something safe: shoes or dishes. Maybe even a towel rack. No one is ever too chubby to buy a nice towel rack.

"I went swimsuit shopping today," I sighed to a girlfriend on the phone. "It was horrifying."

"Oh no," she replied, "Don't ever do that. Don't you know Satan runs a sweatshop down in hell that specifically turns out swimsuits?"

I considered this. "Is it right next to his bakery?"

"Close. On the same street. His Pringles factory is right next to the sweatshop."

"Oh right, right."

We laugh and then, "I'm not liking the way my thighs rub together," I told her. "It's creating too much friction. I could probably start a small fire down below."

"Well, you'd be a hot commodity on *Survivor*. No one would vote you off if you could start fires between your legs!"

This is why girls have girlfriends. This very reason. We are hooting and cackling and shouting things like "Fire in the hole!" when Brad walks in. Wiping a tear from my eye, I wave him away and mouth "Swimsuit shopping…" He has no choice but to raise his eyebrows and made a swift exit. I feel no pity. He can still wear the same swimsuit from high school if he wanted to.

I'm not the authority on swimwear. The last time I purchased a suit, I confused the inside from the outside and wound-up fielding questions about the visibility of the crotch liner. I bitterly recall my post-children swimsuit buys—where I'd search and hunt for the skimpiest coverage. Strings here, patches there—it was a matter of fabric then, not size. These days I'm left wondering when the swim skirt will come back in style. And aren't we ready for a sassy reappearance of the water dresses from 1884?

Home Alone

The phone is ringing again. It's probably the fifth call in an hour. I don't mind though. The little girl next door is home alone for the first time and calls to check in with me whenever she hears anything suspicious. It's actually kinda cute.

"Um…did you hear that?" she asks now, her voice a little shaky. I hear her shudder and then, "It sounds like someone's walking around outside in the bushes. Geez…this is scary."

I'm tempted to laugh, but don't. At this point in my life, I want nothing more than to be left home alone, stranger lurking in my bushes or not. "Do you want to come over here?" I suggest. "You can help me bathe the boys and then we can watch TV." I know she'll refuse the offer, as she has the four times before now, but it's only right to ask.

I wish I had a friendly neighbor such as myself the first time my parents left me home alone. All I had was a bossy older sister who was in fact, being left home alone for the first time as well. She was 'in charge' and took her job very seriously.

"Have you brushed your teeth yet?" Like a little drill sergeant, she stood in her slippers, having had us get ready for bed at 7:00 p.m. Her tiny bathrobe was cinched at the waist, tied in a perfect knot on her belly. She must have been about 10 or 11 at the time, making me all of 7 or 8 and not at all a willing participant in the ruse of playing insubordinate. I rolled my eyes at her and leaned to scratch my ankle. She grasped my arm and yanked me toward the bathroom. She had three years and quite a few pounds on me, so I was basically under her control.

"And wash your face, and put your stuff back in the drawer, and dry off the counter when you're done." She was barking orders over my shoulder as I spit into the sink. So young, and already I knew it was going to be a long night.

A little patience and a lot of manipulation on my part paid me back in full. By 9:00 p.m. I had her convinced that cooking would actually be okay, and that mom's rule to never use the stove didn't apply when we were super hungry. By 9:30 I had us made up like Daisy Duke and Farrah Fawcett, complete with frayed shorts and tube tops, and by 10:00 p.m., an hour past our designated bedtime, we sat crammed together on the sofa watching *Amityville Horror*. Frozen in fear, we were glued to the TV, praying our parents would hurry up and get home just to safely bust us and put us to bed.

"What was that?" she squealed as the wind whipped through the trees and the branches tapped the glass.

"Did you hear that?" I curled in closer to her as I cocked my head to listen to what I swore sounded like a man walking through our backyard holding an axe.

Having recently learned the 'Rosemary…I've got your baby' trick in any darkened room with a mirror, I opted to sit in discomfort rather than get up and use the bathroom. I wriggled and squirmed until Andrea agreed to accompany me and we ran, clutching one another, through the house and down the hall. Shadows on the wall made us scurry faster and

I panicked when I thought, just for a second, I had seen the ghost of my grandmother lurking in my parent's bedroom.

We slammed the bathroom door and stood wide-eyed and panting in the bright light. "I saw Grandma," I gasped, "And I can smell her perfume!" Completely untrue, but I imagined I could. After she had passed away a few months earlier, my parents woke in the middle of the night to find the entire house in a haze of Jean Nate, her signature scent. I had overheard their conversation the following day and had never fully recovered from the knowledge of it.

"Listen…" Andrea put her ear to the door, "I hear her coming…" I too put my ear to the door and with trepidation, struggled to hear our approaching deceased.

BAM BAM BAM! We screamed and our dad laughed. The doorknob rattled violently. "Whoooooooo." He howled on the other side of the door, "It's Grandma Sprenger and I'm coming to get yooooooou." BAM BAM BAM! Then laughter.

Andrea threw open the door and we stood shaking, giggling, and visibly relieved. "You two should have been in bed an hour ago." He wasn't really upset. Probably just thrilled to have the chance to scare the pants off us. Our mom was a different story.

"Cooking? You girls were cooking and playing in my makeup? And what are you wearing?" She obviously didn't recognize Daisy and Farrah in her anger-induced delirium.

"Then you stay up watching 'R' rated horror movies and hide in the bathroom till we get home?" She is beside herself. "Never again! I'm never leaving you two home alone again if this is how you behave!"

"But we were scared…we saw a ghost…" we pleaded and begged for another chance.

"Nonsense," she replied. "You saw no such thing. We live behind a freeway, not a graveyard." As if that would make a difference to a ghost. No matter, we weren't allowed to stay home alone again until we were considerably older.

When the phone rings for the sixth time this evening, I pick up and hear, "I'm coming over!" I definitely won't mention the *Rosemary's Baby* thing.

I Was the Red-headed Stepchild

I grew up being a stepchild and now I have two of my own. Not in the typical blended family/*your mother married my father* sort of way, more along the lines of "All this crap piled on these steps needs to go up!" manner of thinking.

I first became a stepchild in the fall of 1979 when we moved from a ranch style home (circa early 1960s) in San Bruno into a split-level in the suburbs of Pleasanton. It was then that my mother said pointedly to my older sister, "This first step belongs to you," and then to me, "And this second one belongs to you. That makes you my stepchild number one and stepchild number two. You girls are responsible for anything placed on your step and all of it must be carried up and put in its proper place at the end of each day."

Back then, this made perfect sense. All of my friend's parents were still married and I had no understanding of the term stepchild for any other reason. In fact, my strawberry hair deemed me the nickname The Redheaded Stepchild long before I heard it used in any other context. And would our crap ever pile up: laundry, books, school bags, shoes; we constantly were stepping over and around our belongings on our way up and down those stairs.

"Stepchildren!" my mom would yell in the late afternoon, "Get your stuff."

"Stepchildren!" my mom would yell in the early evening, "Clear the stairs!"

"Stepchildren!" my mom would yell at bedtime, "If I have to move any of this myself, I'm moving it straight to the trash!"

That last one would get us stomping down to retrieve our loot and pounding each stair with exaggerated force on the way back up.

"Do you realize," I asked my sister, "That if we had a one-story house Mom would have no place to put our stuff EXCEPT in our rooms? She's fully taking advantage of us."

But now, being a mom myself, as well as a homeowner of a split-level, I pile things at the bottom of the stairs with the expectation that someone will carry it all up. Someone being Josh, of course. I try to sort it all out for him, make his job easier. His stuff on the first step, Ben's on the second, mine on the third. It's all a matter of organization, really. But he's not buying it. He protests, huffs, growls, and carries up the items with a steady stream of complaints being strewn from his mouth as he goes. He too stomps his feet. He too feels the unjustness of the situation. Normally, I find everyone's belongings in the correct room but his defiance is illustrated in where he places it all: on the floor and in a heap.

However, Josh is savvier to blended families and actual stepchildren than I was at his age, so I hesitate calling him my stepchild out loud. For now, I just call him Josh and ask him to continue being helpful.

If You Dare Wear Short Shorts

There are numerous reasons I do not wear short shorts; too many to name, actually. Most young women have fond memories of displaying their tan, firm, teenaged legs for all their male admirers. I'm no different. Once upon a time I lay in a boat, on a beach, atop a towel, on a lounge-chair, just about anywhere and proudly stretched out my two muscular trophies, if you will, for anyone who was interested in taking a gander. Granted, I was a 13-year-old at the time. Years of gymnastics had rewarded me well and I basked in pride and vanity, rather than humility and inner self-worth, which is where I should have had my priorities.

The summer of 1985 had me preparing for eighth grade, while the "Powers That Be" felt I was long overdue for a reality check. I lost myself in clouds of pastel eye shadow, glitter lip gloss, *Teen Beat* magazine and Duran Duran 45s. I was completely oblivious to the fact that while I stood lip-synching in front of my mirror like the narcissistic Belinda Carlisle wannabe that I was, fate had a plan for intervention which would soon put me in check.

My best friend that week was a fellow gymnast. She invited me to camp on a lake with her family and though that may have been exciting enough, we were overjoyed to learn another family would be accompanying us. It included a 16-year-old son, Mark. We were drunk with our fantasies, high on hormonal lust, and giddy with the anticipation of possibility. Sadly, it never occurred to us that a 16-year-old boy would have little interest two preteens that still stuffed their training bras.

Two families shoved into one recreation vehicle ("RV") left little room for privacy. The poor guy had to hike off alone to escape us. We trailed him like eager puppies—giggling, sighing, cooing, and batting our eyelashes. It's humbling even now to think how we must have appeared: our blush in angry streaks across our cheeks and mother's mascara sticking in hard clumps to our lashes.

As embarrassing as all that may be, it would have been okay, the trip would have continued just fine if, in the middle of a campfire one evening, I hadn't been suddenly seized by a sharp pain in my abdomen. Wincing, I bent over in my lawn chair and held my breath. Another one followed and I groaned in agony. Both families sat sprawled in other chairs, all circling the light of the blaze. It soon passed and I was able to return to my normal position, being careful to adjust my very short shorts so that if Mark looked my way, my supple young legs might quite possibly take his breath away. My wishful thinking was abruptly cut short by another cramp and by then, I was quite positive I should be rethinking my Mark strategies in the bathroom of the RV.

Some time passed while I sat in the restroom trying to comprehend the origin of my unfamiliar pain. I decided to exit the RV and rejoin the campfire, hoping to avoid the humiliating question of "Everything come out, okay?" Since my reappearance to the group went relatively unnoticed, I returned to my chair by route of Mark, strategically sashaying in front of him.

As I passed, my rear was met with a ripple of laughter. What began as a low giggle soon grew into a twitching chuckle. Mark fell over in his chair, holding his stomach. I turned to look at him, indirectly giving the rest of the crowd their front seat to a comedic accident. Laughter exploded around me. As I began to panic, Mark wiped the tears from his eyes and snorted, "Nice toilet bowl ring on your legs!"

The moral of the story is: No matter how great you think your legs appear; they will always look ridiculous with a toilet bowl ring on the back of them. And that, my friends, is reason enough to not ever wear short shorts.

3

One Smart Cookie

Just a Trim

A friend and I are chatting. I am perched on my dining room table, she on my sofa. I am swinging my legs and though completely engaged in the sport of keeping my sandal on my foot, I can't help but notice the way she is peering at my hair.

"Are you staring at my bangs?"

She starts smirking. "Why would you cut them yourself?" Good friends can ask these sorts of questions without getting pummeled.

"Is it that obvious?" The look on her face tells me that why yes, it is. I hop off the table and groan. "Really? Do they look bad?" She starts snickering. Not a good sign.

I am not a stylist. I never have been one nor have I ever claimed to be. Actually, that's not true. Once in the seventh grade I convinced a friend that she needed her hair styled more like Madonna's if she wanted to be cool. The look would be impossible, unless she allowed me to trim it up for her a bit. Plus, I would throw in a purple streak, much like the one I was sporting.

We sat cloistered on her bedroom floor, hunched in front of a hand mirror I had tacked to the wall for ambiance. She looked doubtful, but handed me her dad's buzzers. "Just be careful, and don't cut off too much, okay?" Buzzers! I thought I was going to have to use the fabric scissors I had swiped from my mother's sewing basket that morning. Things were going better than expected.

I happily chatted away while I cut and shaved, fluffed and sprayed. I sat streaking her longer locks with a purple Sharpie pen while she gazed into a compact mirror, inspecting the crew cut I had done above her left ear.

Enter Mommy Dearest. "Agh!" she screamed, "What are you girls doing?" I immediately started to scribble on my own hair instead. "No!" she yelled, "No! No!" I fumbled the pen and saw with horror as it descended from flight and made a bright line across my white mini skirt.

"You." She stood fuming and pointed me to the door. I shoved my gear into an Esprit bag and hightailed it out of there. The next time I saw this friend it was post-trip to the beauty parlor where her mother had taken her to clean up my chop-job. Her mother felt that a tightly coiled permanent was a solution to the hair calamity I had created. I winced when I saw her. Angrily she hissed, "I hate you," when she passed me in the hall at school.

I hadn't cut hair again until I had the boys, then I tinkered with an occasional trim. But with Josh's cowlick and my absence of a steady hand, I wound up calling in backup more than once. I stopped cutting hair back in 2002 after being caught red handed with another pair of buzzers and a son who now looked remarkably like Calliou.

Brad looked on in horror as I swept up the evidence. "Zip it, Blondie," I told him, "Or I'll shave you while you sleep." I waved the buzzers around to drive home my point. He exited swiftly, rubbing his hair and glaring at me.

So now I stand examining my bangs in a mirror while my friend sits hooting on the couch behind me. I flick them around and bite my lower lip while contemplating the repair-work needed. A lone Sharpie pen on the desk in the kitchen catches my eye. Problem solved.

Loose Lips Sink Ships

As a child, I once remarked to my aunt that her bottom was considerably larger than mine. I went on to tell her that no matter what, my bottom would stop growing before it reached her gigantic proportions.

"Loose lips sink ships," my mom later scolded me. "You may have really hurt her feelings."

I have since learned to bite my tongue, but am always amazed at the folks that I meet who have not been informed of the age-old adage, "If you can't say something nice, don't say anything at all." Or perhaps they have but choose not to adhere to it at the right time. My vote is to change the expression to read, "If you can't say anything intelligent, don't say anything at all."

Take for example the comment of a very good friend after I suffered a miscarriage after the birth of my second son. "Oh, this is probably the best thing that's ever happened to you. I mean, with all of Ben's health problems, how could you even handle a new baby? Ben's needs would surely get lost in the shuffle..." Gulp. Thanks for your confidence in my parenting skills , and to assume I would allow one child's needs to out-shine the other's is not only offensive, it's ridiculous. Not to mention, we just lost a baby and that is a tragedy no matter when in life it happens. But hey, I appreciate your support.

I understand that children with special needs are somewhat of a mystery to those parents who have healthy kids. Our routines, our sacri-fices, our flexibility. More than once I have been told, "I don't know how you do it. I could never do what you do." To which the only appropriate response is, "True. You couldn't." Smile. Nod. Clear my throat to get through the uncomfortable silence that ensues after such a remark. When I am feeling generous, I usually tell people, "Oh, you'd be surprised at how strong you really are. Especially when you have no choice. When the only option is to protect your child, you will do it without even thinking of the effort until its passed." I think both responses are accurate, neither one unintelligent.

Yet I'm still at a loss when I hear an occasional dumb-as-rocks re-mark: "Fortunately, you will never have to buy two Happy Meals at Mc-Donald's because Ben won't even know what he's missing." Uh—yeah, I'm so relieved to have saved those three bucks. Paying for two Happy Meals is sure a pain in the ass.

More recently I was told by a mother of a brilliant little girl who lives with cerebral palsy, "(Sigh) Sometimes I think it would just be easier if she was mentally retarded. That way she'd never know how much a struggle her life is going to be." I almost laughed at the absurdity of her comment, until I realized her seriousness. My shock quickly turned to anger and resentment when she continued by telling me, "What man is going to be able to love her the way she is? She'll be alone the rest of her life and that makes me so sad." When I said nothing, she concluded with, "You must feel the same way about Ben, except lucky for him—he won't even know he's alone." Hold the phone lady! Excuse me while I throw up. Do people actually think like this in our society? I chalked that conversation up on my list of firsts: the first time anyone ever told me they wished they had a mentally retarded child. Who even uses the R word these days?

Loose lips sink ships. It's a great aphorism to live by. I'll have to remember to propose it the next time someone tells me I'm fortunate to have a non-verbal child because, "My child never shuts up. I'd give anything to have a few minutes without hearing his yapping all day long."

Metaphorically Anorexic

After the normal stretching-of-the-pants exercise (up, down, up, down, pull-pull-pull) I bounded downstairs and caught Brad just as he was leaving through the front door.

"Wait…do these pants make me look fluffy?" I spun around, completely expecting an answer I did not receive.

First, he groaned, which caught me off-guard. Then he said, "Why would you ask your husband that question?"

Dean, our friend and current roomie, poked his head around the corner of the kitchen with his eyebrows raised. "Brad," he paused, "Allow me…no, you do not look fluffy," his hands began making an hourglass figure in the air, "You look curvy…" I wasn't sure how to interpret this because the hourglass he made was wider than his shoulders. In fact, it was making me look pretty hefty.

"Um…" I began slowly, so as to not confuse anyone, "Do these pants make me look extra short and/or stocky?'

"Do you want me to be honest?" Brad asked.

My face felt hot. "I think you just were. Jeez—it's like you don't even know the 'Man Rules' or something." I was mad. "Can't you just say, 'You look nice,' or 'I like how those pants accentuate your (insert word here).'"

"Fine." His jaw clenched. "Those pants accentuate your butt." And at that he bugged out his eyes and held up his hands at shoulder height, but apart at roughly the width of a fridge. Dean smartly ducked back into the kitchen, leaving the two of us in a showdown of glares.

I need to better prepare myself for this kind of thing. I am married to an analytical truth teller, no matter what the costs. I asked and so I received, even though I felt slightly offended. His logic being, "You wouldn't want me to lie to you?" This is true, but every now and then I wouldn't fight off a small fib or slight exaggeration, especially on stretching-of-the-pants day.

What's ironic is that for someone who tries hard to not obsess about overeating, I find food analogies spewing from my mouth all day long.

For example, Josh complains about his lunch containing unfamiliar fruits or vegetables, and I tell him, "Variety is the spice of life" as a way to encourage him to try new things.

Or when a person says or does something I can make no sense of, what comes to mind is "She's a few sandwiches short of a picnic."

Daily I dub my children "Sweet Pea", "Sweet Potato", "Pumpkin'," Honey Buns," and "Sugar Pie." And somewhere along the line our family went from saying "That's how we roll," to "That's how we cinnamon roll."

And then I had an epiphany. I was happily chatting away on the telephone with a girlfriend when she asked what my upcoming week looked like. I rattled off a packed agenda of meetings, lessons for Josh, therapies for Ben, conferences for both, sporting events, and one or two coffee dates squeezed in with friends. "Whew," I sighed. "I have a lot on my plate. I am—metaphorically speaking—stretched too thin." And then I pictured that and started to laugh. No one has accused me of being too thin in quite some time. "I am *metaphorically anorexic*," I told my friend. "I have a disease…"

"Oh yeah me too" she piped up, then lowered her voice to imitate her husband. "Hey baby, pick up my dry cleaning today." And I'd say, "Ooops sorry. I'm already too skinny." We laughed.

I imagined all the times I wished I had said I was too slight of frame to participate in some event or add yet another responsibility to my ever-growing list. Grocery shopping? Can't—I'm a complete beanpole. Pick up kids from school? No can do—I'm already practically emaciated. Coach little league? Oh—wish I could, but I'm withering away to nothing as I speak.

When Brad caught me closely scrutinizing my "Body by Josh and Ben" in the mirror last night he shrugged and suggested I spend more time at the gym. "If only I could," I sighed heavily, "But I'm already too thin as it is."

My Dance Partner

"**Dip me…I said** to DIP ME! Oh, you clumsy old oaf…Why do I bother with you?" I can hardly believe I hissed those words at my fossil of a vacuum cleaner recently. Ordinarily, my vacuum and I move beautifully together…graceful and strategic, all our moves preplanned and memorized. I kicked the too-long cord out of my way as we staggered down the hallway. "Okay, let's take it from the top."

Is it me, or do all women feel as if a dance is occurring while they vacuum their home? My vacuum and I have been together so long, I feel mildly betrayed when it gets out of sync on me. Its roar is an old familiar tune and once heard, my feet automatically step in line and begin their rhythmic strides to keep time with the white noise. I have the most peculiar habit of always vacuuming in the exact same way, from the back of the house to the front. I've never once broken this pattern, except perhaps to suck up a quick spill in the kitchen. Normally, when I grab the "Vac" out of the garage, it's because I intend to commence our routine of comfortable steps through the entire house. "Shall we dance?"

"One, two three, one two three…under….bed…da dee dum…. hmmm…hmmm…one, two, three….kick, step, backslide, step…" I am Carolyn the prima ballerina in the confines of my home. (Well, kind of.) Years ago, after one too many mishaps with a vacuum who shall remain nameless (let's just say it wasn't the upright kind and *my word,* are those little devils hard to handle!) I was introduced to my Dirt Devil. It was love at first sight. Not only did it have incredible power, but it was light and easy to handle. All its attachments came neatly tucked into its back and never once has anything popped out, fallen off, or become wedged inside. It *is* a clever little thing. It twists and spins like a champion, like a born dancer, if I do say so myself.

You can imagine my alarm when out of the blue last week I found myself tangled in cord, taking a few wobbly steps, and then crashing down in the hallway. Stunned, I lay flat on my back looking up into the widened eyes of my 2-year-old son. "Did it get you?" he was baffled. In my fall, I had accidentally yanked the cord from the outlet and its groan was slowly coming to a halt. I giggled, "No, it just tripped me. It must be having an off day." As we unwrapped miles of cord from my ankles and knees, I took the opportunity to explain to my son that all the high leg kicks and twirls Mommy did with the vacuum were part of a carefully thought-out dance number. No need to describe the look on his face. I didn't continue. Perhaps if I had a daughter, she would understand.

Naughty Girls Need Love Too

Trixie is a bad girl. Not your "run of the mill, cause a little riff-raff" type of bad, she's a *baaaad* girl. The kind of disobedient that tilts an entire household on its axis and shakes out any tolerance and patience like excess pocket change. Trixie is naughty, and she is our cat.

I was about finished with kittens when Trixie came to me. Having just adopted out 5 kittens and their Mama, I had bestowed all scratching posts, litter boxes and cans of kitten chow, then sucked up the remaining mice, feathers, and bells with my industrial strength vacuum cleaner. I settled down with the three remaining felines and vowed no more kittens, at least not for another year. That was when my phone rang.

"Please, please take this baby kitty," my friend begged. "Mark found her on 580 this morning." On the freeway? Who finds kittens on the freeway? Must have been slow traffic. I relented to letting her stay until I found her a permanent residence. When she arrived that evening,

I could no sooner turn her out than I could a newborn infant. Tiny, laden with ear mites and fleas, just learning to walk, this wee little calico wormed her way into my heart. Literally. She had worms too.

Fast forward to her first vet appointment. "Hmmm...a calico?" the vet asked. "Know much about calicos?" I shook my head 'no' as I watched her bounce off the walls, bat a pen from the counter, hiss and scratch at lint, attack his pant leg, bite his sock, and then proceed to pee on the exam table. "Is she aiming at you?" I asked him. "It does appear so," he answered politely. I learned a little about my girl that day and went home prepared to teach her who's the boss.

She's the boss. I can see clearly now that while I may have succeeded with her three older siblings, with her I have failed to instill a sense of respect. "That cat has no respect!" I hear this from my husband daily. "Look—just LOOK what she did!" And always, it's something I could have prevented, knowing this little devil I'm raising.

In our hallway we have a cat door out to the garage, where the litter-boxes are. We call it, "The Girl's Bathroom." All of the girls use the door and have no problems. Except Trixie. She had a problem. Her problem was that she didn't like the door. So, she refused to use it. Instead, she'd do her business right outside the door in our hallway. That lasted a day or two before I wizened up and taped the door open. No problem. Except when the litter boxes got too full for Trixie's liking, she let me know by peeing on my bed. And then one morning...

"Carolyn, your pillow smells like cat pee," Brad told me. He was lounging in the sack while I was preparing to jump in the shower. "Oh baloney," I scoffed, "It does not." Maintain composure, I told myself. Maintain composure.

"No seriously, it reeks. Come smell it." Why I did I still don't know. I mean, who wants to smell cat pee anyway? But as I leaned in to take a sniff, I was also removing the scrunchie from my hair at the same time. Enter nauseating whiff of urine into the nostrils and coincide that with a damp scrunchie in my palm. Wet hair fell around my face as realization sank in.

Brad sniffed the air around me and started hooting and snorting. I felt my damp locks and screeched. "TRIXIE!"

Not much has changed in the last six months. Oh sure, she's cute and playful, but the little heathen has graduated from peeing on me to chewing up everything I own. It's like having a dog, I imagine, in some respect. Shoes, socks, toys, toiletry items, and now electrical cords have all fallen victim to Trixie. A once intricately woven laundry hamper has now been reduced to a standing rectangle of cardboard, it's covering annihilated, fanning out like an Awesome Blossom.

I Should Have Seen This Coming

Years ago, I went to a psychic. Bad idea. Seriously. So baaaaaad. I went because it seemed like a good idea. Also, at that time—high bangs, frosted lip-gloss, and teal hoop earrings bigger than my thigh seemed like the right thing to do. My turquoise mascara, though I loved it, never really seemed appropriate, but I wore it anyway to bring out the brown in my eyes.

The psychic lady I went to came highly recommended by my friend's sister whose neighbor's daughter saw her regularly. I drove all the way to Vacaville. Alone. I did have a tape recorder, but I should have brought a friend to marvel with me. I was so naive…

She was a regular woman, which slightly disappointed me. I expected to see all sorts of psychic paraphernalia placed around her house (which I would have thought had been decorated with beaded curtains and crystal balls and stuff). Nope. Regular run of the mill linoleum in her kitchen, typical overstuffed sofas in her family room.

She smiled and said, "You're a little early…" when I entered. Already I was impressed. I glanced at my watch and guess what? I was. All of my past psychic experiences had to do with me, predicting the predictable. For example—after I went on a bender all night drinking beers and eating potato salad. I'd stand on the scale the following morning and predict, quite accurately, that I hadn't lost any weight. Or go further back to high school when I'd come strolling in an hour past curfew—didn't take a psychic then to envisage that I'd be in for a verbal lashing. I could have seen that one coming a block away. (Actually, I did…when I spied the living room light on—a sure indicator my mom was up waiting for my less than stellar explanation.) Gee, come to think of it—I may have been a psychic back in grade school. I distinctly remember the one time I tried my hand at dodge ball. I knew, without anyone telling me, that my prior athletic ability would precede me, and it did. I pretty much foresaw myself being picked last and wouldn't you know it—I was.

I think I may have been the easiest one hundred dollars this lady ever made.

"Someone in your life is causing you discontent..." Wow. How did she know? It couldn't possibly have been my sniveling.

"You're confused about how to proceed..." Holy smoke. She could tell all that?

"You are looking for answers, but nothing seems to present itself as the right path..." Had a studio audience been present, applause would have broken out all around us.

As soon as I admitted to being there to gain insight regarding a boy I was dating—the flood gates dropped, and I was swatting off her revelations left and right.

"He may still talk to another woman...he has thoughts of her occasionally...in his house are remnants of his past with her..." Well shoot. He did live before he met me...wouldn't that vision apply to every one of us?

"How many children will I have?" I interrupted.

She faltered. "One...no two...I see children, but I am not sure if they belong to you..." Meaning maybe one or more, but possibly none at all. Hmmm...

Yes, seeing that particular psychic was probably a mistake. Not only because I left feeling more confused than when I arrived, but because sometimes being given the answers isn't nearly as fulfilling as learning them on your own. I could have predicted that.

School of Hard Knox

Sometimes I feel like cutting. You know—just skipping out on responsibilities for the day. Instead of grocery shopping, I'd tell the hubby I cut instead. Get the oil changed in the truck? Nope—I cut SpeeDee today too. Laundry? I cut on folding and putting away. As for meals, I cut food preparation and dishwashing after that. It'd be fun to call a friend and say, "You wanna cut today? Skip out on mothering and all that jazz…we could go hang out at 7-11 or the mall and try not to run into our moms." I don't know how many times I cut class while in high school, but I do know the exact day my truancy habits came to an end.

March 17, 1990. It was passing period of St. Patrick's Day, senior year. I stood leaning against my locker listening to three of my girlfriends attempt to craft a good reason to skip second period. Granted, we had only been on campus for one class, but the thought of one free hour before reporting to the nearby elementary school for R.O.P. Childcare seemed to overcome us. "Pick me up some donuts while you're out," said Jeff, a fellow classmate, as he stood and grinned, shutting the locker he used beneath mine.

"This is an A and B conversation," was my witty retort, "C your way out of it." We laughed as I grabbed the wad of bills he held out for me.

"Buy yourself something nice," he joked as he walked away. Well, there we had it—our reason for treason: we had some shopping to do.

After hitting the nearby 7-11 and picking up four Big Gulps and a bag of donuts, I drove my friends around town and pointed out some of the biggest attractions: the house that burned down two weekends past, a favorite local make-out spot near the fairgrounds, and the apartment complex of my latest crush.

I might have been speeding. Before I knew it, lights were flashing in my rearview mirror and I heard the blip-blip of a siren. We freaked out. After repeatedly telling one another to shut-up and then doing our best to fasten our seatbelts without looking too conspicuous, I pulled to the side and warned my passengers to look as innocent as they could muster.

"Going somewhere are you?" asked the officer, peering over the rim of his sunglasses.

"YES!" shrieked Angie, the resident drama queen in the backseat, "It's St. Patrick's Day and we were going home to put on green clothing for the children we work with during R.O.P. Childcare." It would have been clever, had it not been so ludicrous.

"Do you live at 7-11?" he asked, "Or is it you have a Big Gulp soda machine at your house?" he leaned in my window and inspected the interior of my VW Rabbit. His sunglasses fell from his face onto my lap. I felt my jaw go slack in shock.

Recovering, I tried not to laugh. He ripped his glasses from my hand and asked to see my license. I handed him the card and smiled as if this were the most common mistake under the sun.

He stared at it and then grunted. "Having a bad hair day, were you?" The gall. I stopped smiling and glared at him. He held the card out for me to take and sneered, "What would you call that style? That big…" he made a claw with his hand and put it to his forehead, mocking my shellacked bangs. I reached for the card, and he flicked it back. Kind of in a TV cop sort of way, minus the cool.

I didn't like this guy. Officer Knox. He saw me reading his tag and said, "That's right—I'm Officer Knox. As in—you just entered the School of Hard Knox." Was he serious? I held back a defiant snort. He made us drive back to school, while he escorted my vehicle. A police escort. Lights flashing and all. We arrived just in time for the next passing period, so our appearance in the front parking lot didn't go unnoticed.

Melanie, the resident crybaby, sobbed the entire time we walked up to the building, making it seem so much worse than it was. Students gaped and gawked as we made our way inside. Once there, we were assigned different principles, but were all handed out the same punishment. No senior trip. Our mothers were called. One at a time, we were forced to explain what we did while the principles listened and nodded at one another. Partners in defending evil.

My mother asked to be put on speakerphone. And so, she was. "You called me at work to tell me my daughter cut a class?!" She was flabbergasted, "You are denying her a trip with her classmates her senior year because she missed a class?!" Oh—she was hot. I saw the look pass between the principles. Uh-oh. Trouble. They gulped and swallowed, shifted in their chairs. "Oh no you don't," she told them, "Carolyn WILL go on that trip with her friends unless you are planning to deny every senior the same opportunity when they miss a class. Do you need me to tell you she had my permission to be off campus? Is that it? Well fine then! She had my permission; I'll call the front office right now and tell them as much. Give me a break gentleman, and please—get back to work." Click.

I replayed this hopeful scene in my head, as I waited to make the call to my mom. When I did get her on the line, she was understandably upset but was pretty busy at work, so the actual conversation was much briefer than my daydream version.

On my way out, I slid a package of donuts across the counter to Jeff, who had been the teaching assistant in the office that period and was witness to the entire scene.

"What? No change?" he grinned.

"Welcome to the School of Hard Knox," I answered.

Sleep Deprivation

I've heard that insanity is a sure destination point when sleep deprivation occurs. Now while I may not be ready for a snug fitting white coat with straps, I am ready for a good four years of sleep, give or take.

Before our first child was born, I was told the horror stories all moms love to share; spit up, ear infections, colic, even projectile vomiting. I smiled and innocently took it all in. But the tales of late hour feedings, night terrors, and children who loved company in the wee hours of the morning unnerved me. See, I'm one of those rare breeds of people who like sleep. Need sleep. Live to sleep, if truth be told.

Our first child was one of those textbook babies. Ate well, smiled a lot, went down for naps with no problems. Actually, slept through the night at 6 weeks of age. We like to think he tricked us into thinking this parenting game was a breezy one to play, and then BAM—along came his sibling just 20 short months later. I haven't slept since.

It just recently came to my attention how disturbing this lack of sleep can be. The first sign was my finding the remote control in the refrigerator the other day. I hadn't even known it had gone missing. Next, my bath towel magically appeared in the bathroom trash. An odd occurrence— sure, but not completely unexplainable. But just last week I accidentally applied acne medication to the bristles on my toothbrush, and sprayed deodorant in my hair.

When later teased about my actions, I meant to retort with a friendly yet witty reply, but instead I spit out a snarl so fierce and sharp, my hand flew to my mouth in shock. "I think I need more sleep," I offered, "My nightly average of…three hours, interrupted, does not seem to be cutting it anymore."

Our family has a perfect balance of sleepers versus non-sleepers. Brad and I like to sleep, our two children do not. See how nice and even that is? More correctly, Brad and I need to sleep, our two children do not. I think they might be vampires. Up early, the boys move freely through the day and do not seem to slow their paces until around 4 p.m. As any parent knows, this is much too late for a nap. It took me a while to believe this rule applied to us, but trust me, it applies to all kids. Allowing a child to nap after 4 p.m. is the same as a written invitation to that child for a late-night pajama party, courtesy of you.

I thought I could get around this nap issue by just putting them down earlier. That decision had me jogging from room to room, answering cries for sippy cups, bottles, and books. Then having to walk the wandering child back to his bed and try to explain, through the sobbing and the begging, the benefits of sleep. Not to mention having to change the sheets of the child who barfs when he cries too much, and shake the other child (who wandered in to see what all the fuss was about) from my leg while trying to keep my pants up. Needless to say, nobody ever slept, and I would be fighting off the urge to sob in unison after an hour or two of that.

Next, I tried cutting naps from their schedules completely and would find myself stumbling over a sleeping kid in the hallway, on the kitchen floor, even curled up next to the treadmill. Around 5, those little buggers would crawl off somewhere to sleep whenever I wasn't looking.

I then began to experiment with the power naps, and would wake them after 30 minutes, thinking they'd be good and tired by 9 p.m. They were onto me. And their little bodies began adjusting to my studies of trial and error.

So where does that leave me? Sitting around with a glazed look in my eye, babbling with my finger in my mouth? Only sometimes. Most days go by somewhat normally and by the evening I am looking forward to a warm bath, a trashy romance novel, a steaming mug of hot cocoa, and a quiet evening knowing the little ones are tucked in their beds. Since that is nothing more than a fantasy, I have settled for a negotiating youngster, a howling baby, a phone call from the out-of-town hubby, and a much-anticipated evening of late night T.V. That little pajama party where I can't un-invite the guests and wish like heck they would go to sleep.

Spontaneous Self-Disclosure

"**And so,**" I continued to the gal in the toll booth, "This party means a lot to my family and I'm hoping I'll get there before it begins…"

She nods and stares blankly out her window. My cue to get a move on. "Well, it sure has been nice talking with you, you take care now…" I smile as I drive onto the bridge. Brad is slumped in the passenger seat, one hand covering his face.

"WHY do you do that?" he drilled. "Why force perfect strangers into having conversations with you?"

I shrug, "They love it." I beam a wide smile in his direction—we have forever disagreed on this point and truthfully, he is most likely correct. I just can't help myself. It's a nuisance I suppose, this giving away of too much information.

For as long as I can remember, I've been reminded "less is more" and "don't talk to strangers." No matter how much prompting I get, I still fall victim to the blabbermouth syndrome and find myself info dumping on whoever is lending an ear. I have the gift of gab, though some may say it isn't much of a gift.

"Don't you just hate it when strangers touch your belly?" I'll inquire of the pregnant cashier, thrusting us into a 5-minute diatribe on how respect for privacy disappears when your stomach is exposed for folks to rub, touch, or generally make a wish upon.

Or "I'm sorry I'm so grumpy," I'll open with when conversing with the telemarketers, "It's just that my son is sick and I'm starving. I haven't eaten since breakfast…" and then we are off on a 10-minute discourse about what you sacrifice when children come along.

My favorite is when a University of California, Davis student working the Alumni Association calls and needs to talk about what's new on campus. They phone specifically to butter up Alumni and then solicit donations, but I'll chat about my college days, give tips on dorm raiding, and ask if the Graduate is still the best place to dance. I inquire about my favorite professors and engage the youngster in a conversation about his future before querying the status of his interview skills. I've been known to offer a pointer or two and wish them well before hanging up. No money lost, but perhaps a youth inspired. (My justification for not donating to the fund.)

"Sometimes you just need to zip it," Brad tells me, "Before you annoy a person to the point of hostility. You are a danger to yourself, you know that?" We are laughing some, but his message is clear: less is more. The same old thing.

The American Flag

The American flag: the stars, the stripes, the feeling of pride that swells up inside each one of us when we now see one. It hasn't changed at all, only we have; and it's this change that has brought about a national feeling of unity I hadn't yet experienced in all my 29 years until this past September.

With pride, I hung a flag outside my home. That, combined with a sense of unison and collective honor, keeps me in a constant state of humility and awe. So, you can imagine I was pretty flabbergasted this week when a car, donning that symbol of "togetherness" cut me off in the Albertson's parking lot and left me with my jaw open. Now, being cut off is no travesty, even I know that. However, being cut off, honked at, and then given the universal sign for "excuse me" (that's being polite) was a bit unnerving. After doing a double take to make sure the small flag on the antennae was American, I fought the urge to follow this vehicle and edge them off the road into a ditch. You see, I haven't been able to find an antennae flag, and for the first time I am glad. I wouldn't want to fall into the same hypocrisy category as this particular person.

At that moment though I realized something very important: although sporting a cute little flag is very patriotic, and it's pretty well guaranteed that fellow Americans feel united when gazing at their neighbor's gesture of patriotism, it doesn't take away the fact that these proud Americans are still *just people*! People who drive fast, live dangerously, lie to their spouses, cheat on their taxes, and even flip off a fellow American in a shopping center parking lot. It made me recall a similar lesson I learned years ago about doctors; I believe the correct term for it is *the white coat syndrome*. Studies have shown that people generally tend to put more faith in someone, say a doctor, if he is wearing a white coat. We tend to believe this person is somehow more experienced, more knowledgeable, more worthy of our trust just because he is dressed in a white coat. Interesting case study. I realized then that I was guilty of stereotyping Americans the same way: they have a flag, they must be considerate, honest, hardworking, and in this case, *careful* drivers. Not true. Again, I have those stars and stripes waving from a post on my front porch, yet I admit, I'm not all good. I get impatient, I get grouchy, sometimes I even raise my voice to my children. I too, have been known to use that same universal sign for "excuse me." And even though I'm not proud of it, I actually once told a petulant cashier that she could kiss my ------. There you have it, and I do call myself an American.

And so, no high-speed chases ensued as a result of the incident. No cars went careening off the road into ditches that day. Just a quiet moment of contemplation helped me to remember that people are just people—flags or no flags.

The Beach Versus the Rock

"Here you go, Carolyn. You'll need these for the summer." My mom shoves a book of tickets into my hand. I don't even need to look. I already know what they are—admission passes to Twain Harte Lake. They haven't changed in size, color, or paper stock since the late 1970s when my sister and I first used them. The feel of them gripped in my fist is familiar enough to bring me back to when I was eighteen, or thirteen, or even six years old and was forced to stay within my mother's sight on the tiny beachfront lake.

Which, it occurs to me, is where I'll be rooted in the sand keeping a close eye on my two boys while attempting to maintain some degree of cool. The realization that I have been demoted to 'beach mom' slowly makes a home in the pit of my stomach.

Twain Harte Lake has always had two areas to house its guests: The Beach and The Rock. The beach, as appealing as it sounds, was home for the families that came to the lake. Parents with canvas umbrellas, inflated balls, sand chairs, and plastic toys spread out the length of it and sat eyeballing the children while enjoying some grown up chit chat. Back in the late '70s, fathers would be seen frolicking with kids in the shallow water, complete with plaid swim trucks and white zinc on their noses. Mothers stayed protected from the sun under enormous umbrellas, squeezed into creaking beach chairs flicking ash from their cigarettes into the very sand their tots would be scooping into buckets. Hidden behind a pair of plastic white-rimmed sunglasses so large they practically covered her entire face, my own mother had a lime green two-piece that she enjoyed displaying, especially while wearing her bangle bracelets and sparkly earrings. The amount of red lipstick she could leave on a cigarette butt before extinguishing it in the sand was a continuous source of intrigue for me. I thought she and the others were like movie stars.

At a very early age, I understood The Beach held no real interest for me. Kids stepping on one another's castles, parents shrieking not to get too close to the water, or the towels, or the adults, or the water fountain where, God forbid, someone could get trench mouth if they actually used it. Somewhere in a photo album lives my favorite picture from that era: I'm standing at the water's edge in a little yellow bikini, the right side of the seat creeping up into my rear. The sky is streaked with red and orange, marking the end of the day. I've got a bucket in one hand, a shovel in the other and though the picture is taken from behind, my head is turned just right so that the photographer caught the look of pure longing on my face as I gaze across the lake to The Rock, where I knew I belonged.

The Rock was actually just that—a gigantic rock, but one could only get to it by crossing a narrow bridge atop of a dam. Teenagers milled about on the rock, spray painted their names on it, lay sprawled on beach towels, and turned their radios louder and louder. From the beach, I could see them dancing and carrying on. Noise bounced off the water and eventually made its way to the beach, where I could make out laughter and music. The Rock had two diving boards housed on an attached dock, and as I looked on, boys would dive off and emerge to the shouts and squeals of the girls perched nearby. Far too young, I longed to ditch the sand toys and partake in that kind of activity instead.

Once I filled out my bikini, I left The Beach for good and never looked back. It was on The Rock where I met my first kiss, had my first beer, and participated in my first criminal act: graffiti. Anyone and everyone who has ever spent a summer in Twain Harte knows about The Rock and has a "Did you ever…?" or "Remember that one time…" kind of tale associated with it.

It's been years, over a decade actually, since I've set foot on The Rock. Even longer since I made my escape from The Beach. The thought of me making a permanent dent in the sand with my own 3-inch off the ground chair is sort of funny. This mom can only hope for two things: that most of the teenagers I met on The Rock will now be all grown up too and stuck on The Beach with their own children, and that noise will still bounce off the water and we can get a little entertainment from The Rock while we're there.

The Little Things

You know what I love? I love washing my face. No, no, no…not just the washing part—the entire thing. Sudsing it up to a real stiff lather, then rinsing with warm water with my eyes squeezed shut. But the best part is if a big, huge soap bubble comes out my nose while I am exhaling during the rinse process. It always cracks me up. It's a tiny, unplanned bonus during my day. Something to make me laugh that I didn't even know was coming. Things like this I appreciate more than I can say.

As a mom, my day comes complete with spilled juice, regular costume changes, picky eaters, slow risers, cranky nappers, and tantrum throwers; sometimes all before 11:00 a.m. This is expected. Though I may crack a smile or two during this routine, it rarely makes me laugh. So, I've learned to appreciate the little things in life that stop me in my tracks and make me realize, if just for a second, that we are all players in the same game.

Out of the blue, our cat will run sideways. It looks unnatural, un-coordinated, and uncomfortable. But no less hysterical…seriously, a cat running sideways has to be the funniest thing I have ever seen.

Sometimes I catch myself ducking as I drive through parking garages. Am I thinking this is helping my car find a spot, unscathed? I don't know, but whenever I feel the familiar downshift in my neck, I always smile. I have a hard time sitting straight up—like a rebel driver, provoking a roof scuff.

Misunderstandings are my favorite. While submerged in a sea of bubbles the other night, I realized I had no bath towel in which to dry off with. I called out to Brad, "Oh Towel Boy…" Imagine my surprise when he sauntered in wearing nothing but his ten-gallon hat and a pair of cowboy boots. "What seems to be the problem, Little Missy?" he drawled, then blew the smoke off his finger-gun. "You called for a cowboy?" Okay, so we are still laughing over that one.

Crossing paths with old friends—that's another favorite of mine. Turns out a resident studying under my son's orthopedic surgeon is a guy I went to summer camp with 15 years ago. We did the old, "Do I know you?" routine, but it occurred to me while leaving the parking garage at Children's Hospital, just who he was. (I was ducking at the time.) At home, I rifled through old pictures until I found one of him, then sent it off with a letter hoping he'd find it just as funny as I did. That he did—he replied to me days later thanking me profusely for the laughs and memories. How could I have passed up that opportunity?

I love it when people think of their car as a sanctuary—I too, am guilty of this. I sing loud and strong, waving my arms in the air, some-times even banging the steering wheel for emphasis. I rehearse speeches I think my friends need to hear (out loud), I relive past conversations I had (out loud) and then come up with the witty one-liners I should have used. The best though is when I look over and see someone singing to the same song I am. Gasp! Connected…to a stranger…by music! I love it!

It's very cool too when that sanctuary is disturbed, and two random people can share a laugh at "being caught." One time I sat in traffic, pick-ing at an unsightly blemish on my face. I was strained forward attempting to get a good look at my chin in the rear-view mirror, when a cute guy in the car next to me yelled over, "If you pick it, it won't heal!" Embarrassed, yes. But I also saw the humor in it.

My oldest son singing in the car, my youngest son reaching for a cracker on his own, my husband coming in the door Friday night after being gone all week for work…I live for the small moments in life that make my smile spread ear to ear. Josh may battle me at bedtime and Ben may never learn to walk, but guess what? Tonight, when I wash my face, I'll blow a soap bubble out of my nose and I'll laugh long and hard, even if I'm the only one who sees it.

The Social Butterfly

The Perfect Diet

"**Where is the** last slice of pizza?" Brad bellows from the kitchen. In the other room I slouch down into the cushions on the sofa and try to appear invisible.

"Carolyn!" He is shouting now and obviously wants an answer. I offer none, slump down even lower.

"The pizza is GONE and I know it was here just a few hours ago. Did you eat it?" This is the question that needs no answer. Did I eat it? Well duh. I seem to be eating everything in our home. I'm surprised our plants don't have little nibbles on the leaves.

Brad flops onto the couch munching on a piece of…what is that… celery? I didn't even know we had celery in the fridge. Hmm…I must have tossed some into the grocery cart in one of my health food fevers. Eyeing me carefully, he says, "So tell me about this new diet you're on. The one where you can eat chips and ice cream. This diet that okays pizza and has you ignoring fresh vegetables, such as celery." He shakes the stalk to bring home his point.

Honestly, I am trying to appear sufficiently apologetic, but the sight of his celery doing a little dance is enough to make me giggle. I lose my composure completely, and hunch over snorting and snickering.

"You asked me to support you. Did you not ask for my help?" he and his stalk wait for an answer. Again, I offer none but just shrug, grin and tell them both, "Okay, okay, I'll try harder."

Dieting sucks. There are no ifs, and, or buts about it—I cannot stand to diet. I come from a long line of food lovers and not one of us is Italian. Irish folk like us are supposed to be pale, frail and looking like we need a meal. No one would even suspect my lineage, given that explanation.

I could blame society, I could blame my mother, heck, if I wanted to, I could even blame genetics. But no—it's nothing more than a genuine case of poor eating habits plus a trip to Thirtysomething. I should have never expected to live in the frame of an athlete forever, especially after having two children and completely wiping exercise out of my life. Who'd have thunk it?

I go to my doctor and tell him point blank, "I'm ready for that prescription. The pill that causes weight loss, high energy, and has the side effects of happiness, patience, and love for all mankind." I came home with nothing. A suggestion to get more sleep and make time to exercise, but hello- in my world, that is the same as nothing. A friend suggested that what I wanted wasn't even legal. Dang.

I do the only thing I can do—make my celery do a little jig before I bite its head off.

The Run Not Done

Recently, I forgot to run in the half marathon I stopped training for months ago. How is this possible that I would forget such an event? Oh, I don't know. In between helping friends move, looking for a husband who's gone MIA, preparing for my son's upcoming IEP, and helping a mother-in-law who fell from my porch breaking three bones in her foot, ankle, and leg, I might have become a bit distracted. When did my life get so crazy?

Two years ago, a friend and I ran the U.S. Half Marathon to raise money for medical expenses for Ben. We cross-trained every day for months on end and still, we finished pretty close to the last of the pack.

In fact, as I neared the finish line that day, I caught up with a group of runners who looked like cover models for *Muscle Magazine*. A tad smug, I matched their stride and jogged alongside them for a few paces. They were friendly enough and asked if this was my first marathon. Trying not to pant and wheeze, I nodded yes, and they told me I was doing just fine. They went on to tell me that they were on their second lap of the 13-mile course. It occurred to me that in the time it took me to run 13 miles, they had run 26. Fricking professional runners.

This time around I was determined to do better. About 6 months ago the same friend and I found a race in Calistoga and registered to run the steep terrain. A month or two passes without us even running to one another's houses. "You better train, you better train," friends told us. We waved them all off and figured we had plenty of time. Another month gone and I am struck with a vision one day while eating a pop tart in my kitchen. The picture I see is this friend and I swimming at 5:30 a.m. everyday as a means of preparing for our run. I call her, worried. "We'll be fine," she assures me.

A few more weeks slide by. "Hey, I have a great idea," I tell her one afternoon, "Lets walk the 13 miles, not worry about our time and get massages afterward!" She wholeheartedly agrees and we decide to re-search where to stay. Apparently, she thought I would find us a place and I thought she would so no, we never reserved our rooms. By now we have stopped talking about the race and hope like hell no one else remembers we are supposed to run it either.

At the beginning of April, I reassure myself that yes, we'll still make it to Calistoga to—at the very least—get our massages. I make the mental note to self to book the appointments. Lost the note, never made the appointments. But while scheduling the time to do my son's kindergarten registration, I flip open my day planner and see that I have a half marathon to run in two days. Interesting. I call my friend. "Um, any plans this weekend?"

"None," she yawns loudly in my ear.

"Want to take a trip to Calistoga with me?" She is silent, then, "Is that THIS weekend?"

I grunt. She immediately launches into her top ten reasons why she can't possibly get away. "Calm down," I tell her, "With Brad gone and his mom laid up with her foot, I can't go either. Who'd watch my kids?" We are both relieved.

"Plus," I continue, "I found this really great looking race in Tahoe in a few months, and I registered us for that one instead."

"Should we start training soon?"

"Nah, we have plenty of time."

The Search for a Phonograph (A Phono What?)

"Ah...but faint hearts never won fair ladies..." the words of a famous poet drift from my son's bedroom, spoken by, none other than—a fox. Disney's *Robin Hood*, to be precise. I smile, not at the line, just at the source of it. At times the sound quality goes in and out, and I hear the muffled scratch of the speakers failing, then recovering, albeit quicker than I would expect.

Earlier in the day I retrieved my childhood record player from the top of my bedroom closet. I had insisted on taking this portable turntable with me when I left home, hoping for a moment quite like the one happening now. Wanting to spare my favorite plaything from the greedy clutches of a vintage toy collector, I packed it and all its accompanying records then hid them away carefully, until I knew they'd be treated with the same admiring heart I had shown. With its gingham cover, cracked white handle and layer of protective dust, I presented the ensemble to Josh, secretly pleased I had waited so long to do this. He's been back there for close to an hour now, enjoying the original recording of such tales as *Brer Rabbit*, *101 Dalmatians*, *Mickey and the Giant*, *Winnie the Pooh* and the *Blustery Day*, and *Sing Along with Mitch Miller and the Gang*.

And when he saw my name scrawled in pencil inside the lifted cover, he shook his head and gasped, "Didn't Grandma ever tell you not to write on your toys?" His shock at my audacity in this childhood act of vandalism would only serve to strengthen his appreciation.

This record player was to me, the equivalent of the Play Station—Portable ("PSP"), by today's standards. Where kids nowadays might save allowance or beg, borrow, and plead for new games, I did the same. Only my plea was for new albums such as story albums, sing-along albums, or the latest and greatest by Peter, Paul and Mary, if my mom was feeling generous.

Yet, I wanted Josh to truly enjoy the stories and that was tough to do, what with the speakers unconvinced to stay functioning and all. Perhaps finding a newer children's record player would be a nice idea…I called my friend.

"Can you help me find a phonograph?"

"A phono what?"

I laugh, "You know—a record player. A kid's one that Josh can carry around."

Silence. I add quickly "Because you know, kids carry these things around all the time…"

"Hmmm…let me ask my sister. She's right here." I hear the mumbled question then her response, "A phono what?"

"No luck," my friend tells me, "But let me make a few calls."

I pop online and begin the search that way. After much investigation I have learned two things. The first is that toy companies have no use for producing record players anymore, not with technology supporting cassettes and compact discs. While it makes sense, I'm still convinced I might find one somewhere. eBAY turned one up—at the tune (ha!) of $150. Absent was the needle, but not the warning which read: Not intended for use. Well shoot.

And second, finding a record player manufactured to appear vintage was easy breezy, but locating one under the price of $165, not including shipping, was not. I'm pretty sure my parents would stop speaking to me if they learned I spent anywhere near that for a record player, even if it did come complete with a fancy plastic carrying handle.

I contemplate my options, forgetting for the moment that I actually have none. It's either fix it, or continue to play the records on the thing until Josh drains the lifeblood out of it in his innocent attempt at hearing a story between varying fluctuations of volume. No sooner do I ponder "Can someone actually repair this toy?" when I get the answer from my first call to a Fix Everything Shoppe. "A phono WHAT?"

Think Before You Act

"Just think before you act." Words of wisdom from my mother. I never much listened to the old gal, perhaps I should have when it came to this.

"Hi again, Handsome. We have to stop meeting like this." I playfully tapped my male neighbor on the rump in the aisle at Safeway. He turned to look at me and I gasped. Not only was this gentleman NOT my neighbor, but he also looked horrified at my bold display.

"I…am so…sorry," I sputtered. Slightly traumatized, I made a quick retreat and slunk back to my cart. I hightailed it out of there and made a mental note to self, "Think before you act."

I have a nasty habit of doing and then considering. I live by my own personal mantra 'I'd rather apologize for my behavior than to ask for permission.' It may be time to alter that mantra. Take for example my roller-blading mishap: While cruising around the neighborhood one day attempting to perfect balance and sheer agility, I took in the sun, the breeze, the sound of a dog barking in the distance. I was high on life. As I drifted down the middle of the street, I saw a car approaching in the distance. Oh, happy day - it was a friend from around the corner! Since I was still in the street, I decided to give him a small show of entertainment. I waited until he had advanced close enough to take in the full effect of my theatrics.

Pretending to lose my balance, I flung my arms about in great circles. I leaned side to side, mouthed, "OH MY GOD," and faked a tremendous spill directly in front of his hood. For a special touch, I bumped my fist against his grill on my way down, just to make him think for a second that he had actually hit me. I snickered at my creativity and popped up quickly, anxious to see his reaction.

I took a majestic bow, waved to my loyal, yet imaginary subjects and pretended to accept the roses I was being handed for such a fine performance. I then squinted, trying to see the look on his face. The first thing I noticed was that the driver was mortified and about to exit his car, thinking he had run over a pedestrian. Somewhere around this time it occurred to me, this driver was not black, and the friend I was trying to entertain just happens to be. Oh no. I smiled weakly and offered a pathetic shrug, "Just kidding…" I tried to look hopeful and sorry at the same time. He gave a deep sigh, glared at me, then drove off, shaking his head and most likely wishing he actually did run me over. Again, I made a mental note to self—*'think before you act.'*

Yet…just yesterday my eldest son took a flying leap off the couch and landed on the back of his brother, who was expecting nothing to fall from the sky and screamed from the shock of it. The two collapsed in a heap, the youngest bumping his head on the tile of the fireplace. I untangled the two of them while Josh chanted, "Sorry, sorry, sorry, sorry…" I tuned out the apology song while inspecting Ben's noggin as he howled.

"I just wasn't thinking Mom, okay?" Josh looked adequately remorseful as he hugged my leg. It appears that we have two budding absent-minded professors in the family. Definitely time to alter that mantra!

When is a Horse not a Horse?

"Ow!" my friend grabbed her thigh and began rapidly massaging one spot. We were working out, so I figured this was a weak ploy on her part to get out of the leg exercises we both so desperately needed.

"Oh, knock it off," I panted, "Just a few more sets…"

She sat down. "No, seriously…I think I have a charley horse."

I love this expression: charley horse. When is a leg cramp not a leg cramp? Why, when it's a charley horse, of course. I had a professor during my University of California, Davis days who sporadically discharged random trivia out to his students throughout his lectures. Eventually I grew more interested in his sidenotes than his actual course material, and until this moment, I had yet to find the opportunity to share what I knew about the origin of the term charley horse.

"Did you know Charley was an actual horse?" I cleared my throat, got ready to impress.

"Oh, please no…I can't stand any stories about horses…do you know one time when my husband and I were dating, I went to his parents' house for dinner and his grandma asked, right as I was scooping salad onto my plate, when the 'little horse' was going to get there. 'Where is that little horse you said Tommy was bringing with him?' she said. I thought it was so cute until I saw how embarrassed his mother was. Then I realized that granny's hearing was bad, and that little horse was me." She smirked.

I laughed loud and hard. "Okay, so check this out though. Charley was a real horse who lived a long, long time ago," I tried to catch her eye during her crunches, "And when he got old his owner loaned him to the keeper of the White Sox ballpark in Chicago in the late 1800s. He put Charley to work pulling the roller that laid chalk lines for the games played there. Because Charley was up there in years, he had developed a limp. Pretty soon the crowd began referring to any limping player on the team as the old 'Charley Horse.' I know this because my sociology of occupations professor told me so."

"Tens of thousands of dollars your parents turned over to the UC system for their daughter to be properly ed-ja-muh-cated and you come away with that bit of knowledge? Is that the best you can come up with?" I am doing sit ups so I pause to respond, "No, by the time I graduated I also knew how to drive a tractor, jump on a trampoline, farm on a co-op, climb a rock wall, manipulate the inner workings of an experimental cow, grow a square tomato, and stock up on a few dozen other random bits of trivial knowledge I'll never get to use unless someone invites me to play *Trivial Pursuit*. Plus, everything else I learned which was an indirect part of the college experience." Not exactly academia, but still, one must familiarize herself with the practical application in the science of beer consumption.

"Excuse me," an elderly gentleman approached me and smiled. "I couldn't help overhearing your conversation. You'll have to forgive me for eavesdropping." He wiped the sweat from his brow, little cutie pie.

"Oh, that's okay," I grinned in return, "Did you know 'eavesdropping' originated in the old country when property owners weren't allowed to build their homes up to their property lines..."

When Your Vehicle Hates You

Life is no bowl of cherries when your vehicle hates you. Take it from me, my truck has been out to get me since I drove it home last Spring.

Though it wasn't brand new, it was new to me and sporting a cool 28,000 in mileage. Pretty good for a 1998, right? Mileage and mileage related issues have not been a problem. It's the electrical that keeps me from my destination points and has me continuously calling friends out on rescue missions.

The first time it died I was downtown. No biggy. Not far from home. A kind stranger took pity on me and helped me push it into a nearby parking lot. I was concerned. The second time, I was in Oakley. Again, not too much of an inconvenience, but for the traffic lining up behind me, it wasn't pleasant. I was embarrassed. The third, fourth, and fifth times I was needing to get my son to important appointments involving MRIs and EEGs. By then, I was annoyed. The sixth time dawned the morning of Josh's birthday party at Pump It Up. We arrived late in my husband's work truck, complete with cake, balloons, and party bags amid cement, work boots, and various tools. By now, our mechanic, his colleagues and some generous neighbors had taken a look under the hood. We had replaced everything from the alternator to the battery. I was losing patience.

Then the front passenger window imploded on me while driving on Highway 4. Covered in glass, I returned home and fuming, pointed to the truck and told my husband, "Get rid of it."

It heard me. It set out to make my life even more miserable. Little nuisances began to occur. The driver vanity mirror cracked while I was looking in it, leaving me with an ever growing complex if nothing else. Random clicking sounds, the glove box sporadically popping open, radio knobs flying off when not in use. While in a carwash the other day, water sprayed in through a closed window. I was soaked, and then mad. I decided to challenge this little truck of mine.

"Bring it on," I whispered into the vents, "Bring it! Come on, you chicken? You got what it takes?" I verbally harassed the truck and hissed insults into the vents whenever the opportunity arose.

For a while all was calm. I thought perhaps I had intimidated it into behaving. I had even forgotten how troublesome the truck could be and began thinking of it as "reliable." That vehicle got me hook, line, and sinker.

"You're where?" Brad asks me. I am pulled over on the side of the freeway, hungry kids in car seats, my bladder refusing to be ignored for much longer and a cell phone battery with one bar to spare. I describe my location and he is flabbergasted. "You missed the 238 connection! How did you do that? Haven't you driven home from the Oakland Airport before?"

"I was watching the gages like you told me to!" I spat in reply. Damn. I had been watching so closely, I missed my exit and now not only was I broken down, but I was lost. Our trip to the airport was fraught with various warning lights on the dash blinking randomly in a colorful holiday show. I thought I could drop him off and make it home in time to figure out my next plan of action. I thought wrong. Watching all the gauges drop to zero was quite a sight, but better than that was the way I steered my crawling truck across 4 lanes of traffic, with a cell phone plastered to my ear. Multitasking at its best. "Oops, sorry hon. The truck just died on me. Let me call you back when I'm off the road."

I made a few phone calls, passed out the Goldfish and Crystal Light to my wee passengers, and then settled in for the long haul. No music. No air conditioning. Even my hazards weren't working. And why was there not a highway patrol in the area? I could really use someone to yap with until my dad arrived.

Now most folks would be furious right now: fed up, done and ready for a new vehicle. Why this didn't upset me, I can't say for sure. Perhaps a part of me expected it from the truck, maybe even admired its surprise attack. Pathetic, sure. But life is no bowl of cherries when your vehicle hates you.

When Ink Meets Skin—Again

The first time I ever got a tattoo I was nervous. I was giddy with excitement but had also been egged on by friends who had been taking a nip of the ol' snakebite, if you get my drift. What I wanted was a simple white daisy on my inner right ankle. And yes, I know everyone has an ankle tattoo, I am fully aware of my lack of creativity in placement. I know. What I wound up with was a colorful mosaic of skull and crossbones which spits a flaming serpent from its open jaw, that winds its way up the back of my calf. Kidding. I have a purple daisy, not a white one.

But there is good reason for it. A tale much more endearing to me than merely white versus purple.

I like body art. There. I said it. It seems to me that one's feelings about such a thing can be broken down into three perspectives: you like it and have some, you like it and have none, or you don't like it at all. And since I've yet to meet the guy who doesn't like body art, but is covered in it I choose to exclude that particular category.

I dig it. I think it's cool, simply put. I'd have more but for my lack of willingness to drive back to Campbell to get another tattoo, or piercing, or whatever I may be in the mood for. Well one day a few weeks back, fate intervened, and I pulled up behind a black truck at a stoplight here in town. My gasp was in unison with my cousin Casey, who was sitting right next to me. We both read the decal on the back of the truck. She touched my wrist and whispered, "Call your husband and arrange for a sitter. We've got somewhere to be." The decal read, "East Bay Tattoo."

Now if there's anyone who can appreciate body art to the same degree I can, it's Casey. And like other sets of BFFs ("Best Friends Forever") out there, we vowed to get tattoos together someday. But with her living in Michigan and I in California, "someday" had suddenly presented itself "that day." And we weren't about to pass it up.

When we bounded in the door, I sort of mentally braced myself. The last time I had perused a tattoo joint the guy who owned it sized me up and said dryly, "You don't look like the kind of girl to have a tattoo." I considered that, then decided to be offended. I don't look like I appreciate a little excitement? A nice piece of art? A little pain for the fun of it? I come from the school of thought that for every tattoo out there—there is a chronicle that accompanies it. No one gets a tattoo for absolutely no reason at all, do they? When I see body art, I see a good conversation opener. And when you put a group of tattoo-ees together, good luck getting your chance to tell your own tale of ink meets skin.

Casey and I saw our opportunity to lay side by side and get inked. Tee hee. Giggle, giggle. Frank and Ed accommodated us, even though Frank was technically there on his day off and Ed was getting ready to close the place up. I suppose it's not every day they see two girls begging for a chance to get tattoos before one of them returns to Michigan the following day. They were cool. Never even commented on whether or not we looked like the kind of girls to have/get/want/ or whatever with tattoos. And after Frank patiently explained just why not he would ever be putting a fairy anywhere on my body, I too came away with a different perspective on pixie-like creatures and opted to be happily content with a modified version of my vision.

When we left East Bay Tattoo, we were smiling. One of us donned her daughter's name surrounded by butterflies on her hip. The other one (guess who) wore the prettiest little snowflake on her inner left ankle. And no, the tattooist didn't even comment on my lack of creativity in placement.

You're Fired!

My friend is sobbing. Between breaths she tells me how she was fired from her job and how humiliated she is. They weren't downsizing, there was no corporate restructuring, her job was in no danger of being eliminated, she was just fired and that's all there is. And no, they wouldn't be giving her any references. I'm dying to know what she did but can't bring myself to ask. I figure if I hold out long enough and say the right things, eventually she'll offer up the goods and I won't look nosy.

"Everyone's been fired," I tell her, "We all make mistakes. I know a guy who got fired from the Alameda County Fair. I mean, come on! Who gets fired from the fair?" This is true. In high school a kid I knew landed a job in a beer booth. He didn't last long. She is unimpressed. "This was a real job," she points out, "One I planned on keeping for longer than two weeks during the summer!" She sniffs, wipes her eyes. "Have you ever been fired?"

Oh God. Immediately I start to giggle because, yes, I have been fired. Canned. Let go. Here's your stuff we packed in this garbage bag for you—that kind of firing. Easily I can justify this and say I was about to quit anyway, which is true, but let's just say it was a mutual parting of the ways with the company taking the first step in the right direction. It was a good lesson to learn in being assertive and forthright, as well as addressing issues as they emerge rather than brewing a rage and acting on emotion, instead of logic.

Years ago, I took a job at a very small, family run law office for the summer. Teaching children nine months out of the year was enough and I happily anticipated a change for that short amount of time. My tasks included filing, invoicing, answering the phone and patching through calls to the correct recipients. Kind of your typical no-brainer. Gradually, the boss began to expand my responsibilities and I soon found myself in the company of her teenaged daughter more often than not. A sort of built-in au-pair, if you will. Truly, it was an insult. Yet, I was too timid to voice my concerns and I focused my efforts on not telling anyone what I actually did during the day.

Then came the fateful afternoon that I chose to brew a pot of tea, rather than coffee in the company coffee pot. The boss acted as if I had created the moon and stars. "Tea?" her eyes went wide, "In our coffee pot? That's brilliant!" She scurried out and went on to meet with a client. Her sing-song high pitched voice carried out to my desk, "I just thought of the cleverest thing..." At my computer, I looked up in surprise, but didn't say a word. Just sat silently irritated.

In the weeks that followed, I said nothing as the boss claimed credit for my ideas both creative and work related. I was even sent in her place to work at her daughter's high school pig-skin roast and when a gift basket was delivered to the office thanking her for all her time and effort, I wasn't even offered a measly chocolate covered macadamia nut. The nerve. I gritted my teeth and balled my fists, but never once did I express verbally how slighted I felt.

I was an impending storm on the horizon. Aggravated, insulted, bitter and frustrated. I stalked around that office popping antacids, muttering my quitting speech. I rehearsed lines like a local thespian, anticipating my upcoming performance with both fear and excitement.

And then I happened to overhear my boss chatting happily in her office while using the speakerphone. The caller said, "That letter you composed was just fabulous! The committee went nuts and actually decided not to go forward with the original proposal."

My ears perked up and I sat a little straighter in my chair. I knew precisely what letter she was referring to. I had been asked to draft a note on her behalf stating why she declined an invitation to some club meeting. She had said flippantly, "Oh, just make something up. Hell, tell them I have ethical issues with the proposal. I don't care!" Laughing, she marched out on her little heels. Click, click, click.

I did just that. I was wondering what the repercussions may be. I listened intently as the caller continued. "That letter really turned heads! No one was willing to go forward with the proposal without first scheduling a meeting with you discussing the entire ethical side of the issue. We had no idea you felt so strongly about it!"

My boss laughed nervously. I knew she didn't have a clue what the letter said and would be flying out to my desk to examine it just soon as she hung up. But then—the unexpected.

"Oh that?" she said nonchalantly, "I just scribbled that out the other night. Truly, I just put how I felt on paper. I had no idea it would be so well received." I covered my mouth with my hand in attempt to prevent her from hearing my sharp intake of breath. "You know," she continued, "I have dabbled a bit in creative writing." Oh! That was it! I'd show her creative writing!

For the next 45 minutes I jotted down in a Microsoft Word document everything both big and little I hated about working there. I used expletives, I got personal. I thought it a healthy, somewhat productive way to express my fury rather than putting a foot through the wall behind my desk. What I didn't do was press "Delete" when I was finished, as I had originally thought.

The next morning, I arrived at work only to be greeted by the boss's husband, my last check in one hand, a garbage bag filled with my belongings in the other. So much for my healthy, productive method of personal expression.

My friend has now stopped sobbing long enough to laugh along with me at this. "See, it was a huge blunder on my part, not asserting myself earlier in the game, and then leaving a hate list on the computer in my haste." "That was so dumb of you," she says. She had just lost her job so

I let it slide. "Okay, I feel a ton better now." She is still snickering as she walks away. I knew I should have asked her why she was fired.

Don't You Wear No Underpants?

"Oh my God, Carolyn, tell them that one about your butt crack!"

Okay, so this isn't what I had planned when a friend invited me to her "Pampered Chef" party and told me she wanted me to meet her neighbors. They were all lounging on oversized, puffy furniture, nibbling on the party's appetizers: miniature versions of real food. They were actual snacks, just 1/100th normal size. I feigned a smile and stammered, "I beg your pardon?"

"Come on! Tell them what happened in Safeway the other day!" A crowd of unknowns sat grinning up at me as I slowly backed away and pretended an unusual interest in the host's centerpiece. A shove from behind moved me back into the room of hopefuls, all anticipating the world's most embarrassing story. "Yes!" said another friend, her palm on my back being my physical escort. I picked imaginary lint from my blouse as I avoided meeting the eyes of these women. I hardly wanted to share this tale of humiliation with perfect strangers, but then I thought—it is pretty funny. I proceeded to fill them in, knowing full well no one was going to top it that night and I might as well take home the prize for biggest disgrace, since it wasn't going to be biggest order.

I had been shopping at Safeway with my infant son one afternoon. With a shopping cart full, I stood standing in the frozen food aisle, scrutinizing the selection of waffles. Out of nowhere a voice boomed, "Oh my GAWD, I kin see yer butt crack!"

Well, folks just stopped dead in their tracks all around me. I prayed that comment wasn't directed at myself and I turned to look for the source of the bellow. A woman of impressionable size grasped my upper arm and literally spun me on my feet to get a better look at my backside. I was too stunned to yank my arm from her clutches and by that time she was on me again, "Don't you wear no underpants? I kin see yer butt crack plain as day!"

I wriggled free and took note of the fellow shoppers gawking in my direction. I retreated and no doubt—my cheeks were met with the frostiness of the glass door. My hand automatically went back to protect my rear and in doing so, I discovered I had indeed split the seam in my nylon sweat pants clear up to my waist. She was still shrieking, "Girl DO something, will ya? You don't want nobody else seein' yer butt like I kin!" I started to say something like, "Sshh…please…sshh…" And I swear she looked right at me and yelled, "Did you just say SHH to me? I'm tryin' to help ya here!"

At that point I wizened up enough to pluck my son from the cart and dart out to the parking lot. No need to explain that I did, in fact, have on underwear, it was just a pair of the skimpier variety. And let me just say, holding a baby and running while trying to cover exposed cheeks is no easy feat. I laid my head on my steering wheel and did a good combination wail-laugh out of pure humiliation.

I tried to retrace my steps and, horrified, I recalled my time spent in church that morning. By myself. Sat up front even because I felt so damn happy. Left church feeling like everyone had been so nice to me. Nice and smiley. I was literally sweating as I drove home and, sobbing, I told Brad what happened. His first response, "You wore sweats to church?" After that he made me turn around so I could model my new style. "Get up off the driveway!" I hissed, "It's not that funny!"

So, wiping their eyes and catching their breath, all the girls had a good one on me. But honestly, what good is an embarrassing story if you can't share it with a few people anyway?

Clowns Are No Laughing Matter

"**I saw the** perfect shirt for you," a friend said recently. "It said, 'Clowns scare me.'" I wish he had bought me this shirt.

Clowns scare the heck out of me and I'm not afraid to broadcast it. This isn't my fault though. I really did have a bad experience with a clown that warrants a genuine terror on my part.

My parents have a sick sense of humor. That, and an absolutely repulsive taste for art. They picked up some wretched oil painting of a hobo when I was about five and hung it in my bedroom. I'll never know why. It certainly didn't match my decor. I had gingham print, for goodness sakes. Oil painted hobos had no place in my room! They disagreed and nailed it on the wall opposite my bed.

It was nothing short of frightening, this picture. A sad clown, with a wilting flower in his hat. I wouldn't even look at the painting, yet when I did, I found myself unable to look away. I stopped going into my room during the day and resisted bedtime like you wouldn't believe. When friends were invited to come play, they would recoil in disgust and point, speechless, at the picture. "Ewwww! That's scary!" Little girls ran shrieking from my room on a daily basis, until kids just stopped coming over all together. I begged and pleaded to have it taken down but my parents would insist I was being silly and that clowns were funny, happy people.

Then, my imagination began to take over. At night, I swear, the hobo would wink at me. I would hide under my covers and sneak a peek every few minutes and WINK. It would get me every time. Even my older sister, who had never sided with me on any issue, begged my parents to show some compassion and take it off my wall. Of course, they offered to hang it in her room to which she replied, "NO WAY!" and I knew then I was on my own.

Well, one night the winking just got the better of me and I bawled for my parents to come and remove the evil clown. Exasperated, they took it off the wall, and to placate me, hung it so I would not have to see the winking. And where did they hang it? Why, right above my head. I was petrified, having this picture so close to me. I laid there sniveling, thinking the worst, when all my fears came crashing down on me. Literally. The clown picture fell from the wall and hit me on the head. Needless to say, the painting was taken from my room and today I hate clowns.

Close friends know this and tease me endlessly. My boys get a ton of jack-in-the-boxes for gifts and at parties, people bring out their antique porcelain clowns for my review. I know though I'm not alone. I grew up in the days where "Pennywise" was a popular horror movie villain and the kids of my generation all screamed with terror when the Poltergeist clown doll came alive. Other folks hate clowns too, right? They just may not have a strong aversion to oil paintings as well.

A Hazardous Life

"**Have you ever** thought how great it would be to live in Hazard County?" I recently asked my husband.

"I think of nothing else," he rolled his eyes.

Hazard County…now that was a place. Most of us would remember it by a few of its more infamous residents: Bo and Luke Duke. The two young men who shaped my image of what a real man was supposed to be.

And growing up in Pleasanton, well, that made finding a Duke about as easy as finding, well…a Duke, of the royal variety. It was no small task.

It was 1982. Mullets were the rage in hairstyle, "Oh Mickey" was at the top of the song charts, and every girl under the age of 20 was plastered to the TV to catch a glimpse of those two outlaws fleeing from Roscoe P. Coltrane, and his faithful sidekick, Flash. The General Lee took to flight at least five times during a single episode, and we got to see Boss Hogg rant and rave while gnawing on a barbequed chicken leg.

Now that was good TV. I memorized the theme song and thought Waylon Jennings was a musical genius. I wanted to find myself one of them "good old boys." Where were all the men who were "never doin' no harm?" The ones who did "just a little bit more the law would allow?" Not in Pleasanton, I can tell you that much. And the ones that were, well now, they looked nothing like Bo Duke.

By the time I was of dating age, *The Dukes of Hazard* were long off the air, yet I had all but forgotten what I wanted in a man. After several rejections of one poor soul, the boy finally implored of me, "WHAT do you want? What is it that I can't give you?"

"Are the doors of your car welded shut?" I asked, "Do you have an Uncle Jesse? Can you slide across the hood of your car? Do you know how to make moonshine? How tight can you get those jeans?"

He said nothing. Just stared at me with his jaw dropped.

I held up my hand, "Wait, wait. I'm not done. Does your horn play a patriotic tune? How do you feel about painting your car orange?"

"You're crazy," he said amazed, "Plus, you watch way too many reruns."

"So, calling your car the General Lee is out of the question? I'm sorry then, I think we should just be friends…"

As time passed, I gradually gave up my search for the next Bo Duke. I realized he was just one of a kind. I was no closer to finding a Boars Nest to hang out in than I was to letting a man named Cooter tinker around under the hood of my car.

Contra Costa County will have to suffice. And Brad, though he's no Bo Duke, is a pretty good catch. He's blonde, looks good in his jeans, and knows how to make his own beer. (While it ain't moonshine, it's still pretty concentrated.) Now if only I could get him to slide across the hood of the car.

5

Jane of All Trades

Laborious Locks

History has a way of repeating itself, or so I've been told. I haven't lived long enough to really know if this is true, but when I think about the 80s, I find myself thinking, "Oh please, no…" The 80s are a blur to me; a neon colored, Pat Benatar impersonating blur. I want to hang my head and hide my face whenever I come across a picture, *any* picture, of me during that ten-year period.

Between the ages of 8 and 18 a young girl is supposed to be very impressionable. And impressionable I was. Disco was on its way out, while what we now call "soft rock" or "easy listening" was coming in. (I recently heard an elevator version of something I danced to in 8th grade.) Only then we called it "cool new music" and we forever tuned in Madonna, George Michael, Hall and Oats, and Joan Jett. MTV was making its debut and peeling ourselves away from music videos was next to impossible. Our generation coined the phrase "Gag me with a spoon" and "Gross me out!" while wearing our Swatch's and putting our Izod collars up. Applying all those different shades of pastel eye-shadow took up a good part of my morning. I think the first time I ever heard my mother mumble the word, "Hussy" was when I tried to leave for school with my sweatshirt torn and stretched, hanging loosely off a shoulder to reveal a thin bra strap, colored of course. In between all the obnoxiously large hoop earrings, a collection of beads that could outdo any friend's and a strong desire to wear pumps with jeans, was my fascination with belting huge shirts at the waist and having the shiniest rhinestone earrings. It was quite a time. I could live with any of that all over again and be fine. It was just the hair of 1980s that I can do without.

It began with the bi-level, a style that had girls chopping uneven layers all over the top half of their head, and leaving the locks from their ears down hanging limply. Soon after, the permed, bi-level became the rage. That hairstyle quickly faded into a craze which saw all the fashion-conscious teens in the midst of growing out their layers. Girls all over had perms, or cheap imitations of cuts straight out of *Flashdance*. For a short time in junior high, I sported an uneven 'do in which my hair passed my shoulders on the left side of my face, but was shaved over my ear on my right. I don't even know if there was a name for this cut, but I can guarantee you, I was a follower with a capital F, because I never would have done this to myself, if all the other girls who were also trying to look like Madonna hadn't either. But no bi-level, no perm and no nameless mistake with scissors, could ever top what I fear most if ever the hair of the 80s finds its way back onto the fashion runways.

After high school graduation in 1990, I don't think I ever wielded a can of Aqua Net the same way I did in years before. Hair spray companies never had it so good as they did during that era. Why it is we women competed to see how high our bangs could get is beyond me. I'm embarrassed I ever partook in such a ruthless and "stiff" (no pun intended) battle of the bangs. We termed it "the bear claw" and tried to get our locks to stand up at least the height of one hand. These days, my bangs hang limply over my brows or I modestly tuck them behind an ear. I wouldn't even dream of taking my comb and raking it repeatedly though my tresses. I'm ashamed to admit I developed a system back then...it was blow dry, curl, rake, rake, rake, separate, spray, separate, spray, separate, SPRRRAAAAAAAYYYYYYY. And to have to take this hairdo out in rainy weather—why that was the tragedy of the week to me. Damage all my hard work? Let my bangs go limp? Be seen with small hair? I'd rather stay home sick then try to get my bangs to behave in the winter. I wouldn't want to relive all that again, just for the sake of fashion.

By observing the teens in our neighborhood, I'm starting to see some of the old styles show up on these young girls. It looks as though Farrah and Bo are alive and well in my small town. My guess is we are somewhere in the 70s in the height of all this "new" fashion. Bell bottoms, platforms, long straight hair…it can only mean one thing…soon the 80s will upon us and shoot—I'm all out of hair spray!

The Big Race

"I need to be there when??"

The young lady handing me my US ½ Marathon T-shirt nodded and said, "With 3,000 runners here, you need to start lining up for the race around 5 a.m."

I tried not to look mortified. I tried to look like I lined up at 5 a.m. to run 13.5 miles at least once or twice a month. No biggy. I failed. She laughed. Told me, "You'll be fine. But again, get there early. You runners ought to know that by now."

I've never been called a runner. Heck, I don't even call myself a jogger. I'm more in the category of a walker, and when I have the kids, I'm a stand-arounder. But with all this training for my son's fund-raiser, I guess I can be called a runner. At least for the day.

Last Sunday I ran the big race in San Francisco. Surprised all my friends and family, even myself a bit. I set a goal to finish before the crew started cleaning up after the event, to not be dead last and to live to tell about it. Mission accomplished! Coming in under 3.5 hours is not any record-breaking time, but for me, it felt damn good.

So back to this "helpful" volunteer who told me to get there two hours before the race started. She was toying with me, I soon found out. My friend and I showed up at 5:30 a.m., thinking we'd see a crowd of athletes, all doing shots of Powerade and helping one another stretch out. We were met with sleepy headed volunteers, loading cases of water onto the tables at the finish line. Granted, it was still dark out, but we sure didn't see any runners up this early.

After a couple of warm up laps around the park, we spotted some folks jogging down to the starting point. Hooray! Nope—just more volunteers. I mumbled a weak apology to my friend. What could she say? She forgave me. Anyway, we were here to run for Ben, not to sleep, right? Around 6 a.m., runners started appearing, all toned and trim and speaking of their previous times in races. I would nod and smile and stretch out my calves, all the time thinking I was in for a world of hurt in just a few hours.

For the first time since planning to do this event, I was feeling nervous. But after that starting cannon blew, I forgot all about nervous and soon was feeling proud. I was in a pack of athletes that trained to do this for months and they too, were here for very good reasons.

Nice crowd, those runners. Every time I would slow down and start walking, someone would shout "Go Number 484!" and get me back running again. And all those cameras! I ran more than I ever dreamed I would, mostly because I didn't want to get caught on film hunched over taking a breath, while tending to my side cramp. No way! If I was going to have my picture taken, Heaven forbid, I would not be doing anything but running and looking like I loved it!

In my delirium, I missed seeing the 11-mile marker. I kept thinking, "This is the longest mile of my life!" until I spotted the 12-mile marker and almost cried with relief. Somewhere during that last stretch, I caught up with a gentleman in tip-top physical shape. I was happily thinking that I must have done good. If someone in that great of physical shape is just now finishing too, well then…that must mean something. It did. I learned later that he had run the race twice, was on his second time through the finish line as I entered it for the first.

So, I did it. Finished the race, wasn't dead last and lived to tell about it. Even met some great folks during the process. Not bad for a first timer. Would I do it again? Not on your life!

Just One Last Cut

How many times have we decided to make that "one last" attempt at something; and thanks to our diligence, we were rewarded with pain instead of pride? That one last chop on the end of a carrot and "Ow!" there you stand with your finger wrapped in a towel. That one last attempt at running the block of cheese down the grater and "Yikes!" all of the sudden you have a set of scraped knuckles.

Back when Brad and I had no children, back when free time was something we thought we had so little of, Brad undertook the task of building a desk for our office. I had cleared out and decided to spend the day at my folks, give him a little time to bond with his tools in the garage. His project just about done for the day, Brad made one last cut on a piece of wood with his table saw and his life—well, his thumb, was changed forever.

"Carolyn, telephone," Mom said and gestured towards the office. "It sounds like Brad, but I'm not sure." She shrugged.

Now this was certainly news. We had been married for quite some time and my mom pretty much knew the sound of my husband's voice on the phone.

"Hello?" (Me.)

"Um, don't panic. But I'm on the way to the emergency room ("ER")." (Brad.)

"Are you driving?!" (Me.)

"No, Joanne is." (Him.)

"Really? Huh." Nod, nod. "Where's Mark?"

"Well, he's been drinking." Yes, this much was true. It was Saturday after all. "Meet me at the ER, okay? I gotta go. I might faint. You might not want to go home first. It's kind of a mess with blood and stuff."

Of course, I went home first. I was a little curious what his definition of, "mess" might be. Someone should have been there to greet me, warn me a little at least. I was met with a trail of blood that led from the garage to the kitchen, and then sat pooling on the counter around the cordless telephone. It looked like a massacre. In her haste to get Brad to the hospital, Joanne had scribbled a note to me, but had pressed the pen so hard onto the paper, the words "It's going to be okay!!!" are still inscribed in our pine dining room table.

I couldn't help it. I went into the garage to inspect the crime scene and half anticipated finding an appendage, a finger or leg, anything they had forgotten to bring with them. Not discovering any missing limbs, I drove over to the hospital and upon entering the ER, was grasped firmly by the shoulders by a wide-eyed Joanne who kept nodding and saying, "He still has his thumb. I think. Yes, I think he still has his thumb."

I left her and went to find Brad, who was at that moment curled up on a gurney in fetal position, moaning and wincing from agony. He brightened when he saw me. "You wanna see my thumb?" he slurred.

"Are you on pain killers?"

"No." Angrily he glared at me. "I wish I was." Then he smiled, "It's really bad. I almost cut it off." Oh yuck. Leave it to a man to think near dismemberment was really cool. I could see it soaking in the cup of solution he was holding, and from my angle, it didn't look like a thumb.

Seventeen stitches and some hours later, I drove him home and was comforted that his thumb was wrapped in gauze and tape, so I didn't have to see it. Kindly, he videotaped himself changing the dressing a few days later, so that I could get a peek, just not up close.

When he tells the story of how it happened, he always gets a round of groans and sighs when he says, "It was just that one last cut I was going for..." As all good craftsmen know, that one last cut will getcha every time.

Breakin' the Law

I was raised with the generation of kids who never wore seatbelts. We leaned against the doors, put our feet out the widows, and my personal favorite—And car seats? Well, that's a laugh.

My mom once confessed that she and my father used to plop my sister and me, as toddlers, on the backseat of the '69 Chevy and tell us, "No monkey business!" By monkey business they meant what exactly? No throwing our bodies against their seat backs when they slammed on the brakes? No hopping up and down on the red vinyl bench? No opening of the doors while the car was in motion? I'm still confused. It was a warning we got—not a seatbelt. Either I was too young to actually recall how we survived, or too traumatized by so many close calls that I've permanently blocked it out.

A two-hour ride to the family cabin usually went something like this: Mom and Dad bicker as they load up the back the truck, tailgate down and shell popped open. Not a camper shell, mind you—just a shell. Sister and I stand close by, poking one another and adding to the irritation level at the scene. We all four squeezed onto the bench seat of the truck, which is covered by a ridiculously scratchy poncho material. I squirm and whine while Andrea feigns allergies to the fabric. An old trick, but one that doesn't require much effort on our part. Before we round the first bend, we have worn down my mom, who wants nothing more than to NOT listen to the two of us moan about riding up front. I mean, seriously— what could be worse? No air conditioning, nothing but country music, and the two of them debating my father's driving skills—or lack thereof.

"Put them in back..." Mom says to Dad; then to us, "No horsing around."

We make neighing sounds as we climb over her and shove one another through the shell window, our passage to the back of the truck. A window like that is made for handing through things such as drinks or snacks, not small children. Do we pull over and safely get in the correct way? Of course not. Dad wants to make good time, and we are "on schedule." Never mind the extra 45 seconds it would have taken to do this right. Plus, he is probably thinking we'll lose enough time in Oakdale when the girls will want to stop at the A&W.

Once en route, Andrea and I will try to surf. You know—stand up in the back but hunched over since we are too tall to do this. We are successful for most of the trip, but without a doubt the following will take place: Dad will unexpectedly slam on the brakes, causing the surfer to lunge forward and slam her face and head into the previously mentioned miniature window.

At this time the window will slide open, courtesy of our angry mother. She will be all keyed up because no doubt the BAM scared her. She and my dad will have most likely exchanged a few cusses in the second it took her to get the window open. In her excitement she will holler something like this: "Your father just had to slam on his brakes! What in the hell is going on back there?" Neither Andrea nor I will mention that it was the slamming of the brakes that caused us to wipe out while surfing, thus the thump on the window. It won't matter and we already know this. We are smart enough to look humbly apologetic and promise no further horsing around.

When we grow bored of surfing, we will move on to rummaging through the bags they have packed. Mom's 'toilet bag,' though the name appears interesting enough, does not contain one item worth five seconds of our investigation—yet there is that one palm-sized case containing a flimsy circular object we can't figure out. (After learning about diaphragms years later, I am still horrified that we touched hers, took it out of the case, flung it around…ewww.) Turning up nothing worth a hullaballoo, we will be forced to knock on the slider window and duck, a pint-sized version of doorbell ditch.

Seatbelts would have made none of this possible. Was it safe? Did we have fun? You betcha. Would I allow my own kids to do this? Not in this lifetime. And to think I once thought my own parents were uptight.

First Kiss

Quite by accident, I stumbled upon two teenagers in a park near my home the other night. Oh boy, were they embarrassed! Was I! Talk about hightailing it out of there…I don't know who was retreating faster, them or me. I have a funny feeling I may have interrupted that all important first kiss. There's something to be said about participating in someone's first kiss, even if the role isn't that of kisser or kissee.

Come to think of it, I don't think I am anyone's *first* kiss. No one has led me to believe that to be the case, so chances are my name wasn't mentioned during any locker room towel snapping in junior high. I'm not sure how I feel about this—I may have avoided the snickers and hoots, assuming this is what junior high boys did, but I also missed out on the starry-eyed wonder and slight twinge of disgust of being a boy's first smooch.

Unfortunately for me, all of my boyfriends came with baggage, even back in the day. Seems to me I singled out those boys who had girlfriends that weren't quite finished with them. I was forever the target of a jealous rage; some little ninny with her ponytails in a bind would either egg my mailbox, toilet paper my house, prank call my folks, or just fall down in a fit of hysterics during "passing period" at school. Twitching and crying, a certain girl would scream obscenities at me while gathering up the spiral binders she had previously hurled in my direction. I dodged more than one thick Pee-Chee in my time. Not that I was a boy thief, on the contrary. I preferred the boys that showed potential, and nobody recognized that more than a female who had recently set him free.

Back to the kiss though…there was a small window of time when I believed my first kissee was experiencing his first smacker as well. After all that fumbling and bumping, laughing and nervous snorting, I had no reason to believe otherwise. This guy was as fresh to the scene as I was. Trevor. I wrote his name on every folder I had. Secretly called myself Mrs. Berner. Lived in between the times I could see him again. Which, sadly, was only once again—the following summer in Twain Harte when he didn't recognize me. Acting as if I was a stalker, he had his friend tell me to stop following him. The gall. I reasoned that had I been his first kiss, he would be begging me to follow me around and kiss him some more.

After that I decided to be a bit more selective when giving my kisses away. Perhaps a bit too particular, I didn't get an opportunity to polish up on my lip mashing activity until the following month when a skinny young man from New Jersey came calling. My dad referred to him as "the pimply faced nerd", but he had my heart. I never went so far as to write his name on any folders, but at least I can recall him fondly and rest comfortably in the knowledge that I never stalked him.

Which leads me to wonder about the two teens in the park…first kiss? Perhaps. I'm just happy to have been a part of it.

Say Cheese! (Steak)

"**You are an** absolute disgrace."

The year is 1995 and I am watching my soon to be husband devour a sandwich. He is grunting and slurping, occasionally grinning through the mass of cheese and meat. The mother in me wants to wipe his face. I fight off the urge to grab the sandwich and tell him to swallow.

"Here…you've got to try this." (Heya, roo rotta fry vrif) He offers me his meal and I decline with a polite, albeit false, half smile. He swallows and says, "Steak and cheese—two great tastes that taste great together." I am not sold on this. He shrugs and wolfs down the remainder in two big bites. Pats his belly, licks his fingers and sighs happily. A man and his cheesesteak can soon not be parted.

It wasn't long before I realized I had been a fool. Steak and cheese are meant to be together like chocolate and peanut butter. As mashed potatoes are to gravy, as bacon is to eggs. Some foods are meant to find mates, and frankly when cheese met steak—it was a marriage made in Philadelphia.

Fast forward a few years. "Oh, my GAWD—is that what I think it is?" Startled by his outburst, I slam on the brakes and mini skid to a halt on Brentwood Boulevard. He is practically in my lap as he points to The Cheesesteak Shop. I shove him back into the passenger seat and sock him in the arm.

"Are you insane?" I howl, "We are *driving* Einstein, do not cause an accident because of a sandwich!"

He is flabbergasted. Acts as if I have besmirched the family name. Slandered his favorite superhero, watered the plants with Guinness. But no—it is worse. I have insulted the all-mighty combination of steak and cheese.

"Now you listen and you listen good, Missy. Sandwiches, Hoagies, and Cheese fries will all be at my disposal in a matter of time." He points in my face. I swat his finger. He jabs me in the ribs with it and starts doing the "McFly" tap on my forehead. "I have waited years for this and you WILL celebrate with your man." (Cue the sinister laugh.)

I made a few calls. He has to wait longer than he thinks. July 15 may be just around the corner for the rest of us, but when you're anticipating the grand opening of The Cheesesteak Shop, time passes ever so slowly. Thankfully, he got called out of town on business. At the end of each phone conversation, I reassure him of two things; Yes, I still love and adore him, and no, The Cheesesteak Shop is not open yet.

Caution! May Be Habit Forming. If only they knew.

School Dazed

Commencement exercises at University of California, Davis, back in 1994 marked the end of my academic career. Being only 21 years old at the time and having two degrees under my belt, I felt pretty self-righteous about my scholastic standing as well as what the future held for me. I envisioned saving the universe, owning a luxury apartment in the Big Apple, and driving some flashy convertible to my posh downtown office. I had worked my tail off and wanted out of school in the worst way. Graduation didn't come soon enough for me and I happily trotted off the campus and into the arms of 'the real world'.

Greetings from the real world. I haven't saved the universe yet; I don't know if I've even saved my diploma. As for a luxury apartment—well, I've never even set foot in one, let alone one in New York City. I drive my flashy Oldsmobile to preschool, gymnastics, and countless therapies for an autistic child; once the window was broken, so that's kind of like a convertible. Not exactly what I envisioned, yet I couldn't be happier. Oh sure, I didn't see the gray hair and the stretch marks in my future either but hey—who plans those kinds of catastrophes?

Shockingly, what I miss the most is school. No psychic could have predicted that one. The binders, the folders, the paraphernalia...I could blissfully get lost in a sea of school supplies. I miss the classrooms and the teachers and truth be told, giggling with classmates, passing notes, and hoping the cutest boy would sit next to me.

My friend's daughter started kindergarten this year. I'm thrilled for her. We sit on my grass licking Popsicles and I scoot closer, eager to hear about her adventures.

"Tell me about when you were naughty in kindergarten," she says instead. I check my pretend watch. "How much time do you have?" I ask. Her mom and I laugh while she squeaks, "Oh I bet you were naughty all the time!" She is giggling all over the place, but I think it's because she knows it's true.

I wasn't exactly a naughty girl; I just had a different agenda than my teachers. I thought school was the place to go to see your friends. Chat a bit, laugh a bit, catch up on old times. Even back in kindergarten. I was mildly irritated by the adult put in our midst, the one who gave instructions and put a halt to most of my conversations. She threw off my groove. I saw her as a pesky queen bee, someone who buzzed around and annoyed me, yet couldn't be squashed without a great deal of harm coming to me because of it.

"Well," I told Hannah, "Once I was yapping to a friend during Art and while everyone finished their Chinese Dragon color by number project, complete with brads to fasten on the limbs, mine was yet to be cut from the ditto and had about 6 of the scales colored in." Her eyes are wide as she listens to my tale of disobedience. "I was talking and lost interest in what we were doing. The bell rang for recess and my teacher told everyone they could go outside, everyone except me. I was to skip recess and finish my dragon during that time."

I remembered this well. Not only was I mortified at the thought of skipping recess (I had so many kids I needed to talk to), but to be forced to color? And cut? And fasten brads? Oh, the horror. I spent the entire recess bawling with my head on my desk and I have no clue if I ever finished that project. I must have blocked it out—post traumatic Chinese Dragon syndrome.

"Tell me about when you were naughty as a teenager," Hannah asks next.

"Yes, do tell. I'd be curious to hear this myself." Another neighbor has joined the Popsicle party.

"Hmm…after spending all of my time volunteering at the orphanage and reading to the elderly after my work at the church, I didn't have much time to be naughty."

Snorting and guffawing is heard all about.

"What? What?" I try to appear surprised and insulted that no one believes me. I lick my Popsicle and tell everyone, "It's half true. I was too busy to be *really* bad. I had to hunt up the right kind of boys to bring home, you know—long hair, motorcycles, shoes torn wide open at the toes…"

Heads nod in agreement. We were all teenagers once. We know. Our gaze shifts to Hannah who is smiling widely.

"I'm going to LOVE school!" she says gleefully. I know just what she means.

Not Bad, Just Different

The phone has been ringing off the hook.

"Carolyn, you should know" and "I have to tell you." And my personal favorite, "Carolyn, I was so scared."

One would think I was becoming privy to some extremely useful information or a bit of juicy gossip at the very least. But no, I have just returned home from a four-day solo vacation and my friends and neighbors have been giving me news from the underground. A slice here and there of what exactly occurred in my home, and outside of it, while I was safely thousands of miles away.

"And when I stepped into your backyard, I saw the youngest wearing a diaper that weighed about 40 pounds and he was chewing on an empty soda can," a friend reported witnessing after a surprise pop-in on Brad and the kids while visiting in the neighborhood. I envisioned Ben, can in mouth, stumbling over the bulging diaper as it ballooned between his knees.

When I relayed this to a group of ladies from my street, one laughed and said, "Oh, that's nothing. I stopped by early one evening to see how hubby was faring without you. Josh answered the door holding a glass of wine and Ben was asleep on the kitchen floor." That was interesting, considering Josh is a 4-year-old.

"My husband told me that he spotted Brad with the boys at the store. Both kids were eating stuff out of the packages, and Brad was drinking a carton of chocolate milk. They hadn't bought any of it yet." Another piped up. I imagined the scene. Brad most likely took the kids grocery shopping while all three of them were starving and they cruised around grazing on snacks and called it dinner.

I was duly concerned, but I know Brad. He is a Father of the Year, if I've ever met one. He is the dad that gets up two and three times a night to check on wailing children. Monsters? Bad dreams? All taken care of. He'll change diapers at 4 a.m. if need be. When Ben was in the hospital for over a week as an infant, Brad insisted I go home to rest while he stayed with Ben to hold him all night long, cords and all. I don't think Brad slept for three days straight.

When he runs errands, he invites the kids to go and genuinely wants them by his side. He calls to talk to the boys when he's out of town and sends home postcards addressed to each of them. He cooks, he cleans, and he does laundry. (Well, he tries…and I do give points for effort.) He plays ball, he swings, he slides and the man sees no difficulty in packing up the gang for a trip to the park.

He lives by the philosophy that little boys don't need baths every night and only girly-men get their hair brushed every day. Mac & cheese might be a complete meal and Jell-O is considered a breakfast food, but so what? Here is a man who loves his kids and welcomes the opportunity to spend time with them.

Another gal dropped in the other day to regale with me with her version of "Four Days with No Mommy." Although amused, I said nothing until she shuddered and sighed, "Oh Carolyn…it was just so bad." I shook my head in disagreement and replied, "Not bad, just different." You see, I know a good thing when I've got it.

Piece of Cake

Thinking Pink
National Newspaper Association Award Winner

"Why do you insist on having all this pink s**t on the counter?" Shoving my hairspray can off to the side, Brad looks exasperated and then glances down into my make-up bin. Something fuchsia catches his eye and he recoils. "This is sick. All this pink and silver…why do girls love this garbage?" He holds a sparkly magenta lip gloss and inspects it, before tossing it into the sink and rummaging through my stuff.

I snatch the disc out of the basin and stick out my tongue.

"You know what the problem is?" He is on a roll. "All you girls love to hate Barbie. You think she is a terrible role model for the little girls, yet

National Newspaper Association
Better Newspaper Contest 2005

Third Place

presented to

Brentwood Press
Carolyn Dodds

Best Humorous Column
Non-daily Newspapers, circulation 12,000 or more

NNA President   Date

September 28 / October 1 2005

you herd like cows through shopping malls to load up on knick-knacks to make your hair bigger and your butts smaller. And all of it comes in PINK cans. It's an illness with you women."

He shudders. Rather than listen to a diatribe on the effects of the color pink on the female psyche, I justify my collection of bottles and tubes by saying, "First of all, hair products and cellulite reducing creams are not knickknacks, they are staples to any woman's toiletry bag. And secondly, pinks and all shades thereof are a sweet reminder to some women of the little girl she once was."

I am sufficiently happy with my witty retort, until he pretends to barf. "Here's what's real, sweet thing. Ain't none of you ladies gonna look like Barbie with this trash. What Mattel needs to do is manufacture a real doll. Create something more realistic to which girls may aspire, especially after they get married. Something like a fatter Barbie."

I consider this. "Farbie?" How about "Charbie," the chubby Barbie? Instead of makeup, she'll have purple bags under her eyes, and own an entire collection of sweatpants to wear with oversized shirts."

He perks up, "Yeah and make her little play kitchen stocked with diet food. Oh, I know! Charbie's house can look like a dive, and she can have all these candy bars hidden throughout the furniture. You know, so Ken thinks she eats healthy all day."

The fact that I know there is no longer a Ken, but a new boy for Barbie to run around with, is something I do not mention. I am still smarting over the fact that he suggests I hide candy in the couches.

"Yeah, yeah, Charbie can have an exhausted look on her face and a bunch of little baby dolls in cribs and swings and stuff. They'd make a killing!" He is so impressed with himself.

"Or," I say, "Charbie can be working at a computer in an office that is littered with Ken's junk and doing all the billing for his construction business. Charbie's babies will all be fed and entertained, while she cooks, cleans, runs errands and does office work."

He stares at me. "No, no, I got it," I tell him, "Charbie can be active in both her kid's schools and do home daycare, too. She'll buy the kids new clothing and shoes, but still wears her wardrobe from the early 1990s.

And Mattel can incorporate all sorts of vintage 1990 styles into Charbie's line of shirts and pants. Wouldn't that be cool?"

Brad says nothing. "Here's the clincher," says I, "Charbie will be the type of doll that may look worn down and tired on the outside but can always find the energy to greet Ken with a smile and kiss after a long day. She'll balance two overactive young boys, feed and water all of the pets, and be more than happy to pick up a friend's children from school, too. She'll be on the telephone all day, not chatting with other dolls, but talking to doctors, making appointments and scheduling the boys for various kid activities. Charbie will never once mention that she earned two college degrees before she was 21, and now doesn't have the chance to use either since starting her family. Charbie is incredibly selfless."

"Hmmm," says Brad, "I don't think anyone would buy her. What kid would look forward to that?"

"And that, my dear, is why Barbie exists. She's a 'here's what you could have been' kind of dolly."

He grins and powders my shoulder with a dusty evening glitter. "Pink isn't so bad."

Mum's the Word

I'm torn. One of my teen-aged 'nieces' confessed to me that she's recently had a bit of a run-in with the law. While I truly believe there are some things parents are better off not knowing, I feel compelled to at least warn this friend that her daughter could be headed down the road most traveled, at least by teens. So, I asked my wise, yet empathetic husband for his opinion on the matter of should I or shouldn't I?

Brad: Are you crazy? I'll turn her over to the feds myself.

Me: How old are you, anyway? It wasn't all that long ago you were spinning donuts with your Bronco in the middle of a neighborhood park!

Brad: True. But I was quick about it. Plus, you're the one who was involved in a police chase. I'm not sure you should be so overly concerned unless you've fessed up to Bill and Paula about your break-in to Shadow Cliffs.

Good point. But it wasn't a break-in as much as it was a "climb-over." I was dating some boy that had some pretty crazy friends. He wasn't half as much fun as they were and I jumped at the opportunity to fix up my friends with his, just so we could do something a little out of the ordinary one night.

"So, ladies…ever been dry sliding?"

Gino tossed the idea to the group. We had all convened at Jan's house, where her parents were out for the evening and she stood smiling in the kitchen, giving Scott the eye. My girls knew nothing about dry sliding; just knew that these boys offered a chance at entertainment. Of course, we were game.

Minutes later, Jan's car, or rather her parents' car, was parked on Stanley Boulevard in Pleasanton, lights down low. The four of us girls sat rethinking our plans, nervous now as we watched the boys jump from their car and start running down the dark stretch of road. They disappeared into the bushes. Jan turned off her headlights and sighed. She was in a tough spot, her crush on Scott being the only motivation for what she was doing. We exited and crept into the brush. I screamed as I felt my arm clenched and a hand smother my mouth. I shoved off my laughing attacker and we joined our friends; the eight of us jogged down a shadowy path and found ourselves at the back of the hill where the water slides were.

Upon trekking up the incline, we were greeted by a rather tall chain link fence, which the boys scaled quite easily. Not to be outdone, the girls—one by one—went up and over as well. Bringing up the rear was Michele, who in her haste didn't notice that her shirt was caught on the fence. As she leapt toward the group, we heard a squeal and turned to see her upper body fully exposed, hanging by armpits. I'm sure our laughter was heard for miles. She wriggled out of her shirt, dropped to the ground and turned to snatch the fabric from the fence.

Like ants, the gang scrambled onto the slides, which didn't bode too well—they were dry, hence the term "dry sliding." We hadn't finished more than a few runs when flashing lights pulled into the parking lot and within seconds, shouting was heard. In a flash the group dispersed, shimmying over the railing, this time not one of us losing any clothing. I lost sight of fellow cons as the eight of us went in eight different directions. Scared, I made my way through the shrubs to the road. Once there, we realized that both cars fled the scene. Four of us had been abandoned. We crouched in the underbrush waiting to be rescued while police off in the distance scanned the hedges and plants looking the stragglers.

A minivan pulled up and the door slid open. "Jump in!" yelled Gino, who had traded his own car for his mother's an attempt to throw off the cops. Without losing a beat, I and three others dove into the moving vehicle. I was assisted by another dry slider, who yanked me in by my wrist. We were panting and nodding and extremely glad to have eluded Johnny New Badge.

I was 15 when I did this. The same age as my niece, who didn't experience nearly the level of illegality that I did during my scuffle with the feds. My parents heard this story years later, told over a holiday dinner, when I felt that time and maturity had provided enough safety in which to share it. Trespassing, illegal parking, an actual police chase on foot, not to mention riding without a seatbelt. My parents would have had a field day with that. I'd most likely still be grounded had I been caught.

With that in mind, I opted to zip my lip for the time being. A girl doesn't be a favorite aunt by squealing.

What's Playing on your iPod?

I opened the passenger door of my girlfriend's car and slid in. She was listening to "The Macarena."

"Oh no," I said. "Oh, haaaail no. 'The Macarena'?"

She nodded and sang, "One knocka, two knocka, three, ah-macarena...knocka four, knocka me, knocka thee, ah-macarena..."

I don't know what was worse, listening to her version of the song, or just the fact that she had it on her iPod. Oh wait--that was my iPod; I had loaned it to her a few days back. Whoops. My bad.

"Oh, listen to this," she piped up and quickly shifted to another oldie but goodie. A little ditty by Travis Tritt, then after about 20 seconds, she was bip, bip, bipping through the menu and we were crooning to *Dust in the Wind* thank you very much, Kansas.

"I can't believe the collection of songs you have on this thing!" She was grinning. "I had forgotten all about the Bronski Beat trio!" Oh. Well, so had I. Until now. That, and so many other long forgotten downloads.

The iPod. It is a good invention. I just had no idea how many people actually used them. About a year ago I took my iPod to the airport with me. I fancied myself clever. I thought, "How many people will see this and wish they too had thought ahead and brought their iPods?'

The answer was none. Everyone there had iPods, even the folks working the check-in counter. Well, shoot. On the airplane I sat next to a gentleman with a smaller, more compact version of the iPod. The Nano, was it? I had to know, had to bond with this guy over iPods.

He wasn't interested.

I leaned over and cooed about its diminutive size. Asked a few subtle questions. Tried to see what he was listening to.

"I'm gay," he sighed impatiently.

Rolled his eyes. Shifted in his seat away from me.

"I'm not trying to pick you up!" I was aghast. "I am genuinely interested in your iPod!" Oh, the nerve of some people. "Seriously!" I told him. "I love to know what people listen to. Don't you want to know what's on my iPod?" I held it up.

"Not really."

Well fine. I sat back in my chair, borderline mortified with humiliation. We didn't speak again the remainder of the trip. Stupid iPod owner. He should be kicked out of the club. The club of cool iPod owners. I'm in it. You probably are, too.

I like my iPod because it's a palm sized version of my true self. Music says a lot about a person and my iPod tells the world all about me, if someone took the time to listen. Most of the songs on it remind me of some part of my life, or inspire me to do better, be better, make a positive change. I imagine this to be the case for most people who listen to music.

There are songs by Dave Mathews, Blind Melon and Alanis Morisette that remind me of house boating, some of high school, even a few numbers by Raffi and Hap Palmer for the kids. I've got everything from Sinatra and Tom Jones to modern hits by Eve 6 and Gnarls Barkley. For any occasion that calls for music, I feel covered.

Last year for Christmas my husband made a movie for me. He took the last 12 years of home video footage, found his favorite clips, set them to music and made what he called "The Mommy Movie." It brings tears to my eyes each time I watch it. It too, is on my iPod. (That and the movie *Elf*, another classic in the Dodds family home.)

My friend hands me the iPod to peruse since she's still driving.

I click back to "The Macarena." I smile at my friend. I forgot how much I actually like this song.

Queen of Denial

Everyone has their thing. A little saying that brings about the rolling of the eyes and the deep sighs from family and friends who know better. Mine is, "Today is Day One!" I say this whenever I'm ready to start eating healthy and exercising regularly. I say it practically every day. People who know me well know to ask, "Another Day One, eh Carolyn?" (Snicker, snicker. Hoot, hoot.)

But enough about me. Let's talk about my mom. Ever since I was little, she has always sworn to have risen by 5 a.m. I've never quite understood this. We all know she sleeps in. But in conversation, it's always, "Oh yes, I've been up since 5 a.m." Self-righteous sniff, toss of the hair, and quaint little smirk. I'm tempted to add, "But then you went right back to sleep, right?" or something of the sort, but have long since stopped being a smart aleck about it. (Sarcasm serves no purpose with people's little things.)

On Christmas we had the family over. While the kids played out back, her and my father sat with me in the living room discussing their morning and describing in detail the production of having my sister and brother-in-law stay with them. They haven't had houseguests for quite some time and act almost unfamiliar with having to accommodate company. I said nothing during the tale of the battle that ensued over the temperature in the house. I smiled politely as I listened about the mess the pair were making in the guestroom, and only shifted slightly in posture when she expressed her displeasure over the all food they ate. It was when my mom complained about how late they slept that my ears perked to attention.

"I knocked on their door at nine and told them to get up…I mean, I've been up since 5 a.m."

Dad's gaze met mine. I quickly lifted one eyebrow only slightly, but it was enough for him. "Oh baloney," he said, "You slept later than all of us."

"What? I did no such thing Bill! You know how early I get up!" Her face flamed red and she laughed nervously. My cue.

"Yeah," I piped up, "I remember you sleeping in past ten some days. I had to wake you to tell you I was leaving for school!" This never actually happened.

"What? What?" she was flustered and had no idea how to handle my father and I. We sat chuckling and nudging one another.

I sat back to enjoy the following exchange.

Mom: "I was up and dressed at 6 o'clock!"

Dad: "At eight you were still in your pajamas…"

Mom: "Maybe at seven, but at eight I was getting in the shower."

Dad: "Must have been near 8:30 a.m. I saw you in the kitchen reading the paper at eight. And you were still wearing your pajamas."

Mom: "Well fine. Either way, I got up before the rest of you."

I find it hilarious that we have had this conversation, or one like it, ever since I can remember. I used to call home from college some mornings around 6 a.m. just to be greeted by her sleepy, gravel filled voice with a touch of alarm in it. Common knowledge states that people don't call before the sun comes up unless it's an emergency. "No, no—you didn't wake me," she'd say, "I've been up since 5 a.m."

It never fails to amuse me: While she's 'been up since 5 a.m.,' my dad 'has only had one beer', and Andrea is continuously 'in the middle of my thesis.'

"Your family kills me!" Brad told me recently. "Are all you guys always in denial?"

"They might be," I tell him, "But not me!" I flex my bicep to make a point. Take a bite of salad and stretch my leg across the counter to drive home the point that now I'm getting in shape. I adjust my sweatpants and tie my hair up into (what I think looks like) a very athletic looking ponytail. "You know what today is, right?"

Calgon Moment Goes
Down the Drain

I recently asked my husband, "Do you know what I do to have fun?" He stared at me. "Because I think you may have a skewed perspective of what qualifies as 'fun' for me."

He looked thoughtful, then offered, "Um…you talk on the phone all day?"

Ah yes. Because making doctor appointments, scheduling various fundraisers and double-checking that others are supposedly doing *their* jobs, that's fun for me.

"You take a bath?" he asked tentatively, then followed with a much firmer, "Yeah—you take a bath. That's what you do." He smiles and nods knowingly, like a kid having just spelled A-C-C-U-R-A-T-E in a spelling bee. Had there been a buddy of his in the room, I would have just seen a round of high fives.

Taking a bath. Fun? That's debatable. Relaxing? Also, up for discussion. The last time I escaped to the privacy of the bath, I hadn't even dunked a toe in the water before Brad barged in holding a coffee mug. "Did you know this mug has a chip in it?" His surprise obviously warrants conversation.

"It will have more than a chip in it should you stay in this room any longer."

Once emerged in billowing suds, the door opens again. "Oh, a bath," says my oldest kid, "I'll get in too…"

"You are seven," I reply, "I can think of 112 different reasons right now why that would not be okay. Be gone. Lock the door on your way out." My eyes have never left the page I'm on. He did half of what he was asked to do.

Soon I hear howling coming down the hall and I sense, that within seconds, I will bear witness to the father-son struggle Brad is having with my youngest offspring. Together they tumble in, Ben pitching a fit and

Brad looking weathered as he restrains him from diving into the water. "He wants you," he gasps. "He's determined to see you," he shouts the obvious above the wailing. In the midst of the bathmat wrestling match, a container of baby powder hits the deck and in an instant, a cloud fills the air. Not only am I clueless as to how the baby powder appeared, since I haven't purchased any in eons, but I'm now so far from relaxed I'd be seeing red, if I could only stop coughing through the white.

Brad potato sacks Ben and hauls him out over his shoulder. His, "Mommy's RELAXING right now," is drowned out by screams of hysteria. Soon I hear the front door slam and the truck start up. Good. They're gone.

"Meow." Says cat Number One, as she enters. Curious, cat Number Two trails in behind her. Sensing a party, cat Number Three trots in, flicks her tail, then perches on the toilet seat. Appearing anxious, she hunkers down and stares into the tub as if ready to pounce on a fish. Her posture is a little disconcerting. I try to read as still as I can. I take advantage of my 14 seconds of serenity before cats Number One and Two both vie for space on the ledge of the tub. Friendly bantering quickly becomes a territorial brawl. Screeching, Number One takes a nosedive into the tub.

Pandemonium broke out as I bolt upright and grapple the shower curtain to get my balance. Number One paddles around, making her way through the suds, hissing and spitting the entire time. I see my book floating in the wake. And that was the last time I had 'fun' relaxing in the tub.

Recalling this more recent episode helps me see the humor in it so I put on a grin and say, "Yes Dear, you're right. I do take a bath to have fun."

Are You Tough Enough? I'm Not

We're only three weeks into the school year and already I've heard enough of Josh's new favorite song. The kid really knows how to kill a tune—a skill he acquired, or so I've been told, from his mother.

It wouldn't be so bad if it were a compact disk ("CD"). I didn't mind repeating (countless times) on the way to and from Brentwood Elementary every day. I suppose the sad part is not that it's Raffi or Barney, or anything else that would be reason enough to drive a sports utility vehicle into the nearest wall; it's that I used to love this CD and am now too old to appreciate its pseudo-gangster lyrics. And I can't decide what's more deplorable: that he truly digs the beat, or that I even owned this CD to begin with.

"Mom!" he said with excitement as he came downstairs one night. "I found the best song in the world! I love it so much! Can you play it in the car tomorrow?" Roughly translated—can it be heard tomorrow, the day after, and every minute until it's hurled out the window?

Thinking that since this was a choice from my own personal CD collection, it wouldn't pose a problem unless it contained some choice lyrics that I would regret allowing him to hear.

He thrust forward his treasure with obvious glee. I didn't even have to turn it right-side up to recognize the faces on the cover. New Kids on The Block. I laughed nervously. Things like this only occur when witnesses are present and at that very moment, a new neighbor friend was standing in my kitchen. Her coffee mug paused halfway to her lips, which were now agape and forming an "O" with surprise.

"Um…where did you find Daddy's CD?" When all else fails blame, blame, blame.

"No, Mama, this is yours. I found it in your 'my-favorite-CDs' pile in the office." His doe eyes begged for reassurance.

"Are you positive this wasn't in a pile intended for donation?" When blaming fails, try redirection. I smiled at my new friend, who glanced anxiously around my kitchen, looking perhaps for that hidden New Kids on the Block boy band potholder or magnet.

I had no choice but to support my kid. "Fantastic choice! Play it upstairs for now and tomorrow just remember to bring it with you in the morning."

We continued our chat, pretending the soundtrack was anything but—Don't worry 'bout nothin' cause it won't take long…we're gonna put you in a trance with a funky song…

Since 1988 I've long forgotten about this boy band, and since that morning I've gotten my fill of Jordan and Donnie and the rest of the boys whose pictures once upon a time wallpapered my room. But Josh hasn't.

Much to my horror, he turned on the CD after a soccer game and sat with his buddies, tailgating in the back of the truck while families exited the park. As the volume increased, so did the stares.

My girlfriends and I chatted a few feet away, laughing at the poses they struck, the moves they "busted," and the fact that the New Kids had temporarily made a comeback in Smalltown, USA. Listen up everybody if you wanna take the chance…just get on the floor and do the New Kids dance…

Corny, no doubt. But a heck of a lot more innocent than today's rap standards.

"I feel the first twinge of regret since throwing away my New Kids sleeping bag," I told my friend.

"If I knew someone would have appreciated them," she replied, "I would have saved my New Kids action figures…"

A soccer dad walking by said, "Right on!" to Josh, and flashed me the thumbs up. "I saw them in concert!" he laughed. "But only because Tiffany opened for them at Great America."

From the back of the truck Josh shouted over, "Are you tough enough?" while his cronies sang backup.

"To hear this song again?" I shouted back, "No!"

But to let my kid enjoy some old-school music, sure. When I can't take this any longer, I'll leave out *A Flock of Seagulls* for him to discover.

Pirate Edges Out Savior

I found my "Book of Questions."

Almost everyone had one of these back in the '80s. It was simply that: a book of questions. Although these questions were designed to provoke deeper thought and eventually perhaps the reader would even "find himself." It cost only about six bucks, tops. Six bucks to find myself? Hey, get me a copy, right? Right.

I opened it up and called a friend. "If you knew you were going to die within 24 hours" (I used my best Mystery Theater voice), "What would you do?"

"Who is this?"

"Funny, what would you do?"

"Oh no, not your 'Book of Questions' again. Give me a different one."

"Umm," I flipped through the pages, "Okay, if you could sit next to any person, living or dead, on an airplane, who would it be and why?"

She thought for a bit and then asked, "Why would I sit next to a dead person?"

I sighed deeply and immediately regretted having finished my glass of wine.

"Okay, Okay. How long is the flight?"

"What? How would I know? It doesn't matter! Who and why, that's all I need. And don't say Jesus. Everyone says Jesus."

She groaned. "I have no clue. I hate flying. I guess I'd say the pilot. Then I could keep an eye on him."

"What if he smelled like alcohol? Would you still want to sit by him wondering if it's Listerine you're detecting or a liquid lunch?"

She was exasperated. "I'd never even fly, so there you go. Who would you sit next to?"

The easiest question in the world for me. "That's simple! Steve the Pirate."

Pause. "Who?"

"From '*Dodgeball*'…" I can't believe she doesn't know this. "I'm a pirate…Arrr…you know, the pirate guy from '*Average Joe*.'"

I absolutely love this guy. One time Brad and I were out of town staying at a hotel. I had come out of the bathroom and saw that he was flipping through the channels. I gasped when I saw my pirate and flopped across the bed. "Oh, my Gawd, it's Steve the Pirate. (Giggle giggle.) I love this guy. Keep it here." I clapped a little and smiled broadly at Brad. "Hee…hee…" I turned to stare dreamily at the TV.

Brad was less than amused. "That is Heath Ledger, and this is *A Knight's Tale*. They are knights," he sneered, "not pirates."

I gestured dramatically toward the TV. "See his red-haired friend? There in the background…that guy behind the horse…him! That's Steve the Pirate."

I don't remember much from that trip; except we did watch *A Knights Tale* all the way to the end.

On the phone, my friend was perplexed. "You'd pick that pirate guy over anyone else? I'd rather poke my eye with a very sharp stick than try to figure that one out."

How do you explain that being funny on an airplane is an absolute must? Dave Chapelle wouldn't be flying coach, so no chance there for a laugh. Neither would Brian Reagan. And while Kevin James may consider it, with my luck I'd wind up sitting behind him and never get closer to do much more than eavesdrop. I wouldn't be a part of an actual conversation…so that leaves me with Steve the Pirate. A fine choice, too, if you ask me: charming, funny, adorable; he even has good teeth… what more can you ask for in a seatmate? (Except, of course, the power to forgive and grant you an eternity basking in all the wonders of His glory. But like I said, everyone always picks Jesus.)

7

Friends in High Places

The No Information Society

I've always been a club kind of girl. As a kid I joined the Spanish Club (I didn't speak any), the Drama Club (they politely asked me to leave), and the Unicorn Club (I started this one myself.) The UC folded after its first few meetings where all the girls sat around, adjusting ponytails and comparing our varying Pee-Chee Unicorn folders. We'd occasionally do pencil sketches of our beloved mascot, spending the remainder of the meeting naming them such things like Cornhulio and Unicyss, but sadly, there isn't much to do that hasn't already been thought of when it comes to a unicorn. Plus, after the terrible screaming match broke out between believers and skeptics, we became a group divided and it would have never been the same.

These days, other than the Red Cup Society, I only belong to one other group/club—The No Information Society, and this membership came without any of the necessary hazing. Currently, there are only two standing members: myself and my neighbor Mark. His club name is Big Daddy Kool, "BDK" for short. I don't have a club name. I haven't reached that stature yet.

While his wife and my husband will sit around and debate politics and government, safety corridor issues and the real estate market, BDK and I take our places opposite of one another at their kitchen table, exchange a nod, clink glasses, and start our dialogue off after a loud swallow and one of us saying, "Whew! That burns going down!"

The No Information Society keeps its conversation black and white. No room for any of that irritating fuzzy gray area:

"Sleep okay last night?"

"Yeah, you?" This is the extent to what we talk about. One time I said, "I like corn." And he bobbed his head, "Yeah, me too." We keep it simple. Seldom one of us will make a mistake and ask, "What are you talking about?" to Joanne or Brad, and they'll just sigh and refill our glasses and tell us not to be bothered with Big Boy and Girl Conversation.

So, we're forced to confer on the merits of lager versus ale and whether or not Jim Beam and Jack Daniels were actual people. "Five minutes alone with Captain Morgan, and what do you ask him?" This is me, trying to be philosophical.

"I'd ask him if there's any truth to the rumors about him, Jose Cuervo, and Johnny Walker." This is BDK, matching my wit.

Sometimes we disagree. "Hey," I told BDK one night, "I think The No Information Society should have its own emblem. I designed one, want to see?"

"Not unless it's at the bottom of a bottle of tequila that you got hidden under that jacket of yours."

And most recently I suggested, "I think the No Information Society needs more members, don't you?" BDK glared at me over his shot glass. By his silence I was to assume that no, we were not accepting any new applications at that time.

The night the No Information Society came into being, the four of us were involved in a religious debate. Within minutes, it became fairly obvious that Mark and I had better things to discuss, especially after he asked me, "You wanna try something that'll put hair on your chest?" It's not every day a lady gets that offer.

Joanne shook her head and muttered, "Well there they sit—the President and Co-Founder of The No Information Society." Leading us to wonder who was which…even today we're unsure and now neither one of us wants to know—because that, of course, would mean we had some information.

Mark said that night, "My club name is Big Daddy Kool. I'll name you later." Eight years and I'm still waiting. Perhaps he meant "I'll name you Later." I'll never ask—something like that would defeat the whole purpose of our club.

An Experiment in Social Interaction

Back in my college days, I studied Sociology. Oh, sure. I studied coeds, frat parties, tractor driving and the occasional pig race, but in truth, there was a degree earned in there somewhere.

I once had a professor who loved to talk Social Interaction: the study of people in any given situation, at any given time, with any given circumstance. It was intriguing, to say the least. Unfortunately for me, I took his class at the beginning of my degree program, thought all Sociology classes would prove to be just as fascinating, and wound up bored to tears later in my academic career over the likes of Karl Marx, Max Weber, and Emile Durkheim. While these guys were geniuses in their field, bringing such issues as capitalism, material economic foundations of society, and the rise of bureaucracy and the rationalization of society into a much broader light, I longed for a more hands on approach to learning social theory and ached for less time with my nose in a book. (This is hard to believe if you know me, but quite obviously saying a lot.)

Enter George Herbert Mead, my Sociology Superhero. This is a guy who believed that the "self" was constructed and reconstructed through interactive behavior. One of the founders of the Symbolic Interactionism theories, he concluded that the "self" can only develop through interactions with other people, so that the "self" is inherently social. I was easily wooed by his theory and mourned the fact that he had died 41 years before I was born, a good 60 years before I could interview him. After studying Mr. Mead, I grew to love his findings of Interactionism and looked for every possible scenario in which to run new studies.

The previously above-mentioned professor, whose name has since escaped me, became keen early in the game to my expressed interest in social dynamics. He graciously granted me the time and space required to test my own newly developed theories "out in the field." Yet, throughout the duration of the school quarter, it became fairly obvious that my field experiments were becoming less of an opportunity to gather data and more of a prospect to just plain mess with people. For educational purposes, of course. Consider it more of a college set version of "*Girls Behaving Badly*," or in my case, GIRL. I like to think Chelsea Handler would be proud.

To be true to my studies I had to wrap Mead's theories into my own hypotheses. Prove somehow that people evolve and adapt given the situation. Twelve years later and I had not yet found myself on the other end—being an unknowing part of a social experiment. Until last night.

Safeway checkout. End of the day. While my two children mistake the cart for a jungle gym, I gaze out the window and let the cashier continue to total my purchases. Tired sigh, quick glance to my watch, mentally I prepare dinner. The children hop and swing around me, chanting nonsense as I drift into thoughts of beaches and sand. Margaritas…painted toenails…

"That'll be $297.62," she says cheerfully. Say what? I look down and see a vast array of food that doesn't belong to me being swiftly bagged and placed in my cart.

"Oh wait! That's not mine!" The cashier and I laugh and start sifting through the items to sort out what's staying and what's going. No word from the lady behind me in line, to which all of this belongs.

"I am so sorry!" I tell the kindly cashier, "I should have put a divider up!"

"No, no…I'm sorry!" she replies, "I should have been paying better attention!"

Still nothing is said by the woman who is, I feel, equally responsible for the confusion. She watches silently as food is unloaded, totals are re-tallied, and a new receipt is issued. I wait patiently, expecting her to offer her own apologies for her lack of attention. Nothing. She is totally devoid of emotion, if anything—acts as if the groceries aren't hers either.

As I exit, it occurs to me that she may not have been being rude, she may have been gathering data. Another fan of Mead perhaps, another girl behaving badly. I've got to start giving people more credit.

Is It All in a Name?

Life is funny sometimes. People cross paths for what seems like no reason, but then years later the significance is learned and the understanding that follows seems to be uncanny. Or, in this case, totally unreal.

I have a friend named Maureen. I met her during a TOPS soccer season when her husband and I agreed to help coach our children's team. Secretly, I was thrilled Jim agreed to coach too—I thought I could follow his lead, be his little sidekick. Not do much more than chat with parents, run the field, bark a few friendly orders. I asked him right away when he donned his COACH shirt, "Have you ever played soccer before?" He replied, "Nope. You?" I grinned and said, "Not a day in my life!" We high-fived to a great upcoming season.

Over the course of the next few months, Maureen happily fed my children, doled out drinks when needed, cheered from the sidelines and somehow, without even trying, weaved her life together with mine. Maureen cut my children's hair for school pictures this year. No small task if you've ever met my youngest kid. Her son and mine both attend the same special day class and we've enjoyed the friendship that blossomed naturally through complete understanding of each other's situations.

During the entire time I've known Maureen I've always intended to tell her that she is one of two Maureens that I have ever known in my entire life. The first one was pretty extraordinary too. In fact, the First Maureen left such an impression on me when I was six years old, I've never forgotten her and have always carried around a feeling of warmth and comfort just by hearing the name. While pregnant, I considered it for both of my children before learning that they were in fact boys, not the little Irish lassies I was anticipating. I specifically told my husband during both pregnancies, "I once knew a Maureen who was very kind to me as a child, she took care of me at a birthday party when no one else did. She played with me while all the other older kids ignored me.

Maureen is a good name, I promise." At six years of age, an older child taking special interest in you makes you feel important, it can even leave a lasting impression.

One day a group of us special day class mommies were standing around waiting to pick up our little charges after school when the topic of childhood geography was brought up.

"I grew up in Hillsborough," said Sherry.

"I grew up in South City," I piped in.

"Oh, me too," said Maureen. "In San Bruno."

"Well, wait a sec…I lived in San Bruno until 1979," I told her. I stared at my friend. "Did you go to Monte Verde Elementary?"

"Yes!" she exclaimed. The wheels in my head started spinning rapidly.

And I knew, I just knew that I was looking at the very Maureen I would have named a child after.

Totally unreal. That discovery lead to numerous conversations, countless sessions of "Whatever happened to so-and-so?" unending laughter while pouring over class pictures, and a few phone calls to our moms, who also remembered one another. She caught me up on all my elementary school crushes, as well as called one boy's mom who she kept in touch with. It was quite the trip down memory lane.

What's most remarkable though is not that we crossed paths once again, this time 30 years later. But that when we did, she again left me with an unforgettable impression of kindness and sincerity. This same little girl who once cheered me up while others around took no notice, grew into the woman I've seen comfort my own son on her lap, before I realized who she was to me. But better than that is the realization that I have, in fact, only met one Maureen in my life, not two.

Moms Behaving Badly

"**Come on,**" I anxiously drum my fingers on my knee, "Can't you eat any faster?" I am squished into a booth at Johns Incredible Pizza waiting, rather impatiently, for my son to down the cone he's been licking for the past 15 minutes. This is such a role reversal. Here is a 5-year-old who wants nothing more than to sit and finish his snack, while his mother is chomping at the bit to get back out and play more air hockey.

"We're never going to get back on our table," my friend hisses at me, "Do you see this crowd?" She gestures dramatically out to the game room. Clusters of children and parents fill the gaps and with a sinking feeling, I realize our chances of playing one more cutthroat match of air hockey are getting slim. We are here for a birthday party and much to our surprise, have found ourselves totally entertained. Our strategy was this: ditch the kids with the dads and go have some fun.

As it was, getting the air hockey table was initially a bit of a challenge. We hung around watching some teenagers play and by the time our presence there made them uncomfortable enough to leave, Joanne was off wrestling with her youngest daughter a few yards away. "Come ON!" I screamed at her, jumping up and down. I dove onto the table and sprawled out in an effort to save it for us. She hurled tokens at me as she ran past, chasing her child. I leapt off and crawled around on the ground finding them as she wrangled the child and eventually deposited her with her father.

This little snack break came unexpectedly during the midst of some heated competition between the two of us. Joanne was leaned onto the table, one arm guarding her goal, the other holding the puck and pointing at me, "You want a piece of me? You want some of this?"

"Bring it sister," I challenged, "You've obviously been playing with your eyes closed today!" We made faces, obscene gestures, and did our best to implement diversion tactics. A tap on my shoulder halted the spirited exchange.

Josh stood with his dad, who looked less than amused by what he just overheard. "Your son is hungry," he said to me. "Can you please stop dancing and listen?"

I waved my paddle in his face, "I am winning," I sang out in my best Will Ferrel, "I am in the middle of John's and I am winning..." It was true for the moment. Joanne and I had been feeding tokens into this table all morning and I had dove, screamed, and gyrated my way to having the higher score. Taking a break now meant we could lose our table to some kid, or even worse, another parent.

"Can't you take him to get a snack?" I asked as I turned my back and launched the puck past Joanne's paddle and into the goal. I squealed and laughed and did an in-your-face motion at Joanne. "Go feed your kid!" she yelled at me, just as her husband walked up, their daughter in his wake. Well then. It was basically decided who'd be taking a break with the children.

As soon as we had the kids fed, cleaned, and loaded up on tokens, Joanne and I made our way back into the game room. The crowd had thickened up considerably during the half hour we had disappeared. She pointed to the bumper cars and raised her eyebrows at me. When we tried to get enter the gate, the attendant inquired, "Where are your children?"

He stood in my path. It was either answer or not get on. "With their dads, why?" I thumbed the air towards him, smirked, and gave Joanne a 'get-a-load-of-this-guy' look. The attendant look genuinely surprised, "You mean, you ladies want to ride this? Without your kids?" He stepped aside and tried not to smile. Once on, I stood in my car to get Joanne's attention. I pointed to a little girl wearing a bright pink bow in her hair. The child saw my intention and stuck her tongue out at me. Joanne nodded in agreement and when the buzzer sounded to start the cars, the two of us made a beeline for the child and repeatedly bumped her around. We were high-fiving and hooting as we exited. The attendant just shook his head.

We hit the virtual roller coaster next, and stumbled out as it ended only to spot our husbands walking by with the kids. They looked haggard and exhausted. Seeing us laughing and nudging one another intensified the looks of irritation they wore. I grinned and waved. Called out, "Hi honey! Having a good time?" then grabbed Joanne and attempted to steer her through the crowd away from them. Snickering, we dodged and weaved the pack around us. A sharp yank on the back of my shirt stopped me in my tracks.

"Times up Sweet Cheeks," Brad told me. "You're back on kid duty." It was fun while it lasted, us moms behaving badly.

Scent of a Woman

Mmm, you smell good. What are you wearing?" My friend sniffs the air around me and grins.

"Desitin," I reply dryly, "You can get it anywhere."

This is a real conversation, no joke. Yes, *Desitin* does smell nice, but I hardly wear it as perfume. I can't seem to completely wash it off my hands and the aroma hovers around me hours after application.

My friend looks horrified, as if I've just fessed up to having a rather ghastly diaper rash myself. "No, no," I tell her, "It's not what you think. It's on my hands." I present my palms for her inspection but seeing nothing she eyes me curiously.

This friend has no children. Therefore, any chance of connection here is nil. She looks confused; is wearing the scrunched eyebrow, perplexed facial feature combination. How do I explain to this person that real perfume goes out the window once the children come along?

Knowing better than to attempt a clarification, I go against my gut and try anyway:

Me (as if talking to a child): *"Desitin* is used for *diaper* rashes and..."

Her (still horrified at my confession, and now a tad embarrassed about her compliment): "I KNOW! I just don't get why you'd rub it all over your hands?"

(Did I say that?)

Me: "I'm not really wearing it (sheesh!). Ben is, if you must know the truth, but it's hard to wash off and then."

Her: "Do you have any *Obsession*? What about *Sunflowers*? Can't you rub in a *CK* cologne or something to cover that up? Here...I have some *Tommy Girl* in my bag."

She begins to rummage around in her purse. Two things: First, I haven't carried a real purse in years and second, people who put perfume samples in them make me nervous. Where is the logic in that? I mean, if it spills, you will forever smell like that particular fragrance and so will your wipes, diapers, and extra snacks...wait, what DO people put in purses anyway?

I shrug off her effort and forgo pointing out that just seconds ago she complimented me on my scent.

Instead, I tell her, "Look, soon it will fade and by then I will smell like fishy crackers and juice, peanut butter and fruit snacks, and not long after that—Costco diaper wipes." She is silent. Her rummaging has stopped, and she slowly looks up at me.

In all seriousness she forms her question and slowly asks, "Why do you rub wipes meant for children's butts on yourself?"

Pause. "Well, to get off all the stickiness from the peanut butter." She stares at me. "And to feel generally…refreshed…" I end weakly.

We are at a standstill in our conversation. I recognize all the signs. Neither of us knows how to continue so we stand there sort of looking at other things and riding out the awkward silence.

"Would you like one?" I offer. In an attempt to appear savvy to *Mommy Loops*, she smiles and says, "Of course, I need some refreshing myself." She dabs her cheeks and the back of her neck. Soon, she is swabbing her elbows and the back of her knees. When she starts completely slathering her shins and ankles, I try not to gawk.

She tries to hand it back to me. Until this point, I almost gave her credit for trying but this little stunt is too much. "Um, no thanks," I say. "Just go ahead and toss it in the trash." I wave her towards the garbage can with a swift flick of my wrist and false smile of encouragement.

"What you really need are little wipes that smell like perfume," she informs me. "Then rubbing them all over your body wouldn't appear so strange and unladylike." Did I say dry off with the thing? No, I told her to refresh herself, not take a bath. "And you'd smell like a woman," she states.

Or an idiot, I reason. I'll stick with baby fresh for now. And perhaps friends with kids, the ones who wear the same scent I do.

Seizing the Day

"**Oh, hi Curly,**" my dad looks surprised to see me on his doorstep at 9:30 a.m., "What are you doing here?"

"Isn't Andrea up?' I ask. My sister is in from Texas for the holidays, and we have made plans to go to the gym this rainy morning. I've dropped the kids off at their schools and am dressed in my running gear, ready to hit the treadmill with my big sis.

"Um…" he looks uncomfortable, "Andrea isn't up yet. She said she has cramps." He offers a weak smile.

I feel my jaw go slack. "CRAMPS?" I hit the road at 7:45 this morning to get the kids to school and stop by my parents' home to grab her in order to work out before having to pick up the two little monkeys. I stomp up the stairs and shove open her bedroom door.

There she lies. On her back with a heating pad covering her middle. An empty glass of what appears to be orange juice is on the nightstand, the straw bent at the neck, hanging its head in shame. She doesn't open her eyes but mumbles, "Mom…? Can you get me some more (sniff, sniff) juice?" She moans softly. This is just too much. I can't even remember the last time I laid in bed at 9:30 a.m., let alone had someone bring me something.

With a running start I hurl myself on top of her. "Ooomph!" I start snickering.

"Get off me you freak!" she screams. It is like we are 10 years old again. I roll to the side and let her adjust herself. "What the hell? Why would you do something like that?" She is pissed but I don't care. She glares at me. "I have cramps, you know." I roll my eyes. "I am in pain, Carolyn. You have no idea." She has apparently forgotten that I have borne two children. I mouth 'blah-blah-blah' and do the quacking hand to show her how affected I am by her pain.

"Oh my God Andrea, look!" When she does, I lift up my shirt and expose my sports bra. She sighs, exasperated, and lays back down. "You act so lame sometimes. Aren't you supposed to be a mother?"

"We are going to the gym. So, get up." I nudge her. She flails a hand across her forehead.

"Go by yourself." Hello. I could have done that at home. I didn't have to drive all the way to Pleasanton to go workout. She pulls the covers up under her chin and turns her back to me. I lean in and blow in her ear. She slaps at me. This is how it is. We have always been like this. Fighting, teasing, never agreeing on anything.

"You have got to be kidding me. I drove all the way here. In traffic. To work out with you. And you want to lay here sleeping?" I bounce up and down on the bed to get a response. Nothing.

She leaves me no choice. I examine her ponytail until I find a stray hair and I pluck it from her head. She yelps and swears at me.

"Girls!" Mom pokes her head in the doorway, looks irritated. "Knock off all the monkey business and either get up or be quiet." I can hardly believe we're getting busted by our mother. We're in our thirties after all. We sit stunned and silent for a second.

Andrea lifts the covers, "Get in," she orders in typical big sister fashion, "And grab that box of See's Candies on the dresser." I do as I'm told and lean back against the headboard.

"Let's talk about Mom!"

Finally, something we can do together. Way better than going to the gym anyway.

Sentiment More Valuable Than Dollar Amount

Though the shirt is rather repulsive, and it's actually much too small for me, I can't seem to part with it. Multiple shades of green and a tad snug in the chest area, I bought it for twenty-five cents at a garage sale my friend Michele had a few years back. When I rescued it from the heap of its peers, Michele looked at me, wrinkled her nose, and asked, "Do you really like that?" I smiled. "I do," I told her, "Plus, this was yours, right?" And it was. She wore it for a long time then decided to pass it on. I was happy just owning something that my friend had cherished for that short time, even if it didn't fit.

Michele moved to New Hampshire last summer and now I'll never give that shirt up. More than once it almost found itself it my giveaway pile too, but I liked to put it on and go to her house, just to get a laugh. The new owners probably wouldn't think it too funny if I showed up at their door now, donning that shirt. They may even call me weird. Chances are I won't be seeing Michele for quite a while, so I keep this shirt and her memory close to my heart.

Sometime before she planned on moving away, I programmed the banner on her telephone to read "DODDSRCOOL." I thought I was pretty clever. She told me recently that she thinks of me every time her phone rings, because the banner lights up her new kitchen. "I'll never erase it now!" She reminisced about me sneaking off with her phone and then reappearing minutes later, smug and grinning expectedly. "What?" she had asked, "WHAT?" I said nothing, just kept smiling and giggling. Her husband had noticed it first actually, and called my house to inform me, "The Dodds might be cool, but not cool enough to be on our phone." We laughed, but lo and behold—nobody ever erased it. I like that. Sentimental value. I think it ties us together as people.

I love that the older I get, the more I cherish the right things. Friends, relationships, children, just people and shared experiences in general. Almost everything I own now is tied to a person, a memory of something we did or said. I like to look at pictures and remember the way we felt at that moment in time. Try to recall—what were we laughing at? Or why were we standing so far apart? Inside jokes hold more value to me than a new couch or any piece of furniture. I like to look at my slippers and know that they came from a friend, or at my earrings, and remember them as a gift, rather than a purchase.

This must be hereditary, this need for connection. My father keeps his true valuables on the top shelf of his closet, yet they are nothing any robber would want: his daughters' cards and artwork, a scrapbook made for him from his family and friends. And my mom pilfers away what she holds dear in an antique chest in their home: report cards, hospital bracelets, black and white photos. I know exactly what they would grab should the house catch fire, none of it clothing or kitchenware. None of it being accessories or even jewelry. All of it more valuable than what can be claimed by insurance.

So, while I cannot seem to squeeze into Michele's size S from Old Navy, I won't pass it on. I have the feeling that while someone may think it's beautiful, and may even be able to wear it, no one will ever come to truly appreciate the shirt, or its original owner, like I do.

Those Hot Summer Nights

The other night at bedtime I turned out my son's bedroom light and asked him, "Are you sure you're cool enough?" He lay sprawled across his bed in only a T-shirt and Scooby Doo boxers. His reply came in the form of holding one hand in the air and giving me a thumbs-up.

"Okay then…good night." I started to shut the door, paused, then opened it back up again. "Are you positive you don't want a cold cloth?" He sat up. "Mom, I'm already freezing. You can probably turn down the air conditioning ("AC"). Good *night*."

Now there's a conversation that would have never happened in my house when I was a kid. My mom and dad didn't believe in AC, though they had a change of heart, ironically, once my sister and I left for college. That's where I got the call at my little apartment in Davis when my mom gleefully announced, "Dad and I broke down! We got AC! Ho, ho, ho. Whaddaya think of them apples?"

I can tell you exactly what I thought of "them apples." I thought them apples were rotten. Those two made my sister and I live through sweltering heat day in, day out. Every night each of us clutched a washcloth soaked in cold water. We'd drape those cloths over our foreheads, our necks, our bellies, our legs and our feet until they eventually felt room temperature again. That little method of keeping cool would last about 7 minutes tops, then we'd meet in the bathroom for a re-soaking, and bicker over who got to use the sink first. Andrea and I were fighters. We fought the heat, we fought our parents, and we fought each other. We'd angrily shove one another away from the sink and wind up with our tank tops and skivvies soaked. "Shut up…you shut up…" Then we'd hustle back to our respective bedrooms before our washcloths heated up.

One night in high school when I no longer felt my washcloth was doing its job, I reached my breaking point and grabbed a beach towel from the shelf. I proceeded to soak it in the sink. The wringing out of the mammoth cloth woke my sister who came in to tell me first what an idiot I was to take a wet towel to bed, then reconsider and order me to scoot over so she could soak her own towel. "We've been using these sissy washcloths for years," I balled it up and hurled it at the wall, "I'm tired of feeling like a greased pig at night."

Our hoots and snickers brought in the always uninvited third party, Mom, who saw the towels and said, "NO WAY." Andrea was standing mummified in a cool *Budweiser* wrap while I was midway through creating my own *New Kids on the Block* toga.

"I don't know how you even heard us over all thirteen of those fans you have in your room," I sneered.

"Yeah" said sister, "Why don't you spread the wealth a little bit and let your daughters get a fan or two?" We angrily deposited our towels into the bathtub and exited in a huff, each of us fisting a washcloth.

Another night Andrea and I met up in the bathroom she had entered rubbing her eyes, her washcloth perched on top of her head. I was on my knees rifling through the cabinets. "Help me find the hot water bottle…"

"Why? So, *you* can use it? No thanks…Mom's probably got it anyway," Andrea sulked, "Remember she confiscated it after our last brawl…"

I paused my hunt, then laughed. "That was a good fight." We had actually wrestled out into the hallway that night, slapping, grabbing, and pulling hair. Being totally uncivilized. My mom broke us up and hollered, "What is the world is the matter with you two? You're acting like wild animals!"

"HOT wild animals," I cried, "Hot, sweaty, wild JUNGLE animals who have no air conditioning!" I was panting and gasping, and my t-shirt was bunched up and twisted.

"We're DYING from the HEAT, *Paula*!" Andrea screamed at her. The water bottle, which had been packed with ice, lay on the ground between us. I can't remember which one of us discovered that while a hot water bottle is good for relieving tired muscles or soothing sore tummies, should it be packed with ice and water, it also served as a great ice pack to accompany a warm child to bed.

"I refuse to allow you girls to bicker over this." She picked up the cold pack and clutched it protectively to her side. "This now belongs to me."

I imagined her cozied up with it in her bed, fans running, the temperature a good 50 degrees cooler than my own room and hissed at Andrea, "Nice going."

She flashed the international one finger sign for "Your fault."

We must have been the only kids who fought over who got to sleep with a hot water bottle stuffed with ice. Normal parents may have spent the additional three dollars and purchased a second one so that each of their two children could reap the rewards. Then again, normal parents may have also invested in fans for their children, or AC while the children still lived at home for that matter. Either way, Andrea and I spent a great many summer evenings covered in cold washcloths.

After double checking that my son would indeed be comfortable that night, I went downstairs and flopped on the couch.

"Did I hear you offer him a cold cloth to sleep with?" Brad raised an eyebrow at me. "Who does that anyway?"

Sweeping It All Under the Rug

A friend dropped in the other day. Marched straight past me into my house and stood to face me in my kitchen.

"What?" I asked. She pointed to the rug on the floor. She raised her eyebrows. Jab. jab. She pointed again. I still didn't get it.

"Um, you like my rug?" I asked weakly.

"I think what you do with this rug is disgusting!" She retorted. Well now, how was I supposed to answer that? What specifically does one do with a kitchen floor rug that may offend another? And she leaned down to lift a corner of it, I immediately knew.

"DON'T touch that!" I squealed and leapt over to stomp down the corner with my tennis shoe. Too late. With her lifting of the corner, out blew dust, crumbs, and bits of animal fur. Not to mention broken cracker bits and cheerios pieces. "Disgusting," she mumbled.

All right, so she had me. My sweeping skills are what my dad would term "half-ass." In my defense, I don't own a dustpan. I never think to buy one. Why would I, when sweeping things under the rug has always worked so well for me? Quite frankly, having two little boys makes my kitchen a black hole for crumbs, dust, fuzz, lint, and small toys. I'd forever be with broom in hand if I insisted on having a clean kitchen floor.

Big or small, anything gets swept under the rug. Why, if anything seems to break the size barrier, I just do a little hop-hop, and within seconds, it has been reduced to bits and flecks. And I don't even have to see it.

This doesn't mean that dirt stays under my rug. Heavens no. When it gets to the point of the rug having tell-tale hills and valleys running throughout it, I grab the vacuum and suck it all into oblivion.

Friends and neighbors don't seem to really mind. Even the gal who comes to cut my hair knows to peel back the rug before she begins snipping away. This way I can easily sweep and cover in a matter of seconds. I have it down to a science.

I stood there facing my friend. She was shaking her head and making small "tsk-tsk" noises with her tongue. Smiling sly, she whisks a small dustpan, complete with ribbon on the handle, from her purse. "Happy Birthday!" she announces. I did what any good friend would do; I thanked her for her gift and after she left, I put it under my rug.

Marriage on Collision Course

The concept of marriage has become somewhat of a mystery to me. Two people together, forever. Thankfully, some of us have grandparents who've been married for decades, having weathered bad times to be role models for those of us who think of marriage as a temporary state of being. Not that there is anything wrong with that, mind you. I've known couples that have divorced when divorce was absolutely the best thing for them. I've also known couples that have stuck it out when all reasoning escapes me.

I hadn't even heard of the term "divorce" before moving to Pleasanton from San Bruno as a kid. I lived in what may be termed a "rough" section of the city by today's standards. In those days, it was totally common to hear neighbors screaming and dishes breaking. I didn't give much thought to parents fighting at all, until I moved to a rather classier suburb and discovered that most of my new friends lived with their moms and saw their fathers only on weekends and holidays. It was an intriguing concept to a kid who grew up thinking marriage was defined by two adults living unhappily under the same roof.

The evolution from romantic courting to resentful avoidance is curious to me. I had a conversation with a girlfriend last week who told me she was getting all her ducks in a row financially now because her husband has no plans of sharing his 401K retirement savings with her. I laughed at the incredulity of this until she said, "I'm serious!" He told me that by the time he retires he should have saved $500,000, and what did I plan to do—since my job doesn't offer such a thing?" I was silently fuming for her when she continued, "After I asked him to help me get the kids ready for bed one night, he said, 'Look—I'm the provider (she works too) and you're the nurturer. Since my work is done for the day, you can finish up with yours while I relax on the sofa.'"

I scoffed and told her, "You should have said, 'No, you're the comic and I'm the audience and that was a pretty funny thing to say.'"

"Or," she remarks, "You're the comic and I'm the heckler and I'm out there screaming YOU SUCK right about now."

We're laughing but the reality of her situation doesn't elude either one of us. Just that evening I had asked Jason to help me clean the kitchen and he answered by scooping more pasta on his plate and saying with his mouth full, "Sure. I'll clean off my plate here while you wash the dishes."

I said nothing, only fought the urge to whack him in the head with the pan I was scrubbing. Just the visual of it was enough to cool my jets.

I can't help but think we aren't too different from most couples. At least we talk to one another. I know a girl who does everything under the radar. She lives in constant stealth mode and doesn't tell her husband a thing.

I hope for the sake of all budding new relationships that everyone's not headed in that direction. One friend of mine is dating a guy that does nothing but romantic things for her, and it's been nearly a year. I wonder if it will eventually taper off and the real boy will emerge from his present "perfect gentleman" shell. She constantly gushes about how he surprises her with cards and flowers, phone calls and pop-ins. One night he showed up with lobster and salad and they picnicked on her down comforter; stayed up all night just talking and laughing. Ten years from now will she be made happy by the mere visual of knocking him out with the frying pan?

I saw a bumper sticker yesterday, "Marriage: Do It 'Till You Get It Right." See? A mystery.

8
Birds of a Feather

The Case of the Missing Underwear

"So, give me the dirt on your underwear…" I snicker into the phone as I settle back onto the couch and get ready for a good conversation with my friend Aimee. She recently emailed me to describe a most unusual occurrence at her house; her underwear had gone missing. And not just one pair, mind you—she continuously could not find multiple pairs.

When she first complained of her panty predicament, it seemed highly possible that she was just being silly. I mean, who really notices missing underwear? I guess I just have so many that I couldn't begin to take an inventory. But the more we spoke of her dilemma, the more I began to see how missing clothing, even underwear, was no laughing matter.

The first indication of something amiss came the morning after a New Year's party she had thrown in her home. Surprised to find that her underwear drawer had been rearranged, Annie saw with astonishment that her "special occasion" hot pink bra and panties had been shuffled into the "everyday" stack. Not only that, but it seemed that her granny panties had mysteriously worked their way to the front of the drawer. Perplexing, but no one she lived with seemed to know anything about it.

The next clue arrived with her roommate's announcement that he let a neighbor of theirs into the garage to "borrow" something. The neighbor was a guy they had gone to high school with; he had also been at the New Year's party a few weeks earlier. Not too comfortable with this particular gentleman anyway, Aimee perused the garage and noted that her basket of dirty laundry had been moved. She thought little of it until she later went to fold the laundry after washing it, and found she only had one pair of underwear in the entire load. The plot thickens.

So, Aimee buys more panties and decides to keep a closer eye on them. One morning, on a whim, she decides to go out for donuts, but skips her shower. Fearful of getting in an accident and not having on clean undies, she does a quick change and kicks the used pair into a corner of her room. Upon returning with a box of donuts, a roommate tells her that a neighbor stopped by for a visit while she was gone: the same neighbor that "borrowed" something from the garage. Aimee ditches the donuts and stomps off to her room. No more undies in the corner!

"Those were brand new!" she shouted, "That's it! I'm calling the cops." To her dismay, the cop that arrived at her doorstep was also someone she had gone to high school with, unfortunately a friend of the neighbor's.

"Oh Aimee," I tell her, "This cannot get any worse." I am on the couch still, listening to the details of this story with disbelief.

"Oh, it does," she tells me, "He went and got my underwear back from the guy and asked me to describe it for verification. I had to tell him it was a G-string and said "Princess" on the crotch." We are both laughing by now, but not completely unaware of the scariness of the situation too.

"Not only that, but they are keeping all the swiped pairs as evidence. I called the store where I bought them to report them as stolen and the people just laughed at me. Now I'm out 30 bucks. But don't worry, he's moved and there's been a restraining order filed."

"But this isn't really funny," I tell her, "Aren't you a little scared? What are you going to do?"

"Well for starters, I've stopped wearing underwear. It's too risky. I suggest you do the same."

Hmmm…something to consider, I suppose. But since the guy has been caught, no need for me to do anything extreme.

The Red Cup Society

While on the phone with a friend the other day, I mention that our neighborhood is having a gathering that evening in the garage of one of our friends.

"Hmmm…" she says, "Another red cup event?" I start laughing, then start really laughing when I think about how right she is. The red cup has symbolized "adult party" in a way that no other cup has throughout time.

"I can just see you now," she continues, "Bounding out your front door, red cup in hand, as you make your way up the block and into the garage where the party is." I'm surprised at her accuracy. "You'll probably wave and chat with all the neighbors on your way." This particular friend has always been in awe of just how close the people on our street are. Sometimes too chummy and occasionally a few have been accused of pushing the limits on the boundaries of friendship, but no matter what—we enjoy one another's company and never seem to be in short supply of red cups or anything that fills one.

But she does get me thinking. Have red cups always been a part of adult gatherings? A look through a few old photo albums gives me my answer. Lake Shasta 1995. Twenty close friends share the confines of one houseboat meant to sleep twelve. Even in pictures, easily seen are the plastic red cups scattered about on tables, next to sleeping bags, some even shoved forgotten onto the shelves in the bathroom. While some lay like fallen lushes, others stand at attention—their dents and cracks like battle wounds, proof of their night spent in the sticky clutches of drinking boaters.

I toss the album and grab another. A cabin trip in 1998. Just a couple of families from the neighborhood and what do you know—red cups abound. I believe we were up there celebrating Thanksgiving, a day to share appreciation for what we have and what are about to receive and there we are—all six of us toasting with plastic red cups.

Next album. This one takes me back farther as it's packed with photos from my college days at University of California, Davis, in the early 1990s. My twenty-first birthday—I'm raising my plastic red cup and grinning at whoever's taking the picture while the unnamed co-ed whose lap I am sitting on holds an enormous 24 oz Mac Tonight plastic number. I remember this night and this guy, who in all actuality probably agreed that red cups were cool, but when it came down to it—they just didn't hold enough beer. Behind us, towers of red cups line the countertop.

I've seen enough. I call back my friend and tell her, "Apparently, I've been a part of this Red Cup Society for years and had no idea I was even a member!"

"How can you gallivant about bringing your red cup to parties and not know this?"

She is *so* not a member. Everyone who's anyone knows that the house supplies the red cup, nobody actually brings their own. I patiently try to explain this. "Is this written in the society bylaws or something?" she inquires. "Did you guys set a statute on what defines proper membership behavior?"

"Look," I tell her, "I didn't start the club, I only joined it. Maybe I should have a party with blue cups just to see what happens—they make those you know."

She gets excited. "Yeah! Do it! You'd probably get all the kids in the neighborhood to show up. Kids like blue, right? Blue cups say 'pin the tail on the donkey' all over them." She has a point. Might be fun to try. But since I am not the one hosting the event that evening, I do the next best thing: saunter in with a blue cup in hand.

Smiling and nodding, I tip my cup to everyone I pass and enjoy the look of confusion that washes over the crowd. Hurrying to my rescue, a neighbor rapidly approaches and hands me a red cup filled with sangria. "You gotta be kidding me," he says as he takes the blue cup and deposits it in the trash. "What are we, Chuckie Cheese?"

Close call. I could have lost my membership.

Wine Down

One of my favorite misunderstandings happened with my friend CiCi. We had been standing around at T-Ball, watching our kids run amuck, comparing our identical looks: tousled hair, baggy sweats, dark puffy eyes, and expressions of unadulterated fatigue. Her oldest daughter and my youngest son were participating in Freedom League, the first T-ball league for children with varying abilities.

She sighed. "You know what we need? Just an evening to relax. Why don't you come over tonight and wind down?"

My appreciation for a good red wine overrode my sense of hearing. "You are so clever!" I slapped her arm. "I love it!" *Wine down.* Throw back some vino and put up our feet. Swirl bulbous glasses of grown-up grape juice. I considered her a genius right there on the spot.

She stared blankly at me. "Have you not heard the expression 'wind down' before?" She looked a little skeptical.

Thinking myself unfamiliar with the lingo of today's hip, sassy wine consumer, I said, "NO! It's great too—wine down!" I threw back my head and gestured to a glass being emptied into my open mouth. "Brilliant!"

Instantly she understood and started laughing. We made plans to wine down as soon as possible, not to mention as often as our schedules allowed.

I get a kick out of everyone's personal expressions for alcohol consumption. While CiCi and I chuckle over 'wine down', I share the expression 'Corona Monday' with another girlfriend, Pam. Corona Monday began when she'd pick up my son from school, take him home to play, and I'd retrieve him later that evening. I'd chat with Pam in her kitchen while she'd make dinner and we'd polish off a few Coronas. This happened on Mondays, thus the name. We eventually gave up trying to squeeze in some exercise during our Monday visits, and opted instead to cook and drink beer. On the last Corona Monday, I spit out my lime and asked, "Do you remember when we weren't old enough to drink beer?" I tossed the bottle into her recycling bin.

"Yeah," she laughed, "Or how about when we didn't even like the taste of it?" She poured some wine in her spaghetti sauce and smiled, "I love being an adult."

As I stood at her counter slicing limes, I thought of my own mother in our kitchen making dinner, when I was a kid. I couldn't ever recall seeing her add wine to anything, let alone suck on the neck of a beer bottle while stirring a sauce. Boy, times sure have changed!

And while it may appear that my friends are all lushes, it's quite the contrary. They're all professional, responsible girls. They all have families, jobs, and hobbies. They, like myself, just enjoy some down time, nothing wrong with that. One of my closest friends has her "Two for Tuesdays" and allows herself two martinis during her dinner preparation. Another gal enjoys what she terms "Bailey's Night" with some of her neighbors, this I found out only recently. "Even though we sometimes drink Emmetts and Carolans Irish Creme," she told me, "We still call it Bailey's Night." She hummed a few bars from 'Ladies' Night' and I got the picture.

Wine Down, Corona Monday, Two for Tuesdays, and Bailey's Night. Call it what you will, it just means one thing. I agree with Pam, I love being an adult.

A Bunch of Girls Did This

"**It must have** been one heck of a party," the carpet cleaner whistled and scratched his head. "You got teenaged boys?"

We both surveyed the damage and I shook my head "no."

"One toddler, one infant," I answered; "but they're not responsible for this." I rubbed the toe of my sneaker on an orange stain and said "Cheese dip."

He pointed to a red blemish of considerable size and his raised eyebrows silently inquired its origin.

"Oh," I nodded, "That's strawberry margarita." And from there I continued to point out the various discolorations, spots, and marks that dotted the flooring of my entire home.

Most people need more than a one-word explanation for the destruction of a house, but for some women out there, BUNCO is self-explanatory. See, the group I play in is pretty hard-core. Wine and cheese served with classical music we are not. These girls like everything from Eminem to Blondie. They eat more than salad greens and have been known to blow M&Ms out their nose (okay, just one girl did that). We even have a designated Head Ass—the one person who behaves more obnoxiously than the rest of us that night. We swear, yell, and throw things. It's the best time I have acting uncivilized once a month.

When I was first invited to play *BUNCO* with a friend, I scoffed, "I'm a little young for tile games with your grandma." She explained it was nothing like *Mahjong* and there was booze involved. Hmmm. Interesting.

After one occasion as a sub in another group, I decided to throw together a few friends and start a troop of my own. I admit it. I was a little worried. Putting together high school friends, neighbors and even a gal I knew from my network marketing days seemed a little risky. But I needn't have feared. Sixteen girls who love to talk, eat, drink and have a good time don't need too many introductions. The night before Mr. Carpet Cleaner came was the first night the group met.

Unfortunately, I had underestimated what a few ladies off the wagon could do to one family's alcohol supply. These girls went through every single bottle in the house. They even uncovered Brad's secret summer stash and someone wound up bringing in a dusty bottle of cognac from my garage. At one point I remember thinking, "Who drinks cognac, anyway?" But at the end of night, the bottle lay empty, next to the others in the sink.

Our men sporadically wandered in for a drink and a snack, then retreated to the "Husband House" down the block, where it was reported later that they had trouble putting the kids to sleep due to the noise from our house. (Boo hoo.) When Brad returned home at the end of the evening, he had to step over four bags of trash on the porch and found me rounding up cans from the planters and crumpled napkins from the kids' rooms.

"A bunch of GIRLS did this?" His eyes were huge. "Are you serious?!"

What could I say? It must have been one heck of a party.

Love: For Some, It's an Animal Thing

"And so," my friend sighed dreamily, "I think I have met...the one." She gazed happily over my shoulder as we lunched at a small table in the corner of a coffee shop. Picturing her beau, no doubt. I returned the smile and cleared my throat, preventing a snicker from escaping my clamped lips. If I had a dime every time this certain friend of mine had met "the one," I'd be fantastically wealthy and far from this coffee shop, I'm sure.

But perhaps I'm wrong. Once upon a time I sat gazing at pictures of Brad telling every living soul I encountered that I had met my prince charming. When, in reality, I actually had. Amazing.

"But," my friend interrupts my reverie, "It's just that we are so different. You know what they say: opposites attract." At this, I let out one obnoxious cackle and snort, then recover by saying, "Of course, of course… so true."

But she does get me thinking. Back when Brad and I had met we were both gearing up to go to family reunions in Nebraska. We thought it a strange coincidence, the fact that both sides of our families came from the Midwest. Being a Husker fan was a bonus for each of us, but I do distinctly remember Brad telling me, "As much as I like you, I hope I don't run into you at my reunion."

And going back even further, the first night he handed me his phone number (I'm a modern woman, so sue me) he had written down the exact phone number I recently had disconnected when graduating from University of California, Davis. Different area code, of course, but still. I looked him directly in the eye and said, "Shut up. This is not your phone number." But it was. Coincidence, you tell me. And after realizing our birthdays were numerical opposites (10/03 and 03/10) we knew we were destined for one another.

Back in the day, we were convinced we had everything in common. What a laugh. A reality check was in order. After eight years together, here's a more accurate glimpse of Mr. and Mrs. Prince Charming: while I eat all the good stuff off my plate first, he saves the best for last. I'm a neurotic cleaner, he's a compulsive collector. I say, "Keep it simple," while he touts, "Lets analyze this situation one more time." I enjoy the sound of silence; he gets a kick out of how loud he can talk. I drive in a hell-bent hurry to get to my destination, he is proud of being called, "Grandpa," when he gets behind the wheel. When holding the remote I stop and giggle to reruns of *The Facts of Life* and *VH I Behind the Music*, he pauses to watch elephant documentaries and *The Journey of the Jellyfish*. It's infuriatingly romantic how different we can be.

I am deep in my contemplation of my current situation when interrupted by another dreamy sigh. (Courtesy of my friend in love.) I feel compelled to grin at her. I have that self-righteous "I'm so much more knowledgeable than you," smirk on my face for sure. And for what, I ask you. I was so far off when I thought Brad and I had everything in common, that my friend may be way ahead of her time in the realization that they are opposites. I should have been so open minded.

She takes one last swig of her latte and says, "But get this, he likes to watch animal documentaries." What can I say but, "He's a keeper!"

The Ups and Downs of Bunking Together

I sometimes walk past my youngest son's room and pause, just long enough to glance in and envision the room configured as my office, my sewing room, my gym, my anything. In a house the size of a large apartment, a person will do anything to find more space. With a 1,200 square foot home to work with, I sometimes get pretty desperate.

My husband caught me leaning up against the doorframe the other day, pure want written all over my face. I was mentally arranging the selection of Pottery Barn furniture this time. (When I dream, I go all out.)

"I'm thinking the boys will love to share a room…" I began.

He held up a hand and stopped me there. I know, I know. There are two stands' people take on kids sharing a room. Ask anyone who's ever shared a room and they'll tell you they either loved it or hated it. But most will tell you, now that they are all grown up, that some of their favorite memories involved same room antics.

My sister and I had to share a bedroom only when we spent time at our family cabin. And looking back, those are the memories Andrea and I find most hilarious.

There was a window of time that lasted about five years, when I thought my sister walked on water. I absolutely idolized this girl. Of course, she wanted no part of me and thought everything l said came straight from the mouth of a bleating baby sheep. I was ignored, made fun of, beat up, lied to, and every once in a while, asked to do her a personal favor. Wanting nothing more than to impress her, and prove I was capable of gaining her respect, I continuously jumped at the opportunity to do her bidding. Take for example the mouthwash incident.

At 15, Andrea had realized what a gem she had in a small sister who was willing to do anything to be noticed by her. At 11, I had been awaiting the opportunity for ages. One night, she entered the bedroom we shared and pulled a Tupperware container of green liquid from her shirt.

"Here," she shoved the container at me, "If Mom or Dad find this, tell them it's yours."

I shrugged. Easy enough. "Why are you hiding mouthwash in our room?"

"You are suuuuch a dummy. It's not mouthwash, it's Creme DeMenth." She grabbed my shirt collar and pulled me close. "And it's YOURS, remember?" She released me and punched my arm to make a point.

Rubbing my shoulder, I nodded and was secretly filled with pride at such a big responsibility. I tried to play it cool though and not let my enthusiasm for the task at hand blow my position. I mean, if I pulled this off, who knew of the possibilities?

The next day, Mom entered the room with a stack of folded clothes while I lay across the bed reading my latest Judy Blume novel. She opened the dresser drawer and proceeded to pull out the Tupperware container.

"Oh." I said nonchalantly, "That's mine."

Pause. "It's my mouthwash…"

I pretended to read with one eye closely watching my mother. First confusion, then a look of all knowing passed over her face.

"You are 11," she reminded me, "You have no reason to hide booze. Now, where is your sister?"

Okay, so the woman was smarter than we thought. Andrea got busted and I got slapped around a bit by the sister who didn't hide her mouthwash very well.

I can't help but wonder what kind of memories my boys will make by sharing a room. For now, though, it's out of the question. If I can't fathom the thought of putting two toddlers in a room if for no reason other than because of the smell, what would I do with two teenage boys? I knew we needed a bigger house.

Aggies, Aggies Everywhere

"Here," my brother-in-law, Paul, handed a small book to me. "This will be the most useful book you'll ever read."

I snorted. Aggie Facts and Figures. Yeah right. These Texas Aggies, I tell you, they take themselves pretty seriously.

When he wasn't looking, I skimmed through it. Curiosity got the best of me. It was your average, touristy, stocking stuffer kind of book. A little bit of history, a touch of tradition, the school songs, a map of the campus, even a few trivial facts. But a useful book? Rolling my eyes, I tossed it on the nearest table.

Months later I am standing in line in Burger King somewhere in Las Vegas, when the man in front of me says, "Hey! A fellow Aggie! You can cut in here…" I absentmindedly touched the Texas A&M hat I was wearing, smiled at the gentleman, then moved my place in line. Before I can say, "Thank you," a man from behind me boos and with his thumbs down jeers, "Boo Aggies. Longhorns rule!" Oh my gosh. A battle of the schools in Texas, right here in Vegas.

I turn and say sweetly to the boo-er, "Oh, Longhorns! That's right… isn't your school sign the broken bull horn?" and I proceed to show him the Aggie's version of the Longhorn hand sign, Courtesy of the Facts and Figure book.

More recently, Brad and I were shopping at Costco. As we stood in line, we noticed a lady giving us sly little looks and sneaking in an occasional conspiratorial grin. Slowly, she breaks into song, her eyebrows upward, prompting us to join her. We don't get it. I am doing all l can to not crack up. Finally, she stops and says, disappointed, "It's the Spirit of Aggieland, you know. The A&M's song." She points to Brad's hat, and clearly embarrassed now, swallows and looks away. Giggling, I explain our confusion and inform her that my brother-in-law is a professor there, but we aren't familiar with the song itself. I don't mention, though, that I recognized the words from the Facts and Figure book. I am a little surprised at this myself.

Fast forward 20 minutes. I am now helping Brad load groceries and children into our truck. A car approaches, slows down, and then a completely different woman hangs out her driver's window and screeches, "GO AGGIES! WHHOOOOO!" She waves, then drives off laying on her horn. We are dumbstruck. I would have thought her insane if I hadn't caught a glimpse of a Texas A&M sticker on her back window.

I immediately call my sister to relay the funny incidences to her and Paul. She tells me, "That is nothing, Carolyn. Paul and I were waiting to get on a flight last week and some man saw the A&M logo on Paul's shirt. He gave us his spot in line. Then, on the plane, the flight attendant saw the same logo, and before we knew it, we had free drinks for the duration of the flight."

I am beginning to understand the serious school pride those Aggies feel. It's trickling slowly into my blood. Why, just last week, I spied a Texas A&M bumper sticker on a car in a parking lot. The occupants of the vehicle were emerging and it was pretty obvious there was some tension between them. I approached the car and said cheerfully, "You guys' Aggies?" Initial shock from the male driver, then genuine glee as he answered, "Yeah! You?"

"Nah, but my brother-in-law is a professor there. Hey, do they really do that elephant walk I've heard about?" No reason not to throw around a bit of trivia I picked up from the handbook.

"Yeah, it's crazy too…" The conversation continued and I was able to toss in one or two more little facts I had gathered from my skimming. I departed rather proud of myself.

You know us Aggies, we take ourselves pretty seriously.

Hard Habits to Break

Some people leave the cap off the toothpaste, others pile their dishes on the counter. Still more dump their dirty laundry next to the hamper rather than inside it. Me? Well, I have a bad habit too. More than one, if truth be told.

I buy food with the intention of eating it, yet days later Brad will pick rotten bags of salad out of the fridge and hold them at arm's length while carrying them across the kitchen to the trash. Guiltily, I watch him toss the sacks and see dollar signs going right in the can as well. My intentions are good, I swear, I just seem to be lacking on the follow-through when it comes to eating healthy.

It seems that I choose to grocery shop when I am feeling pumped up about being a healthy eater. Buckets of cottage cheese, bags of greens, containers of nonfat yogurt all get tossed into my cart, while I happily envision the slimmer, trimmer me in a few weeks' time. Then I get home. Chaos ensues. Children are screaming, the cat is in heat, the toilet is clogged, I've left the hose on in the yard, and what choice do I have? I reach for a licorice rope while I plot out my escape.

While in deep contemplation, I'll yank open a bag of fruit snacks and dump the pouch into my mouth while I lob my hissing feline into the garage. As I wander around and put out the small fires in my home, I've thrown back a Coke, nibbled on a Ding-Dong, munched on a handful of chips, and topped it off with a chewy granola bar. Of course, now I'm not hungry for dinner, so I skip it. Then by 10 p.m. I am absolutely ravenous, so I devour one of those yogurt containers, yet can't help but think, "I already ate bad today, I might as well start tomorrow and just eat whatever I want for the last time right now." Munch, munch. Well, it's nice to see you again, Little Debbie.

I do okay in the morning. I always start out with a clean slate. But by mid-afternoon, I am no more willing to load up my blender and whip out a fruit-shake, than I am to strip down and start doing Tae-Bo. If I'm really raring to go, I might take a vitamin and wash it down with a bottle of water, but I seem to peter out in ambition by say, 1:00 p.m. I even have a sign posted on my fridge that reads, "WALK AWAY FROM THE FRIDGE. There's nothing to see here." Of course, it's now covered up by pictures Josh has drawn and a reminder card from my dentist, but my rationale is that if I can't see it, it must not be there. Therefore, I don't have to heed it.

Oh, I know, I know. This is not a good life plan. I am going to start eating healthy tomorrow, I swear! Feel free to drop in anytime and offer words of encouragement. If I don't answer the door, chances are I just can't hear you over the blender.

Growing Up Process is a Battle of the Grasses

Well, it's that time of year again. The sun is up, the sprinklers come back on, and we will begin our annual process of trying to re-grow our front lawn. Now, I'm not pointing any fingers here, but I don't think I'm the one who killed it in the first place.

Sometime around May, when the weather started changing for the warmer, I started dropping hints:

"Wow, it's getting warm. Should we turn the sprinklers on soon?"

"Hey, here's an idea. Let's have green grass this summer!"

And more recently, "Turn on the sprinklers! I don't want to look like I live behind a field of wheat!"

My seasonal begging and whining are always met with the same reply, "Be patient. I know what I am doing." You know, it just occurred to me, perhaps I've had the wrong idea about Brad. I've thought all along he wanted green grass, when in truth, brown may have been what he was shooting for. I'll need to ask.

Brad just recently mowed the wheat, and in there I can see a few blades of green grass. I am hopeful. In my excitement I forget that this is a process and I shouldn't rush it. I shout, "Shall we fertilize now?"

Brad is calm. He looks up at me from over the mower and says, as if teacher to pupil, "Remember Grasshopper, the process. Always remember the process."

Here's a thought, I think, screw the process. Fertilizer can only help. Brad's fear is that it will burn the grass. But I am one of those wives who will respect her husband in his presence, then haul out the bag as soon as he disappears. Which is exactly what I intend to do. This battle of the grasses—hey, he brought it on himself.

Okay, so far, I've discovered we don't own a bag of fertilizer. I am slowly catching on to how he thinks. Knowing full well I may attempt to sabotage his efforts of a fertilizer free summer, he failed to purchase a bag. No matter, I am resourceful. I can live without it and so will my lawn.

It's his "water the lawn twice a day" notion that I am going to de-bilitate instead. Turning the sprinklers on twice a day hardly seems like enough water to even turn this brown grass a deeper shade of tan. I scoff at his ideals.

As his truck disappears around the bend each morning, I scamper outside in my slippers and robe to hold the hose over the parcel of brown I have come to call my lawn. I wave at the morning joggers; I smile at the early commuters. After putting the boys down for their afternoon nap, I am out there again, this time fully dressed and completely alone due to the heat. I do this for what seems to be 40 days and 40 nights. Slowly, particles of green are appearing. I say little chants when the sprinklers are running, praying to the Grass Gods that they are kind this year.

In the evenings, Brad stands over our newly growing lawn, and with pride tells me, "See? It didn't need anything except the sprinklers on twice a day." He puffs his chest out just a little to make his point. Nods in the general direction of the lawn and whistles, "Sure feels nice to be right all the time." (Chuckle, chuckle.) He knows nothing of how I stood, holding a hose for hours at a time every day for the last few weeks. I won't tell him either. I'll let him wonder when the water bill comes.

This battle of the grasses, it comes at a heavy price. But so far, the score is me one, Brad zip.

It Must Be in the XX Gene

"Hey, what happened** to your butt? Did a cat scratch you?"

Ah, men. They never know just how close they are to getting creamed. "No, dear," I answered through gritted teeth, "those are called stretch marks. I got them after our sons were born."

I can't count how many times the men in my life have said something that made me want to cover my head with a bag and walk away.

A week after a neighbor of ours had given birth to her little girl, Brad met up with her while retrieving the mail out in front. I listened through an open kitchen window as my hubby, in all his charm, asked, "When will you be having that baby?" I felt her embarrassment, then his, as she answered softly, "I already did. She's a week old."

Now, that's not the first time Brad's been caught with his foot in his mouth when it had something to do with a baby. Years ago, I sat holding the plump toddler of a very good friend and Brad exclaimed, "Look honey. Lindsey's legs look just like yours!" Had I not been holding a child; I would have belted him. As it was, I fought off the urge to clobber him for months after, every time we saw a baby

My dad is no better. Once, while rehashing some memory of the family cabin, my dad reminded Brad of the time he and I were caught in the fog all night and had to call for help because we got lost. I hung my head and covered my eyes as Brad answered politely, "I don't think that was me."

"Ah sure it was!" Dad slapped him on the back, "I even remember you drove that old Camaro." Now that definitely was NOT Brad and even Dad knew it then. "Um, it was your truck, your blue one, right?" Quick recovery, but not quick enough.

Moving right along, I have a son. A 3-year-old. A very precocious child who never misses an opportunity to converse with strangers about their gender, or mine for that matter. And body parts? Well, body parts are the topic of many a discussion, no matter our location.

Take for example our trip to the store one day last year. Josh is sitting in the front of the cart and without warning, suddenly reaches out and clutches the "V" of my T-shirt. Pulling it into his chest, he announces loudly, "Those are some BIG boobies!" I struggle to release his grasp of my shirt and righting it, say to the young gentleman cashier, who is blushing furiously, "They're not that big, I swear."

And then most recently, again during an outing to a grocery store, Josh is overheard telling his mother how much he loves her. An innocent bystander, who happens to be in her late 60s or so, exclaims, "What a sweet little boy!" Upon gaining this compliment, Josh approaches her cart, peers in, and then bellows, "Are those your DIAPERS?" I quickly gather my son and whisk him away to another aisle.

I look to my youngest son with the hope that he will put an end to this ungodly tradition of saying precisely the wrong thing. Given where he comes from though, I'm not crossing my fingers.

Another Pet Project

I dial home as fast as I can and when Brad answers I blurt out, "How do you feel about the kids having a science experiment?" He is quiet.

I am in the middle of the Tracy mall, watching one kid of mine do battle with the snack tray on the stroller, the other climb a pole on the display of hermit crabs and plastic cages. "What kind of science experiment?"

I try to read his tone; it sounds hesitant with a hint of curiosity. I decide to capitalize on the curiosity portion, but before I can answer, Josh's foot knocks a plastic cage to the ground, sending sand and fake palms out into the passing foot traffic. "Josh, pick up that cage," I hiss.

Brad cuts in and says, "Cage? We don't need another pet. You have a frog in the kitchen dying from malnourishment and some fish in the office now, active participants of cannibalism." I barely hear this as I am sweeping sand into the cracked cage and smiling sheepishly at the attendant. I wave her away mouthing, "No problem."

Okay, it's true. I don't have a particularly stellar record of keeping things alive in our house. Plants, small animals, they don't stand a chance. I once brought home a small cage of mice and within weeks, I learned that mice have no issues with inter-family breeding. "Get rid of these things!" Brad would yell, as all 15 or 20 would be fighting for a turn on the little wheel in their cage. Scuffles most often lead to the death of two or three. I soon came to my senses after finding the cage looking like a battlefield, one too many times. Mice would hobble around, war wounds open and bleeding. I wound up letting them all go in a field behind my house.

Once we had a turtle named Vinnie. Lethargic little guy. I'm convinced he died either of boredom or was sick when we brought him home, because honestly, I did all I could for him, and he still kicked the bucket. In fact, he so rarely moved around on his favorite rock, when we did discover he had passed on, it was because his eyes had been shut for so long. Not because he was belly up or keeled over in a food dish.

Before Vinnie was Ziggy, the iguana member of the family. He may actually still even be alive; we wound up paying the East Bay Vivarium to take him off our hands. Iguanas grow fast and are incredibly territorial, so when good old Zig started calling the shots around our house, we knew it was time for him to go.

Who wants to live in fear of a reptile?

Josh is hopping up and down, pulling on my shirt pleading, "Mommy! I neeeeed a hermit crab!" I watch my girlfriend wrestle her daughter off the display while asking about cost and maintenance. She politely nods her head as she tucks one wriggling kid under her arm like a sack of potatoes and pops a bottle in the mouth of another. I know the look. She can't wait to get out of here.

"What did Brad say?" she calls to me as her hair falls slowly out of her ponytail. My son and her daughter are now circling her, shouting in unison, "We want to get crabs! We want to get crabs!" The hilarity of that statement is almost too much. We are both exhausted by just standing at this display. I toss my phone back in the bag and answer, "He said to let you get one." We both crack up.

It Takes Two to Tango

What is in a Nickname?

Funny little pet names have a way of following you through childhood and ending up, if you're lucky, on the headstone of your grave. I say, "If you're lucky," because isn't a nickname someone's special way of identifying you; a personal way of separating you from the rest of the world? In our family, having a nickname is a privilege, an honor, and sometimes… an embarrassment.

I was dubbed "Curly" as an infant, due to the head of unruly ringlets that sprouted at varying lengths from my skull. As I grew, "Curly" was sometimes altered and became "Curls," "Curlygirl," or the dreaded "Curlymonster," when I misbehaved. It could have been worse. My sister was called "Goat" all the way through high school because, as a toddler, she ate everything in sight. She gobbled down money, safety pins, paper and paste. You name it. She downed it like a goat.

Mom wasn't as fortunate as her daughters. Years ago, the family played an intense card game of *Phase 10*. Dad, having a handful of SKIP cards, generously gave her one each time his turn came up. Thus, she was left with a handful of cards, whose points would count against her, and a slowly growing rage. That and the sound of her family's laughter every time she was skipped eventually got the best of her. Furious, she threw her cards across the table and screamed, "I HATE this game! I hate playing this game with all of you!" She pushed her chair away from the table, and angrily marched upstairs. We heard a door slam in the distance. After a moment of silence, Dad thumbed the air and did the old "get-a-load-of-her" shrug, before he shouted, "Ah, you'll be beggin' to play cards with us!" We exploded in hoots and snorts, giggles and snickers. She returned to the table minutes later, red faced and still slightly steaming. Dad patted her chair and said, "Have a seat, 'Skip,' join the game…" A nickname that's stuck, even to this day.

While some people get christened with only one pet name, few are the fortunate recipients of two or more. Again, in our family, this is something special. Our mother. Poor thing. She had a love affair with a can of hairspray that made her the butt of our family jokes for years. She took it all in stride until my sister and I secretly started calling her "The Brick," due to the stiff bob that surrounded her face. "You two are just plain cruel," she would say, to which we would reply, "Say it, don't spray it…" and then start cracking up.

Nicknames aren't just for family members either. We love calling our friends by made up terminology. A close friend from New York we named "Brooklyn Joe," or "Jo-Jo Bronx." Shortened to "Jo-Jo" years ago, our kids think of her as Auntie Jo-Jo. I don't think they'd know who we were referring to if we called her by her given name, Joanne. And her husband? Well, he's Big Daddy Kool ("BDK") to those who know and love him. BDK by a chosen few. A neighbor who seemed to trip over, step on, and eventually destroy whatever was in his path was dubbed "Breaker," a play on his last name—Baker. And his highly dramatic daughter we lovingly teased as "Faker Baker," when her crocodile tears would start rolling. Our extremely nurturing and responsible teenaged neighbor we think of as "Molly-Mom," because of the way our sons love her. I could go on and on…

Josh is "Joshie-Otter," due to a favorite children's book, Ben is "Ben-Bear" because of his size, and Brad was nicknamed "B-Dog" back in high school. It's a regular zoo around here. It's a privilege, an honor or an embarrassment. We'll have to let the kids decide!

Ahhh, the Good Old Days

They say there's nothing like a visit from an old friend. Who are they, anyway? Because they are absolutely right, and I should tell them so. Isn't this the truth—just when you think you have your life in order and you are officially a grown-up, someone waltzes back onto the scene and those long buried memories come floating up to the surface. I suppose when you spend most of your childhood with the same person, both of you are left with hours of laughter, buckets of tears, and a load of future blackmail material just waiting for the ideal time to be presented.

"Remember when you found that furry thing in the street and gave it a name then made a home for it in your sweatshirt pocket?" My long-lost friend visiting from out of town starts snickering and takes a sip on her drink. "Then you showed your mom and she screamed and said it was a cat's tail?"

I am amazed she remembered this, and I didn't. After all, it was my mother who had a panic attack and made me wash my hands about 100 times while my friend stood watching and rolling her eyes. "Leave it to you to pick up a cat tail and try to make a pet out of it…"

We are on my back deck, reminiscing about our days of youth, when she blurts out, "And then you had the bright idea of sneaking out one night after our parents went to bed and YOU fell asleep while I hid in the bushes in front of your house!" It was true, she had waited and waited for me and wound up getting a front row seat to the final 10 minutes of my older sister's date instead.

I start giggling and chime in, "Yeah Andrea saw you, too! She woke me up to tell me there was a little boy hiding in our bushes. I got all excited thinking it was Jeff Fox until I got down there and found you."

At this, Brad joins us and flops into a deck chair to hear all the things I have purposefully excluded from my bio when we met.

Wiping the tears from her eyes, Inez turns and says to Brad, "She used to make up these raps…what did you call yourself? "Rap C." Well, she'd make up these raps about the tragedies in her life and test them out on me during lunch hour…it was painful."

I am humiliated beyond belief. I haven't called myself "Rap C" in 20 years or so, and I would never admit to doing such a thing now; but with my star witness sitting five feet away and choking on her laughter, I have little choice but to succumb to her stories.

I am struggling to recall a tale in which to embarrass her but unfortunately, she has dominated the stage and has a quite a bit she plans on spilling. In Brad she has found the perfect audience. He is laughing when laughter is called for, nodding with encouragement, and slapping his leg when she hits her punch lines. It's a bit much, but I say nothing. He slugs me in the arm and cackles, "Wasssuuuuupp Rap C?" They both crack up and start hooting and snorting. I silently sip my diet Dr Pepper.

"Once my dad convinced her…(laugh, chuckle)…he had caught a leprechaun but she wouldn't…(wheeze, sniff, snort)…look in the trap because she was too scared!" Inez and Brad are beside themselves now, bent over in their chairs and unable to breath correctly.

"Oh, please!" I cut in. "If you recall, we had watched *The Leprechaun* right before that and everything green freaked us out for a while…" They don't buy my feeble excuse but so what? Is it really necessary to explain why little green magical men who hoard money, dance jigs, and speak in accents would make me uneasy?

I am wondering if this visit was such a good idea. As Brad sits, all ears, and listens to her regale us with her stories of days gone by, I raise my glass and silently toast them before slinking down in my seat in a sulk. How dare she. Before the afternoon is over my husband will have gathered so much material on me, I may never be safe again. And in my own home! They leave me no option but to make up a rap about them.

Bicycles, Babies and Staying in Touch

While on a walk one evening with my two sons, a commotion up ahead on the road caught my eye. It was a scene that sent me reeling back to when I was 12 and had a fisted grip of what I believed life was all about. Two girls came careening around a corner on one bike. The one on the handlebars was wide-eyed and screaming, "Slow DOWN!" while the one in charge was laughing insanely and purposely making the bike dip to the left and right. As the two went head over heels onto the pavement after one dip too big, a scene straight from my heart of memories flashed in front of my eyes.

Nicki and I were two of a kind. We had that special kind of love hate friendship that started when we were 7 and by age 12, we had mastered all the goofiness that came along with it. We loved to be together, but always wound up fighting. When we were joined at the hip, one of us always seemed to get into trouble. Usually me; my mom had a much tighter grasp on my whereabouts. We avoided playing at my house because of this, so playing at Nicki's meant freedom with a capital "F" and room to grow, explore, and learn what being a kid was all about.

On this particular day, "being a kid" meant convincing Nicki that I was a safe bike rider and to pleeeeze get on the handlebars. It took some sweet talking, but on she got and off we went. It was a ride we'll both never forget. She was hollering for me to slow the hell down—we always swore whenever we weren't in earshot of our parents—and I was wildly laughing, screeching, and dipping very close to the pavement as we picked up speed. She knew she couldn't jump ship without risking bodily harm and I knew I had, for a moment, control of my untamed friend who normally controlled my every move.

I took full advantage and then got greedy. Yelling, "Whooooo," and then tipping the bike as I steered around a bend, I lost control and Nicki's slight weight couldn't counterbalance fast enough. Skidding quickly turned to fishtailing. Down we went in a tumult of shrieks. All I saw was black. Black pavement, black tires spinning, black grease from my bike chain covering our two scraped up little bodies. Nicki was fuming between tears.

"You IDIOT! You almost killed us!"

I was laughing and crying and inspecting all my abrasions. We sat in the street hugging our knees and sniveling. Her eyes flamed as she shot me a few hot glares in between all of the theatrics, but to me it was worth it. I wish I had a scar from that day to remind me, although I don't need one, and neither does Nicki.

As I approached the two girls sitting on the curb, I wondered about their friendship.

Were they new friends, or did they have history like Nicki and I had? Did these girls name their bikes? "Violet" and "Cactus Flower" covered much terrain for us. Had they laughed yet at another's attempt at cutting bangs? Have they seen each other through the loss of a pet? Are they yet to discover the thrill of sliding downstairs in a sleeping bag?

I eyed the girls and estimated their age to be about 12, tops. I remember 12 pretty clearly. Slam books, eye shadow, boys, slumber parties, training bras, and waiting, waiting to become women. We had those, "When I'm all grown-up..." conversations, naturally presuming we'd be sharing one another's lives just as closely in the years to come.

Yet, while now I juggle bottles, change diapers, and battle with children to go to bed, Nicki juggles paperwork, changes flights, and battles with CEOs to get ahead. A little different than what we had planned. I could hear the apologies in between the giggles as I passed the crash victims. I felt a slight pang of sadness and hoped these two wouldn't let one another slip away in the same fashion Nicki and I had. Oh, it's not really so bad. We occasionally talk on the phone, but I don't ride my bike to her house to play before dinner anymore. I can't recall the last time she asked me to come and trim her bangs. I'm dying to show up one day on her doorstep, my sleeping bag tucked under my arm and say, "Let's slide down your stairs!"

A Voice from the Past

"Yep, ain't she a beauty?" My dad hiked up his pants at the waist and proudly swelled out his chest. "They don't make 'em like this anymore."

Well, there you have it. Some things never change. My folks are still shopping for antiques and displaying their purchases all over the house. Not that I blame them. This is their hobby, and frankly, if these two can find something they enjoy doing together after 38 years of marriage, then good for them.

As for me, I'm loaded with memories of being dragged into countless auctions as a kid and sitting, under protest, as my parents bid on everything from tea sets to bedroom furniture.

"Don't move, don't raise your hand, and for goodness sakes, whatever you do, don't scratch your nose." The sermon I received upon entry to each barn, auditorium, or warehouse that was unloading estate treasures. I shudder at the thought.

Granted, I was pretty lucky. Not one of their great bargains ended up in my bedroom after a certain clown painting fell from my wall and whacked me on the head, but my poor sister wasn't as fortunate. She became the proud owner of an antique dresser, complete with adjoining mirror.

Now, about that mirror. We all thought it must be a joke; that a smart aleck auctioneer or some young employee got the best of us. When the smudge HELP ME appeared in the center of the glass once positioned in Andrea's room, our family sort of tilted our heads to one side and chuckled. Dear old Dad tried to wipe it off with a rag. Mom marched in with the Pledge and soon wound up with a strained tricep muscle from her effort of buffing it off. Me? I'm not so refined. I spit on the mirror then patted the message with a dirty sleeve.

Hmmm. A few seconds of silence then Andrea said, "No way. Get it out of here." Nothing would remove the words and as evening set in, the message appeared stronger and clearer: HELP ME.

"Why'd ja go in buy somethin', so old in da first place?" the glass shop owner asked my mom. I had insisted on tagging along on the outing to see what an expert had to say about the matter. I stood next to my mom, silently agreeing with the man, and nodding my head in approval.

"Don' cha know better than to buy somethin' that's haunted?"

I eyed my mom, wondering if she knew better. We had a whole house filled to the brim with things this man would most likely declare possessed. My mind went to work. A collection of ancient tools lined the walls of our mountain cabin: daggers and forks, claws and sharp hooks. Just what kind of parents did I have anyway?

"We're just interested in replacing the glass." Mom replied, paying no mind to the warning we had received. While she wrote him off completely, I returned home and broke the news to Andrea, "Your dresser is haunted, the guy said so. Plus, ALL of our stuff has ghosts in it and he told Mom not to buy anymore antiques." Not entirely the case, but I was inclined to exaggerate, even then. I grinned, "Enjoy the dresser."

While Andrea scanned the new mirror each night for further messages from beyond, I slept peacefully with the knowledge that none of my furniture was trying to communicate with me.

"Well," Dad beamed as he showed me an antique gas pump he planned to restore, "What do you think?"

"If it doesn't say HELP ME on it, I think you did good!" We laughed. There you have it; some things never change.

Copycats for Every Type

"She's copying me!"

I watched as a neighborhood friend of Josh's mimicked his every move. Even as he tattled, hands on hips and headed tilted to one side, she struck the same pose. I worked hard at keeping my expression neutral, because, in all honesty, it was pretty comical.

"Stop copying me!" he screamed at her.

"Stop copying me!" she screamed back.

Well, what do you know—we have a copycat among us. And a Type A personality at that. For those of you who aren't familiar with the various personality types of copycats, allow me to elaborate.

The Type A Copycat, otherwise known as the "Blatant Mimicker." This is the person who literally follows your every move. Small children, annoying relatives, the new kid in class—all are Type As at some point. Example 1: a friend purchases a pair of new shoes; you can't seem to resist the urge to go get the same pair. You are now a Type A. Also falling into this category are the bandwagoners: those certain folks that seem to latch onto an idea and run with it, without any realization of why. ("I'm becoming a vegetarian!" "Yeah! Me too!") In third grade I pushed the limits of the Type A—I copied so much off a friend's spelling test paper; I had actually written her name on my sheet! Pathetic, but true.

The Type B Copycat, also called the "Furtive Friend." This is the person who seems uninterested in something you have, yet winds up being the proud owner of another in the near future. You know the kind—you show a friend or neighbor your new barbecue and they own it a few days later. Maybe even have a party to show it off or something. The Type B personality usually suffers from short term memory loss ("You have one too? I had no idea!") and are rarely children. Having mastered the poker face, usually Type B personalities are found casually observing one's interior design, but asking nothing more than where a certain item can be purchased.

And lastly, the Type C Copycat. This is the worst type of copycat. There are a million names to dub the Type C personalities of the world, but I'll stick to the clean ones: the "Hypocrite, the Fraud and the Imposter." A Type C personality is the guy who scoffs at what you have, informs you of why its purchase was a mistake, gives you a dissertation on how it will disappoint you, is somehow familiar with the history of the product and its real value, then arrogantly shows you his, a week later. Type C personalities are quick to justify their position and will interrupt your line of questioning continuously with a series of "Yes, BUT..." (s). They are infuriatingly frustrating, as they will never admit to anything more than seeing yours. They too suffer from short-term memory loss, but as an added personality quirk, they like to insult your intelligence by suggesting you may have remembered the exchange incorrectly.

All types of copycats can be guilty of all types of imitation: ideas, purchases, you name it. But let's be honest here. Nobody likes to be copied. What is at stake is one's individualism. Most folks take a genuine pleasure in being original and strive for admiration for their attempt. Sometimes that admiration may become irritation if the copier isn't too careful.

So as Josh sobbed in my shoulder about his loss of self, I smiled and whispered in his ear, "It's okay son. She's a Type A. We'll just have to work with her."

The Kindness of Strangers and Friends

As I stepped onto my porch, a bag with a note caught my eye, "Carolyn, hope you can use these! Michelle." People are really too kind to our family. It was a bag of clothes for my boys, some pants, shirts, and shoes that her kids had outgrown.

I brought it in and Josh and I happily rifled through it, he wrestled a Buzz Lightyear sweatshirt over his head as I lay out all his new treasures.

Now, this isn't the first time we've been the recipients of people's generosity. Once, I sat in traffic on Oak Street, my car dead and my arm flailing about outside my window, waving cars by. I stayed seated, wondering what in the heck I was going to do, when a young lady came running across Highway 4 to my rescue. She pushed me down Oak Street and into a parking lot. My hero. She disappeared without ever even telling me her name.

Another time, I had taken my boys on a stroller walk and came to section of sidewalk where construction was being done. Three sections of sidewalk were missing, and the entire area was roped off. I contemplated my two options: Off-road my stroller through the landscaping, or turn around and head back home.

Before I could decide, two construction workers jogged over, lifted the double stroller, and carried the boys to safety. They carefully released the stroller on the other side of the marked area, tipped their hats, and bid me a nice day. I was impressed.

A girlfriend asked me a short time ago how often I have bought clothes for my sons. Honestly, not including shoes, I can count the number of times I have bought clothing on one hand. This even includes trips to consignment stores. Thanks to the generosity of a few families in particular (you know who you are) the Dodds boys are dressed and joyfully don the fashions of years gone by.

They don't know the difference, and truthfully, I like it better this way. Sifting through Hefty bags of "new" shirts and shorts, why I can think of no better way to spend an afternoon. I am forever in amazement of the kindness and generosity people show one another.

Recently, Pump It Up hosted a fundraiser for my youngest son Ben, who lives with a multitude of issues including cerebral palsy, sensory integration dysfunction, global dyspraxia, global developmental delays, and Pervasive Developmental Disorder ("PDD"), a form of autism. The people that came out were amazing! Folks I knew, folks I didn't know; all people I hope to see again.

Thanks to the kindness of the friends and strangers, we raised money for Ben that already has been put to good use: Special leg braces and an appointment with one of the country's best pediatric orthopedic surgeons. It is darn near impossible to say in words how appreciative we are of everyone's kindheartedness.

Kindness. Generosity. Thoughtfulness. It all goes so very far. Far enough that, in an effort to keep the ball rolling, I now have bags of clothing and toys that my little ones have outgrown, stacked high in my garage, ready to go down the street. I am delighted to see the kids I know wearing Dodds-Me-Downs, rather than brand new. This pay-it-forward mentality only serves to make us all better humans.

Goodbye 1819

While cheering on Josh during his swim lesson a few weeks ago, I make eye contact with the father of a child in the same class. A familiar blip of recognition, so I trot over and begin the standard parental chit-chat. After a few minutes we realize not only did we both grow up in Pleasanton, but he's also he's a friend of the older brother of a girl I called my best friend for the greater part of my childhood years. I love this sort of conversation, albeit we missed a majority of the swim lesson. We did, however, catch one another up on life and times of Todd and Nicki.

While we stand laughing and nodding, my attention gets diverted by a colorful bunch of balloons being released in the parking lot next door. And though he is still talking to me, I hear nothing as I watch, with the rest of the water park, as the balloons slowly hover above us and float overhead. Because of the sweet distraction, I catch only the last fraction of his parting sentence, "…yeah, you know the house went on the market, right?"

I stare at him, gaping. By 'the house' he means 1819, which is what we called the two story, five-bedroom home that withstood three kids, two marriages, one stepchild, and countless tenants after the children left home. This swim lesson dad and I most likely have the same menagerie of memories, substituted only by his friends and mine.

"What?" My surprise is only surpassed by a sinking feeling of sadness. "They're selling 1819?" He chuckles, yet the look on his face mirrors how I feel. "Yep, and from what I hear its already sold and the folks are retiring up North."

Just this month, friends of ours moved to New Hampshire. During their last night in the house, I watched from across the street as neighbors went in and out of the front door. I stood there wishing to never hear that door slam by the hand of anyone other than a Larkin child when another neighbor said sadly, "I can't imagine never going into that house again." Same feeling, different day.

Never entering 1819 for me is comparable to never going home. Though I haven't set foot inside it in ages, the last time I had was akin to a time warp. Nicki and I had sprawled across the sofa, catching up over the holidays. Content, I happily soaked in the familiar sights and smells from my youth while sipping out of a cracked coffee mug that read 'Damn I'm Good!', the very mug I insisted on using as a kid because it had a cuss word on it. There's something about that house still having the same phone number I learned in the 1970s that continues to give me a deep sense of security and belonging.

Within its walls I mastered my backbends and handstands, gleaned insight on the cons of tucking your shirt into your underwear and answered the question of whether or not a child should trim her own bangs. (No.) The house was a liberating safe haven for me, as I was allowed to do things my own mother would have never tolerated. Nicki and I perfected gymnastic stunts on the second story banister, cooked entire meals without a mother's watchful eye, and were forced into entire summers of creativity and imagination. The garage housed her brother's dirt bike, which at age 12, we stole and wrecked three streets away. The front lawn at one time was dotted with steppingstones, which I had stumbled over while storming out of 1819 one hot summer afternoon. Awkward thing to be falling flat on your face while in the middle of a tantrum.

I like to think the house has history, theirs, and mine. I consider it as much a home to me as I did to the entire Mickels family.

"You know," the swim dad says to me, "They got over a million bucks for it." Doesn't surprise me at all. The buyer got a great deal.

Crazy Soccer Moms

I'm running with a bad crowd. I've fallen in with a few tough characters. I might even be deemed one of those "undesirables." Car thieves? Nope. Night stalkers? No siree-Bob. Drug dealers? Not even close. Try "Soccer moms." We're a rough bunch, and we don't take lightly to strangers.

Okay, okay in all seriousness here, my 3-year-old son started soccer last Saturday and I found myself feeling a bit like Sybil. A personality I never even knew dwelled within me, presented herself for dozens of Brentwood parents to see. I'll call her, "The Over Involved Lady." Let's just leave it at that.

Most parents stand on the sidelines and cheer for their offspring. And honestly, I intended to do just that. But upon arrival I learned first-hand that parent participation is mandatory and I wasn't going to be excused from running the laps or even doing the warm-up exercises. Thank goodness I had my 16-month-old in a backpack and my camera securely wrapped around my neck. I was thrilled I had asked Brad to tag along because when cued, he relieved me of the 28-pound backpack as well as photography equipment. This freed me up to give high fives, roll balls, and yell orders to Josh and his teammates. I was a regular one-man show. Until I got the sign from Brad that I was in desperate need of backing off a bit.

See, I'm not used to team sports. I was an ice-skater until junior high, then redirected my focus on gymnastics. Two sports that carried very little risk of me being pegged by a high-speed ball at any given moment. I steered clear of the ball essential sports. Years of being placed in the outfield (the waaaay outfield) during the time I played softball, taught me that I had no talent for ball retrieval, ball capture, and just plain keeping my eye on the ball. And as far out in left field as I was, the only time a ball ever really came my way was when an overzealous coach wacked one in my direction with the false hope of my actually being able to stay in front of it. Coaches never learn. At the end of one season, I gladly turned in my bat and ball and petulantly told the folks, "No, THANK YOU. I hate balls. I always will." I now understand why that certain remark had my parents snickering. Still, it was ages before I picked up a racket and gave tennis a fair shake.

So, there I was last Saturday with a ball in my hand. Not for me, mind you. For the children. I wanted to be good. I tried to let my son have his space and to not overstep his personal boundaries. And in all fairness, with parent participation being a necessity, I was in good company with seven other moms and dads, all wanting the same thing. We did our best to help the coach, assist the kids, set an example of team spirit, and look as if we knew what we were doing. I must say, we did good.

As our practice wrapped up and I surveyed the departing players being hugged by their parents, I felt proud of the crowd I had fallen in with. We're not so tough after all.

Night of Disaster Ends in Peace

Now I'm no Columbus, but I did make one pretty significant discovery the other night. Our backslider has a faulty latch on the screen. I may never have known this if it weren't for my innate ability to sense a crisis brewing in the wee hours of the night.

Our 3-year-old had slipped into our bed, which meant simply one thing: sleep was next to impossible, as young Mr. Dodds is a bed hog and a cover thief.

Slightly annoyed, I threw off the sheet and left the men snoozing while I searched for a better place to slumber. Exhausted, I flopped into Josh's empty twin bed and tried to unwind. I should have known better. Scooby Doo makes a horrible pillow, and the faint flicker of the neon blue nightlight across the room was growing brighter by the second. Not only was I sharing these quarters with the family cat, but Josh's blankets are all toddler sized, so I lay there exposed from knee to toe.

And that sound…what was it? Water?

Had Brad left a hose running from earlier today? Well now, sleep was unthinkable. I needed to investigate. I crept through the house and opened the backslider, only to glimpse a rather sizable puddle on the patio. Just as I suspected, the hose had a telltale drip trickling from the spigot. Exasperated, I stepped out onto the cement and closed the screen door. (Unnecessary, but I am a girl of habit, and I can't seem to break the one where I shut every door behind me.).

l scurry over to the nozzle and in my attempt to shut the valve, the water pressure gives way and I find myself in the center of an icy blast. I cover my mouth to conceal a screech and stand there wrestling with an angry hose. It's spitting water at every angle. Soaking, I grapple the enemy, strangle it, and throw it to the ground. It seems dead and the drip has ceased. I'm safe. Secure, but reminded of the time a toilet exploded on my mom years ago and now I have a bad case of the giggles.

Chuckling with the memory, I return to the slider and CLICK... it won't open. The family cat is on the opposite side and greets me with a friendly, "meow." Is she mocking me? Shock sets in as I try the slider again and realize with horror that I am locked out.

I smile at the kitty. I speak in a high falsetto voice; the kind people use with children when they aren't quite comfortable, hoping she won't recognize my anxiety and turn on me. "Hi Tooter! You wanna go get the kitchen chair and slide it over here? Then you can jump up and unlock the screen for Mommy?' My voice is so high I'm afraid I'll break into song. She ignores my request. The gall of this animal. I feed her every morning at the crack of dawn, and this is the thanks I get?

As I am pondering my situation, it occurs to me that I saw Brad eating malted milk balls earlier today. Mmmm. I am hungry. Chances are, if he left the hose on, he may have left the bag of candy out too. I must investigate. Under the dim shimmer of the streetlight, I spy a pink bag on his workbench and am almost positive there's a bunny on it. Score! I practically skip across the yard and snag the bag of loot. "Hee, hee," I snicker out loud. There's something so devilishly enjoyable about a stolen moment such as this one.

I mean, how bad is this really? I flop down on a lawn chair and stretch out. Tossing a malt-ball in my mouth, I look up at the stars and realize this is probably the only moment I'll be afforded to unwind before I begin another day with two small children, tomorrow.

And miracle upon miracles, when I tug on the screen again a few minutes later, it opens.

Being Neighborly

"It's a beautiful day in the neighborhood, a beautiful day for a neighbor, would you be mine, could you be mine, won't you be my neighbor?"

Until 1996 I thought this was the biggest crock of hooey I'd ever heard. Where would anyone ever find a neighborhood like that? I mean, outside of Mr. Roger's studio? Nothing against Mr. Rogers, of course. Personally, I thought the man was remarkable. But his neighborhood? Come on. Take it from a girl who grew up in an area where folks yelled at kids to get off their lawns, where grown-ups didn't buy Girl Scout cookies, and where every once in a while, some grouch found their trees lined with toilet paper.

Then, in 1996 Brad and I bought a humble little starter home here in Brentwood. I have photos of moving vans lining the street while couples up and down the block carried their belongings inside their homes. We all casually attempted to sum up our new neighbors in the process. Having an entire block move in on practically the same day was cause for celebration. Everyone shared the same idea, and that idea has carried on for almost seven years.

Celebrate! Party! Gathering! Food! Drink! You name an occasion, the folks on our street will be there with a case in one hand and a plate of food in the other. Case of what? Doesn't matter. We got you covered.

This group comes prepared.

The folks are friendly enough that there is never a question of whether or not to bring additional family or friends to anyone's house. It seems the "Open Door" policy is alive, well, and in constant practice in this neighborhood.

Take for example one Christmas a few years back. A neighbor of ours was hosting a party. Apparently, word of the shindig got out, because before he knew what he was doing, the host found himself sharing glad tidings with a man who introduced himself as "John," from a few streets over. This isn't uncommon around here. Folks seem to drop in anytime, anyplace, for no reason at all. Sometimes just to say hello and grab a bite to eat.

Now while it may sound like Mayberry, or at least an adult version thereof, our neighborhood has seen its share of sadness. I've never liked to see anyone move, no matter what the reason, but I have to admit, the new residents all fit in as perfect pieces to the puzzle that make up this crowd. (Once we chose New Year's Eve as the night to introduce ourselves to some new neighbors, and after crashing their party, we spent the evening carrying on with these folks as if we've known them forever.)

While some people may live years not knowing who lives next door, we have been fortunate enough to become godparents to our neighbor's children and bestow the same honor on them. We've vacationed with neighbors, seen the births of their babies, the growth of their children, even witnessed their vows of holy matrimony. We've cheered at their kids' sporting events, swam in their pools, and helped them find their lost pets. We've laughed when they've made it and cried when they haven't. We've been able to share in many a families' sources of pride, elation, sadness, and mourning. We've done more in our lives in the last seven years with people we never even knew 10 years ago; it just seems more than coincidental.

History in the making, that's what we're doing. Not even trying, and we're setting the foundation of what our kids will hope for when they settle down. The men share their tools, the women their secrets. And since we're a tight group, there's not much here that someone doesn't know.

Mr. Rogers knew what he was talking about. I'm a cynic no longer.

When Plans, or Priests, Go Up in Smoke

While flipping through a magazine the other day an article about wedding day disasters caught my eye.

I grabbed my glasses and with a swift flick of the wrist, had them on my face and was peering closely at pictures of couples who complained of their day being "ruined."

Come on. Ruined?

I scanned each paragraph and looked for an announcement that either someone had died, was injured or was left at the altar. Nothing. A-ha. So, it just boiled down to a matter of perspective.

I have a friend who, on her wedding day, got thrown up on in the limo on the way to the ceremony (nervous flower girl). We thought that was a bad sign, until we arrived at the church and discovered the air conditioning had malfunctioned, and we had to sweat through a long Mass in the heat of July. That too, a bad sign.

The clincher though was when her priest stood a little too close to the unity candle and then caught fire right before our very eyes. A groomsman leapt from his position in line and flung himself onto the elderly gentleman. Riding this priest piggyback, the groomsman beat out the flames with his bare hands and grunted wildly while flailing his arms about.

It was quite a show. Both escaped unharmed, a little ruffled up and a tad worse for the wear, but all that couldn't have been a sign of anything positive. To this day the bride still insists it was the best day of her life. Perspective.

Back in the days of Brad and I discussing the "Big M," he presented me with a choice not too many girls get. While on a drive one day he told me to close my eyes, that he had a surprise for me. Since I was the one driving, I told him, "No."

With that, he proceeded to put a tiny velvet box on my shoulder and chuckled. I eyed the box, and then pulled off the road. Breathing heavy, I got all teary eyed and opened the box. "Oh my..." I stopped. The box was empty. No ring. What? I looked at him and was ready to slug the beast for his insensitivity.

"Before you panic, I thought I might ask you...do you want an engagement ring, or an engagement Sea-Doo?" he said.

Well, that changed everything. I loved water sports. What girl would turn down a Sea-Doo? It was the kind of gift that kept on giving. Of course, I made the right decision in the end. I chose the Sea-Doo. I eventually wound up with both, plus two great engagement stories. How many girls get to say that? You don't find a girl with a ring and a Sea-Doo plus a matching tale for acquiring each, every day of the week you know.

A few friends couldn't understand it, nor could they understand how I could smile and be thrilled with my wedding day, when the wind blew my veil over my head in the middle of the ceremony. I just thought it was funny.

I didn't mind that all 200 chairs showed up at my house, rather than at the reception site, nor did I mind that due to a florist in a hurry, my bridesmaids and I had to race to the bathroom with a pocketknife and trim the thorns off the roses we were carrying right before the ceremony.

No matter. As long as my pastor didn't go up in flames, I was happy. It's all about perspective.

10
Ball and Chain

Fire in the Hole

Not a lot surprises me when it comes to cleaning a house. I mean, I've been scouring and polishing just like Cinderella since I first decided to be a stay-at-home mom. So, you can imagine my astonishment when I happened to be strolling past our guest bathroom one day and a mark on the toilet seat practically screamed at me. I did a doubletake and then left to fetch the *Formula 409* cleaner.

When I returned, I went eye to eye with this baby. Although I must admit, it was in an unusual place. Not often do I see tan smudges on the seat; obviously, most folks know where to look in order to uncover the real problem areas of a toilet. Perplexed, I held my breath and leaned in for a closer inspection of the perpetrator. Although oddly colored and bizarrely shaped, I sprayed it in attempt to free the bathroom of this interloper. Nothing. Not even a smudge removed. I was mystified. No technique seemed to be successful. Scrubbing, rubbing, picking and scraping; this mark was clearly not going anywhere. Frustrated, I blew my hair out of my face and continued to do battle with a spot. As my bicep throbbed and I worked up a sweat I must have inhaled some weird combination of the various solvents I was using, because before I knew it, I was lightheaded and ready to pass out. Over a spot, mind you. I wasn't willing to be found half dead in the bathroom with a sponge in my hand so I retreated and decided Brad must know something of this.

I wasn't crazy about calling Brad at work to ask him about a spot on a toilet. I knew how pathetic it would sound, but I thought he had to know. I'd like to think it was the funky concoction of ammonias I had taken in that drove me to make that call, but it was a good thing I did. I found my answer. The conversation went something like this:

Me: "Um, hi. (Sheepish) It's me."

Him: "Yes?"

Me: "I'm calling about that spot on the toilet you made. (Better to accuse than be accused!)"

Him: "Yes?"

Me: "You KNOW what I'm talking about?"

Him: "Go on. This sounds pretty good."

Me: "There's a spot on the seat I can't scrub off. It's like it's permanently there. I can't figure it out."

Him: "Oh, you must mean the burn mark."

Me: "The BURN mark?" (Clearly, he must be joking.)

Him: "Yes, you see there was a small fire in the bathroom."
Even I know that fires don't just happen in the bathroom. Someone starts one.

Me: "You started a fire in our bathroom? Why?"

Now he sounds a little sheepish and says really fast, "Well, I was sick one day and was sitting there so I lit some toilet paper on fire, you know, for air freshener. Then it burned my fingers and I dropped it on my thigh. Then it burned my thigh, so I hit it onto the seat and, well, I had to put it out."

Two things cross my mind at this point. First, what this actually looked like as it happened and second, I have found something that surprises me in housecleaning. I stand corrected.

A Slight Tendency to Overdrive

"**Will you just** let me drive?" I hiss, them slap Brad's hand off the steering wheel.

My husband always does this. He's got the worst habit of trying to drive for me, when I am a completely capable woman of the road. "Brad, I don't know. Stay on your side of the car."

He has me sounding like a 10-year-old fighting with a kid brother. I turn to tell him to cut it out. As I do, I knock the steering wheel and we swerve into the next lane. I hear a squeal as the car next to us also swerves. The car honks wildly and I slam on the brakes. We both lurch forward in our seat as Brad shouts, "Watch it!"

I point at him and say, "Zip it, Blondie!"

"Fine, fine." He's mumbling but I am ignoring him. Talk about a side-seat driver, this guy has no concept of the word, "DRIVER." I explain that he is the, "PASSENGER," therefore his job is to passage. You know. Sit there and say nothing. Navigate at the very most. Fold the map if he wants to be helpful. Pump gas. Play with seat buttons. Adjust the climate. Just be there. No need to reach over, grasp the wheel, and career us off the road into a ditch.

So now he's slumped over in his seat, arms crossed and glaring out the window.

"Here," I toss my purse at him. "Find some candy or something. Maybe there's a bag of fruit bites you can snack on." He is in disbelief. He snatches the purse and rifling through it, mutters, "I'm no kid…I don't need your stupid candy to eat." Finding something, he unwraps it and pops it in his mouth.

So maybe I'm being harsh, I don't know. But let me tell you about a drive we took to L.A. a few years back and you be the judge.

It's my turn to drive. All is well. Interstate 5 has little traffic, and we are making good time. We're in Brad's truck, a 1994 lifted Chevy Z71. Metallic blue, all the bells and whistles. It's his baby. Music is playing softly on the radio, and since this was before we had kids, no toys were being lobbed up in the front seat at us and no one was wailing for more milk. All in all, I'd say it was a dream ride.

Out of nowhere, Brad leans over and peering at the dash, says, "Here…you need to put it in overdrive for this stretch of road. Let me…" He then takes the gearshift, which is over the steering wheel and attempts to bump it up a gear for me. Tap, tap. Nothing. Harder now—TAP, BUMP. He shifts it right into reverse. What a champ. The truck lets out a loud THUNK in the undercarriage. The tires lock up and we start fishtailing down 1-5 at 70 mph.

"What did you do?" he yells. He leans to get an arm in and try to adjust the gears, and I smack him. HARD.

I howl. "Get away!"' I then shift into neutral and, totally ruffled, pull off onto the side of the road. "What are you thinking?" I sneer. "Are you totally crazy?" I am on a tirade now and he is helpless. Has no choice but to let me finish rambling on about how he almost killed us.

After a minute, we start laughing. Out of pure incredulity, I am sure. We made it down to L.A. no problem, but we did drive slower and had a higher sense of awareness to every sound the truck made after that.

Brad is sucking on a lifesaver and feels better now. "Sorry," he offers. Grins like a kid. "Just don't put it in overdrive and we'll be okay."'

A Tale of Two Bathrooms

"Aaaghhhh!" A screaming child exits our outside bathroom and runs past me. I look pointedly at Brad.

"You really need to do something about that," I told him. "Kids are afraid to go potty here because your bathroom is so scary!"

"That is entirely untrue," he responds, wounded, "Kids love spiders and dirt. They must just be goofing around."

I raise my eyebrows. A few years back when Brad suggested the addition of an outside bathroom for our guests to use, we had a completely different vision of how it would be accepted.

The idea of an outdoor potty seemed a good one, especially since our yard houses so many neighboring children. We predicted parties where our friends fawned over the concept of "bathrooming" outside and saving that cumbersome trip through the house to do their business. I especially liked the idea of the little sink, and saw the numbering times I mopped up dirt, water, and toilet tissue from the indoor bathroom coming to a joyous, sparkling end. With kids playing in our yard, I was partial to group potty trips and overflowing sinks and toilets being confined to an outside area.

Brad, on the other hand, enjoyed the idea of the outdoor shower. "I can get clean in nature," he told me, "Listen to the sounds of crickets and see the stars…"

"Can you really hear crickets above the noise of the shower?" I inquired. He said nothing. "And how do you actually see stars with water pouring down on you and a door shut?" He glared at me, "It will be the talk of the hood, just you wait and see…"

And it was. Having been given a few windows by a neighbor, Brad constructed a shelter that can be peered into from every angle imaginable. My lady friends see this as a design flaw, as they should. I have yet to actually use this bathroom myself, since no curtains have been hung. A roll of toilet paper sits hunched on the sink, slightly damp from the moisture of Brad's evening showers, and the stray wires from the outlets seem to me to just be inviting danger, though I've been promised they are safe.

And the dirt. Our little outhouse is not too unlike a shack—grime multiples out there and a family of spiders have laid claim to all the corners. Brad's men friends see this as rugged and tough, as they probably should. Women and children politely ask to go inside. I go inside too. Brad is so fond of his little potty hut that in recent months he has taken to doing all his "man-business" out there full time. I don't mind. He can be as slovenly as he wants and I don't have to see it, clean it, or give it any thought at all.

"Your bathroom is no better!" Brad fires back, "I've seen it! Hair everywhere in the shower, and I don't particularly feel like cleaning out that drain again. If children saw THAT, they'd run away screaming too!"

Point taken. The hair issue in my bathroom equals the spider/grime issue in his. Once my shower got all clogged up with my locks, and when Brad pulled the decrepit clump from the pipe, I saw it and barfed. True story. I glimpsed what he was holding and for a second, imagined being forced to eat it. I gagged and then darted from the room. He chased me with it, thinking I was kidding and laughed at me until I flailed myself over the kitchen sink and heaved.

"But it's *your* hair!" his confusion was understandable. I now string my discarded tresses all over the shower walls to avoid another clog.

"I think my bathroom looks decorative and ornamental!"

"And I think mine is what an outdoor bathroom should be!"

We both think that separate bathrooms are a good idea.

Let the Games Begin

Is there really such a thing as healthy competition? I'm sure there must be, I've just not had any experience with it. Board games, card games, drawing games, you name it. I've played with people who are ready to knock out their competition. They'll lie, cheat, steal and go the distance just to say they've won. Absurd.

My personal favorites though are the folks who stomp off and throw in their cards, chips, or whatever it is they may be holding. Nothing beats a good huff when playing with friends. But family—whoa, step aside. In family games, there's just no holding back. In the midst of a *Monopoly* game a few years back, my brother-in-law abandoned the game during a dispute about rules, stormed up the stairs swearing and fuming and then tossed in his properties from the top of the landing. The rest of us dove to catch what we could and wound up bickering over who deserved what. We ripped colorful cards from the sweaty hands of one another which launched us into a full-blown attack over fake real estate. Wheezing, we lunged onto each other like puppies, scrambling to steal as much as we could. It was a pathetic display of human greed.

One time my own mother left the table in a similar state during a card game with Dad, Brad, and myself. We were only dating, and I was nervous that after witnessing my mother while during a brief stint of true identity, he may decide to opt out of the relationship. On the contrary, he foresaw the comedic relief my family offered and was probably more attracted to me than ever.

Twice the board game *Cranium* has provided amusing memories for me: once when I peed my pants while laughing at a friend do a charade of Dances with Wolves—Tatanka, and the other while I cried in a bathroom when my feelings got hurt after a teammate screamed at me for not doing a better humming rendition of "Schools Out for Summer" by Alice Cooper.

But the best of the best was played the night of August 13, 1999. Brad and I were invited over to partake in a friendly game of *Monopoly* by our friends Mark and Joanne. Joanne was nine months pregnant and not a minute closer to giving birth than I am right now. She thought an exciting board game might be just the ticket to kick her into labor. She had no idea how prophetic her idea actually was.

About an hour into the game, Brad is a hair away from filing bankruptcy, has sold off all his property and is finagling deals with anyone willing to be a pawn in his scheme to stay in the game. Mark's 10-year-old daughter was playing too, and she was more than willing to cut deals and save her favorite uncle. At some point Brad noticed I charged a player less for rent than what I had previously charged him a half-hour earlier. I had no clue how he remembered what I charged him and think this is a trick on his part to wrangle up some sympathy, perhaps even a bit of cash.

When his insistence level increases, I decide it's possible I made an error, so I apologize and kindly offer him an extra two hundred dollars for his trouble. This is where the game gets interesting.

> Brad: (Smacking the money from my hand) "I don't want your money NOW. I wanted it an hour ago. When I wouldn't have had to sell off my property to stay alive."

> Me: (laughing nervously) "Did you just hit me?" (I pick up the scattered bills) "Here. Just take it. I want you to have it." (Smile. He swats it from my hand.)

> Brad: "You can keep your blood money now, you little cheat. This game is obviously over." (He pushes his chair back away from

the table.) "We can't play because the final result is now different than what should have happened. You intervened with fate."

We are silent, all of us eyeballing one another. Truth be told, the rest of us were doing pretty good and have racked up properties galore. I'm fully aware that nobody wants this game to end…yet.

Me: (addressing Mark) "Am I in the wrong?" (It's always good to bring in a third party.) "Shouldn't he just take the money and zip it?"

Mark: "I ain't saying nothing."

Me: "Just TAKE the money Brad. It's only a game." (I fling the bills across the table, clearly getting more agitated by the second.)

He tosses them back and says, "I want five thousand dollars for my trouble, an additional two thousand for your error and I'd like half of all your properties as a good faith gesture on your part. I think that's fair."

Me: "You crazy son of a…no way. You have got to be kidding."

Brad: "If you want me to play, you'll pay. Pay to play baby— that's the rule."

Smug, he sits and glares at me, folds his arms across his chest and starts inspecting his fingernails. Joanne says softly, "I think I'm having a contraction."

The game is at a standstill while I make my decision. Stacks of money are piled up in even rows in front of me and tucked neatly under the edge of the board. Easily, I can afford his offer, it's just the principle that annoys me. I do a mental inventory of my hotels, houses, and railroads. I make my decision.

"You selfish little baby! Here! HERE…take ALL my money you cry-baby brat!" I hurl bills in his face. Then properties, then hotels, then my houses are soaring at him next. I clear off the board in seconds. He is stunned silent and wide-eyed, completely caught off guard by my reaction. The 10-year-old disappears to her room. I upturn the board saying, "You wanted to end the game? Well then—it's OVER BUDDY!"

Hours later, my goddaughter Jamie Daryl Flynn arrived. Right on time, the doctors say. Joanne always says she was induced. I like to think she's the result of a little healthy competition, that's all.

Little Neighbor Boy

One of life's biggest treasures, I think, is when people you've crossed paths with as children somehow emerge later and then integrate themselves into your adult life. (Unexpectedly, of course and in a positive, non—stalking sort of way.) Our friend Dean chummed around with a buddy, Kevin, in their late teens and early twenties. Even now, a decade later, they still touch base and communicate, albeit sporadically. But at my wedding, after dancing with Kevin, I cooed to Dean, "I just *looove* your friend!" His reply was a low whisper, "He wasn't always so nice. When we were kids, he terrorized me on my bike. I'd ride home as fast as I could to avoid getting the crap kicked out of me. Ask him. He'll tell you it's true."

That story reminds me of a girlfriend I have today. We live in the same neighborhood, our families know one another well, and as adults—we get along great. But when Brad and I met her 10 years ago, I had gulped nervously and prayed she wouldn't recall me, or what a reticent little kid I had been. She didn't. Years later, I later confessed to her husband at a Red Cup Event that I was the girl she followed home one day, taunting. She had thrown tanbark at me. Threatened to beat me up. I was so scared of her then; now I adore her. Now we laugh about it.

But my all-time favorite "kid from the past pops up in my adult life" tale is that of "Little Neighbor Boy." In junior high a friend of mine, Jan, had a mad crush on a boy that lived on her street. Being two years our junior, it was the sort of thing we didn't advertise, no matter how cute he was. We called him Little Neighbor Boy and watched him from afar. On his skateboard in the street or playing basketball on his driveway, it didn't matter. If Little Neighbor Boy was out, we made it our business to see just what he was up to.

Once I entered high school, friendships shifted and I didn't see much of Jan, or any of her neighbors after that. I had all but forgotten about Little Neighbor Boy until 15 years later when my soon-to-be husband introduced me to a group of his friends, we'd be house boating with that summer.

There stood Little Neighbor Boy, grinning at me and shaking my hand. Oh, if Jan could see me now. I recognized him immediately, even with the goatee and impressive post-teen muscle mass. I tried frantically to whisper this in Brad's ear while a round of introductions were made. I tried to look inconspicuous but felt like I was in the company of child star. Giggly and nervous, I kept chanting, "Little Neighbor Boy, Little Neighbor Boy," until he told me to knock it off and not embarrass his friend by saying that out loud. "Don't call him that," he advised me, "Wait till you know him better..." So, I did.

Turns out Little Neighbor Boy was a good friend of the man I was about to marry. We vacationed with him a lot. He was in our wedding, and we were in his. I know his wife and sister so well. I consider them two of my best friends. I call his house just about every week. We spend every Christmas Eve at their parent's house, and my children don't know any different. One of my sons has a name for Little Neighbor Boy too—it's Godfather. I was there when Little Neighbor Boy called himself "Jimmy Copperbottom," donned a black wig and did a pole dance, minus the pole, in the middle of a ski boat one night on Lake Shasta. I've seen him chug beers, try to breakdance, and get a crowd of strangers to sing "Boys in the Hood" with him on a bridge at Yosemite. I've also seen him cry when his first son was born. He's dressed as Luke Skywalker for both his boys and called us to proudly announce the birth of his daughter.

Recently my 6-year-old drew a picture of himself being born. (It was intriguing, to say the least.) When explaining it to me, he pointed out the doctor, his father, myself, and him all in the room. "And who is this other person?" I tapped the paper, genuinely curious of who was portrayed with a big smile and one hand on my baby.

"It's Uncle Darren Johnson," he answered, "He was there too." Actually, he wasn't, but I didn't tell Josh this. I like the thought of Josh feeling so connected to his "Uncle" that he assumes Little Neighbor Boy has been present for everything, including his arrival.

I rarely look at him now and think "Little Neighbor Boy." If anything, he's just Darren, Uncle, Godfather or occasionally Jimmy Copperbottom depending on the crowd. His family is our family. They're the friends you don't ever remember not having. And at best, you can picture them as they were—cute and scrawny with knobby knees, learning how to shoot hoops, not even knowing you were watching.

And the Cupboard was Bare

"**Is this for** real? Your mom said there was FOOD here this time!" Brad shuts the fridge in exasperation.

In Twain Harte, few things change over time. The lake still rests between a beach and a rock, downtown remains home to Pee Wee golf, the smell of pine and smoke linger in the air no matter where you are, and my parent's cabin will be void of anything edible whenever you arrive.

"I mean *come on*, there is nothing here but condiments!" He's reopened the fridge and is now sliding jars and cans around the shelves, in the desperate hope of finding something to shove down his gullet that isn't intended for added flavor.

"I see plenty of Mom's homemade jam," I suggest, "Plus that can of Pepsi Lite down there and look— isn't that a bottle of Tab?" I move the Tabasco and peer towards the rear of the fridge. Brad leans in to survey the scene.

"Your mother frightens me," he says, "They don't even make Pepsi Lite anymore and when was the last time you saw a bottle of Tab? The logo isn't even really pink, it's so faded with age! Do you think she's trying to poison us?" He raises an eyebrow. "Remember the salad dressing?"

I consider this. "But technically, she would have been trying to poison herself then, right?" Our previous trip to Twain Harte had the four of us sitting down to dinner with Mom setting out a few choices of salad dressing. After the obligatory opening round of "How old is that?" and "What year did you pick this up?" followed by predicable snickering,

Mom answered smartly by ignoring us and rolling her eyes. "Very funny you guys." She poked her knife into a jar of Blue Cheese and gave a pre-emptive stir. "I just bought this last week." The dressing poured out as expected and we began a normal dinner.

When Dad went to pour the same dressing on his salad just moments later, it ran out thin, yellow, and slimy. He gasped and hollered, "What the?" We glanced up to see him scoot his chair back and point at his salad as if it were alive. I immediately started giggling nervously. "Woman, you did NOT just buy this!" Dad starts inspecting the jar, looking for an expiration date. Mom defends herself adamantly, insisting the jar was brand new. She stops and realizes she just consumed a healthy portion of slime on her very own salad. The conversation then turned from Dad's near death-by-dressing experience to Mom's assumed ingestion of cheesy toxins.

Brad and I took turns rationalizing her intake and assuring her she would be okay. "Clean out the G-D cupboards for once Paula!" my dad bellowed, "Before you wind up killing us all!" It had always been a family joke that when my parents restored the cabin, Mom boxed up—then moved back in—all the original food from the cupboards and fridge. She denied it, but this incident with the dressing certainly didn't instill a sense of security in anybody.

"I am starving!" Brad tells me now. He pulls what looks like a gallon sized can of chili from the cupboard and searches for a can opener. Meanwhile I inspect an antique box of Crunch 'n Munch and wonder about its 'stay fresh' pouch. I contemplate whether or not Brad has a case if I died while eating a product that's no longer manufactured. At what point does common sense come in? Too risky.

The phone rings in the other room and Brad takes his 64oz bowl of cold chili with him to answer it. I scurry along with a can of pineapple tucked in my armpit as I wrestle a tube of Pringles. "Oh, hey Paula," he says with his mouth full. "Yep—we have plenty of food."

It is *their* cabin after all.

But It Had My Name on It

"Why is your name on this bag in here?" Brad is leaned into our fridge, assessing our food supply.

On the couch with a magazine, I don't even look up. "It's my sandwich."

"Yes, but why did you put your name on the bag?" I can hear jars scooting around on shelves. Obviously hiding the sandwich in the rear of the fridge wasn't the brightest idea I've had to date.

"Because it's MINE. And I don't want you to eat it." All logic points in my direction. You write your name on the bag, i.e., no one else can stake a claim to it. He starts snorting. Shuts the fridge.

When I hear the rustle of paper, I glance over, a sharp pang of disbelief quickly becomes anger. "What are you doing?" I stand to defend my bread and meat. "That's mine, I wrote my name on it!"

"Wah-ding yo numb on a bahg meefs nufink," he says with his mouth full. The gall. He swallows and wipes his mouth with his sleeve. "You eat all the shrimp out of the shrimp salad, the chicken out of chicken-chow-mein, the meatballs out of the spaghetti sauce and every ball of cookie dough out of a gallon of ice cream."

I see no connection. We're talking in parallels here. "So what? Was your name on any of that?" Because if it had been, I would have respected the name-on-the-bag rule. Trust me, I grew up in a house where people had to protect what food they brought home. Not that it always worked, but at the very least, as a family we tried to respect the possession of outside food decree.

During high school, the fridge was stocked with various colored boxes and bags that had names scrawled all over them. Andrea and I always brought home food and stuffed it in the fridge, but too often found only greasy wrappers and crumpled paper when we later returned to claim our loot. We started writing our names on our things, as a means of safeguarding our treasures. Her and I would rarely eat one another's provisions, it was normally our father that would ransack the fridge and scarf down anything that looked remotely new and exciting. Occasionally, one of us would succumb to the temptation of a half-eaten burrito or the all too enticing slice of apple pie, but then all hell would break loose, a fight would ensue, and someone would wind up getting hurt in the scuffle.

"Girls! Agh! Stop it! Andrea let go of your sister's hair!" my mom found us entangled on the kitchen floor one afternoon. We were screaming and panting and clawing at one another. She pulled my sister off of me and I jumped up and pointed at her. "She attacked me!" I was frantic. I smoothed out my skirt and adjusted my hair. My barrette was nowhere to be found and I had a deep scratch running the length of my shin.

Andrea straightened her blouse and stood glaring at me. Her lip was swollen. I felt a twinge of pride at that. "You ate my slice of cheesecake. It had my name on it!" Yes, I did. But I had also taken the time to wet a washcloth and erase her name from the plastic container, then write my own name in its place. I retrieved the container from the far end of the kitchen, where it had landed after she hurled it at me in a rage. I showed her. "See? It says 'Carolyn' on it." I grinned and tried not to laugh. She swatted it out of my hand and shoved me. Girl fight, round two.

"That is ENOUGH!" my mom was holding her back. "You are supposed to be young ladies!" The three of us wrestled for only a second before a stray palm collided with Mom's cheek. We froze. I wriggled out of the chokehold I was in and opened the fridge.

"Okay, okay. I'm sorry," I said to Andrea, "Here, you can have my cinnamon roll, all right?" I searched the fridge and to my surprise, found nothing. As I continued to look, I heard her say with feigned innocence, "Oh, was that yours?"

So no, writing our names on our food didn't always work, but it usually did. Foolishly I assumed that as an adult, living with another adult, stolen food wouldn't ever be an issue. I stalked into my kitchen and held out my hand. "Give me back my sandwich," I demanded.

He handed over the second half and looked duly apologetic. Good. He wouldn't have expected what would have come next if he hadn't.

Cold Tired Hungry

"**...And then I** told her I'd appreciate a redefining of the term 'team' if this was a Team Meeting and I didn't have a chance to say jack..."

"Have you eaten yet today?" my friend cuts me off in mid-sentence. "Because you're being kind of ornery, and it's annoying." Well. A good friend can say these sorts of things and suffer no real consequence. Plus, she has a point. I tend to get a little edgy if I'm hungry. Actually, 'edgy' is putting it lightly. She's lucky I'm only hungry right now because God help her if I was tired or cold too. And if I was tired, cold, AND hungry—she better run in the opposite direction. Fast. The very nature of me transforms and suddenly my evil alter ego appears. My ordinarily composed self scampers off and hides under a bed somewhere. Gone from sight, unavailable for conversation unless muffins, warm attire, and just 15 minutes of sleep are offered up. Or so I've been told.

Just the other night I'm on the phone with Brad and I find myself interjecting his segment of the conversation with little snorts and huffs as I pick my nails and listen. He pauses and then, "Hon—do you need to go put on a sweater or something?" The man can't even see me but knows enough to guess what my problem is. Just needing a little warmth.

And during a visit with the parents, I tried to describe my recent trip back to Michigan to attend a Christening for my goddaughter. I babbled incoherently for a few moments, then began to waver between catty comments about a friend of my cousin's and emotionally blathering about the ceremony. I caught the look of confusion pass between my mom and dad. With a knowing smile, Mom leaned close to pat my shoulder and tentatively suggest, "Are you tired dear? We're having a bit of trouble following you here…" Just needing a little sleep.

But the worst is getting nailed for being the nasty combination of all three. Separately, my being cold, tired or hungry can be dealt with. But cumulatively, the three are a dangerous combination and my only defense to is to plead insanity.

"I did what?" I am shocked as I overhear Brad's description of my behavior at The Boardwalk. He's complaining to his buddies how crabby his wife was while they spent a family day down in Santa Cruz. "Oh, you should have seen her, shoving kids out of the way in ride lines," he raises his voice an octave in attempt at mocking my tone, 'And these crowds are too thick, this sand is too hot, that water is too cold!' She was just a pleasure." The image strikes me funny. I only remember being a little weary after a day of doing laps on a long dark stretch of asphalt, weaving through small children, strollers, and sets of parents who lumbered about in slow motion. I do recall a few requests on my part for a pretzel or measly bag of popcorn…had I been anything less than joyous? I'm suddenly struck with a flash memory of our final few minutes at the boardwalk. I'm walking behind Brad, slightly hunched while I hug myself to keep warm. He had recently denied my request to borrow his sweatshirt. I am making faces behind his back while I try to trip him. I wound up accidentally kicking my thong off and stepping on a jagged piece of pavement. Tears sprung behind my lids as I held my foot and hopped up and down, gritting my teeth and muttering every swear word I could dream up.

"Are you okay?" He called back cheerfully over his shoulder.

"I am HUNGRY!" I howled. "And TIRED. And COOOLD!" Then I started bawling. "And I hurt my foot—waaahhhh…." So, it wasn't my proudest moment to date, all right? I'm not too insane that I can't fess up and make fun of myself.

A Lesson in Self Control

I married a man who likes to teach. If someone needs instruction, Brad is there to give it. If someone doesn't need instruction, the same applies. If there's a lesson to be had, he'll be the one to hand it out. Your objective? He'll know it, or even better—define it for you. My mother once told me, "You just talk because you like the sound of your own voice." She hadn't met Brad yet.

"I want to teach you to play tennis," Brad recently told me.

"I played for four years of high school."

"Then you should be familiar with the basics. I'll teach you the rest."

"I was on the tennis team. Varsity. I'm pretty sure I could show *you* a few things…"

He chuckled, "No, seriously, Carolyn. Come on…"

There we stood on the courts at Heritage High, opposite one another, me facing the sun. He smiled and waved his racket at me. I was confused. What was that? Would he shout, "This is a racket," and insult me further?

No, he spared us both the lesson on equipment. On his first attempt at a serve, he swiftly tossed the ball up and sliced the air as the ball came down and bounced at his feet. I cough/laughed into my palm.

His next serve shot right past me. Well. The following one came at me so fast I had no choice but to turn and protect my head. I'm lucky I did because it nailed me on the back of my shoulder. I raised my racket to signal 'I-surrender' and whimpered, "Wait…wait…"

He didn't. A fastball thwacked my raised racket, caught me off-guard, and without choice, I hit myself on the side of the head.

He grinned, squeezed a long stream of water into his mouth from his sports bottle, wiped his face with the back of his hand and suggested, "Why don't you fetch the balls?" I woofed in response. And then, "Isn't this great?" I didn't answer.

I had a vision of greatness. It was me pelting him repeatedly with tennis balls as he begged for mercy. I fantasized being at the helm of a ball machine I could set to "Dangerously Rapid" while he danced across the courts, ducking and squealing.

Rather than be a poor sport, I set out to retrieve our balls and wound up hunched over and panting as I chased the elusive little devils across the court after I'd accidentally kick them right before picking them up. Happily, they'd scoot out of my reach each time, as if fueled by kitten motors.

Once all three were successfully gathered, I planted two at my feet, watched with disdain as both rolled off, then lobbed a serve back at him.

"Out!"

"What are you crazy?" I had flashbacks of this very thing from high school. "It was in by a mile! Get your eyes checked!"

My next serve bounced near his feet. He smiled sweetly, "Out again."

Once we got past the preliminaries, we actually had a few good rallies going. I managed to ignore the double-edged compliments ("You'll get the hang of it again!" "Hey—did you play all *four* years? Just wondering…" and "What do you call that kind of serve? It looks interesting!") and did what I could to maintain composure.

No matter. While all I could see was the glaring sun, what he saw was his wife struggling to grip her racket, hold onto three balls at once, and repeatedly dodge shot after shot he took at my head. I was hardly having a good time.

"That was great!" he told me after. "You want to do this tomorrow? I'll go easy on you..."

"Sounds fun." He lies, I lie.

The Death of a Water Heater

That blasted 'drip' is going to kill me. As if doing office work isn't bad enough, I'm stuck in my little hole with a bothersome 'drip' to help me lose my focus. I continue click clacking away on my keyboard until my 'drip' has become a 'drip, splash' and then I stop all together and tilt my head to the side in an effort to better detect the source.

Drip. Drip—drop, splash. Uh oh. Knowing an investigation is at hand, I groan and push myself away from my desk with an exaggerated sigh. I can do this when no one is around to question me. Sometimes I love to be dramatic, even if I'm the only one to enjoy the effect. Unaware of the cause, I begin to play the hot/cold game with myself. I peek into the laundry room and expect to see my washing machine having an accident. All is calm. But as I go to make my exit, 'drip.'

Now I'm no plumber, but my guess is that water should not be cascading down the side of my water heater. Soggy insulation is hugging my heater and appearing sadly apologetic, as if it could hang on no longer. It takes me a second, but once I realize I am standing in water, I yelp and fight off the urge to panic. My breathing begins to sound as if I am in labor as I quickly consider my situation.

I break into my alarm jig and start flapping my hands around like I'm on fire. This rarely helps me solve a problem, but it is fun to do. I consider my present situation: Sprinklers—went on strike over the weekend and killed a nice patch of grass in the front of my house. Backyard tree—I saw it lying on the ground this morning. It's fallen, and it can't get up. Garbage disposal—stubbornly jammed until a neighbor with a screwdriver appeared and scared it back into behaving. And now this: the death of my water heater. It's a mere 8 years old, that's just 56 in dog years. Still a spring chicken if you ask me.

I want to punch my out-of-town husband. Gone for weeks on end and I'm left to nurse our appliances and foliage back to health and then plan for the removal and replacement of a trusted piece of equipment. After speaking with the coroner (plumber) I'm aware of what is involved in the process. It's no small task when you have an "I can build anything" kind of husband, who built a room around the water heater and then stuffed the space with various work-related construction debris.

After spending the morning emptying the area of hazardous materials, reorganizing the garage, and swearing like a truck driver while I move a dresser, I step aside and let the plumber do his business.

Within a few short hours, I go out to meet our new water heater. He's big and brown and tough looking. Seems like a sturdy fellow. Doesn't need that sissy insulation. Has fancy buttons and knobs, not to mention a nifty panel and crank. I'm immediately impressed and smile at him. The plumber goes over the proper care and feeding of my new friend, while I stand there grinning.

The water heater is actually so nice that I decide not to crowd it with hubby's work materials. I'm trying to win it over. The thought is that if it likes me, it will perform for me. I'm staying out of its way, letting it adjust, trying not to ask too much right at the beginning. And tonight, when I take my shower, I'll know whether or not I'll be stuffing debris around it when I get out.

11

Settle Down

The Role of the Side-seat Driver

"Who's driving here anyway?" Ah, the famous expression of my dad, the one who hollered that very phrase at whoever was lucky enough to be his passenger. Are they lucky, brave, or naïve? It's all the same.

If you were sitting on his right, you were akin to being his sounding board, his navigator, his whatever the moment called for. You were not a wall though. Make no mistake. "What do you think you are? A wall for Pete's sake? Move your head, I can't see a damn thing!"

I grew up traveling in the backseat of a '69 Chevy Impala. My parents drove that thing into the ground. However, before they did, they left me with me a quite impressive mental imprint on the woes of maneuvering a vehicle. While I sat looking at the fading upholstery on the back of their bench seat, I concentrated on memorizing the grooves in the fabric as they argued about who knew how to drive.

"Who are you anyway? Mario Andretti?" Mom would screech as my father dodged in and out of traffic on his quest for that 2-car advantage. "Agh! Bill, slow down!" She'd cover her eyes as he waved her off and repeatedly checked his mirrors for the feds. For a long time, I didn't know what 'the feds' were. I'd been taught that even though my parents couldn't see what I was up to at every waking moment, that Santa Claus could.

I naturally assumed that the feds worked for St. Nick, they were his eyes and ears. I liked the idea. I told him one day, "I hope you get caught by the feds!"

"You better bite your tongue young lady." He eyed me before passing another car.

These days, I have a side-seat driver of my own. I have a couple of them if you include the one that sits perched in his booster seat barking out traffic laws as I drive.

"Mom—did you stop there? I swear that didn't feel like a complete stop."

"Mom—don't take your hands off the wheel like that. You need to be a safe driver." Never mind that I was merely allowing the steering wheel to complete its post left turn rotation by grazing my palms as I rounded the bend.

And "Mom—always look at the road. Quit looking at yourself in the mirror." This one got my attention. I tried to patiently explain that I continuously check my mirrors for safety, not for vanity, and that they're placed on the sides of vehicles for that very reason. He was hardly convinced, especially after I was caught red-handed applying Chapstick at a stoplight soon after.

He was in all his glory when I got stopped by an officer last year and piped up from the backseat, "Are you going to take my mom to jail (dramatic pause) *again*?"

I laughed nervously and tried to assure the gentleman I had never actually gone to jail, just warned my son I would if he refused to stay in his car seat. Ha ha…ho ho…he didn't even crack a smile.

I prefer to drive when the family goes on outings. This way we actually arrive to our destination within a few minutes of our goal time. When Brad drives, I become the side-seat driver. But unlike my frantic mother who begs and pleads for Dad to slow down, I am practically clawing at the windows for my husband to hurry up and get us there. While Brad does have his other skills, he has yet to master the old 'talk and drive' operation. When he opens his mouth, his foot eases off the pedal. I have learned to say nothing until cars start passing us, then I just point and raise my eyebrows. Calmly, he'll say, "Let them go. We have all the time in the world." Then * click * on goes the classical music. It's enough to make me develop a tick.

I should have known to expect his new stock reply after I implored, "Just please speed up a little bit, okay? At least go the speed limit…"

"Who's driving here anyway?"

Food for the Road

"Wrap this up, will you?" Brad mutters under his breath. He is bundled up in an oversized sweatshirt and curled into a ball on the front seat of our truck. His eyes are closed as he patiently waits…and waits…and waits some more as I go around saying my goodbyes.

I understand his tolerance wearing thin. This process of leaving has taken us almost a half-hour and the children have yet to kiss the relatives farewell. We may be here a while.

It started in the kitchen. When we announced we were leaving, a chorus of groans and sighs were heard all around. No one likes to see the kids depart, we understand. Lots of nodding, a few pats on the back, topped off by a hug or two, and then we move our send-off mob into the entryway. But not without our parting gifts—plastic containers filled with salads, potatoes, veggies, and a few baggies loaded with sliced meat. We are not allowed to make tracks without taking some small memento from the meal home with us.

In the foyer, we exchange miniature snippets of conversation, engage in the 'got everything?' kind of small talk, and help the children put on their socks. A hunt for a lost shoe ensues, which guarantees the start of a new conversation and a few more minutes of idle chitchat. Soon, firm instructions to "Find your shoe or we're leaving without it," will be heard. Bantering between parents and children comes next, then the interception from a friendly grandparent, who stuffs another container of leftovers in my armpit.

We congregate on the porch next. "Wow! Look at those stars." The remark that initiates another dialogue that keeps us standing around, now out in the cold. Grandma tells a story about the stars and the kids listen, enthralled—as Brad and I linger there, shivering. At this time, I will be given *the look* from Brad. *Get this show on the road.* I oblige as best I can and manage to wrangle up my two little stargazers and head for the driveway. But not before someone balances a baggy of mashed potatoes on my head.

Once there, I hunt for my keys and ignore Brad's deep sigh. The process of unlocking doors, wrestling the children into their car seats and tossing all accompanying gear through the back hatch is exhausting. I thrust toys, cups, and books into pairs of sticky, flailing hands to placate their tired wails. The tactic works and they seem occupied, if just for a moment. I turn and am greeted by a cooler with drinks to take "just in case."

At last, the chance to say our real goodbyes. We hug, we rub backs, we tousle one another's hair. We are handed two twelve-ounces of Capri Sun, 4 cans of creamed corn, and 1 prickly pineapple picked up at the supermarket. Before I get into my seat, I will be holding two more cartons of soy milk for Ben and a week's supply of his favorite yogurt.

Once seated, I lean to carefully place my loot on Brad's lap. Because of his positioning I am forced to start balancing bags and cans around his shoulders. It's a bit of a challenge due to the watermelon he cradles like a baby. "Steady…steady…" I whisper. He tolerates this until a large jug of tomato juice falls and hits him in the groin. He bolts straight up heaving the can in my direction. Our melon rolls to the floor.

A sure sign to get a move on. Another visit complete, another shopping trip avoided.

Getting into Training Big Time

If you've never met a man who knows how to find a great deal, please come to my house. I beg you. Come into my home and have a look around. Most of what you'll see is part of the Brad Collection, a compilation of various riff-raff he's picked up over the last 32 years.

Now while I might say most of what we've gathered isn't necessary, he'll argue that it's all been worth hanging onto.

Take for example our new train set. Might it be an ordinary little wooden train set, the kind enjoyed by small children in preschool classrooms? Of course not. This is a part of the Brad Collection, and ordinary plays no part in this.

One afternoon he called home from a job site, excited to tell me about a train set we were being given. Now I know a train set is a find, especially a free one. And I am a girl who loves a good choo-choo. He warned me it was large, but I pictured something the size of say, the average Brio train table. He mentioned we might have to have the children share a room, so this train set could have a space in the house. My reply, "Interesting." while in reality I thought, "That'll be the day."

Weeks passed while he touted the pros of getting this treasure ASAP. He bragged how the owner had made it himself, and estimated its worth to be around a few thousand dollars. I was forever being described the detail of the tunnels and hand-crafted mountains. Holding back giggles, I gave it all little thought and only when the owner started phoning repeatedly to inquire when we would be picking it up, did I start to really wonder why, if it was so great, did he want to just give it to us? And why was he in such a hurry to unload it?

The arrangements for pick-up were made and much to my surprise I found Brad, measuring tape in hand, out in the garage, moving boxes around. When he removed the shelving from the wall I piped up, "Ummm…how big is it again?" He skipped around my question and vaguely answered while making sure his head was deep in a box, as to muffle his voice. I knew this trick, and I knew too that it was better to just leave well enough alone and let him continue to sweat out the process.

He and a friend, Scott, left to retrieve the toy in our dually work truck. I was a tad surprised when they later returned, minus one train set. Brad jogged past me, gave me the double thumbs up with a wicked grin, then happily said, "The bed of the truck isn't big enough! Whoo-hoo, this is gonna be GREAT!" I did what I could to keep my facial expression neutral as he proceeded to whip out the measuring tape once again and then toss a few more boxes from the garage up into the attic.

Scott proceeded to rig up our work trailer to the dually, shouting over his shoulder, "I hope this thing is big enough to hold it!" Fear set in. The two guys exchanged excited remarks on train size and manliness, while I fought off alarming thoughts of hand-crafted Styrofoam mountains.

Fast forward a few months. We now have a 12-foot by 6-foot ensemble in our garage, unused and gathering dust. Brad had the bright idea of building "Train Town" in our backyard, then he and Scott, who has amazingly said nothing insulting by now, began construction on a rather sizable building in which to place it. Three quarters of the way through this project, Brad decided it wasn't worth the effort, and that what we need more is a shed.

So have we enjoyed the train yet? No. Do we have an extra, not yet completed, building in our yard? Yes. Can we walk in the front half of the garage? No. Are we looking for takers to donate a train set to? Yes. Will we charge anyone to take this off our hands? No. Was it worth the time spent moving it, storing it, then building a spot for it? Sure! And if you believe that, I've got a train set to give you.

A Night to Remember

"I want you to be there," my friend Liz grabbed my hand, "When this baby comes, I want you to be in the room, okay?"

There is no greater gift than the witnessing of a new life come into this world. Having been on the giving end twice already, this was my first time to receive a baby, fresh from his mama's womb. I wanted nothing more than to be there; I was honored to have been asked.

This is Liz's fourth baby. The knowledge that Liz's third child shot from her body like a cannon in a Triage room after a minimal 2-hour labor never escaped me, and I knew that when Baby #4 was ready, I would have to act fast. This time around, the baby would be a boy. This time around, Daddy was court ordered to not be present. This time around, things would be very different for Liz and for the first time in 4 pregnancies, Liz was happily anticipating her birthing experience.

Her due date came and went with the two of us gritting our teeth in anticipation. Each time I saw her name illuminate the Caller ID, I would snatch the phone from its hook and gasp, "Are you in labor??" Time after time I was met with "No, hee, hee. I just need a couple eggs," or the like. I became a nervous mother hen, checking in with her daily and reviewing her symptoms. "Are you feeling nauseous? They say you might start to feel sick when you're close. How about your feet? Are they swollen yet? Let's go for a walk or something." So on, and so forth.

By the time she was three days overdue, I had gnawed the inside of my cheek into a nice pulp. On the 5th day, I started taking ulcer medication. By day 7, I had removed my fingernails with my teeth. At 10 days overdue, I began to question the validity of this pregnancy. Maybe she was just getting heavy. On the 12th day past her due date, her doctors decided Jr. needed some prompting and they gelled her cervix at a weekly appointment.

"Hi," Liz grunted over the line, "I'm at the hospital. Can you come?" We exchanged words of excitement and then, "Oh!" she breathed, "My water just broke! I gotta go. At least I think it broke…I don't know. My legs are all wet…what do you think?" Before I could answer, she whimpered, "Ow…bye." Click. Oh dear. I grabbed Molly, her teenaged daughter, and we were off.

I half expected to enter the room and hear the coos of a newborn when we arrived. I fought off my disappointment of missing his birth, but joyfully anticipated meeting the bundle. I needn't had worried. Liz was still in Triage and her labor was extremely slow.

When Liz was admitted to her private room, I was amazed to discover her nurse was a girl I graduated high school with. Small world! I chatted and laughed, filled her in on my life, and showed her pictures of my children. "Um, who are you again?" she asked. I couldn't wait for her shift to end.

After several hours of adjusting Liz's blankets, playing with her cords, peering at her monitors, and entertaining her younger daughters, we were given some news. Liz was ready for an epidural and could sleep for a few hours. I saw Molly eyeing the fold out chair next to the bed. "Don't even think about it, sister," I sneered at Molly. "That bed has my name on it."

"Bring it on," she challenged. She poked me in the gut. We chick slapped one another for a minute before collapsing onto it together, laughing. Two girls snuggling up on a chair designed for a small child—at best, opened a door of memorable conversation.

"Is it cold in here? I'm freezing! It's like fricking Alaska in here…" (Me)

"Is that your butt? Can you move it over PLEASE? I'm falling off my side." (Molly)

"You look like a keeper of a crypt—get that blanket off your face. Unwrap your head before you suffocate." (Molly)

"Can I borrow your sweatshirt? Is it even yours? Or is it (high pitch sing song) *Aaron's*?" (Me, making kissy face noises)

Enter the rustling of blankets and squeals as we wrestled one another. Sleep was out. We got up and walked the halls for a while and came back to find Liz propped up in bed, holding her legs, pushing. "Where have you been?" she barked, in between pants.

When we left, she had been sleeping. We stood there holding two coffee cups, three chip bags, one Danish, a package of Lunchables, and an empty cookie wrapper.

"We got hungry," Molly offered weakly. We dropped our goods and sprang into action. Less than 10 minutes later, Jacob Joseph came to us, 10 pounds, 21 inches long—perfect in every way.

Happy birthday sweet child. What an honor it is to meet you.

If You Give a Dope a Rope

There's a cabin built in the ravine where I used to swing from a tree on a rope tied to an uneven branch. The brambles are long gone and the knoll us kids used to hike back up once our turn was over has been leveled so that a driveway could be born. Though the cabin is quite lovely, the tree, I think, held a great deal more charm.

I have a history with trees swings, a menagerie of memories, all of them ending with me landing flat on my ass. Oh sure, they all start the same way…the child grins broadly, laughter carries through the air as her hair blows in the breeze. Little tube top, cut off jean shorts and thongs (we called them thongs way back then), as the hot summer sun shines down on her face. She swings out, back, and out again. But on her second decent from height, just as she starts to head back towards the tree—SNAP. The rope breaks. And the child's laughter becomes a panicked howl then an 'OOOMPH' as she hits the deck. I shudder at the memories, I can recollect quite a few.

So, while I love the idea of a tree swing, what I love more at this time in my life is watching others partake in that good old-fashioned fun. Which is why I said, "No, thanks," when my husband and son begged me to test ride the one last summer while we were out looking at model houses. "No, thanks, no thanks" I shook my head no, time and time again.

"Oh, come on, please…" they begged. They beseeched and they implored and finally, they broke me down. We braved the weeds and brush and hiked to the top of a hill where someone had so cleverly wrapped a thick rope around a massive branch and made, for the neighborhood kids, a swing in a tree. Complete with wooden makeshift seat. It did seem sturdy enough, but still. I hesitated.

Josh went first, the anticipated vision of youth—laughing, spinning, kicking his feet off the truck of the tree to make it last longer. Brad went second. Same thing, only older. And heavier. I should have made note of this. The swing was offered to me. Surely times must have changed. Certainly, this time I'd be all right. This rope did seem pretty thick.

"Well…okay." I made a big production of relenting and climbing on. I demanded that Brad pull me back as high as possible before running and pushing me out as far as he could. If I was gonna swing, I might as well swing big. I swung out, then back, then out again, spinning to see them as I swung backwards high in the air. Then, as fate would have it, the rope broke. "I knew it!" I screamed angrily on my way down. Brad told me later the look on my face was classic.

Because I had been launched out backwards over a steep hill, I landed with an already rapid momentum, and felt alarmed as I went heels over head down the hill. I think I actually picked up speed. When I came to a stop, my hood was on and there was dirt in my mouth. "I told you!" I shouted, spitting out pebbles. I swore a few times and then started brushing myself off.

My poor kid was more traumatized than me. I was half laughing and half crying, Brad was bent over, hysterical and Josh was bawling with concern for his mama. We three made quite the scene as we entered the office of the models and asked to use their restroom. "Remember that rope swing up on that hill?" I pointed in the general direction. The lady nodded, her eyes wide with shock. "Well, it's gone." I left it at that and went to pick burrs from my socks and shoelaces.

A new swing hangs from that very same branch today. I know this because we bought a house nearby and we can watch the kids use it every day. And while I walk Josh up there to swing whenever he wants, I refuse his invitation to give this one a shot. "No, thanks," I tell him, and this time I mean it.

Incident in the Hall

Ok. I admit it. I'm quick to panic. I can't help it though; I can detect even the slightest bit of hysteria in someone's voice when they are relaying a story and I can't fight off the urge to gasp. I have even mastered the art of bringing my hand to my mouth in a dramatic gesture. (Widening my eyes in appreciation of a good punchline, well that just comes naturally.) Perhaps it's because my life, in a nutshell, is just one bizarre accident after the next.

Take for example that time when Josh was a baby and had "that incident" in our hallway. You see, I never actually witnessed what happened, I just had to guess, according to what I heard. And I suppose it's safe to say I have a pretty active imagination.

Having recently learned to crawl, Josh is everywhere in the house, all at once. It is impossible to keep an eye on him at all times. Am I justifying that I lost track of the little devil for a minute or two? Well, perhaps. If I was quick, I would catch a glimpse of his padded foot pajamas as they disappeared around a bend. And that's if I was lucky! Normally I would depend on the slobbery babbling I could hear in the distance, or the occasional thud of his wrecking ball head against a wall or a door when bumped enroute to his destination.

So, when his curious coo was drowned out by a piercing scrape, then followed by a clatter, a thump, and then a howl to rival Jamie Lee Curtis' infamous scream in *Halloween*, I immediately went into panic mode. In the kitchen, I flung the dish of grapes I was munching on into the sink and with a gulp, started yelling in unison. Hoping Brad could hear me while he showered, I began my sprint to the back of the house.

"Aggggghhh! Oh MY GOD! Oh NO! Brad HEELLP!!"

I was hysterical before I even reached the hallway. Had I just shut my own mouth for half a second, I would have realized that Josh had finished his own cry for help and was listening intently to mine. Panic stricken and breathless, I rounded a corner in the hall, only to find Josh on all fours, atop of a fallen baby gate. Pride flushed his cherub face—he had finally overcome this barrier, this nemesis of his for the last few weeks.

Instantly, I realized my blunder.

Whoop of pride, not shout for aide. Oopsie. And all would have been fine, but remember, I called Brad out of the shower for assistance. Again, oopsie. Hearing my hysteria, he had thrown open the shower curtain, leapt from the tub, and in a mad dash to save me, lost his balance on wet feet and tumbled down to the floor. A whack to the skull on a nearby towel rack didn't seem to greaten his mood. Neither did the cookie size bruise on his outer thigh, which appeared in record time.

Having found his footing, he limped wet and naked out to us, one hand rubbing the sore spot on the side of his head. I smiled weakly, then got the look. Silent, he turned and departed, back to the shower to prepare his lecture on overreaction, which I was to get later that evening.

I took it pretty well though. I even widened my eyes in appreciation.

A Family Bed Equals Little Sleep

There were three in a bed and the little one said, "Roll over, roll over," so they all rolled over and one fell out.

As much as I like the little children's ditty, I would never volunteer to have it be the premise of my every evening. And, oh, but it is a…cute song and all, but dreadful bedtime ritual. Only at my house, it goes a little something like this:

There were three in the bed and the little one said…well, nothing because he is non-verbal. But he does shriek a great deal and then whaps me in the head with his empty bottle. Grasps my hair in his sticky fist, wails in my ear, then tries to head-butt me to get me to move. You gotta love autism.

So, they all rolled over and one falls out- the big one, me. Not too far a fall, though. Recently the big one removed her headboard and footboard from the bed and put the entire ensemble on the floor to prevent late night injuries from headers off the mattress.

I go around to the other side. Climb in. There were three in the bed and the middle one said, "Ow! Mom—Ben is kicking me! Ugh! I can't sleep…waaaaahhhh…" So they all rolled over and one fell out. Again, the big one. Now the big one gazes down at her children and tries to remember what a full night's sleep felt like. Did she like it? Probably. Most likely had no purple bags under her eyes then either, or possibly thought eight hours under the covers just wasn't quite enough.

I go back around to the side I originally fell out of, move Ben carefully to the center, and then remove a bunny, a pacifier, a bottle, one sock, and the book that was jabbing me in the ribs a few minutes earlier. Who brought that in? I lie curled on my side, shivering on my slice of mattress and reach to cover my ankle with the remaining one-inch triangle of quilt I've been rationed. I concentrate on that tickle in the back of my throat. I can't decide—is it a cough, or a scream? There were three in the bed and the big one said, "I need sleep, I need sleep." Wide-awake, I stare at my wall and think, "Is this really my life?"

The family bed is killing me. The children start out in their own beds, then like thieves in the night, they steal under my covers and spread their little limbs in all directions. I'm left with no pillows, no blankets, and two little boys that interrupt my sleep with bony elbows in my face, sharp toenails on my calves, grunts, snores, coughs, and enough gas to heat the house. One a deep sleeper and the other who wakes when someone thinks too loud, the boys' conflicting snooze patterns keep me wondering how I function with such little sleep.

I obviously don't. Which is why I can't get that darn song out of my head!

Not So Itsy Bitsy

It's been said that fear is learned. If that's the case, then I have to wonder what my first experience with a spider was. What interaction could possibly have transpired that has me 30 years later horrified at the sight of one? As a child I had a bedtime routine that differed from most little girls. After completing the usual scrubbing up and getting changed, I did a thorough, wall-to-wall room check for spiders. Upon finding any, Dad was called in to terminate the intruder and then a recheck was instated. Sometimes a spider got lucky. The spider of '77 is the one that lived to tell.

I had awakened from a deep sleep with a heavy feeling of dread. Upon opening one eye I discovered that my automatic anti-spider defense had kicked into gear and roused me. On the wall I slept next to sat a baby spider. No matter how small the villain, it had to be removed. I was torn—I knew not to wake up Mom or Dad unless it was an emergency, and I also knew our definitions of emergency greatly differed. Fear won over and I scampered out of bed to retrieve my mom. She wasn't thrilled but followed me back to my room so I could show her the "big spider." (I also understood that she would never get up if I said baby spider; this slight exaggeration was an unfortunate yet necessary part of the automatic anti-spider defense.)

I was horrified to discover an enormous spider directly overhead when the light came on. Mom used a shoe to dispose of him, but then sleepily returned to bed without my having made mention of the original intruder, who I could not find after she exited, leaving me to the first in a series of worries about spiders that got away.

More recently there was my spider-in-the-shower experience. What we term here at the Dodds home, "Hell in a confined area." So, there I was showering one day; joy was all mine as there were no children pelting me with Legos or inquiring if I wanted company. With no shower chaperones present, I leisurely shaved a leg.

As I finished, I stuck the handle of the disposable razor in my mouth in preparation of applying soap to the other. (Any person who has shaved their legs in a shower can appreciate the exact position I am referring to.) After properly lathering up leg # 2, I removed the razor handle from my mouth and leaned to apply it to my shin. At that very moment, the hairy black spider that was residing in the hollow of the handle decided to make his departure and, in a flash, darted out onto my wrist.

Words cannot describe what happened next. I have to wonder what the spider must have thought when he saw what his exit brought about. Screaming, I threw the razor at the nearest wall. Pandemonium broke out. I fought violently with the shower curtain in my attempt to escape the tub. Smacking my arm repeatedly and sobbing, I hurled my body out over the ledge and onto the bathroom floor. In my panic, I lost sight of the spider and then having no bearing whatsoever on his whereabouts, I started slapping my entire body while I lay writhing on the soaked carpet. When I later tried to explain the carpet burns and stinging handprints on my upper body, my husband's only words of comfort were choked out between laughter, "You almost ATE it!"

Being a Brentwood resident has afforded me ample opportunity to fraternize with arachnids. On more than one occasion I have had to photograph the eight-legged intruders just to prove to skeptics that the spiders out here are impressive in size. I've even gone so far as to capture a few (with the help of Brad) which led to an array of multicolored Tupperware bowls labeled "Do not open" all over our freezer. Having an entomologist for a sister has certain advantages. She gladly accepts my cold, stiff offerings and assures me they are harmless. Ugly, yes, but safe enough. As for me, I use razors with solid handles now and still do a room check before turning in for the night.

Uncomfortable in a Bee Cup

I'm a magnet for disaster. Chaos seeks me out and then snuggles down in my very being. I never even see it coming. You'd think I'd be more prepared for the unexpected, but that must be why catastrophe can jump out to say, "Gotcha!" yet never fail to catch me unaware.

Take for example a leisurely drive down Vasco Road last spring. Hubby and I are sitting in some slow crawling traffic, approaching Camino Diablo on our way toward Livermore. A soft melody purrs from the radio, my window down just enough to allow the gentle breeze in to casually toss my hair around. I am enjoying being the passenger for once. All is calm.

That is, until I feel a nice sized pebble thud against my chest, then fall directly down into my T-shirt. Puzzled, I peer into the neckline of my shirt and look around for what came in contact with me. Seeing nothing, I drop the neckline and continue humming along with the radio and occasionally turning to smile at Brad and the kids. Until I feel something tickle my chest, then do a slight bomp-bomp against the fabric of my shirt. The warmth of panic starts to trickle down into my gut as I gaze into my shirt and see, this time, a big-fat-fuzzy-yellow and black bumblebee, attempting to find a comfy place to rest between two hills and valleys.

I scream. Brad hits the brakes and the car jerks to a halt, leaving a slight skid mark on the asphalt. Since traffic is stopped anyway, we are really in no danger of being rear-ended. I start to haphazardly slap my chest and pull at my shirt. I am near sobbing and can only choke out, "Bee…" I reach for the door handle and flail myself out onto the side of the road, still clawing at my shirt and shaking my head violently around.

Brad jumps in to the rescue. He too flees the truck and jogs around to my side. I have now spun myself towards the tailgate and in my delirium, have lost my bearings all together. Since I am pulverizing myself and cannot maintain sanity, Brad does the only thing he can think of to do. Something all the cars stopped in traffic probably appreciated. Who wouldn't want a little entertainment while stuck on the road?

Brad pulls my shirt off over my head and starts spinning me around, in an attempt to find the bee. This gives all on lookers a 360-degree view of my now scantily dressed upper body. He shakes out my shirt and offers it back to me, but not having seen the bee leave the scene I refuse to put it back on. We are still on the side of the road. This occurs to me, so I snatch the shirt and after inspecting it closely, decide to pull it back over my head.

We say nothing to each other as we both get back into the cab of the truck. I am embarrassed beyond words. "There was a bee…" I offer weakly, "I swear."

"You think they knew that?" he asks, laughing. He thumbs the air to point to the row of cars behind us.

Probably not. So, I'll set the record straight: that girl in her bra being spun in circles by her husband on Vasco Road was me. And there was a bee. I swear.

12

Babe in the Woods

Travel Mugs (Which Came First?)

My mug!" I am aghast. On the floorboard of Brad's work truck lies a travel mug that has, like its predecessors, fallen victim to Brad. I wouldn't mind if he borrowed my mugs were his intent to be actually drinking from them, but he uses them as 'spitters' for his tobacco. (Don't get me started.)

But travel mugs are expensive and one by one, they are ruined by my husband. "Use a can," I tell him, "Or spit into a cup or something…" but he constantly grabs a mug because he likes their crafty little openings on the lids. And as any wife of a spitter knows—once a spittoon sits long enough, it's only going to be thrown out. Not washed or scrubbed or salvaged in any way. So long, bye-bye, nice to know you little travel mug.

"You have plenty of mugs left," he rationalizes, which is true, but totally beside the point. His justification is this: *My wife is addicted to purchasing travel mugs. Unnecessary, superfluous travel mugs. We do not have enough cupboard space to house her inane shopping paraphernalia, therefore I become, by chance—not by choice, an active participant in the law of averages. I simply remove from the cupboard what she places inside.*

Which touches upon another relevant issue: my own addiction. Travel mugs. I just can't seem to stop bringing them home. I can be anywhere at all and come across a new, sassier version of travel mug, and instantly think—I need that. I should have that. That really wants to come home with me. And it will.

I have travel mugs that range in size, shape, and color. They have varying design, heating elements, and fancy flip top lids. It seems that the travel mug industry tries to snazzy up the mug bimonthly, just for people like me. And quite obviously, their strategy works. I swipe up new and exciting mugs all of the time.

But like a pesky neighborhood child, this matter of whose addiction is worse comes into play all too frequently.

"Your addiction is disgusting!" I tell Brad, shaking his hockey puck can of chew.

"Yours is expensive!" he replies, fisting a brand-new travel mug.

"So is yours! *And* it's dangerous!"

"Yours is too! Have you taken a look at these things? You have a weapon now! You carry a PIECE!"

We are at a loss on how to resolve this—it's a case of which came first—the travel mug or the spit? And while I justify my collection by way of rationale, "You use them for spittoons, therefore I am entitled to replace my damaged property." He stands firm by his own, "You have dozens on hand—a few less won't be missed." And his latest counterpoint, "You never even know they're missing until you find them on the floor of my truck." Well.

Yesterday I just bought my first travel thermos. It's pink and plastic and pretty. It's for cool drinks only. It has a straw and no fancy flip top lid. I'm already hiding it.

A Cool Solution

"You're doing WHAT?!" my girlfriend shrieked as I held the phone away from my ear.

"I *said* I am taking the kids out of the fridge; can I call you right back?" Ordinarily, I don't keep the kids in the fridge, really, I don't; but on this particular afternoon I certainly wasn't against them sitting on the shelves to cool their little bodies. We've had record heat out this way in

Brentwood and smack dab in the middle of all of the sweltering, our AC betrayed us and conked out. At first, I refused to believe it, I mean, I've always been nothing but nice to our AC. So, with perspiration dripping down my sides, I went from room to room with a stepladder to feel the air pouring from the vents. Warm. Hmm. Had I accidentally turned on the heat in a delirium-induced sweat? Apparently, I had not, I had just worked my poor little AC until it could work no more. Like a greedy, overzealous slave driver, I forced my AC into an early grave with each of my demands for a chilly interior.

I slipped into my sandals and went outback. "I'm sorry Little Guy," I whispered to our AC unit, "Please work just one more time. Please." I reached to stroke the top of what may have been its head and, "OW! Dang! You are HOT!" Shaking out my hand I went back inside to put my head in the freezer to think about how to solve this.

I let the cool mist envelop my face while I mentally counted how many hours were left before dark. Dark equals cool, right? Not necessarily in Brentwood, but I'm a hopeful girl. The last time our AC broke down was in 1998, before the kids. Brad rigged up a one-room AC unit, a tiny window box that was coughed out of the bowels of someone's apartment back in the 70s. How this decaying, grimy ramshackle managed to put out cool air is beyond me, but it did the trick. The only catch was that we had to live in our kitchen for the time being.

AC repairmen were few and far between during that heat spell, so for nearly two weeks we existed within about 200 square feet. We left only to use the bathroom and to answer the door, which were mostly our neighbors dropping by to inquire about the hideous mass of tin we had mounted to our front kitchen window. Before I could explain the tin mass, I would have to rationalize the comforters hanging in our kitchen doorway and then defend the mattress on the kitchen floor. Not one friend could hide their shock when learning of our setup. "Look," I'd say as politely as I could, "Our AC is BROKE, we are doing what we can to survive here. If you want to help (and no one had offered) please bring us some fans." We wound up with six fans and periodically had to leave the kitchen, it got so darn cold!

Now some would say that is really stretching it—how could we even consider doing such a thing? But truthfully, how bad is it to sleep within a foot of a refrigerator? It got so I had even mastered the art of reading a magazine and grabbing a soda without having to look up from the page I was on. Brad and I played cards, boardgames, even charades. We had a blast.

So, what to do with two small children during this stretch of heat? I closed my eyes and let the cool mist rise up around my neck and shoulders while I contemplated my dilemma.

No need to think very long—not more than three seconds later I heard my 3-year-old son say, "Excuse me Mom," and then he proceeded to tug open the door to the fridge while I scooted out of his way. He sat on a lower shelf and let his upper body drape across another at his midsection. "Ahhhhh, this feels GOOD!" Problem solved. I grabbed the baby and joined him.

An Unexpected Gift

Children were running amuck, all screaming and laughing. The noise level was almost deafening, and in the middle of it all, stood my three-year-old son pulling on my shirt and begging for me to fix the ticket-eater machine. This was excruciating.

On a whim, Brad and I had stopped off at the giant castle on Highway 580. On our way home from Pleasanton we were suddenly possessed by an overwhelming urgency to smell smoke and look frantically for our wandering children. (Or so I'm guessing.)

Before I knew it, I was dashing through a wet parking lot, driving a stroller that kept wanting to careen off onto the grass, and dodging the raindrops that were pelting all four of us. I couldn't fathom why we were doing this, especially since I had no bottles for the youngest, but my sense of adventure overpowered my sense of logic and I soon found myself tossing skeet-balls with a crowd of unruly teenagers.

The night wore on. We soothed the fussy toddler with rides on the carousel and continuously fed bills into the greedy token dispensers. Josh accumulated quite a stash of "winning" tickets and wanted desperately to trade them in for a prize at the end of the night. I've been to Chuckie Cheese. I know how this works. What I wasn't expecting was the line of angry parents at the ticket eater contraption and a teenaged shift manager sweating profusely as he tried to fix the problematic machine.

And so the story goes, Josh whining and thrusting his body about as we watched and waited. And waited. And waited some more. Ben crying and thrashing in the stroller, and me; me watching his diaper leak and proceed to soak the crotch and inner thigh of the only outfit we had for him. I was ready to go home. I gave Brad the eye. Catching on, he took Josh by the hand and led him, crying loudly that he needed a prize, over to the anxious looking teen, working the gift counter. Counting the tickets by hand, Brad told his son to pick out whatever he wanted.

As 3-year-olds often do, Josh had a hard time deciding. He couldn't find what he was looking for but wouldn't tell me specifically what he wanted. Exasperated, I shuffled off with the stroller, the wet baby, and the aroma of urine and sour milk in my tow. I opted to pass on the choosing process and let Daddy handle the indecisive tot instead.

Moments later, all four of us were dashing through the rain once more and with the pandemonium of loading the kids and ourselves back into the truck, I failed to see what Josh had chosen. I had little desire to loot through a bag of small plastic insects, miniscule candy, and the ever-popular packet of stickers I had fully expected to see.

It wasn't until the next morning that I learned of the treasure Josh had chosen. Still in the clothes he had fallen asleep in on the ride home, he tiptoed into our bedroom and stood quietly staring at me. As I awoke, I smiled and opened my arms as an invitation to crawl up and join us.

"Here Mommy," he said shyly, "I wanted to give this to you last night." In his hand was a heart-shaped stone on a string necklace. It was adorned with a hand painted flower and…a woman perhaps. It was hard to tell, but I tenderly accepted this gift and wrapped him in a warm hug. All the crying, all the fussing, all the time it took for him to make a decision last night had boiled down to this. He had been shopping for me, and selfishly, I had not even taken a moment in the truck to inquire of his selection.

I wear the necklace every day as a reminder of two things: the most special of presents are the unexpected ones—the ones that come straight from the heart, and the thought behind the offering will always be worth more than whatever price the gift came at. I appreciate both of the gifts Josh handed to me that morning; a necklace and a lesson I'd soon not forget.

What is Normal Anyway?

"Do you ever think," my friend asked me, "About what it would be like if Ben were normal?"

Deep sigh. How do I answer this question without lying?

"Normal meaning what?" I reply, disregarding for the moment that Ben remains undiagnosed without the discovery of a missing key genetic component in his mystery syndrome, but not forgetting that he holds a multitude of varying labels for his symptoms, has a trying 36-hour therapy week. I asked her this not to make her uncomfortable, but to genuinely get a feel for what her perception of normal is.

It's true that I entertain the thought of someday having more children, as well as find myself smiling at the random but somewhat sporadic incidence of Josh and Ben playing side by side in our yard. I've even born witness to an occasional game of hide–and-go-seek, the boys seeming— at least for the moment, to be "normal" brothers. It's even true that I wonder what Ben would say to me, to any of us, should he ever grasp the concept of spoken language. Every day I wonder what occurs in his head to make him fearful of ordinary items, terrified of the inexplicable. And of course, I speculate why one day he'll smile at the sight of Josh's school, when on the very day before he screamed and writhed in his car-seat as we neared it. But no, I do not remain there, caught up in the thoughts of what could have been.

Normal for Ben has become normal for the rest of our family. We accept these differences and go forward, finding pride in areas such as not buying into the stereotypical image of Nuclear American Family. While it may be easy to say, and even easier to write, there is no ease in trying to live it and carry it out. Yet, it has become systematic for us. I imagine it's much like having four children, or more. The busy schedules, the run around, the sleepless nights, with someone forever needing something at some time or another. The chaos that you dub "my life." You take it and run with it. What other choice as parents do any of us have?

And what is normal anyway? While I chauffer my kids to schools and lessons, sports, and therapies, my friend does the same, minus the conversations regarding IEP goals. I imagine both our cars are filled with the same sounds of laughter, talking, kid's music on the CD player. I like to think we shout the same things at our kids: Share with your brother! Don't look at me like that! Let your brother have a turn! LET YOUR BROTHER HAVE A TURN! I SAID…yes, thank you! Good job!

I like to think we aren't the only family that sacrifices a good night's sleep, so that a child's breathing can be monitored closely. The Dodds can't be the only ones here in Brentwood who struggle with getting their children to eat healthy meals, to arrive at school on time, fed and dressed, to keep bathwater inside the tub, and to remember their courteous manners. I know we aren't the only ones disguising vegetables under cheesy sauces and inventing new wrestling moves just to get a kid diapered. And don't we all use sign language in some form or another to communicate with our kids? Our normal just doesn't seem too unlike most families I know. Perhaps, it's just a bit more involved, a tad more emotional at times, to some degree. We have a couple of extra Plan Bs and Plan Cs lined up just in case.

People tend to be very adaptable, and I'm thankful for the simple joy of that. What we gain by even the smallest measure of support and encouragement is invaluable. Ben may never talk or tag alongside his older brother at school, and that's okay. What he can do is love. He gives it. He accepts it. That's our normal.

Just Kidding Around

"Aaaaahhhhhh!" I screamed loudly into my friend's ear. I gripped her arm and squealed as we rounded a corner. She returned the scream, then we laughed and looked at one another, both of us a tad nervous and more than a little embarrassed.

The roller coaster came to a screeching halt. As the bar holding us in was raised, I lifted my leg from atop hers and she shoved me out of the miniature car by my rump. Giggling, we stumbled onto the sidewalk and smiled widely at the gentleman controlling the coaster as we passed.

"We really gotta get out more," I said to Joanne.

She nodded, "Yeah, if a roller coaster made for kids 36 inches in height is this much fun, that's a sure sign something needs to change."

We were at Pixieland recently, an amusement park made for the wee ones in the world, though it was the two of us that were racing from ride to ride and leaving our children in the dust.

"Keep an eye on the kids!" our husbands yelled after us, but we were off...

"Keep an eye on them yourself!" we yelled back, then rushed away snickering and punching each other in the arm like two 10-year-olds. I half expected a spitting contest to ensue, or to be sprayed with Capri Sun, what with the way we were behaving.

"Hey, let's do the Frog Jumper," she motioned towards the kiddie lift ride, her eyes wide and bright with anticipation. With that, she grabbed my upper arm and pulled me into the line of toddlers waiting to get on. We smiled at them, then at their parents who were all wearing identical looks of concern. The gentleman controlling this ride was amused. "Only one of you can ride at a time," he apologized, "Due to weight limitations and all..." his voice petered out a bit. He glanced at my bag of cotton candy, so I quickly hid it behind me. Looking regretful, he smiled and shook his head 'no'.

"Nice," she hissed in my ear, "Ever hear of Weight Watchers?"

I socked her in the shoulder and looked around for something else to ride. Suddenly, I felt a little tug on my coat, and I looked down to see my small son gazing up at me. Trailing him was Daddy, gasping for air as he hurried to catch up with us. He carried the baby on his shoulders and as he caught his breath, scolded me, "You MUST wait for everyone, Mommy. Families all stick together, right?" His tone implied much more than the words.

Okay, okay, so we were here for the kids. I know that. Yet, I couldn't recall the last time I felt so free, so young, so full of energy. Perhaps it was a sugar rush from all the cotton candy I had consumed, but I like to think it was something more. Darting in and out of lines, dashing from ride to ride, gobbling down junk food, shrieking in a good friend's ear, cheering on your buddies and their spouses as they too, hopped on rides and relived their youth. Witnessing good friends share good times and not worrying about who said what and which kid to watch out for…it was a perfect day. But above all, it reminded me I really need to get out more.

The Twenty Dolla' Jacket

"**Do you still** have your twenty dolla' jacket?" I recently asked my friend who has moved out of state.

"Are you kidding me? I'm wearing it right now!" Since we're on the phone, I can hardly verify this statement, but I smile at the thought of her in it, since my own is wrapped snuggly around me, zipped up tightly to my neck. I put my hood on and say, "Put your hood up then!" She giggles, but I hear the rustle of her adjusting the coat, and then the distinct zip of the drawstring, even across the telephone lines.

"Mark still has his too," she says, "Does Brad?"

I snort. "Of course! His one little act of defiance…remember?"

Ah…the twenty dolla' jacket. The year 2000 saw a large group of family and friends camping in the rain at Lake Shasta. Between the downpours we set up tents, unloaded supplies, cooked food, and tended to children. We docked our boats, arranged equipment for music, cleared the site of debris, and shivered under makeshift shelters. All this and not one of us had packed a proper jacket. Having anticipated sunnier weather in June, we were ill prepared for the thunder and lightning, wet showers, and cool temperatures that came our way once our convoy rolled into the campgrounds.

"This sucks," was the general consensus, so we squeezed eight adults into an SUV and headed down to Redding, where we happily located a Costco. It happened that luck was on our side and 2000 was the year that Costco accidentally released its waterproof winter coats a few months ahead of schedule. Having held out hope for, but not expecting to find any, eight of us gleefully dove onto the display and began rifling around to ensure everyone got the proper size. The coats were lined, fluffy, and exactly what we needed.

"And they're only twenty dollas'!" someone shouted and after a chorus of whoops and a round of high fives, The Johnsons, The Flynns, and The Bakers all uncovered the right size jacket...in blue. I found my right size jacket...in blue. Brad found the right size jacket and plucked it from the stack. It was green.

"No!" I pleaded.

"Don't do it!" said his buddies.

"Be like us!" the group implored. He held his ground. "Boo! Hiss!" We were relentless. We hounded him endlessly. He remained steadfast and was the only green olive in a troop of blueberries. Though it was his master plan, none of us respected his decision to be different, each of us mocking his individuality. We wanted unity, power in numbers, a statement of our brotherhood. What we got was a seven to one ratio of blue to green out in the rain, but no one was shivering anymore.

We shuffled around the campsite like Oompa Loompas, unable to distinguish one person from another. While it got to be confusing, it made for a lot of laughs and much more colorful conversation.

"Hey, you—in the twenty dolla' jacket!"

"You lookin' at me, or my twenty dolla' jacket?"

"Can you hand me a hot dog? And my twenty dolla' jacket?"

In all of the years we have had them, not one of us stopped using the dollar amount as its primary description. And while we couldn't tell you who made the jackets or what size any of them actually are, ask any one of us from that camping trip how much they cost, and we could tell you. But not without laughing.

Boom Huckjam

My 5-year-old says to me recently, "Look at my new trick. Tony Hawke does this all the time." He's on his skateboard and though nowhere near a Tony Hawke level of stunt completion, he does seem to have a certain knack for agility.

But it's the name Tony Hawke that gets my attention, more than the 'ollie' he's trying to emulate. It's intriguing to me that I grew up running with skate punks who lived and died by what Tony Hawke was saying and doing, and now here's my son—well on his way to following the same path.

I'm not totally out of the loop. I now know all about the Tony Hawke Boom Huckjam, but in my generation Tony Hawke wasn't an established founder of a successful enterprise. He wasn't a father, wasn't an icon, wasn't much more than a kid my age who was gaining fame and notoriety by his skateboarding talent. My friends idolized him and now, as a parent myself, I can see and appreciate what a great role model he was then and continues to be today.

Because my boyfriend in high school skateboarded and was into anything and everything that revolved around the sport, I too, albeit indirectly and mostly feigned, held a certain degree of interest. While he and his buddies would sit and watch the *Bones Brigade* movies, studying the moves and trying to copy the lingo, their girlfriends and I would roll our eyes, grit our teeth and then quickly flash our fake smiles whenever they looked our way. Though he was cute, I never thought I'd see or hear too much more about Tony Hawke after I dumped that particular boyfriend.

Fast-forward 15 years. I haven't seen or talked to any of the former skate punks I used to know, though I have heard they are all professional engineers, photographers, attorneys and business owners these days. And my mother was worried I'd end up as some druggy cling-on if I continued to hang out with them. What a laugh. She'd never recognize any of them now, or their salaries, I'm sure. I've just tossed Josh's Happy Meal to him in the backseat when I hear his squeal of delight, "It's Tony Hawke! I love Tony Hawke!" I do my best to not slam on the brakes. Lo and behold, his included toy is a Tony Hawke action figure, complete with skateboard and ramp. What do you know?

"Let me see that!" I snatch his Tony doll and begin a thorough scrutiny. At the time I was surprised to see that someone from my teen years had made it to action hero status. I hadn't familiarized myself with the Boom Huckjam nor had I followed Tony's apparent road to success. I hadn't given him too much thought, truth be told. I watched in the rearview mirror as Josh made him do tricks in the air as we drove away. Grinning, Josh chanted, "Tony Hawke...Tony Hawke..."

I did a little self-education. Funny how one of those skinny, little skater boys who repeatedly flicked his hair out of his eyes while he boarded grew up to create a lucrative business. He also formed a launch pad for young athletes in a variety of venues to perfect their skills and gain a little recognition in the process. Very cool.

I watch Josh breeze by on his board, a wide grin on his face as he waves and rounds a bend in our yard. The crash I hear is a minor one. A small groan then he's back up and going. I'm proud of him for a couple of reasons: everything he does, he gives it his whole heart and no matter what the sport is, he's convinced he is already a professional at it. Self-confidence is a good thing when you're five years old. Brad's most proud of him because he chose a role model who is a multimillionaire. Go figure.

Bracing for the First Day

Recently I picked up a calendar of the academic school year for Brentwood. Wanted to see just how soon kindergarten started. The exact day. This might be comical coming from a mom who once thought she'd home-school her children and participate fully in her youngsters' education. Strange how five years at home with two little boys will do a number on one's perspective.

Before I actually gave birth to anyone, I had visions of first days of school. Shirts tucked in, backpacks on straight, lunchboxes in hand, clean faces grinning broadly at me while the camera goes click-click-click. The reality of what's to come is just a tad different.

"Brad, will you be in town for Josh's first day of school? I may need a little help." I toss out the question while stacking papers and binders on what was once my dining room table. Rifling through the scattered sheets, and then discovering more paperwork that needed to be turned in to the district office, I groan but don't look up. Hearing no response I continue, "I mean, I'd like to get a picture if I can." A picture. One. Poor kid. He deserves so much more. Brad looks at me and makes a face.

"Yikes. How will you do that with Ben there?" Good question. Being autistic, Ben has a few quirks that don't go unnoticed. His fear of cameras is a biggy. Just as long as we don't start singing 'Happy Birthday' to anyone while we're there, I'm sure the moment will pass without anyone getting disfigured. Namely me.

When I started kindergarten, I walked to school with neighborhood kids. My older sister escorted me to my class. I was surprised to see that parents had come to capture the moment on film and see their wee ones off with a big fare-thee-well. Hugs, kisses, cameras clicking wildly. I was pissed. By the end of the day, I had worked myself up into a full tizzy and stormed into the house, slamming the door behind me. I was bawling by the time I choked out my reasoning to my mother. She replied, "I did your teachers a favor by staying home, trust me. Here…we'll take a picture of you right now." And she did. The nerve of that woman.

She loved to pull out the photo and tell people, "This is Carolyn on her first day of school." I grew up listening to that line followed by gales of laughter. She snapped a shot of me weathered and worn, eyes puffy and face blotchy from crying. My hair is sticking up out of my barrette and my skirt is twisted and raised. One knee sock is pulled tightly into the correct position, the other is in a crumpled heap at my ankle. I look like I have just gotten pulled off another child in a fight. To think that I looked that disheveled before even leaving for school always got a big laugh from my mom's friends.

I promised myself that when I had a child, I would make a big hoopla out of his first day of school. If I could possibly stop crying and carrying on, that is. I thought I'd have a hard time saying goodbye and turning him over to 'the other woman'. I didn't foresee his last year at home with me being one where we raced across the planet getting my second child to therapies and specialists, Josh tagging along bored and full of angst. I envisioned at-home art projects, outings to the zoo, T-ball and leisurely trips to the park. Bonding, the all-American way. Not mad dashes out the door, breakfast and lunch in the truck, and dinners sometimes being Lunchables or hot cereal. Josh will sometimes wear socks from the previous day, get his face 'washed' with baby wipes, and has to skip parties and school activities so that his brother can attend doctor appointments and evaluations during those times. In an attempt at being a good mom, I enrolled him in preschool and gymnastics, purely for socialization.

"You're having fun, right?" I once asked him, kind of desperate to find out if I was a terrible mother, "You like your school and sports, don't you?"

"They're okay," he replied, "But don't forget—I still want to go to kindergarten." Forget? Not a chance. I'm counting down the days with him.

Spay Dodger

"**Come on, isn't** she cute?' I implore one of my son's in-home therapists to hold a feisty calico kitten. She is taking a break from an Applied Behavior Analysis ("ABA") session with Ben and has come out to see the litter of kittens born in our home three weeks ago. The five babies bring the grand total to nine cats living under our roof. I am beginning to feel like I am walking a fine line between devoted animal lover and schizophrenic cat lady.

Last year I rescued a stray female cat off a neighbor's roof. She thanked me by appearing at my backslider with her two kittens the following day. "Aww." I was beside myself. I fed them, played with them, and eventually decided to keep all three as indoor/outdoor kitties and get them spayed and vaccinated. Both my husband and our original indoor cat were less than thrilled with the executive decision. On the day I was due to haul the little family to Martinez for their surgeries, only the two babies appeared while Beatrice, the mama kitty had elected to be truant. Thus, she missed her ride, and I was down to transporting only two felines which repeatedly barfed, peed, and caterwauled the entire ride to and from the animal shelter.

Fast-forward a good six months. The kittens have acclimated to our home, our original cat is no longer suicidal, and we haven't seen Beatrice since the day before the girls were spayed. Three days before Easter we are expecting out of town guests. The rain is coming down heavy and the winds are cold and strong. In my rush to get the last of the trash out before our company arrives, I dash out to the porch and stumble over the fattest cat I have ever seen. Beatrice. So pregnant she can't even sit up straight. Change of plans. With a meow and a purr, she makes her way past me and flops her protruding self down near the fireplace to dry out. "Awww." I am such a sucker.

After a bit of sweet-talking, Brad is persuaded to make her a warm bed in the garage. I refer to it as "the birthing room." We supply the food, water, and kitty bathroom facilities, while awaiting their impending births. In less than two days, five babies are presented to us by a very exhausted Beatrice and it seems our little family has grown. Again, I am beside myself. A slave to mews and peeps, I can't keep myself away and find that I am reporting every minor detail to anyone willing to listen.

"They opened their eyes!" I tell a neighbor. "They mew when they hear my voice," I proudly brag to a bagboy at Safeway. "They're trying to stand on their own," I whisper knowingly to another mom in the pediatrician's office. Perplexed she had asked, "Who? Your kids?"

"No silly, our kittens. We have five!" I am grinning broadly. She shuddered. "Uh, yuck. I don't envy you."

Within days, Brad has left the state on business, and I have moved everyone in from the garage. I always do what I am advised not to when Brad leaves town. And still, I can't seem to suppress the growing feeling of pride and delight when I see the babies doing everything little kittens should be doing, kitten milestones if you will.

The boys and I watch daily to see the growth and progress of our newest family members, the ones who will stay with us the least amount of time. For now, we hold them, love them, and make sure everyone is well fed and snuggly warm. While we get to enjoy everything that having five kittens will bring to a household, we know the time is coming soon to help them find homes of their own.

In a few weeks our kittens will be ready to venture out on their own. And though she escaped a spaying once before, Beatrice will not be so lucky this time around. That wild girl is getting fixed before I wind up writing a repeat column this time next year.

13

Mama's Boys

Loose Teeth

I wasn't with Josh when he lost either one of his first loose teeth. Good thing too, I may have barfed. While he's one of those kids that pulls, twists, and toys with an unsteady tooth by its roots, I was the exact opposite. My loose teeth would sit in my mouth while I did everything possible to not disrupt their looseness. I barely ate, I hardly drank, I didn't talk too much at all. I did what I could to avoid that undesirable fall out and shaky roll across my tongue.

"Mom look!" Josh had proudly opened wide and displayed a mouthful of ivories. "My toof if woof!" he wiggled the tiny pearl and raised his eyebrows up and down knowingly.

"Oh hey! Whaddayaknow? That's great!" I forced a smile.

He nodded but didn't pull his fingers from his mouth. "Yep, it's rarey fantathtic…"

He was filled with pride, as he should be. The prospect of losing a tooth and entering the unknown realm of "Big Boyhood" was something he had been anticipating for a while. I tried hard to match his enthusiasm. Really, I did but the struggle of not allowing my face to distort and slide into a grimace was a huge one. As the days went by, he had trouble keeping his fingers off that tooth. Constantly, he twisted and turned his wee treasure, just hoping that it would pop out in his palm. The hanging root, the repulsive manner in which his tooth just dangled from his gums got to be too much for me.

Loose teeth make me queasy. It stems from the feeling of amiss I had whenever one of my teeth started to wiggle. Even as a kid, it just didn't feel right. It nauseated me to think that one of my pearly whites was just an apple bite away from breaking free of my gums. I ran from my dad, hand covering my mouth protectively when he'd try to yank out a wiggly tooth. "No!" I'd tell my folks when they'd beg and plead to just have a look-see. I didn't trust them. I soon learned not to tell my parents when one was ready to go, I knew they'd hound me until I offered them a shot at glory.

Only one person's loose tooth has affected me any differently. In second grade I had a mad crush on a boy in my class. I did not find his loose tooth repulsive in the least. I would sneak glances at him poking the tooth with his tongue while working at his desk. Oddly, I felt this was charming. He, like the rest of the second-grade population, had a habit of leaning back in his chair. I sat one day watching the careful way he balanced on the rear two legs of his chair, while tempting fate with the toe of his sneaker brushing the edge of his desk. One careless miscalculation and back he went. "Agh!" he whacked his skull on the desk behind him. I sat forward in my chair to get a glimpse of my love interest sprawled out on his back, flat on the linoleum. Though it wasn't too uncommon in second grade to fall out of your chair, it was uncommon to lose a body part while doing it. What awed me was that as soon as his head made contact with the desk, his tooth took flight and arched perfectly through the air. I had never seen anyone lose a tooth by hitting the back of their head. It intrigued me. It gave me something to consider.

The next time I felt a wiggler coming on, I started whacking the back of my head with my hand. "What are you doing?" My mom screeched, "STOP hitting yourself!" I knew better. I had seen what a smack to the back of the head could do for a loose tooth. It never worked for me, but it didn't stop me from trying.

I eyed Josh as he taps on his tooth with one finger. Slowly I creep up behind him and smack his skull. "Did it work?" I ask innocently. He looks confused as he alternates between rubbing his head and wiggling his tooth as he departs.

Lost and Found Pup

I've got my youngest son pinned to the floor in his bedroom where I am wrestling him, attempting to change a diaper and keep him from turning onto his stomach. He flops around like a fish out of water, bucking and writhing and making me work up a sweat. It's a wonder at all that I saw a flash of black at his window.

Having a bedroom in the front of the house certainly has its advantages. Ben's window looks out onto the street. In the summer children congregate in the shade and sit on our porch-swing with their Capri Suns and Pringles. Ben watches from inside, grinning broadly, but happier to be at a slight distance from all the action. That window tells us who's coming up the walkway, when the mail has arrived, and what the neighborhood kids do while their parents are at work.

On this particular day, I glanced up during the grappling to see a fluffy black face panting on the glass. Forget the diaper. I conceded to the Desitin and baby powder, let Ben fidget and rise to his feet, then watched his naked backside disappear around the corner as he staggered out of his bedroom. As I approached the window, the puppy ducked, then popped up again and barked at me. It cocked its little head then pawed at the screen. I made a beeline to the front door.

I clapped and squealed like a 6-year-old when I saw the little fellow come running. "Oh puppy-puppy, my puppy boy…" I cooed as I swept him up and spun him around. It was love at first sight. But in this house, one doesn't say "puppy" without getting a reaction.

"Puppy?" asks Josh, rounding the bend in the living room and scratching his leg. "Is there a pup…" he gasps seeing me holding the black fluff which is now nuzzling my neck and sniffing my ears. He leaps and does a little jig before coming to us and fussing over the new baby. "Can we keep him?' he begs. I feel it too but shake my head 'no'.

Before he has a breakdown, I try to explain to Josh that baby black Labradors don't normally appear out of the blue on rainy days. The puppy settles down in my lap and starts tapping at my ponytail with his paws. "Sweetie, this little guy (tap, tap) has a home somewhere. The best thing (swat, pat) we can do is to help him find his family."

"But we can be his family," Josh pleads. I know this feeling. It was because of this passion to rescue needy animals that we have had another puppy in the past. Also, some mice, a rabbit, two kittens, and an iguana. Plus, a turtle, a frog, and a few dozen fish we took from a stream down on Marsh Creek. I'm not totally unfamiliar with what Josh is feeling. But I also realize that black labs are rarely strays. Plus, the tummy on this little guy tells me he is well fed and most certainly, very missed. Keeping him might be fun for us, but devastating to another family.

Enter Josh's father. "Oh, you have got to be kidding. Where did he come from?" I start to answer, and Josh blurts out, "Mommy gave him to me! She said we could keep him!" I do a cartoon double take as Josh does his puppy dance again. I know he is a much better listener than that.

"We can keep him until Mommy finds his real home," Brad tells Josh. At least we are on the same page. "Start making fliers and call the paper," he tells me. I nod and watch the two of them take the pup to the backyard. I call Joanne.

"Neener-neener-neener, we got a puppy…" I sing. "And he's black and he's cute and I just love him!" Might as well enjoy the interim, right? I am going on and on with what we'll name him, where he'll sleep, and who he'll love best when I wander into Ben's room and look out his front window. Through the smudge marks left by paws and drool I can see something. A girl. Crying. Looking under cars and pacing frantically up and down the sidewalk. "I'll call you back," I tell Joanne.

I meet her out in front and give her a hug. Tell her the puppy is with us and is just fine. She cries harder now from relief. Doing the right thing is sometimes easy.

So, we had a puppy for all of 15 minutes this week. I still can't stop myself from looking out that window. Who knows what will turn up next?

No More Sweet Moves

"I'm not sure that's such a good idea," Brad looks skeptical as I position myself to do another backbend. I wave him off with a flick of my wrist.

"Yay Mommy!" cheers Josh, "You can do it!" I nod smugly at him and bend over backwards, sticking my tongue out at Brad while upside down.

Josh high-fives me when I return to upright. I ignore the burning sensation that starts creeping down my shoulder blades.

"Seriously Carolyn, you're not in college anymore. I think you should quit while you're ahead." The husband begins to look worried as he spies me rubbing my bicep. To prove that I am just fine I begin walking on my hands and while overturned tell him, "What we really need is a trampoline." I have been gunning for one of those since we bought our house nine years ago.

Josh starts bouncing around as if on a springboard panting, "We… want…a…trampoline!" Brad is shaking his head "No" at him, then at me. If looks could kill, I'd have fallen from my inverted position and lay in a heap at his feet. I grin and shrug, then bound back up onto my feet. I bow to my applauding son. Something pops and my neck starts to tingle. With a little effort, I can keep this smile plastered on.

"Have you ever been on a trampoline?" My father-in-law asks me. We have gathered at the in-laws' for dinner and thanks to Josh's prompting, a few gymnastic stunts as well.

"I took it in college," I reply, "Along with tractor driving." I see his eyebrows go up, a smile playing on his lips, but it's true. My friend Julie insisted that taking a course on tractor driving was the ideal way to meet nice young cowboys. Twenty-three other girls thought this same thing and we suffered through an entire quarter of hauling dirt and hay to the only males in sight: the pigs in the pig-barn.

"Your parents ship you off to Davis and you take Trampoline and Tractor Driving?" Brad is incredulous, "They must be so proud." Actually, they are. My dad being a farmer was more impressed that I came home knowing the inner workings of a tractor, than he was of the diploma I was holding a few months ahead of schedule. "I didn't *major* in either of those classes, I took them for fun." I'm getting a little annoyed.

Josh is trying to pull off a headstand as we bicker. Seeing this, I decide to forgo further participation in the debate and join my young son instead. On our heads we make faces at one another. This is more my style, Josh's too.

"You're making a huge mistake, being like that. I don't know who you think you are," Brad's warning tone just eggs me on.

"Check me out, Brad," I call, "I'm Mary Lou Retton!" I beam hugely, using my entire face. "No, no wait! I'm Kari Strug," my voice is high and animated, "I saved the 1996 Olympic games with my vault onto a fractured ankle." I start wriggling and thrusting. "Look at my sweet moves!" Josh is cackling at the show. Not amused, the hubby saunters out.

Five minutes later I lay with my head in my mother-in-law's lap. "Ow, ow, ow…" I whisper. Sympathetically, she pats my arm. "I can hardly move my neck." She is quiet, nods occasionally and rubs my throbbing shoulder blade for me. I'm not quite ready to admit that I crashed and burned during one of my sweet moves.

"I was doing headstands with Josh over the weekend," she tells me. "I know how you feel. I just didn't gyrate and flail about like you. That might have been your downfall." That and the apple martini I had with dinner. Liquid valor. I should know better.

"Come on Mary Lou, go get an icepack. I'll distract the peanut gallery." I overhear her in the living-room say, "Check out my sweet moves," as I steal into the kitchen and raid the freezer. I put the icepack on my head instead.

The Kid Writes It Like It Is

I received this little ditty after I told Josh that I would like to finish watching American Idol tonight, then it would be bedtime.

> Dear Mom,
>
> I do not like the TV. I want to smash the TV. Why do you have to watch something that is ADULT CONCEPT every night? Can't you just let me watch what I want to watch just for one night?
>
> From Josh

I invited him to join me...I even offered to make us popcorn. But no, *American Idol* was not to be outdone by *Sponge Bob Squarepants*. Not that night. Not with David Cook singing "Day Tripper," are you kidding me? Sometimes I just have to put my foot down.

In the past, when my kid has been upset, I've encouraged him to write down his feelings and share them with a person he trusts. And while I'm glad he is following instructions, I'm a bit surprised that I am the target of his frustration.

Dear Mom,

The pasta you made tonight was sticky. I like harder oodles. Tomorrow you can try again.

From Josh

PS: white sauce ONLY! REMEMBER??????

Dear Mom,

I do NOT like going to bed so early. You stay up EVERY night and do whatever you want. I think you are not right to do that.

From Josh

And my personal favorite:

Dear Mom,

I wrote you this song...you are so beautiful. So beautiful. When you come home from work you look pretty. Is that a baby in your tummy? I think you are pregnant. I think you haven't told me yet. Wahoo. Will it be a sister?

From Josh

PS Why didn't you just tell me?

Oh, dear. Not pregnant, just slacking off on my workouts. And aside from the fact that I don't work outside my home, it was kind of poetic. Very delicately, I broke the news that no, Mommy wasn't having a baby anytime soon...he responded by writing something down he never shared with anyone, including me.

Age eight must be a frustrating year, I don't remember. I do know that I never wrote down how I felt, I just drew pictures of me living with another family, my *real* family; I was pretty much convinced the one I was stuck with couldn't possibly be mine. Switched at birth, adopted as a baby, it didn't matter. I just knew there had to be a bigtime blunder that occurred in the early 70s which left me living with these meanies and my real parents endlessly searching for me.

That fantasy bubble popped when I demanded to see my birth certificate and my mom produced it. Stunned, I read the cold hard facts: they had created me. They had control. The 'puppet masters', I called them. I didn't like being controlled. And as parents normally do, they let it slide. They weren't offended. Somehow, they understood my irritation, even though I battled them point for point on everything until the day I moved out for college. Then the 'puppet masters' became the 'investors' and I developed an entire new appreciation for the folks subsidizing my education.

But with Josh, I don't know what to expect for future letters. I do know though that soon I will have a little chat with my boy and suggest the written word can also be used as a way to communicate your pleasure with someone, a way of showing gratitude. Then perhaps I can look forward to some kind words regarding my noodles.

Not a Peddler by Choice

"Let's have a garage sale!" my husband suggested. "Get rid of some of this stuff, make a little money. Come on—it'll be fun!"

Fun. Going ice-skating is fun. The beach is fun. I'll even take a trip to the dentist with my 6-year-old son and make that into an enjoyable adventure, compared to having a garage sale.

I'm not the hugest fan of peddling my wares. I can't sell. It's not my gift. While some folks can sell ice to an Eskimo, I can't even sell a bad idea to a naughty child. Those who know me well just accept it as the norm, possibly even write it off as a personality quirk. I think I'm the victim of a traumatic selling experience.

It probably started back in the 1970s, when my parents forced me to participate in their garage sale ventures. I dreaded the almighty garage sale, with its one-day massive event status. With the garage sale looming ahead, my whole week would be ruined, if not by mere thought alone. When I knew the upcoming Saturday was going to be spent sitting at a table watching perfect strangers debate the worth of something I own, I would sink into what I thought was, a noticeable depression. No one noticed.

"Tomorrow morning! 7 a.m.!" my dad would bellow and rub his hands together. "Buyers a'comin!" Big smile. Playful smack on mom's butt. Chuckle, chuckle. I did what I could to keep my dinner down.

Why on earth those two loved selling crap escapes me, even now. Year after year, they insisted on my involvement. And how does any 7-or 8-year-old kid really determine the value of anything when questioned by an anxious buyer, someone willing to pay either more or less than the marked price? I had no such skill in negotiation. The garage sale was my earliest experience in second guessing myself. Was $5 too much? Or was it worth 50 cents? I wound up just giving my stuff away. Even now, I shudder at the thought of having to debate, bargain, barter, or enter squabbles based on the cost, or perceived value of anything.

One of the last garage sales I partook in was a memorable one. I sat sulking behind a card table piled high with knickknacks and trinkets I just dumped on it by persuasion of my mother. She, again, insisted I sell, sell, sell! I hid my nose in a book and prayed for a slow morning, vowing to never again sit in a beach chair on my driveway and watch people fondle my semi-valuables.

"Carolyn, are those some of your school chums?" my mom sang out gaily. She waved them over. What? I fumbled my book and as I leaned over to retrieve it, whacked my head on the corner of the table. In eighth grade, the last place I wanted to be spotted was exactly where I was. My sister clued in on this immediately. She smiled widely and then bounded from her post to feign interest in what I was displaying. Oh, no. Nervous now, I eyed her carefully. I wasn't happy that kids I knew were going to see me in this predicament. As they neared, I saw that while I did recognize them from school, they were NOT my chums. These were girls who made fun of kids like me, they didn't need to see my nerdy garage sale items for added ammunition.

I felt my 'fight or flight' reflex kick into high gear. I bolted. In my haste, I didn't correctly gauge the distance between my hip and my card table, and as I shot from the beach chair, I again made contact with it. My display launched into unexpected flight. Within seconds, a shower of scented erasures dotted the driveway. I may have avoided the girls all together, had I kept my cool. But no, I needed to upend my table and hurl the things I had dug from the depths of my drawers out at them. The sound of all things plastic rolling along the cement, combined with high-pitched giggles and snickering still haunts me.

Brad unfolds a card table and tells me now, "See? You can even sit behind this and read if you want to, it'll be great." I stare blankly at him and shake my head 'no'. He tries to break me with pleading. My resistance is just as strong. And since I'm too grown up for 'flight', I choose my other option and put up my dukes.

Oh, the Horror!

In all the years I have been a homeowner, I can't recall one time that I have been properly prepared for Halloween. And that's even living by my own mantra of the 7 P's: proper prior planning prevents piss poor performance. I have Easter and Christmas in the bag, St. Patty's and Valentines all mapped out a month ahead of time. Shoot, we even make cake on the Presidents' birthdays. But on All Hollow's Eve, The Dodds can never seem to have anything scary decorating the front of their house except for maybe ladders, tool boxes, and filthy work boots that Brad has left strewn across our yard during his "construction process." And that's the thing. When you're married to a guy who owns his own construction company, your home, no matter how hard you fight it, becomes a construction zone. Every place becomes the right place for spare tools.

Each fall, Brad embarks on a front yard project, finishing up with a lovely look just in time for winter, but leaving our property in shambles all through Halloween. This year we're putting in a walkway, a retaining wall, and expanding the driveway. Scatter a few cement boulders, redwood trees, and decorative ground cover and voila, *projectus completus*. However, we are not at that point quite yet.

"Our front yard looks horrible!" I told him last week. "It's actually frightening little children."

"Perfect." He wired together more rebar and told me to watch myself on the drainage ditch.

"It's like a creepy maze you have to go through just to get to the front door..." I kicked aside his drill, then shimmied over a flat of concrete. "How will we ever hand out candy?"

"We're handing out candy this year?" He looked surprised. "But we never do."

That's not entirely true. We do hand out candy, we've just done it from afar in years past. Before we moved, we belonged to a group of rowdies in the old hood. All the neighbors would cluster together in lawn chairs on someone's driveway, drinking hot cider and passing out treats. It's always been a group affair with the kids running amuck and the parents hoping everyone makes it home safely. (Sip, sip)

One year we were considerate enough to tape a sign on a ladder in our driveway pointing to where prospective trick-or-treaters could find us and how many people are that thoughtful, I ask you?

A few years back I hadn't done much in the way of decorating for Halloween, but I did have Brad put up our big fake Christmas tree in October, since he was traveling so much with work. I didn't want to be stuck with that project while he was out of town. He did it with the expected amount of grumbling. When I opened the door for the first trick-or-treater, the kid said, "Oh that's cool—it's like *The Nightmare Before Christmas!*" to which Brad replied dryly, "You have no idea..."

So far, this Halloween is shaping up to look kind of similar. We're still totally unprepared for trick or treaters, which is fairly expected, if you know us. But I did catch Brad dragging out of patio furniture the other day, which can only mean one thing: I need to make some cider and meet some neighbors.

Passing the Gymnastic Torch

Perhaps it was the backflip Josh did off the couch, or the flying leap he took from the dresser to the bed, either way—I knew this kid was in desperate need of an outlet for his physical energy.

"Mommy, watch me!" he proceeded to strike a pose on the edge of my dining room table, gather his balance, and then bound from his platform to touch his toes before landing on his feet and bowing at me. He grinned.

"I think you need to be in gymnastics," was all I could say. Yet, memories past of Josh in gymnastics were not all good ones. We quietly un-enrolled when Josh was two before we were kindly asked to withdraw him, I'm sure. His love affair with the trampoline left little desire to try anything else. That combined with his fiery temper was not a combination for success at that time.

Since a few years have passed, I'm willing to try it again. Plus, Josh's knack of pulling off stunts that may take other kid's months to perfect is an adrenaline pumping reminder that he has a natural ability which really should be nurtured.

"It makes sense," says a friend, "Weren't you a gymnast as well?"

I suppose that's using the term loosely. Gymnastics didn't come so naturally for me. I took more delight in wearing leotards and tights than I did in doing stomach crunches and laps around the gym to warm up my muscles. I adored perfecting gymnastic feats that I had worked hard to call my own but loathed the time period before when I crashed and burned at the foot of a beam or a vault while learning new routines. Too often I lay stunned and panting under a set of uneven bars wondering how I slipped, how I missed my mark.

Boys and school dances won out in high school, and I didn't do another roundoff back handspring until I got to college. By then I was ready for the serious commitment it took to be a gymnast, but unfortunately, my body was not. Routines proved harder the second time around and I learned the hard way that not only had I missed my opportunity to be a serious athlete, but with age comes more aches and pains that a younger body may find easier to shake off. For the second time, I walked away from gymnastics.

And yet, here's my son, soaring from couch to couch, walking on his hands, turning cartwheels without knowing what he's doing has an actual name. Then to see the boy on a trampoline! Well, anyone would think he was born to jump and flip, turn and dive, and move his little body in such a random sequence of flowing motions. It's almost unnatural.

Watching Josh fills me with pride, but also a sense of familiarity. My body remembers moving like that, though I'd be far pressed to ever get it to do that again. And so, I'll sign him up. Why not? Without saying so, I'll pass him the torch with the flicker of hope that he keeps it lit for the both of us.

Sharing the Goods

For the first time in the history of Halloween, I have not once raided my sons' buckets after all of the hoopla. Candy doesn't look good right now and it's not because of any amount of will power. It's because I have a sore throat. Brad did the honors for the both of us though, and left Josh wailing "You're eating all the good stuff!" In perfect fatherly fashion, Brad replied, "Ok then, pick out what you don't want and I'll eat that."

Stooped, Josh said nothing for a minute, then piped up, "Well, it's all good. And it's all MINE!" With that he snatched his pumpkin full of loot and tried to make a run for it. Although he may have been dressed as Buzz Lightyear, he didn't move like Buzz Lightyear. Especially after being weighted down with layers of clothing. Brad caught him by the tie-on helmet string and said smoothly, "Since your mother and I took you out to get all this candy, technically it was a group effort. Therefore, it's all of ours. So, find me something to eat Buzz."

I rolled my eyes at the scene and then had a vivid memory of what went down at my house after I went trick or treating as a kid. Dad always inspected the booty while Mom feigned interest in finding something dangerous in our sacks. Like an apple with a razorblade or some poisoned cookie. My bag was returned weighing considerably less than it did when I handed it over. I was understandably suspicious but had no proof of their thievery.

This method was successful until I hit 9 years of age, or thereabouts. I charted my candy after that and made lists of what I had reaped, and how many of each. I would faithfully check my candy stash when returning home from after school, only to be shocked and sickened that my parents had been looting my treasure.

"You are eating my candy!" I yelled one night. "Eat Andrea's instead!"

No, no, they would lie. You must have counted wrong. Tally over, recheck your charts, surely you are mistaken. I heard it all, always told to me with little smiles lurking beneath their serious demeanors.

One year they made the horrific suggestion to put all the candy acquired into one bowl and then the entire family could have a treat every now and again. Both Andrea and I vetoed that proposal, which landed us back to charting and grafting our spoils.

Another year my mom got so tired of me sneaking candy, she went on a mission, determined to make me get sick of it. I opened my lunch box at school and found not a sandwich and fruit, milk and a cookie, but loads and piles of candy. When my box opened, it was like a piñata broke open and candy spilled out onto the lunchroom table. It silenced the crowd around me, but only for a second. Then 10 fifth graders around me screamed in delight and dove into my stash. I was lucky to have wound up with a single rectangle Bit-O Honey that day. Mission unaccomplished; the only thing she succeeded in doing was making herself look super cool in the eyes of a bunch of fifth graders.

After watching Josh squirm and shriek while trying to hold his pumpkin out of Daddy's reach, while Daddy held a firm arm around Josh and attempted to ransack his bucket, I was thankful for only one thing: my throat was sore and I had no desire to help Daddy.

Silky's Hijinks

Someone once said there is no reality, only perspective. That's especially true when it comes to what one finds enjoyable about homework. Our 5-year-old is at the age where the prospect of real homework looms before him and his excitement is barely containable.

In preschool, Josh's 'homework' was a once a month or so assignment that included taking home the class mascot: a mangy stuffed skunk that looked like it had been coughed from the bowels of a stuffed animal graveyard. On rotation, it spends the night regularly with all 25 kids in the class and when Silky comes home with Josh, I fight off the urge to disinfect, delouse, and thoroughly sanitize the thing.

"Ew!" Brad made a face and held it at arm's length the last time Silky was brought home. He shook it by the ear, "This thing probably has fleas…" I nodded in agreement. Then he sniffed Silky and dry heaved. Still gagging, he dropped the skunk to the floor and punted it across the room just as Josh entered the scene.

"Silky!" Josh wailed and then scooped him up and covered his matted face with kisses. I made a mental note to wipe Josh's lips off as soon as possible. "I'm making you write about that in Silky's book!" Josh stormed out. That was part two of the assignment: each child was to dictate to a parent what Silky did when he had a sleepover.

"That thing is disgusting," Brad shuddered. "See where it's been before here." I grabbed Silky's journal and page-by-page went through each of his adventures. With horror, I read aloud about Silky taking trips to flea markets, zoos, doctor's offices and riding around on various pets. It was no wonder he smelled like an outhouse.

When I next saw Josh and Silky, they were in the backyard. Silky had been buried in the pea gravel and Josh was proceeding to cover him with dirt and army men. Interesting. I half contemplated returning Silky to school without a bath, but then thought better of it. I don't need the next parent wondering where Silky had been last and why he smelled like… well…a skunk. I just needed to find my opportunity to snatch the dirtball and toss him in with a load of laundry.

From the pea gravel, Silky went swinging, sliding, and then became the "ball" in a game of catch with a neighborhood child. Brad brought out a bat to the boys and told them, "Here, make this game really fun to watch for me and your mom."

Silky narrowly escaped a beating. Josh and his buddy abandoned the bat and opted to take turns racing with the skunk on their heads instead. Nervously, I looked on and prayed that I wouldn't be receiving a call from his mother in a few days telling me her son had contracted lice somewhere.

That evening I sat with Josh as he went through the day's events. I was scribbling his words as fast as he was saying them when I feigned that a great idea just hit me. "I know!" I told him. "Let's give Silky one more adventure! A ride in our washing machine!" Josh looked horrified.

"No! Nobody ever bathes Silky!" You don't say. "We all like Silky the way he is!" That seemed true enough. Josh certainly hadn't complained about Silky's aroma, the dreadlocks on his back, his missing eye, or the popped seam on his underbelly. What to do? When all else fails, offer up a disclaimer. The concluding line in Silky's journal reads: "...and although Josh's mommy chased me down and tried to bathe me, I successfully dodged her efforts and escaped the soap and water. Signed, Silky"

No reality, only perspective.

That Man Makes Me Nervous

Every holiday season I'm entertained by how my son's perspective of Santa Claus changes. Now, at age 5, he's still a believer, but a skeptical one at that. We are extra careful in our conversation, tone of voice, and explanation when he questions us about The North Pole, St. Nick, elves, and reindeer. It's an interesting position for parents to be in, explaining the ins and outs of Christmas, especially when prior to the holiday season, we work hard at being honest and encouraging children to do the same. Throw in the true meaning behind the holiday, and it's a recipe for confusion for children of Josh's age.

"Mom," he asked the other day, "Is Santa coming this year?"
"Yes."
"And is he coming down the chimney?"
"Um...yes." I can already see where this line of questioning is going.

"Why don't you just let him in the front door like a normal human being?" He asks, "And why does he have to come when we're asleep? That man makes me nervous, being in our house like that. What if he steals something?" Okay, we've obviously not allowed Josh to watch enough Christmas television fare yet, if he thinks good old St. Nick is a thief. But truly, it can be confusing. Take for example his view of elves:

While waiting in line at a furniture store with me last week to see Santa, Josh grew bored and began a conversation with one of the festively dressed employees. "Are you really an elf?"

She flashed me a nervous smile, said, "Sure!" and gave Josh a big grin.

"Hmmm…" says Josh, "Do you like it? Working at The North Pole, I mean." She's quiet and then answers, "I do! But we're extra busy this time of year…" He cuts her off and asks, "You're taller than the other elves, right?" I steer him away from her and attempt to focus his attention on his upcoming turn with Santa. Even still, he pondered aloud, "Do you think the elves are happy?"

I appreciate his train of thought; I wondered the same thing as a kid. Were they held at The North Pole against their will? Did they really want to make toys? Certainly, all elves couldn't like that line of work, could they? The classic Christmas cartoon with the elf who longed to be a dentist got me thinking as a kid.

I wonder how much longer we have with Josh and his belief, albeit it's a cautious one. It may be silly, but I'd like to make the magic last as long as possible. Kids learn too early on in life about hardship and struggle, the reality of responsibility. I suppose I'm one of those mushy parents who want to see joy light up the eyes of her children when they spot their own home decorated in lights. Witness the wonderment of the moment when they spy boot-prints near the fireplace. Knowing that all families celebrate the season differently, I'd like to teach respect for diversity and hold close the little treasures of tradition. Someday, I would like to overhear Josh say to his friends when he's older, "Yeah, my parents always decorate the heck out of our home," and catch the touch of embarrassment in his voice, mixed with a twinge of pride.

My sister and I had a tradition every Christmas, it's something we still laugh about. We'd work out intricate plans of sneaking downstairs in the wee hours of Christmas morning. On Christmas Eve, she'd walk me though our entire strategy, counting our paces from room to room, and then jotting down notes as she went. I'd tag along, nodding in full agreement. Then we'd sprawl out across her bed with our notebooks and draw up different floor plans to the house and brainstorm how we'd get from point A to point B. The real tradition though, was what occurred the following morning. I'd get up and tip-toe into her room with my pages of diagrams and charts, rouse her from her sleep, only to be told to go back to bed. Happened every year. Never once did we act out our plans.

Last year Josh surprised me by dragging a garbage bag full of toys out of his room. He said, "When Santa comes, can you have him take these toys and make sure other children get them?" And just last night I saw him rifling in the cupboards for a garbage bag. Could it be that he's starting a tradition of his own? Holiday magic in the making...and perhaps still a little belief.

Chip Off the Old Block

The 10 Second Rule

Caller ID is a popularity contest that everyone has lost at some time or another. There you are chatting happily away about your new hot pants and the sassy 5-inch Peg Bundy heels you want to buy to complete the look and…

"Oh, can you hold on a second?" your friend cuts in, "I have another call."

Usually before you can even offer a reply, you'll hear a "click" and be on the waiting end of Caller ID. I normally use this time to inspect the dry skin on my heels or do my jaw exercises to rid myself of that bothersome double chin. I don't ever get very far in any task I perform while on hold because of a simple decree a friend made up which we implement religiously, but only with one another.

Termed "The 10 Second Rule," it's the unwritten law that once you are made to wait for 10 seconds, you have permission to hang up and then be phoned back with an apology and promises of free Starbucks coffee and/or Diet Pepsi. Depends on who owes whom.

Most of the time the rule works just fine. Occasionally, a situation arises when one party is in disagreement about how long 10 seconds really is. Consider this charming little exchange that took place a few weeks prior:

Me: "So, there I was riding my bike with Ben in the kid-seat and he was grabbing at my jeans and pulled down the waistband! I was so embarrassed! My crack is out for all to see, and I can't reach back to swat his hand away when a teenager in a car drives by and yells, 'CRACK KILLS!' (I start snorting and hooting.)

Joanne: "Um yeah...that sounds great. Hey, can you hold on for a sec?" (Click)

Knowing Joanne will be a while I immediately hang up and anticipate her return call in a few minutes. Imagine my surprise when the phone rings right away.

Me: "Hello?"

Joanne: That was NOT 10 seconds. I owe you nothing. I am *soooo* not bringing you coffee. You fully cheated and deserve to be thirsty.

I agree. I did cheat, but she has a bad habit of stretching her 10 seconds out to 30 or 40. Even more if it's her husband beeping in. I do understand. I've been on the other end of it too—when a relative calls long distance or an old friend you haven't talked to in a while. It normally takes a lot longer than 10 seconds to tell them you'll call them back. After chatting for 30 seconds or more, I rationalize that Joanne has probably hung up anyway and I might as well finish my conversation and just bring her a drink when I can.

And how do you even try to explain the 10 Second Rule to anyone in less than 10 seconds? It doesn't work. Even more maddening is when the party who has put you on hold doesn't expect you to wait longer than 10 seconds, and you do, and then THEY hang up with their second call before even checking back with you. Happens all the time:

Me: (calling Joanne) "You never clicked back over."

Joanne: "It was my Aunt Mary calling long distance, sorry about that. (Pause) Why? Did you wait?" (She is incredulous.)

Me: "Well, kinda. I had nothing really going on here, so I thought...well maybe...I don't know." (I start to pick at the dry skin on my heels.)

Joanne: "I was on for over a half hour! How long did you wait?"

Me (lying): "Only like 10 minutes or so, don't worry about it." (Was it really 30? How is that possible? Gee, am I pathetic or what?)

The 10 Second Rule—you can call it whatever you want. But in our case, someone winds up with a free drink and the other is left with a reminder to cut it short next time. How can you argue with a rule like that?

The Child Tells a Joke

"**What did the** mama tomato say to the baby tomato?" my 4-year-old son asks me. Before I can even offer a guess, he spurts out, "Ketchup!" This is how it goes. Josh tries to tell a joke but forgets half of it and then bombards his listener with the answer so as to avoid losing his big hurrah when someone actually guesses right. The first few times were funny. It's evolved into slightly painful by this point. We sit, under minor duress, listening to him work through his repertoire, repeat himself a couple of times, change his answer, shake his noggin to clear his head, mutter "Oh yeah, oh yeah," then revert back to the original punch line. We force smiles. Our support is met with another barrage of chopped up riddles. Imagine sitting through a very long movie, being two minutes from the end, then having it start over because it wants to change its plotline midway.

This time he has caught me in the middle of counting ketchup bottles in the pantry, and the irony of this doesn't escape me. I'm trying to remember buying eight bottles of ketchup, and while racking my brain, I am entertained by the one-man show I call "Son".

"Knock, knock,"

I don't answer.

"*Knock, knock!*" he persists.

"We don't want any," I sing out. He giggles. Then tries again. I respond, "Nobody's home."

One more attempt gets him, "Try the doorbell…"

Now he gets mad. "MOM! Say, 'who's there?' Okay? Just say it."

"It." I can't help myself. He's too easy. I can hardly believe I am torturing my own kid like this, but the evil side of me is internally snickering. Plus, still trying to justify the number of ketchup bottles I am staring at. I don't know why I would have so much ketchup and in trying to figure this out, bad wins over good. Until I see the look on his face and realize I am one step away from pushing Josh too far. Oh okay.

"Who's there?' I counter.

"Salt and Pepper."

I can't imagine where this is going. "Salt and Pepper who?"

He buckles over as if he's heard the most hysterical one liner, belts out a slew of fake laughter, starts smacking his forehead with his hand and then hops around on one foot. I stand slack jawed watching this and waiting for the punch line.

He reels me in. "Salt and Pepper who?" I ask again. He drops to the ground and starts spinning in circles while he lay on his side. He holds his gut and laughs long and hard. Physical comedy is about to become one man stronger. It is here that I understand we have a small miscommunication. He thinks my response IS the punch line and has no clue that his joke requires one more sentence. Oh dear.

He pops up and wipes his forehead. The kid was made sweaty by fake laughing. "That was a GOOD one Mom!" he tells me. Goes so far as to slap me on the back, congratulating me for my part in this little exchange. "Salt and pepper who…now that's funny!"

What I find humorous is that a 4-year-old child feels confidently that he can discern between good comedy and bad. A true joke and something that warrants canned laughter.

"I've got another one for you," I tell him, "You'll love this. Why did the silly mommy buy eight bottles of ketchup?"

His face is curiosity mixed with hopeful anticipation. He licks his lips, breaths in deep, and whispers, "Why?" His hands cover his mouth as tiny giggles escape from behind closed fingers. He hunches his shoulders, my cue that he is about to launch into another fit of hilarity.

"Because she is losing her mind and needs a vacation!" I squeal. That did it. As he squirms and writhes at my feet, his body convulsing with snorts and hoots, I realize something. We all love a good joke every now and then. Especially the ones with a hint of truth to them.

The Escape Artist

Exasperation has reached new heights in our home. It was bad when at 15 months, Josh learned how to hurl his tiny body over his crib railing and find his way to our bed…but now…at 26 months, he has learned to free himself from the custom designed bed that Daddy built. I suppose we should be grateful we have a clever little gent among us. I'm sure it's a blessing that his creative streak is in full force right now. I constantly remind myself of the studies which prove mischievous children actually have high IQs. Never will I anticipate full nights of rest and uninterrupted naps with two boys who will let me sleep without worry of escapes and explorations.

Josh's discovery of mastering the latches on his bed was a surprising and delightful event. For him. For us it marked the beginning of an all too familiar dilemma. How do we keep him in bed? It wouldn't be too bad if he wasn't such an early riser. I'm probably the only parent thanking God for the time change right now- since starting my day now means being yanked out of my warm cocoon at 5:45 a.m., rather than 4:45 a.m.

God bless him, he doesn't make a sound until one of us opens an eye, but normally…just feeling him in the room is enough to make me wonder with panic filled curiosity what he may be up to so quietly. It's always the same thing: staring. He's staring right at me, waiting for an eye to slit open and peek at him. Upon seeing that eyelid quiver, he's shouting and jumping, "Get up! Get up! Hot cocoa, hot cocoa!" I have yet to convince him to go back to bed or even to get in bed with us…when he's up, he's up, and darn it, it's for most of the day too.

Naptime has become a whole new battleground for us. There once was a time when I'd tuck him in, and he'd simply say, "Bye-bye Mom," and roll over and be out. Just like that. I thought I was the luckiest Mom alive. I may have been. But now I am just like all the other moms who have to find creative ways to convince their children for a few minutes of quiet time during the day. Recently, after leaving Josh in bed with toys, stuffed animals, books, and his own viewmaster projector, not to mention soft music playing on a cassette recorder nearby, I walked away from all the pleas to stay up longer and embarked on the mission of getting my 5-month-old down for a nap simultaneously. Ben was just being laid in his crib when his bedroom door opened slowly, and I was confronted with a smiling toddler. Happily, he entered the room, carrying a bunny, a book, a ball, and his milk cup. His spit out his pacifier and said loudly, "Hi MOM! I'm UP! I go play now, bye-bye Mom!" Not so fast little britches. As he leaned to grab his pacifier, he began the lengthy process of dropping and grabbing each item his was holding. I ushered him out the door softly hissing, "Out-out- Ben is sleeping- let's go!" as he shouted for various necessities. It was a disaster. Needless to say, we left Ben crying as we began round two in the naptime battle.

See, I can handle rising early and avoiding naps. It's just that I can't seem to get a drink in the middle of the night or use the bathroom without being surprised by a little visitor, wondering what I'm up to. Rubbing his eyes and scratching his buns and telling me in a tired, squeaky voice, "It's *bwight*- no *yight* Mama." And then back to bed we go, where we begin round whatever it may be of the bedtime battle. Oh, I do love my son, don't get me wrong. He is as funny and goofy as the day is long. And let me tell you—the day IS long—especially with a toddler who just can't seem to keep himself in bed!

The Evolution of the Slumber Party

"Please, please come and help me chaperone this thing!" My friend is begging me, nothing short of it. "Ten teenaged girls up all night, giggling, talking, and carrying on. I can't stand to do it alone…" She is desperate for an ally in her own home. Her 13-year-old daughter is hosting a slumber party this coming weekend and being a single mom, my friend is in need of some support.

"They won't be up all night," I begin to console her, "They'll be OUT all night. You won't even hear them. Unless of course, the cops bring them home, and they're all pretty good about ringing the doorbell." Silence.

"It's true," I continue, "Usually the police will deliver a kid to his or her doorstep if they're out past curfew. At least they did back in my day." As I am saying this, I can hardly believe the words are coming out of my mouth. I hardly feel old enough to be reminiscing about my youth, let alone advising peers on their teenaged kids.

"What did you do to be brought home by the feds?" she is laughing.

"Which time?"

Well, that's not totally true. I don't have an entire menagerie of memories involving the police that I can choose from, just a handful, and even then…most occurred within a two-year time period. In fact, my early slumber party days were void of law enforcement, if memory serves.

The evolution of the slumber party is worth noting though. In elementary school, an invitation to one is sought after with a passion. Once obtained, the partygoer must follow all elementary school slumber party etiquette: Have in her possession one My Little Pony or one Care Bear sleeping bag. Cheap knock offs don't cut it as girls have long acquired their cat claws by sixth grade. She must be wearing or have packed her pink, frilly baby doll pajamas with corresponding animal slippers, any species. Upon arrival, she must be clutching one Esprit or Guess brand overnight bag stuffed with sticker collection and slam book, and lastly— she must come ready to partake in and contribute to long conversations about training bras and shaving.

By junior high, the slumber party had slightly evolved. Games such as 'light as a feather, stiff as a board' took high priority, as did playing the Ouija board and freezing one another's underwear. The prerequisites for this party included having extensive knowledge of hair and makeup courtesy of *Teen* magazine, knowing the home phone numbers of the cutest boys in school, and boldly walking around the neighborhood in the wee hours of the night transporting an arsenal of toilet paper and eggs, after any parents went to bed. Junior high slumber parties always had the same girls in attendance: the know-it-all, the chubby shy one, the follower—a.k.a. the know-it-all's sidekick, a few gigglers, one grumpy girl, and without a doubt—the bawler. There's always one who goes on a crying jag because her parents fight all the time and she's afraid they might get divorced. Occasionally, the fibber might be in attendance at the party. This is the girl who lies incessantly but was extended an invitation by the kind hearted party thrower who wanted to offer the fibber a second chance at being a part of the group. It is at the slumber party that she tells another whopper of a story and gets 'dumped' again by her peers. She will wind up sobbing and begging forgiveness, but don't confuse her with the bawler, whose presence there serves an entirely different purpose.

In high school the term "slumber party" takes on a whole new meaning: one friend spending the night and the two girls sneaking out only to be brought home by local law enforcement. This is why the words "slumber" and "party", when spoken together—say in a request for permission to attend such an event, had my mother halting all activity just to clench her jaw, shut her eyes, and apply deep pressure to her temples. If provoked during this time of self-reflection, the antagonist risked bodily harm or at the very least, the removal of any previously earned privileges.

"Yeah, you'll need some help." I tell my friend. "They're all thirteen or about?" I think for a minute. "Hide your toilet paper and eggs. Maybe you'll get lucky and they'll just stay home and keep you up all night."

No S'mores

Six of us decided to go camping. We decided to bring our children. We decided it would be fun and relaxing and decided that while we were at it, we should all drive separately and have just one more thing to contend with (limited parking) once we arrived.

Okay, so that's not entirely true; the convoy happened at the last minute. Someone forgot a tool, and someone else needed an extra air mattress and before you could say 'This tent smells like mildew', five cars and one trailer were making their way out to Del Valle. Setting up camp doesn't make the top 10 list of fun and easy things to do in the dark with friends. Knowing this, I thought it best to leave last. Last enough to be about three hours behind everyone else. My plan to arrive at a campsite filled with frolicking children, happily drinking men, and women gaily laughing while making s'mores around the campfire seemed like a smart one.

I pulled into the campground and thought for sure my group would be easily recognizable by its roaring bonfire and collection of sport utility vehicles. Nothing. I rolled down my window and listened for the sounds of bass and guitar, positive that by this time, someone would have turned on a little music. Not a peep. I rounded a bend and recognizing Brad's truck, sped up—happily anticipating my entrance to a large group of laughing adults, toasting one another with red cups and playing a serious game of Grab Ass. Instead, I see my husband standing in the road holding a hatchet. I have to assume Grab Ass hasn't started yet. He uses the blade to signal where I should park and huffs back into the wooded underbrush. Upon closer inspection, I see one of Brad's work torches lighting the area. This tells me one thing: six adults and not one of us packed a flashlight.

I hop out and wave, wearing a perma-grin since my youngest son has fallen asleep on the ride and I have the entire evening to goof off. Brad points the hatchet at me. "Don't talk to any of these kids!" he hisses, "They're all on time out!" I look to the campsite and see, in the dark, four small, shadowed bodies. One in the kayak, one on a cooler, one sitting at the picnic table and Josh—picking at the bark on a tree. Three smile widely. Three wave and say, "Hi, Auntie Cawayin!" Not Josh. He glares at his father and then whispers angrily to me, "Where have you been?"

I am secretly pleased that I hadn't missed any fun. But a little bummed that I have to help with the setup. Had I known this, I might have stopped for a snack on the way here. The evening progressed with such comments as "Catherine peed her pants, AGAIN!" and "Where's the G-D Hatchet?" becoming commonplace. By the twelfth time I heard "Can we have s'mores now?" I was ready to inflict a little "Time Out" of my own. Plus, it was cooling down fast.

By midnight our camp was complete, and we were ready for bed.

The Laundry Bunny

Ah…Spring is in the air…trees are blossoming, children are laughing, and laundry baskets are piling up around my house. Not Easter baskets, mind you…laundry baskets. How I wish I could waltz into a room and be taken aback by the sudden 'putting away' of my clothing. No such luck.

Of all the household chores I do, only two do I truly detest: putting away clean clothes and unloading the dishwasher (I'll save the latter for a future column). Ordinarily, I love doing laundry; the eventful sorting of lights and darks, the comforting swish and whirl of the washing machine, even the aroma of warm clothing, fresh from the dryer makes me feel all fuzzy inside. I've even been known to smother my face into the stack of heated fluff, as it sits and waits to be folded. Mmm, I'm easy to please.

But laundry fondness ends here. After the folding part, I lose all delight in the chore. I have absolutely no desire to put clothes back where they belong. And so, they stack up, the laundry baskets. And I do what I can to disguise them. If I'm really desperate I'll stick one in the middle of my dining room table and shrug it off as a centerpiece.

What I really need is a visit from the Laundry Bunny. While some folks wait all year for the Easter Bunny to come to their house and leave baskets filled with candy, artificial grass, and plastic eggs, I hold out hope that someone will show up and take my baskets away. Not too unlike Linus and The Great Pumpkin, I believe in the Laundry Bunny. She WILL rise up and come to a worthy house, bringing the patience and keen eye it takes to get all clothing correctly filed in appropriate drawers.

Through the months I do the laundry, taking the proper steps in getting clothing back where it belongs. True, I'm due to start another load before any of my baskets have been emptied of their folded treasures, but in my defense, it does get accomplished. This time of year, though, I start getting anxious. A tad giddy, a little over excited at the possibility that I may be that worthy person who receives a visit from the Laundry Bunny. I start getting sneaky—leaving more filled baskets in varying rooms, an attempt to demonstrate a dedication to the task, yet a lack of time for completion. If nothing else, perhaps she will take pity on me. Oh, I do have a few tricks up my sleeve that I plan on executing this year: more fabric softener—who wouldn't want to put away soft shirts and pants? An extra dryer sheet—nice smelling towels and socks are hard to resist. And the oh-so-casual slip of the tongue about the Laundry Bunny to my children. If she knows who's been good or bad, as I suspect she does, then

I'm definitely going to try to get on her good list. A bedtime story or two involving the silly antics, yet generous heart of the infamous Laundry Bunny can only win me points.

And so, I wait. With my open mind and my overflowing laundry baskets, I am filled with a joyful anticipation of what may come. So go ahead and mock my efforts, call me crazy, scoff at my determination…and just you wait and see who has empty laundry baskets this Easter Sunday. The Great Pumpkin has nothing on my Laundry Bunny!

Trampoline Love

I had never seen a real trampoline before 1978, and even then—I had an innate feeling that piece of equipment would forever change my life. In 1978 there was no such concept as a "safety regulation." There even may not have been such a thing as a "safety precaution" or a "recommended safety procedure" when it came to the trampolines of the 1970s. I know this because the one I jumped on didn't have a net, it didn't have a pad covering the springs, it didn't even have a nifty little ladder for easy access. I was seven. I could've cared less about safety.

I was pouting that day. My parents had dragged my sister and I into (what felt like) thousands of houses they wanted to inspect before purchasing one, and making us—at long last, residents of Pleasanton. I flopped onto a sofa and slouched over while they went to oooh and aaah upstairs. Scowling, I glanced through the aluminum blinds, and then I saw it—the very thing acrobats used to launch them in flight under the Big Top. Immediately I straightened up. "Andrea, look!" I pointed and tapped the glass. "These people work at the circus!" Well, probably not, but I didn't care. We bolted out the back door and, hooting like thieves, clawed and crawled our way onto the top of it. Our squealing brought our father through the very door we left open when we stole outside just minutes before.

"What in the hell do you think you're doing?!" he shouted, "Get off that thing before you break your G-D legs!"

I risked one more flip. Then a bounce down on my rear. Then an, "Okay, okay, I'm coming!" before I feigned an exit and wound up in a pike position right above his head. I knew one of two things would happen; either he'd scare me into following his orders, or he'd have to come up on the tramp to get me. He chose the latter. I sprung him before he reached me, and we wound up all laughing on our backs. This is how my mother found us.

"What in the hell do you think you're doing?" she shouted, "Get off that thing before you break your G-D legs!"

We knew better than to expect Mom to join our impromptu tramp party. Panting and giggling, we shuffled down to the ground and once again heavy with gravity, made our way back inside. I scurried ahead and left Dad to get the verbal lashing.

Ten years later I dated a boy whose parents believed in the gift of flight, and they purchased him and his brother a look-a-like trampoline. Though we had progressed by a decade, safety standards did not. No net, no pad, no ladder. We used it for years and I'm still convinced all my time on that trampoline helped my gymnastic skills considerably when I got to college.

In 1994 I was ready to graduate from the University of California at Davis but decided rather than go through the ceremonies, I'd stay and get my Master's Degree in Nursing. I'd enter the program as a continuing student and bypass most of the red tape associated with being a new applicant. I was accepted into the program and was happily planning my medical future when a trampoline incident intervened, changing my course of action forever.

While home for a visit, that previously mentioned boyfriend was practicing a snowboarding stunt, while barefoot, and launched himself and his board from the trampoline, landing in his mother's flower garden. That may have been all right, had she not secured her flowers with a beautifully laid brick flowerbox. I watched in horror as he limped, foot split open underneath, broken bones exposed, over to me and asked for my medical assistance. It took less than one second for me to decide to withdraw from the nursing program and graduate with my classmates after all. (And to think I was *this close* to becoming a nurse.)

Fast forward twelve years and thankfully safety standards have progressed nicely. The trampoline we own has the net, the pad, the nifty little ladder. None of that has prevented the bumps and bruises, the occasional black eye, but the kids know the rules. They keep an eye on me. I haven't fallen off yet.

Where is the Love?

A friend of mine sat with her three children in a restaurant the other day. Her youngest, a 2-year-old boy, was tired and cranky and repeatedly, he let her know of his intention to end the meal and get home. She was patient. She was kind. She gave him room to be himself and still managed to finish her meal and tend to the older children, ages six and seven. As she exited the restaurant, an elderly woman touched her arm to gain her attention.

"Yes?" My friend smiled down on her as she shifted her 2-year-old in her arms. The woman said coolly, "I sure hope you have someone at home to help you *discipline* that child." She peered over her glasses and tapped the child on his knee. "Why you would allow him to behave like that is beyond me."

When told of this story, I scoffed. I snorted and huffed and went through an entire litany of "I can't believe that!" and "What gave her the right?" I was offended on behalf of my friend. Offended, but reminded too that sometimes people cross lines that aren't intended for passage. Though it happens every day, it still never fails to surprise me how critical we are as a culture of one another when, in truth, the little decisions we make rarely affect the course of another person's life. Such as—was a child's behavior in a restaurant cause for comment? For insult? I find myself wondering, where is the love?

Often, I'll be in conversation with someone, when one party—and it may be myself, is inquiring *why* of the other. Why would you do that? Why would you say that? Why did you let that happen? Having to explain and/or justify our actions can at times be irritating and tiresome. The principle behind general acceptance is a rule I remind myself to follow daily.

There is a fine line that exists somewhere between accepting people for who they are and tactfully making inquiry as to one's thoughts and actions. We are taught early on that 'there are no stupid questions', and though that is true, perhaps the tone behind the inquiry is what can be altered so as to be less offensive.

This must include random comments. Being a parent means keeping a constant watch on your children in public places. Restaurants, grocery stores, libraries—doesn't matter. Sometime, somewhere, one of my kids will offend someone by talking too loudly, walking backwards into them, stepping in front of their grocery cart—any general kid related activity.

"I'd like to get out of here today."

"You may want to put that kid in the cart instead of letting him push it."

"I leave my children at home when I shop, just to avoid what I'm seeing right now."

Those are just a few comments that have been muttered with intent for me to hear. While I do feel slightly insulted, it's more surprise and confusion that I battle with. Whatever happened to the old adage, "If you can't say anything nice, do not say anything at all?" I recently changed my strategy and have gone from diplomatically explaining why I allow my child the lenience of questionable behavior in public places to just simply handing the offending party a business card. It's a glossy black and white photo of Ben that reads:

My Son Ben Has Autism

Children with Autism are sometimes unpredictable. Please don't be alarmed if Ben suddenly screams or has what may look like a tantrum.

He is non-verbal, so his physical cues are what helps him to communicate. He won't answer you if you ask him a question, but don't stop trying to engage him in conversation.

I'm not being a bad mommy by allowing him to lay on the ground, as his sensory integration issues are quite severe. Laying helps regulate him, as thumb sucking does for other children.

I like to see Ben explore a world that is extremely challenging for him. Allowing him to have his own learning style includes patience and tolerance, repetition, and a whole lot of time.

We go at his pace wherever we are. Please forgo your irritation if we are moving slowly.

It's been a real problem solver for me, and an obvious eye opener for those who are left standing there reading the card. I'd like to not have to employ shock tactics when it comes to explanation. What I'd like even more is to not be put under scrutiny. And still, I can't help but wonder. Where is the love?

Without Becoming a Mother

Without becoming a mother, I may have never felt the agony of childbirth, or the elation that follows just seconds after.

Without becoming a mother, I may have never known the inner peace of watching a sleeping baby or felt the quickened heartbeat when the baby stirs and you think you've woken him.

Without becoming a mother, I may have wondered what the stains were on some women's shirts. Now I know… it's barf and that's perfectly okay to wear in public.

Without becoming a mother, I would never have known what interrupted sleep was. I may have never discovered I can survive on three hours of sleep per night.

Without becoming a mother, I would have never lifted my shirt in public to feed someone. I would have never picked up a fallen pacifier and licked it off. I would have never considered my saliva a sanitizer, without becoming a mother.

Without becoming a mother, I would have never tried to quilt. I may never have known the precision it requires or the fact that I lack precision entirely.

Without becoming a mother, I may have always had my fridge decorated with silly magnets, not priceless works of art.

Without becoming a mother, I might think that moms who buy their kids toys at the grocery store just to avoid a battle were weak, now I know they're not. They're just too polite to scream in front of an audience, and that too is perfectly fine.

Without becoming a mother, I wouldn't know 1000 children's books by heart and be able to discern who was a gifted writer and who just plain got lucky. I would never have known I am a woman of many voices, each one hysterical to a child under four.

Without becoming a mother, I wouldn't know that T-ball requires a certain amount of skill, indoor soccer can be intimidating for a first timer, and the folks who teach gymnastics will kindly ask you to leave if your toddler cannot stay off the trampoline.

Without becoming a mother, I may never have laughed at a joke with no punch line, fought off imaginary monsters, fallen asleep in a bed 10 sizes too small, or just stood silently watching as my child sprayed a neighbor's car with our hose.

Without becoming a mother, I would not be able to recognize a five-point harness, distinguish a good monitor from a cheap one, or understand that a binky, a buppee, a nuk, and a suckee are all the same thing: a pacifier.

Without becoming a mother, I would have thought multitasking meant doing only two things at the same time.

Without becoming a mother, I would have missed 100 meaningful conversations about chicken pox, ear infections, RSV, diaper rashes, fevers, potty training, and colic. I would have no idea how important plain old Tylenol really is.

Without becoming a mother, I would not know the panic of losing sight of a child, nor the relief so great you want to cry and scream at the same time when that lost child toddles back into view.

Without becoming a mother, I would have thought stretch marks only happened to other people.

Without becoming a mother, special education acronyms such as: Individualized Education Program ("IEP"), Individualized Family Service Plan ("IFSP"), Resource Center of the East Bay ("RCEB"), Comprehensive Community Services ("CCS"), Individuals with Disabilities Education Act ("IDEA") and a thousand other terms and labels might have sounded overwhelming to me.

Without becoming a mother, I might have stylish clothing, new shoes, clean furniture, a sporty car and a sassy hairdo. I might experiment with bright make up, talk on the phone for longer than 5 minutes, eat at restaurants with no mention of a kiddy menu, and say witty and clever things. I might not try to cut everyone's food into bite-sized pieces and judge a person's home as worthy or not by if it was childproofed. I might still be a size 5. Without becoming a mother, I might have lived the rest of my life without ever knowing the real reason for my existence. How sad I would have been, had I not become a mother.

15

The Apple Doesn't Fall Far from the Tree

Look! Up in the Sky

For as long as I live, I shall never have to fear anything ever again. I live with a Superhero. Actually, I live with a couple of them. Truth be told, I live with one 3-year-old little boy who masquerades as everyone from Buzz Lightyear to Superman, himself.

I'm never quite sure who will stumble into my room the early hours of dawn, rubbing his eyes and scratching his buns. With a yawn and a stretch, he will notify me of whom I'll be spending the remainder of the day with. Some days it's Woody, others it's Buzz. Most days I hang around with Superman and on a rare occasion I see Bob the Builder, or Blue, from Blue's Clues. Costumes make all this magic possible.

Just recently Josh informed me, "I don't like regular clothes anymore." You don't say. At least his laundry hamper doesn't overflow as often as it used to. I once thought raising little boys was going to be easier than little girls, if only because of the lack of accessories. Nowadays I find myself constantly on a mad scavenger hunt for matching hats and masks, mittens and tool-belts. Yep, accessories.

Not that I mind. On the contrary. I rather like having a little person parading around my home, "fighting crime," as he calls it. Now, some kids may call what Josh does as "tattling," but I know the truth. He's keeping our neighborhood free from harm. Why, just the other day he marched in the house while I was fixing dinner and with his hands on his hips he announced, "Some dog took a fat crap on our lawn."

I was stunned silent. He had been outside with Daddy and a few of Daddy's friends right before this recent news flash, so I was pretty much aware of where this information stemmed.

"Where is your father?" I asked. Both his hands flew out and up as he shouted, "Did you NOT hear what I said?" I understand his disbelief. I mean, it was an exceptionally significant broadcast on his part.

I played along, "I heard! And I am just amazed! Now run along and tell Superdaddy that he needs to remove it from our grass immediately. That is your assignment! Good luck!" He saluted me and then flung his imaginary cape over his shoulders and flew from our kitchen. Ah… imagination. I didn't want to squelch even a smidge of it by suggesting alternative vocabulary. I let it slide. It won't be the last time, I'm sure.

Being a Superhero is a big responsibility. I'm reminded daily that his job is an important one. He stands looking in his closet for long periods of time, wearing nothing but tiny underpants, contemplating just who to be. Does he want to help people today, or just be a cowboy? I see him eye his boots, then his tool-belt, then his mittens and finally his helmet. Who am I…who am I? I know this because I have X-ray vision. Being a mom of a Superhero is a big responsibility. I take my job pretty seriously.

A Special Gift from God

Though numerous gifts have been bestowed upon me, there is none I hold so dearly as that of being a mother of a child with special needs.

And yet, I have been doubly blessed. I have two children, two boys. Some may ask, is this really a blessing? Indeed, it is.

For those of us who have wanted nothing more than to have the love of a child, it is a blessing beyond words. With the birth of my first son, I learned how to wear stained clothing and still feel stylish. I made up songs, tripped over toys, went days without showering, and relished in the fact that I was a mother. This son was changed regularly, bathed daily, and wore matching socks. He continuously smelled of baby lotion. Yet, he grew too fast. Rolled at four months, walked at 10 months, talked articulately by 15 months. Even told us he was too big for a baby crib. We believed him. When he was a year old, I learned I was pregnant again. After a few months, God said, "I'm sorry Carolyn, I'll be needing Jr. up here again for a while. Seems I'm not quite ready to let him go."

I understood, and 10 weeks into that pregnancy suffered my first miscarriage. I believe it was a part of a bigger plan. Within the month I was pregnant again, and this time, because of complications, I was afraid. This time, God said, "Don't worry, Carolyn, I trust you. I trust you so much, I am going to send you someone very special. It's my way of saying, 'good job with Josh. My way of saying, I believe in you." Again, I understood.

Twenty months after Josh was born, Ben arrived. Broken and blue and desperately needing medical attention. I remembered that God had told me this was my reward, not my burden. I believed it then, and I still do. Having a child with special needs is not a punishment, as so often I've heard. Many have vocalized, "What did I do wrong? What did I do to deserve this?" When in fact, the right thing to ask is, "What did I do right? What did I do that God looked directly upon me and said, "This is the person I will trust with such an enormous responsibility?" I have often thought, "What have I done to have this honor bestowed upon me?" Instead of asking, "Why me?" I have tried to ask, "Why not me?"

Before I was a mom, I had visions of my children, all healthy and happy and frolicking together in the sun somewhere. I saw my kids bickering in the backseat of my car, dressing up for Halloween, waving goodbye from their classrooms.

I hadn't foreseen hospitals and medical equipment, surgeries, and recovery times. I never visualized myself standing over a child, fresh from the operating table, wiping the tears off my cheeks as they flowed down my face. I never anticipated the feeling of worry and the sour stomach of 'what if' when it came to a child. I never saw walkers and therapists, people looking upon my family with pity. I saw none of this.

But God did. He saw it all. The plans for me were so different, His and mine, yet together fit perfectly. I am beginning to see His plan, and how it weaves together with mine; with time, our two dreams for one life intertwining as they should. I do not feel sad now when I see children much younger than Ben, doing all he should have accomplished many months ago. Instead, I remind myself that Ben's plans are different, as are mine. Society tells us what children should do and when, how they should learn and why. It's up to me to help my young son overcome his obstacles and salvage his self-esteem in the process.

I do not know what I would have done if not for the last 18 months of research, study, application of technique, trial and error, and thousands of hours on the telephone. I never saw myself as advocate of children with special needs but since He did, I gladly follow Him and accept His design for where I need to go.

I am doubly blessed. I saw healthy children and God gave me Josh. I saw sports teams and costumes, laughing and learning. Milestones reached and growth going too fast. And God gave Josh. But He also saw what I did not—appreciation for progression, patience for the process, eagerness to learn and desire to succeed. And God gave me Ben. He saw my love for family, a determination to overcome, the ability to rise above ignorance and prejudice and an opportunity to teach others. And God gave me Ben.

Inquisitive Kids Leave Their Parents Behind

"Where's Josh?"

Brad and I exchanged a worried look and then Josh popped out from behind a clothes rack. "BOO!" I first felt relief, then anger as I hugged my small son to my chest.

"You need to stay with us. We were worried about you!" I held him and saw Brad shut his eyes with the combined feeling of hysteria and relief.

"Where's Josh?" The phrase has kept Brad and myself in panic mode since he was able to walk. Like most toddlers, he has that innate ability to seek out fascinating objects wherever he is. Needing no prompting, he'll stop to observe a bug on the sidewalk, to watch an ant struggle with a crumb, to stand under the umbrella of a tree and look upward or just to examine the extra skin on his elbow.

These interval pauses never pose a threat, unless we don't happen to know he has stopped—and we, of course, have continued our walking. I used to look at kids on leashes and think child abuse, now I have a better understanding of why parents keep a harness on roaming children. I should know better. I, too, was once a wanderer.

Years ago, my parents would drag my sister and myself on excruciatingly boring outings. Under protest, I would meander the streets of historical towns and partake in re-created western scenes. I could imagine no worse punishment than having to sit in some hot, stuffy saloon and sip sarsaparilla from a warm mug. Come on, even I knew it was root beer. And to have it served by a teenage barmaid smacking her gum and looking more bored than I was…it was painful.

I distinctly recall one time in particular I had been fed up with stagecoaches and cowboys, so I detoured into a candy shoppe in the historical town of Columbia. The rest of my family continued onward while I browsed through jawbreakers and licorice ropes. From there I went into a jewelry store and enjoyed looking through the pins and bracelets worn by the ladies from the 1800s. I had no more than set one foot out on the porch as I exited, when I was snatched by a stranger who grasped both my shoulders and asked, "Little girl—where are your parents?" Why, I had no idea where they were. I hadn't even thought about them the last 15 minutes or so. She led me by the hand, out into the dusty street and started scanning the area for frantic parents.

I saw them before she did.

Immediately, I was scared. They looked furious as they approached us; I quickly scampered behind her skirt. I was grabbed by my upper arm and dragged out from behind my robust savior.

"Ma'am," she said sweetly to my mother, "The poor child is more frightened than you are…" True, but not for the reasons she assumed. One week prior, my mother had been paged over the intercom at Gemco to come retrieve me at the front of the store and boy had I gotten it then! And before that, a kindly stranger had returned me to my parents in the Lost Tot Lot at the San Jose Flea Market, so I basically knew what I was in for.

"You are soooo busted," my sister hissed in my ear. I barely heard this as I watched my mother politely thank the lady. Her jaw firm, the smile stiff and false on her face. I could tell by the grip she had on my arm, that and the way she had me half standing/half hanging in the air, she wasn't done with me yet.

I honestly don't remember what happened next, perhaps I blocked it out, but I am completely aware of how it feels to lose sight of your child for just one second in a public place. Nothing is scarier. I have apologized profusely to my folks for causing them so much grief in that department. I can imagine they've said, "Where's Carolyn?" many more times than we've had to say, "Where's Josh?"

Say "Cheese" for the Camera Please

Well, it's been a year since we've had our second child professionally photographed; I suppose we're due to go back.

I feel mildly ashamed of how we've slacked off photographing Ben, whereas when Josh was a baby, I went through three rolls of film a week easily, just on him. Plus, I lined the walls with his Sears Smile Saver pictures, and forever had wallets to hand out to perfect strangers. Every three months Josh was dolled up and sat in a wagon, a basket, a bucket, or was merely propped up against another adorable prop at a studio. While some term this "first child syndrome," I find myself having to agree.

Once child number two entered our world I began to see there was more to life than catching every three months on film. I vowed, I swore I would never become one of those moms whose second child went without baby books and numerous photos, but here I am. Now that's not to say Ben doesn't have a baby book, he does. He also has letters and cards that his brother does not. In my determination to treat them fairly, I remind myself that to do that also means: Do not treat them the same. Respect their differences and celebrate their individual needs.

Back to picture taking then…I am a baaaad mommy when it comes to dragging my kids to a mall and fussing over them to sit still, be quiet and smile BIG. Call me crazy, but I'd rather have the pictures that look real: the ones where Ben is crying, and Josh is scowling. Or Josh is heaving Ben off the table and Ben is slugging him.

My personal favorite is when Josh got a hold of the spray bottle I had tossed in the diaper bag with the intention of wetting down his cowlick, and he proceeded to spray himself, his brother, me, and then the photographer. Now that is art.

True moments caught on film. But even I know that these are not the ones folks prefer to hang on fridges and send out in holiday letters. Plus, I could take these for free at home. When I am paying for pictures, I want my kids to look like the well-mannered, perfectly poised, little gentlemen they are not.

The last time I tried to get my boys to behave in a studio was a year ago and I have never gone back. I left sweating and panting, close to tears and inwardly pledging never to set foot in one again. I was close to a meltdown myself when the young girl behind the counter asked me, "Are you okay?" I had sniveled, "I have a college degree. You'd never know that by looking at me, would you?" I was completely disheveled, and my hair had fallen out of my clip during the battle to keep Josh's hands out of Ben's vest. The two had romped like puppies and wound up screaming and biting one another, before falling off of the table they were posing on.

"Can you get one of them on the ground?" I had asked the photographer. She looked at me disbelieving. A bit annoyed, both with my kids and more than likely with me, she answered, "Ma'am, pick up your kids and tuck in their shirts. We're through here." Well, la-dee-da. She had to go dry herself off I'm sure, Josh had gotten a bit squirrelly with that spray bottle.

After that experience, who can blame me for not going back? But it has been an entire year. And we are due for some excitement around here. I'll make sure to fill up the spray bottle.

In Training

"**Um, Carolyn,**" **my** friend is giggling in the water, "I think your swimsuit is on inside out."

I look down and sigh. It is 6:30 a.m. and I have just emerged from the pool, where two friends and I swim laps a few mornings a week. Lo and behold, the cups which are supposed to support my chest are banging out, flopping around on the outside of my suit. If that isn't bad enough, the peach crotch liner is adding a nice contrast to the black suit down in the appropriate area.

"Good thing I'm not here to impress any guys," I reply and with that, I shake the support cups wildly.

I have no good excuse for this fashion faux pas. It was dark when I pulled on my suit this morning, I suppose that's about all I can offer in the way of justification. Although, why none of us had noticed any of this before I jumped in the pool is unexplainable.

What I can explain is why we are rising at the crack of dawn to swim. Lap swimming is a part of the cross training I am doing in order to prepare for a half marathon in the fall. October 19, 2003, I will be running a mere 13.5 miles in order to raise money for my son, Benjamin. The U.S. Half Marathon takes place in San Francisco and draws in about 2,500 people. This year, including me.

After clutching yet another Denial of Services letter from our insurance carrier, I started to see the writing on the wall when it came to medical expenses and Ben. Like so many families before us, we came to the realization that in order to get your child the best possible medical care available, a constant "hunt and kill" attitude must be adopted. This isn't to say that early intervention services haven't been provided for us, indeed they have. But because of Ben's various and significant conditions, we are more often than not caught in the web of referrals, denials, appeals, consultations, and forever lasting phone calls.

Because Ben has multiple diagnoses, including cerebral palsy, sensory integration dysfunction, and significant developmental delays, we work closely with specialists including geneticists, neurologists, therapists and caseworkers. All who have a life of their own, none of whom have Ben at the top of their priority list.

Now I can't and don't expect Joe Doctor to slam my son into every open appointment when one is necessary, but I do expect our insurance system to, at the very least, approve just one of the tests he is constantly being referred for. Whether it's a renal ultrasound or a brain EEG, our perspective is that if a doctor orders it, it's probably relevant, especially given Ben's medical history. So as a parent, my take on the situation is that if I must fight to get Ben what he needs, then I will go down kicking and clawing. Anything else would be robbing him.

With that said, I was cruising through Starbucks a few weeks back and had an epiphany while sipping on a Tuxedo mocha with raspberry. Those drinks must be magical because before I knew it, I had pulled off to the side of the road and was jotting down notes in my day planner. I would have a fundraiser to get Ben the equipment he needs! I frantically scribbled and scrawled, thinking who I could send fliers to. Friends, family, friends of friends…Ben would not be denied any therapy or equipment as long as I was his mom.

One thing led to another and now I am in a cross-training program, in preparation to run 13.5 miles. Some folks have asked, "Are you crazy? Run 13 miles? Whatever for?" My only answer is this: having a child with special needs is a rare and wonderful thing. I would run 13 miles, I would run 1,300 miles, in order to get him whatever he needs to improve the quality of his life. Completing a half marathon and asking friends and family to sponsor me is small potatoes in comparison to what other moms have done for their children. And as parents, isn't that what we need to do? Stop at nothing to deliver to our children what they need? It's going to hurt, I'm sure. But it would hurt worse to do nothing.

Balloon Love Can be a Fragile Thing

"NO!" **Josh yells** and jumps off the shopping cart. He throws his head back and stares upward at the Safeway ceiling. His red balloon has drifted skyward and come to rest on one of the panels above us. Devastated, he falls to his knees and begins sobbing uncontrollably. In between fits of tears and gulps, he looks at me as if I have delivered the ultimate betrayal. Perhaps, I have. I was, after all, the one who tied the balloon to the cart and assured him it would be safe.

It takes a few minutes, but I gather him up and get him to the checkout. A kind employee has fetched him a new balloon, also red, complete with matching ribbon. He shrugs off this offering and announces loudly he doesn't want a balloon with a *ribbon*, he wants a balloon with a *string*.

Then he taps the Safeway logo on the balloon and says sniffling, "My other balloon says SpeeDee." We hightail it out of there and I load him, crying, and his brother, crying in unison, into the truck.

Don't get me wrong, I do feel for the kid. Since I am partly responsible for this situation, I drive back to SpeeDee Oil Change and get another one. I'm kind of embarrassed to admit this, but that short drive was way better than listening to him carry on for the rest of the afternoon.

Later in the day, I phone my friend Liz to relay the story in an attempt at gaining some sympathy. She is laughing but swears her story of balloon love is better than mine. She is a mother of four daughters, ranging in age from 13 down to 3. Molly, the eldest and a great big sister, had drawn a big smiley face on a balloon one day and the youngest, Katie, fell in love with it. She named the balloon Tia, and carried it everywhere with her. Tia became a member of the family. A big-headed, lopsided grinning, float around the house and startle Mommy, member of the family.

After a few days, Liz felt that Tia may have worn out her welcome. "She always caught me unaware," Liz explained. "Every time I turned around, she would be slowly bobbing her way into the same room I was in. It was eerie." So, one day, after Tia had drifted into the kitchen and surprised Liz by lightly brushing up against her calf, Tia met her fate. In one fell swoop, Liz had Tia under her arm in a football hold, and a fork jabbing the side of her "head." Katie entered the kitchen just as Tia went POP and was tossed into the trash. Liz was left holding the fork and feeling incredibly guilty.

"NO!" Katie screamed, "You killed Tia!" She threw her little body onto the floor and started writhing in agony. Liz had no choice but to put down her fork and try to soothe Katie. Katie would have none of it. She cried and yelled and carried on all afternoon. Liz reported that Katie had shot her looks of contempt throughout the day. They did finally reach a compromise; Liz fished Tia out of the trash and had Katie tape her to a piece of paper. Molly wrote the date and time on the paper, and Tia was hung above Katie's bed, as a sort of memorial. She resides there to this day.

Liz tells me Katie is a little more jaded now when it comes to balloons, "She has never given her heart and soul to another one since. Balloon love, it's a complicated thing." I believe her.

Herculean Effort (Not)

Halloween is just around the corner and for most children the idea of dressing up and parading down the street is exciting.

Some children wait all year long to get that "just right" costume and show it off to their buddies. Some kids even keep their costume a secret until that very night, in order to surprise their chums and bask in the glory of being the scariest, the prettiest, or the most creative.

This is not my son. This has never been my son, nor will this ever be my son, from what I can predict. At 3 ½ years of age, Josh is familiar with donning costumes every day and parading through the neighborhood. Sometimes he rides his bike, other times he travels by scooter. There are even occasions he chooses to walk.

But nevertheless, he is always dressed to the nines, by standards of imaginative 3-year-old boys. I don't think he has worn play clothes in months. Our friends and neighbors know to ask him how he would like to be addressed, rather than call him Josh. Waiting for a particular season to dress up has never occurred to my son.

This time of year is a mystery for him. He cannot fathom why, for just a short period of time, others join him in costume, while the rest of the year he remains the only Batman, Buzz Lightyear, Spiderman, or Woody on the street.

Months ago, I overheard him inquire of a friend, "Who are you supposed to be today?" as he realized his friend was wearing jeans and a collared shirt. When watching a sporting event on TV, he'll pipe up, "Look Mom! They're dressed up like football players!" The knowledge that most folks are not pretending to be something hasn't quite sunk in. For now, I can't do much but encourage this innocent bit of naivete.

This time of year, I see him wander slowly through the aisles, carefully looking over the selection of costumes. Reaching to feel the fabric, running the thin material through his palms while deep in thought, he is a regular costume connoisseur. I dare not stand in his way. I recently stood silently by; waiting for the nod of approval from him as he selected his favorite. Instead, I got a sullen shake of the head and a deep sigh. "No," he told me regrettably, "None of these will do."

Dang. That means I'll probably have to spend more than 12 bucks on one.

After watching Hercules a few times last week, he informed me of what I knew I would eventually hear. "I need a Perciles costume," he lisped. So, I made him one. I took a big pillowcase and cut out three holes, two for arms and one for his head.

I dimmed the lights so that he wouldn't see the shade of the case, mauve, and hoped for the best. I dove into my old craft bin. Elated, I came up with a few fake leaves from an old wreath, quickly spun into a crown, and a braided rope I had peeled off some revolting lampshade back in college. Wrapping that at his waist I happily announced, "Ta-da!" and spun him around to see his reflection in the mirror. It was a pathetic attempt at creativity, not one I'll soon repeat.

His face registered horror, then curiosity. Had I really been serious? Was this a joke on my part? Assuming so, he undressed and left it in a heap at my feet without saying a word. Standing there in nothing more than his little tighty-whities, he finally mustered up the courage to ask, "Can we buy one instead?" But of course. It may be Halloween, but I'm no monster.

She Got More

"Hey—he got more!" Josh examined his pile of whipped cream, floating on a mug of steaming cocoa. Then he looked at his friend's with horror. "Do you see how big his cream is?!" He pointed at the boy's mug.

Deep breath. It was true. Yes, I gave his friend more, but it was quite by accident. I smiled tightly and said nothing as I topped him off with an additional dollop. His friend gasped. "No fair!" he wailed. Suddenly, I was overcome with a powerful sensation of déjà vu.

Rewind the clocks a good 25 years. My sister and I had come to the breakfast table in the wee hours of the morning. We padded into the kitchen in our identical robes and slippers. I rubbed the sleep from my eyes as she pushed her bangs out of her face and we looked up expectantly at our mom to bring us our mugs of hot chocolate. A few dishes had banged around and we heard her swearing softly. Andrea and I exchanged a look. We knew well enough not to fight before Mom had her first cup of coffee.

She stalked in and put the warm mugs before us. Mom was wearing a grim expression but Andrea obviously hadn't noticed that due to the fact she was examining her hot chocolate. "There's no whipped cream," she boldly stated. It was a show down between the glares. Mom said nothing. She turned sharply and returned to the fridge, where she grasped the can and slammed the door. I thought this a very brave move on my sister's part. I would have been willing to forgo the whipped cream, just to stay on Mom's good side this particular morning. Andrea, obviously, was not.

Clutching the can, Mom filled Andrea's mug, then turned to do mine. I counted in my head, one…two…three…four! Wow! I knew how to time the familiar *FFFFFF* on a can of whipped cream and I had gotten more than my sister. I could hardly believe it. This little fact didn't escape Andrea. "She got more!" she exclaimed. Silent, Mom turned the can to Andrea and unloaded on her mug. Cream piled up in a small mountain. This was too much! She had way more than I did at that point.

"Hey!" I shouted, suddenly upset that the unfairness was turned in my direction, "She got MORE!"

She squirted my mug again. At this point, the pile of whipped cream fell over on the table and that was the breaking point for my sister. "That is NOT fair! She…" she didn't get to finish. Mom sprayed her in the face with whipped cream. I started laughing until I too, got a face full. Stunned, we were both silent, our faces hidden by a mask of cream. Mom wasn't done. Shaking the can furiously, she hissed, "You still want more? Huh? HUH? Is the whole thing enough for you two?" She took aim and fired the entire can on our mugs, the table, and our faces. She slammed the empty can down in the center of the table and walked out.

Josh's little friend was glaring at me, then thrust out his arm to present me with his mug. I smiled as I shook the can as hard as I could. I took aim and fired.

Multitasking on the Road

"**Oh, these idiot** drivers!" Exasperated, I swerved to pass the car in front of me. It had unexpectedly slowed to 35mph, causing me slam on my brakes and in turn, sent a jolt of adrenaline straight through me.

I peered into the window as I passed and realized the cause for the decline in speed was due to the driver's need to dial her cell phone.

Annoyed, I reached for my own phone and unconsciously slowed as I dialed a friend's number. Reporting this scene of lunacy took top priority. Oh. It would appear that I too, am an idiot driver. Realization washed over me and I lowered the phone back into my bag. Now would probably not be the best time to make this call.

Normally I do not multitask in the car. I know the dangers. I once rear-ended a Mercedes while applying mascara at a stoplight. Clueless, I had lifted my foot from the brake pad during my intense concentration of wand-to-lash activity. Not only was I embarrassed, I was left with a huge smudge of black on my eye and could barely see to pull off the road.

Upon entering motherhood, I quickly mastered the "rummage through the diaper bag while driving" game, and excelled at lobbing everything from bottles, toys, books, and small crackers from the front seat to the back without a hitch. Thus, my older son learned early on to "think fast." It is a skill that he will undoubtedly thank me for later.

It was my incident with hand lotion while driving that taught me a lesson I'll soon not forget: skin creams are meant to be applied and absorbed before one needs to grip a steering wheel. A little something for all you ladies out there to remember, take it from me.

Common sense would tell you not to oil up your hands and then attempt to drive. Not priding myself on being common, I felt confident I could get to Pleasanton as well as let the healing begin…steering quite safely with my knee, I managed to get the little cap off the lotion bottle and after fumbling with it for a second, proceeded to lose it in the crevice between my seat and door. Undaunted, I shook the little jar into my palm, while keeping my eye on traffic. Nothing. I advanced to pounding and in one fell swoop, had lotion in my palm, on my steering wheel, dotted across my dash and splattered diagonally on the windshield.

In the backseat, the boys didn't miss my sharp intake of breath. Instinctively, I brought my hand up to cover my mouth as I gasped, and wound up with a mouthful of cucumber and aloe. (No matter how great it smells, lotion never tastes good.) Traffic was slowing, thankfully, and I was awarded an opportunity to simultaneously spit lotion, knee-steer and rub vigorously my arms and face. Feeling much like the child whose parents apply 10 times the right amount of sunscreen needed, I sat in oily distress, a bright white version of my former self.

As traffic picked up, I abandoned knee steering and grabbed the wheel. Or at least tried to—my hands slid forward and I wound up steering with my elbows for a brief second. Composing myself, I groped around in the diaper bag, found an extra T-shirt, then draped it across the wheel to stabilize my grip. Pretty resourceful if you ask me. This from the same woman who had to hunch forward, lean at a 45-degree angle, and cock her head sideways in order to see through the lotion-streaked windshield. Incidentally, I was also able to wipe my face on the shirt each time I rounded a bend.

No longer do I multitask while driving. Who needs that stress? I just stick with the road, the kids, the music, the phone and the gas gauge. Keep it simple, you know?

Happiest Place on Earth

"**Get over here!**" the woman yanked what I assumed to be her daughter back into the line ahead of me. The child bit a quivering bottom lip and avoided my eyes. Stepping back, I fumbled my Minnie Mouse Ears and looked with surprise to my husband.

"Aren't we still in Disneyland?" I whispered and pretended to scan the area, double checking. Had this been our first experience with mean behavior, I might have let it slide. But since our check-in a few days prior, we kept finding ourselves rubbing shoulders with folks not feeling the love here in the happiest place on earth.

Yesterday morning in the concierge room, a sweet little girl named Juliana played with our sons while Brad and I inspected the selection of hot scones. I know her name because her mother repeatedly hissed it while the child tried to initiate conversation with us. "Juliana, stop it! Juliana, come here! Juliana, calm down!" Her younger brother toddled around, examining the plates of other guests while their father snapped the newspaper loudly from his overstuffed easy chair. I had stepped over his sprawled legs earlier and was surprised that he hadn't moved them and offered even a simple, "Excuse me." Nothing. He occasionally cleared his throat, but not once glanced up to see the whereabouts of his charge. Until the man-cub pulled a pile of magazines to the floor, then Daddy shot from his chair and bellowed, "No, James! No! Come James! Come!" The room watched as James, being the 2-year-old that he was, ignored his father and continued on his drooling, smiling, curious way. Good for you, James.

When I later saw this same family in the hallway, the children darted away from their parents and came to my side. I knelt and listened to Juliana as she described her autograph book, and then toyed with the idea of helping James as he tried to maneuver his way into my double stroller. The parents were mortified. "Children, come!" Neither child looked up. James continued to climb and grapple his way into the front seat. I smiled warmly at Big James Senior and said, "I think Junior is holding out for a ride!" He didn't even meet my eye. I felt my smile begin to disintegrate. And because I knew they weren't interested in conversation with me, I began one. Just for fun.

That was nothing compared to my brief interaction with a different couple in The Disney Store. I had seen these two off and on all day in both parks as well as in a restaurant. I pointed them out to Brad throughout the day, saying "Look! There's that couple again!" and we had marveled that you can see the same people all week long in a vacation spot that suits thousands. By the time we encountered them in the store, I felt compelled to approach them and share that information. My thinking being had it been us, our response would have been gracious and friendly, and we would have been flattered that someone felt bound to tell us. I envisioned a fun conversation that led to a departure with warm fuzzies.

I tapped on her shoulder. "Hi!" I began with a big smile. They stared at me. "Um...it's just that my husband (I pointed to Brad, he smiled) and I have seen you guys everywhere for the last day or two, and..."

"No, you haven't," the man cut in, bored. "We just got here today." They turned and left.

I was still talking when they departed. I looked to Brad for help. He shrugged.

"Disneyland, right? We are in Disneyland, aren't we?" I was flabbergasted that people could be less than courteous to their fellow Mouseketeers. I cheered up considerably when I spied a young couple making out wildly while in line for The Haunted Mansion. "They are happy to be here!" I told Brad. "We should be following *them* around for the rest of this trip!"

16
Mother Knows Best

How to (Not) Catch a Leprechaun

When Josh came home from school holding a small paper which instructed parents to help make a leprechaun trap, I got very excited. I love building things, especially with my kids. I had visions of green paper, glitter, and glue. Stickers, shamrocks, and little candies wrapped in gold foil danced in my head. At least for the day. After that I kind of forgot about it. The paper got lost in the shuffle of the other dozen or so piles that stack up weekly on my dining room table. When we compiled everything to prep the room to paint, I found it. Ooops. One leprechaun trap due the following day. I raced out and bought my youngest son a pair of shoes so that we had a box to use for our trap.

"A shoebox?" Josh's dad asked me, "What for? I know what to do, just leave it to me." I was worried. Especially when he added, "We won't even need all that extra crap you left out for us." I eyed the stack of green paper, markers, glue, glitter and candy. How was any of that considered extra? How does one create a trap for a leprechaun without the standard lures? Curious now, I inquired of his plans and then added, "Don't get out of control. Use the shoebox…" I needn't have worried.

I have a friend who, when she heard about the project, got to work with her husband and made a "Leprechaun Idol" trap with their daughter.

Complete with a fancy stage, steps, mini microphone, and all the hoopla to make it look close to the real thing. When the unsuspecting little fellow got on stage to sing—wham! Down he went through the trap door. I thought it was pure genius and wished we had been so creative. We weren't. Though I wasn't home to help with the project, what I found when I returned later in the evening was pretty much a 3-D version of my vision as well, minus any decoration.

"Where's the trap?" I had asked in hushed tones, so as to not disturb the sleepers.

On the couch, Brad didn't even open an eye. He said nothing, just pointed to the hallway. There on the hutch was Josh's trap. One box, one pencil, a little dental floss, and a gold coin. "That's it?" I was incredulous! "How long did that take? About 5 minutes?" I was hot, "Did Josh do anything? It looks like you did it all, in about 10 seconds!" True, I had the same blueprint for the trap, I just wanted to splash on a little paint, cover the thing in paper, sprinkle glitter haphazardly around…make it look inviting. This looked like a box propped up with a pencil, which was attached to some floss dangling weakly around a coin. Even worse, Elmo's face was grinning at me from the top of it.

"Elmo doesn't exactly say St. Patrick's Day," I told Brad. "Couldn't you have covered that?"

"Sure, he does! And look—the box is green."

Well, okay. I'd give him that. "What did Josh think of it?" He paused before answering.

"Josh made this himself. He used his imagination, his tools, and his patience to come up with a design that he could build without any help from me. I think you'd be interested in knowing that while it may look like something I would make, I did not. I let our son do everything. He opted not to use anything you supplied him to create a trap that fit your vision, rather made something that fit his own with the instruments of his choosing."

Silence. I hadn't planned on a slice of humble pie tonight before bed. I inspected the trap with a new perspective. Upon closer scrutiny, something caught my eye. A wee little shamrock had been glued to Elmo's hand, Josh's attempt at appeasing me, while still working from his heart. It was the best trap I had ever seen.

Girl Fight

My friend's daughter got in a fight with a friend at school. She lays curled in a fetal position sobbing into a pillow on the couch. "Nobody even likes me anymore," she wails. Though her voice is muffled, I can still interpret most of what she is choking out. Her mom and I make eye contact and exchange a sympathetic glance with one another across the sprawled and quivering body of 11-year-old Morgan. "She's turned everyone against me and now nobody talks to me!" Morgan is bawling and hiccupping so I rub her back, I can totally relate.

The first time I got dumped by my friends I didn't see it coming. Sixth grade. They just stopped talking to me one day and ignored my presence until I got the drift. I was devastated. Went home sick and willed my body to catch some rare disease so they'd all be sorry. I visualized each of them at my bedside begging for my forgiveness while I oh-so-generously bestowed small tidbits of kindness upon them. I vowed to stay in bed until they all liked me again. Unfortunately, my mother was the type of mom who would, rather than bring me soup and read me poetry about true friendships, tell me instead to 'quit hanging out with spoiled brats and make some new friends for once.' Two days later the group dumped another girl, then another, then another. We formed a coalition of sorts, joining forces as one by one we accepted the girls as they too met their fate by peers. Eventually, only two girls remained and we wouldn't let them hang out with us no matter how hard they rallied. I think it lasted less than a week.

In junior high fights with friends became more complicated. When on the outs with a friend, one could expect secrets to be revealed, lies to be spread, and bad words to be scrawled across lockers. I think I worked harder at staying on the good side of my peer group than I did at any homework assigned to me. I even joined a church youth group with the expectation that goody-goody church kids didn't dump their friends. I have since learned two things: the church kids are more knowledgeable of things like drinking, drugs and fooling around, and that they too dump their friends when so inclined.

I want so badly to prepare Morgan for the really big fights—the ones that come later when young men are involved. Right now, she is arguing with her friends over who sings which song and what boy is cuter on which reality show. Enter real men and she may be in for a world of hurt.

"You've probably never been in a fight in your life," she says accusingly. "You're a total do-gooder that everyone liked." Not true. I snort and laugh. I have actually only been in one real fight. The only reason I came away unscathed was because I could outrun the girl who's head I dumped a beer on in college. Seriously. There are many reasons girls who are from Pleasanton that wear pink jeans and white leather boots, complete with fringe, should not attend parties in Dublin where female attire consists of large team jerseys and baseball hats turned backwards.

The Proof is in the Wood

"Ha! Nice table!" my friend Michele snickers as she flops onto my couch. With her 1-year-old daughter on her lap, she balances the child, a bottle, fourteen fluffy stuffed toys and one quite weathered Winnie the Pooh diaper bag, seams pushed to maximum capacity. By the look of it, an explosion is looming. Eyeing it cautiously, I half expect an eruption and then the spewing of various baby paraphernalia around my living room. I step back, and wince—a slight attempt at protecting myself against the sudden pacifier to the forehead or God forbid, the other full bottle hitting my square in the guts.

"I remember when you actually protected this coffee table from the hands of children!" she hoots as I pass the baby a hammer to pound against the wood. I vaguely recall ever caring about this table, but since her insistence is adamant, I nod and listen.

"Remember all those candles you had everywhere? With the iron holders? And your coffee table books—you had, like *nine* of them!" Oh my God. I sit back, stunned. I've completely blocked out ever having décor in this house until this very moment. I look around the room and see, in flashes, what used to garnish the shelves, the fireplace, the tables and walls. The room *did* have ambiance! It *did* have a feeling at one time— something stylish and sassy that didn't say 'kids dwell here and forever will so death to all interior design and tranquility.'

"Whatever happened to all your pretty things?" It's a fair question. I just have no answer. With the arrival of my children, the fancy knick-knacks I used to treasure gradually made their way into boxes, bins, and onto tables at garage sales. I hadn't even missed anything. Known artists' works have been replaced by Josh and Ben Originals. Down came Ansel Adams and up went local photographers. Hand sanitizer and plastic utensils are now scattered across the same counter top that used to house vases of fresh flowers and palm sized books of poetry.

"And didn't you get your carpet cleaned a few times a year?" she is laughing at me—not with me—but for good reason. My floor looks as if twelve to eighteen people parade through this house on a daily basis juggling leaky sippy cups, sloshing wine around in short glasses, and sawing together graham crackers just for the sheer pleasure of making crumb dust to dance on in the living room. Slight hesitation, then I answer meekly, "I still do…"

Michele cackles and shifts the drooling cherub on her lap down to the floor. She kicks a few gnarled kitty toys across the room in order to spare her child from a faux-fur induced episode of toxic shock. The baby grips the table leg and starts gnawing away in true Pebbles Flintstone form. Rather than stop her, as I once might have, I lean over instead to coo, "Does that taste good? Is it yummy? You likey?" A few bite marks can only add to the charm.

Once close enough to the table to lick it myself, if I were so inclined to, its past six years are clearly visible. Ink scribbles, sticker residue, and the remaining color—albeit faded, from Josh's 'washable' markers beautify the surface. Countless nicks and scratches in the wood, impossible to tally, along with the ground-in wax from crayons have created an original tabletop that at that moment, becomes priceless to me. Upon closer inspection, I can make out the name of the culprit scrawled messily, and now permanently in the pine. JOSHUA.

Not much to look at, I'll give her that much, but I wouldn't sell this table for anything. Instead, I nod to the Winnie the Pooh diaper bag as Michele rummages through it, trying to locate wipes and a diaper. "Nice purse."

Girls Gone Wild

It is 3 a.m. and I am lying face down on the couch. On my back is one kitten, nibbling on the blanket and pulling it away from my face. She is working hard, too, so I don't disturb her. Near my feet, her twin is pouncing from ankle to calf, doing battle with my toes, now uncovered as well. They are The Girls, and I adore them.

I started out in my own bed tonight, really, I did. Somewhere around midnight The Girls woke me by sharpening their claws on my hamper, then launching into their nocturnal routine. Chasing one another through the house, knocking plants and dishes into the sink, and shutting themselves in the bathrooms. The all-too-familiar sound of the doorstop being flicked is enough to rouse any good sleeper. It might be cute, if they did this during the day. But after 11 p.m., kitten antics slide down the adorability scale.

Any movement on my part is an invitation for play. Adjust a shoulder, and I have a Girl on my arm, springing into action. Feigning sleep is preposterous; they are onto me: meowing in my ears, licking my nose, tangling their paws up in my hair. I tolerate it for a while, before grabbing a pillow and making tracks out to the couch.

Brad misses all of this. Safely tucked in with his eye-pillow and earplugs, the guy is immune to all activity between 10 p.m. and when he rises. It wouldn't matter. The Girls never even put a whisker to his face at night. They know better; how—it is still a mystery, but even our older, wiser kitty never disturbed him after dark. Before I exit, I nab a kitten and toss her on Brad's middle. Nothing. She flees as if burned and he is so cocooned in his rat's nest of pillows and blankets, he doesn't even flinch. Whatever.

On the couch I cover my head with my pillow and groan. Someone bites my big toe. Throwing off the blankets and rubbing my eyes, I am up and on the hunt for two little Girls.

"Mary Kate and Ashley!" I hiss.

They scamper down the hall. I hear a soft "whump" as one of them doesn't round the bend with much agility or skill.

They hate their names, but who can blame them? So do I. It made sense at the time…twins, one thinner than the other, both girls. It was too perfect. I try again, "Lilly? Daisy?" They like those names. Tentatively, both girls creep back out to the living room, but not before I have rustled a bag of treats, set off a musical toy by stepping on it, and buried my face in the crook of my arm to muffle my scream after bumping my hip bone on the corner of our hutch.

I toss kitty candy onto the porch and happily shut the front door behind them. I do this every night; one would think I would have learned by now. They certainly have me trained well. My little girls gone wild.

Painful Hero Worship

I can hardly believe there was ever a time when I thought the sun rose and fell on my sister's face. Sure, she's a great gal and yes, I do think she is intelligent, but to worship her in the way that I did when we were children. Well, that was just wrong.

Tap, tap, tap. The signal. I was 6 years old and waiting patiently for the three knocks on the wall that separated Andrea's room from mine. Once beckoned, I carefully slipped from my bed and on tiptoe, crept down the hall to peek in her doorway. "Yes?" I whispered anxiously, so proud to have been summoned by my elder sister.

"Dummy!" she cackled fiercely, then started hurling a collection of stuffed animals at me. Dumbo, Garfield, and a big stuffed dog—BAM BAM BAM—all hit me square in the face. I squealed and hightailed it back to my room, only to get busted for being out of bed when Mom and Dad heard me running through the halls. "Mom," Andrea would call sweetly from her bed, "Tell Curl I'm trying to sleep and please stop spying on me!"

I'd lay there hating her until I heard it again: tap, tap, tap. When I refused to respond, it came louder: TAP, TAP, TAP. I sniffed and wiped my eyes, then stood up for the call of duty. Surely, she needed me, if she was tapping again. Needed me for more target practice and a good laugh, that's all. "You are so stupid!" she hissed as she pelted me with another round of fluffy ammunition.

When Andrea wasn't planning hoaxes to practice her aim, she was inventing new games for us to play. Boarding School: where I was the secretary and wasn't even allowed in the same room as her. Angry Maid: where I cleaned her room and wasn't compensated. Dentist Office: where she flossed my gums into a bloody pulp and then told me to brush more often. And her personal favorite: Dolly Hair, where she dragged me around our house by my hair. This is 100 percent true. I let my older sister drag me around by my hair. This is painful, if anyone is wondering. Hurts like hell, truth be told. Yet I endured, hanging onto the hope that she might actually invite me to play with her again sometime.

And she did. Invited me to try a new game she invented called The Optometrist, where she was the eye doctor and I was the blind patient. I allowed her to continuously poke me in the eye, while she giggled and stabbed, I actually thought I would wind up wearing one of her contacts and looking pretty nifty. I was such a sucker.

My stretch of hero worship lasted until high school, where it faded into silent admiration without verbal affirmation of her coolness. I was trying hard to establish my own sense of style, without the connection to her being obvious. She feathered her hair into a Farrah Fawcett 'do; I feathered mine and looked remarkably like an elderly yard duty. She glossed her lips and looked sleek and flirtatious; I glossed mine and looked like I had just eaten a pork chop with my hands tied behind my back. She dabbed a little Charlie on her wrists; I over splashed a bottle of Love's Baby Soft on the back of my legs. It was a feeble attempt at flattery, but she would never see it that way. Only saw a chubby kid sister copying her every move and failing at it every time.

Hero worship is a painful thing. I cringe each time I see my second son ignored by his older brother. I may have to impart younger sibling wisdom to him when the time comes. Such as, no matter what he tells you, do not EVER let him drag you around by your hair. Ever.

An Unexpected Adoption

Our family got some big news this week. It seems I was adopted, as was my husband and my children. We didn't plan on being adopted, heck—I didn't even know we were up for adoption. And yet, we were chosen. I'm flattered of course, and I treat my new family members with gentle hands, a soft voice, and a friendly face. Out of nowhere, a mother kitty and her teeny baby appeared in our back yard.

Thin, hungry, a little scraggly—the twosome romp and play and act as if they've stumbled onto Feline Club Med.

As soon as the slider door creaks open, eight twigs come running and can't wolf down the kibbles and water fast enough. Oh yes, I've fed them. How could I not? I know they have no plans of leaving now that they've found their meal ticket. And such gracious guests they are—lick the bowls clean, never leave so much as a crumb on the ground. Mama even helps Baby wash up after the meal.

We've had a few cats in our yard before. They stroll into town, stay a day or two and then mosey along on their way. The traveling sales-men type—never stay long, never cause a scene, "…just passing through, Ma'am," is all I get. But a mother and daughter pair, well, that's enough to make me break out the fine plastic dishes and set them up on a flowered dishtowel. I don't want to appear anything less than a cordial hostess.

Our 4-year-old is beside himself.

He's made a bed for the pair, checks on the kitties three and four times a day. Brings them ample supplies of water and food. Our indoor cat, Tooter, looks on with a mounting feeling of disgust. She sits and stares through the screen, ears back, a low growl in the base of her throat. She's upset, all right. Has every reason to be, I suppose. But I'm at a loss of how to convey to her that she is not threatened. She is just in the midst of a tough lesson on sharing. We all go through it; now is her time.

"Aren't they cute?" I gush to Brad. "Very," he replied. "Just give it a few months—all the other kittens they have will be cute, too."

Oh. Good point. What to do? What to do? For now, I supply food and water, loving hands and a warm bed. But I'm thinking someone, somewhere is probably looking for two beautiful, friendly, affectionate kittens to share their home with. Mama isn't even a year old yet…she's a bitty little girl herself. Perhaps we can help.

Working the System

I found myself eyeing my children differently the other day. I saw them not as the little drippy-nosed bandits they are, but as the future chore recipients they will become. I wickedly chuckled and rubbed my palms together, knowing soon, very soon, I'd be handing down a good load of responsibility to these boys. There's only one problem. Is sneakiness hereditary? If so, I'm in for it.

I learned at an early age how to manipulate "the system." Chores were given at various stages of our lives and I soon discovered that doing laundry only appeared to be fun. In reality, it wasn't Mom's Golden Rule: As soon as you could reach the buttons on the washing machine, you were old enough to be responsible for your own clothing. Many a time I missed a neighborhood game of kick-the-can while I sat grumbling and muttering as I folded my laundry. I often wished I hadn't stood on tippy-toes wildly reaching for the machine buttons, proving I was tall enough for such a grown-up task. That was my first lesson in "with age comes sacrifice." On the plus side, it did teach me to think creatively and later provided me with many opportunities to weasel out of chores.

Take for example our dinnertime routine. Age was my only ally, for being the youngest allowed me to have a tad less responsibility. My job was to set the table. I truly enjoyed this duty. Setting plates, napkins, and silverware I believed to be a job of artistic nature. I took it very seriously and was continuously disappointed when my parents insisted on having matching place settings. I saw no point in this, and would choose various colored napkins, mis-matched utensils, and (my personal favorite) I would turn the flower pattern on the plate to be upside down or sideways.

This little show of imagination was mistaken as a display of immaturity and I was excused from having to clear the table and put everything away at the end of a meal. Since that required much more effort arid no creativity whatsoever, I gladly relinquished that job to my sister.

Cleaning bathrooms was a different story. My sister and I shared a bathroom, much to my displeasure. While she was perpetually messy, I was neurotically clean. Mom noticed this personality variance early on and cashed in on my cleanliness. Knowing full well my sister was going to botch the job, it was I who applied the Soft Scrub and Lysol and then I who nagged like a little hen when she left toothpaste blobs on the counter. I did learn when scouring a bathroom, a simple sign that read "Cleaning in progress" hung on the closed door left me undisturbed for up to an hour in which I would gab on the phone, listen to music, paint my toenails, or just perch on the edge of the tub with a good book and occasionally dip my toes in the water to feign a first-rate scrubbing for any passersby.

Sister, on the other hand, had allergies.

An excuse I believe to this day that liberated her from many a chore. While I would be violently sweeping the pollen from deck in Twain Harte, she would be watching me from inside the cabin, sitting in a recliner, flipping through a magazine, and waving. At times she would pretend to pout and wipe a tear from her eye before laughing and mouthing, "I have allergies" at me through the window. Her "allergies" excused her from any chore that required a fleck of dust to be in her presence, because Heaven forbid she may get something in her eye. While I hauled up deck furniture from under the cabin, she'd catch my eye (easy enough to do when I'd be glaring at her) and hold up her drink as if to toast me, then mouth, "Very refreshing…mmmmm." So, she too, knew how to work the system.

I consider the line of system workers my boys come from as I watch them. Manipulation runs deep through their veins. I have no choice but to think I'll be stuck cleaning bathrooms for the rest of my life!

Sizing up Adolescence

My, oh my…my good friend Liz's daughter is now wearing a bra. Where has the time gone? It seems like just yesterday she was telling me about her scraped knee and the wheelies she could do on her bike, and now this.

I mean, I would have noticed it anyway; she didn't have to keep reaching to hike up the straps while we spoke. Nor did she need to continuously adjust her shirt, so that the telltale cups would poke through. Every so often; I saw her glance down to make sure her little chest was still there. I suppressed a giggle.

First bras are big deals. Especially to those of us who had no big deals to put in them. When I first mentioned needing a bra to my mom, she laughed long and loud.

Wiping the tears from her eyes, she asked, "Whatever for?" Not to be outdone, I replied sharply, "For my teats, what do you think?"

Well, that did it. She wasn't laughing anymore. "Smart mouthed young ladies don't need bras," she said, "but girls with breasts most certainly do. You, my dear, are not a girl with breasts."

I disagreed. I had examined my chest every day for over a year, and now, at 12, I was positive I needed one.

It took some doing, but I finally convinced Mom to take me bra shopping. Perhaps it was all that walking around with my shoulders hunched, so as to give the impression of all that extra weight out front. Mom ignored that ploy, as she did the "my chest hurts when I jog," tactic. Most likely she probably grew exhausted of seeing me stand sideways in the mirror, sticking out my chest. I had grabbed her sewing tape and measured myself, then marched downstairs to make my final case. "I'm a 28!" I announced. "It's high time to put a bra on these things!"

Bra shopping is quite an excursion, even now at 30 years of age. Back in 1984, the selection of bras for young ladies with no need for them most likely offered a lot less to choose from than today's standards. I wound up with three soft cotton bras, one with padding "for special occasions." Oh, I knew of a special occasion, all right. The seventh-grade end of year dance was right around the corner, and if there ever was a night I needed a little assistance with my chest, that would be it.

From then on, I never left my room without putting on a bra. I tried to slide the word "bra" into as many conversations as I could, feeling without a doubt, I would be seen as much older and mature than my mere 12 years.

"Oh," I'd sigh, "This bra is killing me..." yank, yank. Or "I think my bra is too tight," wriggle, wriggle. Every so often, "Is there a tag on this bra? Something is scratching me..." I was a one-woman bra-expo.

A lot has changed in 18 years. For one, none of my bras are padded— for crying out loud, my chest needs NO help anymore. After two kids, I'm considering a reduction somewhere down the line. I avoid looking at myself sideways in mirrors, and that hunched shoulder look is for real—no ploys here! I rarely use the word, "bra" in conversations these days, except of course when giggling with a friend over her daughter's first bra. Then there's no holding me back!

A Glimpse of My Future

I like teenagers, always have. Maybe not so much when I was a teen-ager, because I lived all the drama, the attitude, the dishonesty and the embellished tall tales to the parents, but I did develop a certain appreci-ation for the culture once I outgrew it.

My teen years were pretty typical of anyone's who grew up where I did, the suburbs of middle class America. We had parties, went to concerts, cruised around in cars late at night, we even attended football and basketball games showing our school spirit. My friends and I cut classes, erased messages from the school, forged sick notes from home, and dodged detentions countless times. Nothing stands out in my mind as being all too original except for my one-time offense of breaking, entering and trespassing, which of course occurred while I was running with a 'wild crowd'. Even so—without ever being arrested, it does lack a certain appeal when regaling any group with that tale.

These days I eye my oldest son suspiciously and wonder what his future, and mine, hold for us in a few short years. I have a good friend Sherry who has the best relationship with her teenaged son—it's a real one. She's totally upfront and so is he. They openly harass one another, but there's love behind it. It may provide a little frustration from time to time, but it gives more comic relief than anything else.

She once told me how bad she felt because after years of listening to him over-dramatize all his injuries, she ignored him one time and found out two days after the fact that he had indeed broken his arm. "Do you know how crappy I felt about that?" she later told me, and we laughed. He forgave her because he knew better than anyone how unbelievable he'd been in the past. I love this kid and I've never even met him. Sherry has a dozen stories about the trouble he gets into at school because 'he was just standing there, not doing anything at all.' She rolls her eyes and smirks every time she's needed at the school to retrieve a skateboard, meet with the principal, or reclaim some item from home which got smuggled onto campus. "Oh, but he had nothing to do with it…*he's innocent*…"

He called her in the afternoon the other day after telling her that morning he planned on skateboarding home from school.

"Hey Mom."

"Hey. Where you at?"

"Up at school still. It's hot." He pauses while he awaits an offer for a ride that isn't coming.

Sherry smiled. "It sure is. We're all out by the pool. You should get home and come swimming."

He scoffed. "Like I want to swim with a bunch of old ladies."

(When she told me this I said, "Where is he? Where is that punk?")

When he got zero response he said, "But I broke my arm…"

They both laughed and she told him she'd see him when he got home.

Now that's a good mother-son relationship. Josh and I get along fine now and that's mostly due to the fact that he's eight. Give him five more years and I have little doubt that I won't be retrieving his skateboard from school, meeting with his principal, and reclaiming smuggled items from home. I try to be as much of a straight shooter as humanly possible, but even so—the kid has a mind of his own and I want him to use it. For now, I'll just keep try to keep it real and still look to Sherry for what to expect in my future.

17

Following in Their Footsteps

Remodeling a Sacred Place

"Well, you'll never believe this, but your dad and I have decided to remodel the bathroom," my mom sings into the telephone. A missed beat and then, "You know...*your* bathroom."

By 'your' she means the one I shared with my sister growing up. The one I cleaned. The one I fought for time alone in, the very one I got shoved out of repeatedly while my brushes and hairspray were tossed out after me.

"My bathroom," I reply dryly "Yeah, that's funny." I still have visions of Andrea and I wrestling each other up against the sink and threatening to burn one another with our crimpers and curling irons. If I never see another granite slab with gold marble weaving through it again, it will be too soon.

"All except for that lovely countertop," Mom purrs, "We're keeping that."

Oh, good Lord. The woman will never learn. Glittery showers of gold interlacing with creamy swirls went out with rust colored carpet, which incidentally, my parents still have too.

"It's valuable," she informs me, "And people will just die when they see it!"

I nod and smile, "Oh they sure will." My parents are thinking of moving and they know their home could use a little fixing up beforehand. Remodeling the bathroom is a good place to start, I don't think it's been touched since Andrea and I lived there and that was a good 15 years ago.

When they bought the house in 1979 the bathroom was papered in a soft back velvety material, psychedelic butterflies flitting all over it. I thought the room was the prettiest thing I'd ever seen but, "It looks like a bordello!" my mom had shouted when I begged and pleaded to let it stay. She relented to allowing butterflies, but only on white paper with sprigs of lilac floating around it. Good enough. The walls were recovered, a shower door was added and then no other improvements have been made since.

In fact, to this day the drawer that held bathroom stuff still needs to be shaken and sworn at just to open. Once open, one needs to reposition it then with bated breath, very slowly advance it along the runners in order to get push it shut. My fault. During my fluffy hair stint in the 80s, I used to blow dry my 'do upside down to give it that much sought after added lift. One morning I had my drawer open so I could easily access any one from my collection of brushes. Our pink radio was shoved off to the side, plugged in and blaring out the newest *Wham!* single when, in my lip-synching daze, I threw my head over to blow dry the underneath and CRACK, I bashed my forehead into the open drawer. I rocked it so hard that the contents were bucked up and dropped to the floor. My sister ran in but, upon seeing me writhing on the floor holding my head, the blow dryer still clutched in one fist, had figured out what happened before I could explain. The irony of the situation struck her as hilarious. "*Wham!*" she pointed to the radio, which was still going strong and "Wham!"—she pointed to the open drawer, all cockeyed and empty and then bent over cackling. We both cried, but for different reasons.

Cruising for a Bruising

My parents have left on a cruise. Finally. Ten days at sea and I'm happily anticipating the lull in phone calls I'll be receiving about their cruise preparations. One can only listen to the same concerns about clothing, cameras, accommodations, food and entertainment for so long.

And to have a non-cruise conversation flip to become one in record time is something only a person who won't be joining them on the ship can fully appreciate.

Mom: (phoning me) "Oh. hi dear, what are you up to?"

Me: "Well, I kind of have a bit of a headache and…"

Mom: "Oh, that reminds me! I hope I don't get a headache on *the cruise*…I don't want to be stuck in my *stateroom* missing all my *activities*, not being able to wear any of my *new clothing* you know…"

She managed to sneak in three of her favorite cruise conversation topics in one sentence. Impressive, if not mildly annoying.

A week before my parents left, they came out to Brentwood for a visit. Up until this time, our conversations had centered on all pre-cruise preparation as well as the collection of suitable paraphernalia for the trip. Eight long months were spent organizing, hunting, gathering, and on my part—just listening to the endless possibilities. This trip was like a pregnancy, and I was the friend of the mother-to-be. My "I'm so happy for you" attitude evolving into one of "Please, not another story about the cruise" as we neared the final stretch.

After a relatively short stay Mom decided they needed to get home and 'get ready' for the bon voyage. She had to "practice packing." I quickly glanced around the room. Was I the only one who thought this unusual? Having never heard of such an event, I inquired how one goes about such a thing.

Mom: "I don't know why you're laughing young lady. I need to make sure everything fits in my suitcase. And wipe that look off your face."

I pictured her standing over a neatly packed suitcase, smiling and nodding. Then removing everything, only to repack it again the exact same way. Rinse and repeat. I snickered.

And there was this exchange on the night before their departure:

Mom: (again, phoning me) "Hi dear. Just wanted to let you know we'll be leaving on our cruise tomorrow morning. (REALLY???) I'll be sending you our itinerary in the mail before we leave."

I'm thinking this is totally unnecessary but—whatever. I cradle the phone between my shoulder and ear, continue slicing grapes, and attempt to shake Ben off my leg, signal Josh to turn down the TV, and slap Brad's hands as he eats the fruit I am cutting for the kids. The phone slips, I fumble it and swear, then return it to my ear just in time to hear her add, "I'm also sending you a list of all the activities on the ship. You should see it! The games, the dancing, the dinners! It's high time I had a vacation you know—I've been doing nothing for years but working my ass off for everyone else!"

I smile. My mom works because she wants to. Because she causes trouble when she finds herself with too much time on her hands. A little part-time office job keeps her out of the house, out of my dad's hair, and gives her the spending money she enjoys.

The next morning, a mere 12 hours after the last call, my phone rang again. "Hi Carolyn!" Dad sounds excited. "We leave today on our cruise." I'm wondering if he and my mother ever talk to one another at all. "So, uh…can you take care of the cat?" Since I live 45 minutes from them and happen to know my mom has already contracted with a house-sitter, my answer is obvious. "Love to." What he doesn't know won't hurt him.

And then later that day:

Mom: "Hi hon! We're in our *stateroom*. (Giggle giggle) It's sooo nice. We're watching the fellows put the luggage on board. Oooh, they look so strong! Here, talk to your father!"

She passes the phone and I hear Dad, albeit muffled, chuckle, "Oh ho ho…don't drop it overboard!" They share a long laugh, then "Oh Bill!" in the background. (More giggles)

Me: "Have you two hit the bottle already?"

As I iron a shirt, I balance on one foot while the other is pressed against the round belly of my overzealous tot in an effort to keep him at bay. The boy is laughing and pushing his tummy forward, trying to knock me off kilter. I signal to his older brother for a little help, while trying not to iron my hand. Due to the howls of the child who is yanked by the arm down the hall, I missed a majority of the conversation. But I did hear, "And go by the house and check on the cat."

Three days into their cruise my sister calls me. She is the one other person who can relate to the last year with these folks. Plus, she stayed with them for one week prior to their departure. Poor thing.

"Well, give it to me straight. How many breakdowns did Mom have before they left?"

She scoffs. "I don't even know. She had a different reason for each one every night I was there. Did you know the day before they left, she made me shop for her? I picked up film, cat food, and even a pair of shoes! Do you know how hard it is to buy shoes for someone?" I am laughing already. "Carolyn, she made me buy her shoes." Sister is beside herself.

"Wait," I cut in, "What was Mom doing for the last eight months? All she talked about was how she prepared!"

"Yeah, well. She's all talk. She spent over an hour one night just eye-balling her suitcase. I was going crazy! I finally screamed at her, 'Pack the damn thing and be done with it!'"

We both are hooting and cackling. "And why does Dad think YOU are taking care of the cat? Mom hired someone."

Neither one can say much, we are laughing so hard. "They called me from the ship you know," she continues, "I think they were drunk." I can't even sit up on the couch. I'm making little snorting and gasping noises in my hysteria.

"They called me too." We calm down a bit. "You think they're having fun?"

"Yep," she says, "I'm so jealous. I wish I was on a cruise."

"Me, too."

But You Had to Have It!

"**What do you** want to do with this?" Brad holds up my Thighmaster and raises an eyebrow. We're cleaning out the garage and thus, treading on some shaky ground with what goes and what stays.

I barely look up. "Toss it." He gasps. "But *you had to have* it. You begged and pleaded, cried practically, until I gave in and bought you one."

I am incredulous. "I did not. I bought that myself before I even knew you. You're obviously confusing this with the Stair Stepper." That baby I did whine and cry for, back in the day. I just *had to have* one of those and when I did finally become the proud owner, I used it and the accompanying video two or three times before I grew bored. I felt embarrassed being the only person in my garage stepping and sliding around. When I brought it inside, I became subjected to snickers and hoots from the peanut gallery. I tried once again to step my way back to the pre-baby weight I enjoyed, after the kids were born, but trying to kick and slide with babies attached to my lower limbs became too much of a different kind of workout. I lost track of it until today, when we found it supporting boxes of books and albums.

"What about these?" Now he raises my Tony Little VHS tapes up for scrutiny. "Make a decision, *you can do it...*" he mocks Tony's catch phrase and we laugh. Then I groan. All these things I had wanted so badly, and here they were, hidden among other cast away items we had long forgotten about.

It reminds me of my mom. I wonder what ever happened to her yogurt maker. The one she *had to have*. She dropped hints for months before Christmas one year, showing us pictures in magazines, telling us which stores were carrying them. She'd smile and nod, tap the glossy ads and shake her head. "Just think...homemade yogurt, girls. No more buying little cartons. Now you can have any flavor you want." None of us were totally sold on the idea. Especially my father.

"Ugh, yogurt..." Dad made a face. "Why buy a machine that makes sour milk? Just leave some Half and Half out for a month and there you go—homemade yogurt." He laughed at his own quick wit. But Mom was relentless in her pursuit. She got her coveted yogurt machine that year and made one batch. Just one. Never again has that machine been used. The yogurt, if that's what it actually was, turned out so awful she couldn't put us through a second attempt. I think she still has it though, probably stashed away in her kitchen cupboards somewhere.

Not too many rooms away from my *had to have* prom dress and Andrea's *had to have* OP jacket, I found a dress my Junior year of high school that I needed for the prom. It was perfect and was, what I thought, unique. Strapless black velvet, layers of shimmery purple organza, a gi-normous bow in the back. I envisioned being the belle of the ball. And so did about 25 other girls who wore the same dress that night. So much for standing out in a crowd.

And Andrea begged and moaned about getting an OP jacket one Christmas, only to not get it and throw the tantrum to beat all tantrums in the Joyce family. She went and bought it herself at a sale the day after, just in time to learn that the style had died over the holidays and kids no longer wore them. She wore her OP jacket back to school the day after the break, then never again.

"What are we going to do with all of this?" Brad asks, mildly annoyed.

I shrug. "Toss it in the cement mixer on our driveway. You know, the one you just had to have."

But My Mom Always Says

"You've got more problems than Carter has pills!" My hand flew up to my mouth and I gasped. Had I really said that? Horrified, I asked Brad, "Did I just say what I think I said?" He nodded and smirked, "You sure did, *Paula*."

Oh my gosh. I have become my mother. It's finally happened. After 30 years of fighting what has obviously become a futile battle, my hips have widened, my thighs have lost their definition, and my mouth is spewing forth terms from the olden days. Before you know it, I'll be applying rouge to my cheeks, looking for records to play on my phonograph, and be telling my friends their wire was busy when I phoned them. The thought of that just made me break out in a cold sweat.

I can't pinpoint the exact moment of transformation. Perhaps it was the first time I told Josh to mind his P's and Q's when we had company. I later learned, via an email, how that expression came into being, and made the concerted effort to fight Mother Nature and be me, not my mom. 'Years ago, at the local taverns, pubs and bars, people drank from pint and quart sized containers. A bar maid's job was to keep an eye on the customers and to keep the drinks coming. She had to pay close attention and remember who was drinking pints and who was drinking quarts. Hence the expression "minding your P's and Q's." Fascinating little piece of trivia…

Now while I might go forth barking various expressions I picked up from my mom, I'd like to think that's as bad as it'll get. But I can't say for sure. I was the only kid I knew whose mom had, in a moment of frustration, pulled the car to a skidding halt on the shoulder of a freeway when my sister and I were fighting, and told us point blank, "Get out." We sat stone silent in the backseat, the earphones from Andrea's Walkman hanging limply between us, evidence of our scuffle. "If you two don't stop all this fighting, you can walk home." We were miles from the city we lived in. Although I know now it was an empty threat, the prospect of having to march along the highway was sobering. We reserved our fights for when we were closer to home after that.

My mom also grew tired of hearing us bicker over what was fair, who got more, how something happened, where were so-n-so's favorite Sergio jeans, and why weren't we allowed to go to the mall? Red colored nail polish was worn by girls who were easy and high heeled sandals gave off the wrong message, a couple more of mom's favorite little sayings. I'm sure raising two daughters who constantly rolled their eyes at her and threatened to run away forever was no picnic. But she always had her expressions to keep us in line.

"Name brand clothing is exactly like the stuff being sold at K-mart. I'm not spending an arm and a leg on a tag." As if we ever asked her to cough up a limb for the sake of fashion. As a kid, I wondered what specifically was the price of an arm and a leg? Which cost more? The leg was my rational. I never knew for sure. When I did inquire about such things, I was told to not get "sassy". (Still a favorite word of mine.) And to "watch my mouth." If I dared to even whisper, "But I can't see it," I would get a smack on the hand and be told to "mind your P's and Q's." I only wish I knew then where that expression had originated. I may have ordered myself a pint, just for the heck of it.

"Who's Carter and why does he need pills?" My young son is genuinely curious. I hug him close to me and tickling his ribs, I tell him, "Now don't be sassy…"

The Mysterious Long Black Line

In the good old days, back when I went on outings with my own parents, one of my favorite places to visit was my godparents' house. As far as I knew, John and Fran Maness ruled the world. Never mind their own two children, they welcomed me with open arms and made me feel like a part of their family each time. Not only was I allowed to stay up late, they let me watch scary movies and do midnight freezer raids for ice cream and Popsicles when I felt compelled.

Knowing my love for reading, they gave me books—the ones filled with rows and rows of LifeSavers candy. Since I adored cooking, they supplied me with my very own Pizza Hut mini-bake oven. I was showered with hula-hoops, barrettes and toys my own parents would never buy. I adored these people. There was just one thing I could never figure out.

"What is that long black line?" I asked my mom one night. She sat reading the paper and barely looked up. "Huh?"

"You know, the one on Fran's chest."

Mom glanced at me looking oddly curious. She eyed my father, who wore an identical expression.

With my finger, I made a straight line down my front in between where my future bosom would reside. "There is a black line right here and I want to know what it is." My mom and dad could not stop laughing. They leaned over their papers, whooping and slapping their knees.

I came away from that experience with a new word: cleavage. Still, I really didn't understand. I decided to ask Fran the next time I saw her.

"I want to know about your cleavage," I told her one night over dinner. John choked on his food and reached for a glass of milk. She smiled and asked, "Are you sure you know what you are asking?"

"I'm serious," I said, putting down my fork and swallowing my meatloaf. "I saw the black line and I want to know more about it." I sat silent while they did a repeat episode of my parents.

She explained to me that sometimes women's breasts grow bigger and bigger and the space in between them closes up. The little valley between breasts is called "cleavage" and that I too, would have my very own cleavage when the time came.

"Oh, not me," I replied. "I'm only to grow my boobs so that they are this big." I held my hands in little cups over my chest and made the size of say, a 38 DD. As impressed as I was with Fran's mammoth breasts, I didn't want any of my own. She laughed and told me that if I ever learned to command my body to stop growing in certain areas, to please call her and let her know the trick.

After that I was on black line patrol. I spotted cleavage everywhere I looked and was astonished at how it varied. Big gaps, little gaps and gaps with dark shadows. Too often, I was told by my mother to lighten up on the cleavage conversations with my sister. Andrea was interested too, but since she would come into her own cleavage years before me, I saw her as a threat: someone who would join the upper ranks and leave us cleavage-less girls to fend for ourselves.

I had nothing to worry about. With time came cleavage and all the backaches and scratchy bras that accompany it. I only wish I could call up Fran and tell her that no, I hadn't learned how to command my body to stop growing in certain areas. Maybe by now she could tell me.

White is White

I'm a girl of color. I like bold statements, rich textures, and contrasting hues- especially when I paint a room. Our kitchen is a deep Cherry Red and soft Canary Yellow. It's warm and comforting and very lovely if you ask me. But if you ask my mother, she'll tell you it's outlandish. That is, of course, after she rises from the heap she just crumpled into after fainting dead away.

When I first painted my kitchen, I chose a passionate blue. I believe it was called 'Blueberry'. I sponged and slathered until my heart's content and then invited my mother to come over for a little look-see. I opened the door with great flourish and announced, "Ta-da!" then watched as her smile wilted clean off her face.

"What?" I asked. "What?"

"I don't see what's wrong with white," she told me, "Or go bold and paint with 'Eggshell', but these colors…well they're just so suggestive…" She fanned her face with her hand. She looked at me, eyes wide. Blink, blink.

"Are you implying that my kitchen is a hussy?" I started hooting. That was years ago. Since then, I've redone the kitchen in shades of green, and just recently again in the red and yellow. While I say 'Martha Stewart" or 'Pottery Barn', she insists its décor is more 'Turn of the Century Bordello.'

Last week she told me that her and my father are repainting the interior of their own home in order to put it on the market. I couldn't help myself, I had to ask, "And what colors are you thinking of?" Innocent shrug.

"Why, shades of white, of course," she replied coolly. "But not just any white—we have those contrasting hues you like so much."

Contrasting shades of white...the intrigue is all mine.

"We've already painted our bedroom and bathroom 'Navajo', and went for a more updated modern look in the hallway. It's called 'Paper Lantern.'"

I kept control of my smile.

"Then, your father—you know your father, he always wants to go against what works, well—he insisted on some color for the kitchen so I gave in. We went with 'Snowflake.'"

I felt a twitch coming on near my mouth.

"For the family room I thought a soft and easy look would be best. I chose 'Lily'. But to pull out the baseboards a tad, I painted them 'Antique'. I'm concerned though—that Antique is starting to look a little yellowish in certain light."

I covered my mouth with my hand to hide the ear-to-ear grin I was sporting.

"In the dining room, I want to stay neutral. 'Cool Cream' is a good choice for such a small space. But we'll do the ceiling beams a little darker—just to show some depth. It's called 'Cotton'. Or was it 'Cloud'? No, that's right, we're doing 'Cloud' in the upstairs bedrooms..." She tapped her lip in attempt at remembering.

"Really? 'Cloud'?" I cut in, "Isn't that a bit bold when you're trying to sell a house?"

"*Oh, I know.* I thought the same thing, people looking will probably just..." she caught my grin. Saw me chuckle. Now understood the sarcasm. She swatted me with her dishtowel.

I had to understand, then just accept, that she and I differ on color schemes, that's all. While I tend to drift towards bold and shocking, she'll always lean toward soft and passive. Steer clear of making a statement. I have a theory on paint preferences—colors probably tell a lot about people. I suggested this to her, while she stood refolding her towel and glaring at me from the corner of her eye.

"You're right," she said. "Preferring white says that I am clean, organized, and simple. It says I am orderly, innocent, and ready for excitement. Just not on the walls." Well…okay. I tell her I agree, but what's my other alternative? Tell her white is white? Nah—she's not ready for that kind of excitement.

18

It Runs in the Family

I Was Born with It

"**Where did this** come from?"

My son is finger tracing the diminutive tattoo of a daisy I have on my inner right ankle. He's almost three and until this point my husband and I have been pretty honest with him about everything out there. I knew this day would come and I've known for a while just how I would answer—truthfully.

When I was little, my dad proudly showed me the tattoo of a donkey he had on his leg. I would stand wide-eyed in wonder of just how amazing it was. He loved to flex his muscle and make it do tricks. At times, he'd pull his sock down slowly and feign surprise that it was gone—only to reveal it and laugh, much to my relief. Whenever I asked him where he got it, he always said the same thing, "I was born with it." And when I'd inquire, "But why a donkey?" My mom would pipe up from another room, "Because your father is a jackass." (I later learned of her extreme dislike for tattoos, but had no understanding of the sarcasm of that particular moment.) I was pretty easily impressed, I suppose. That, and easily fooled. There's a short stretch of time in there when good old Dad had me thinking he carried a special gene for body art, and perhaps mine would appear in due time.

The notion that a person could actually be born with a picture on their body was too much for me. I repeatedly looked over every inch of myself to see if I had been lucky enough to have even the slightest trace of an image. While I prayed for things like flowers and rainbows to appear overnight, I feared I would be branded with a skeleton or the dreaded rodeo clown.

"When will one ever turn up on me?" I whined to my dad, after a close inspection of the skin behind my knee one day. "Never," interrupted Mom, "Not today, not tomorrow, and not even when you are eighteen!"

Well, she was half right. Nothing turned up on my body until I was about 23. Good friends of ours accompanied my husband and I to a damp hole in the wall in Campbell where I paid way too much money for a microscopic version of my favorite flower to be permanently put on my ankle.

Even then, I knew the day would come when I'd have to tell my future children why I got that tattoo. Not that I'm ashamed, on the contrary. I rather like my little flower and I do take a certain amount of pleasure in the fact that I did something I've always wanted to do. Yet, as candid as I am, even I know that trying to explain the fine line of individualization versus replication is an exercise in insanity.

"Where did this come from?" he asks again. I quickly sneak a peek at Brad, who sits nonchalantly flipping through a magazine on the opposite couch. He glances up at me and slyly grins. "Yes, Sweetie. Wherever did you get that?" I take a moment to match his smirk, then looking my son directly in the eye, I smile and answer, "I was born with it."

Malt Jar Hide and Seek

During a visit to my parent's house recently, I opened the pantry and there on a shelf, looking me straight in the eye, was a jar of Carnation Malt. Stunned, I stepped back and looked at my mother in surprise.

"What is this doing here?" I asked. "Why do you have it in plain sight?"

All she could do was smile and say, "Carolyn, you don't live here anymore. We no longer have to hide it."

Okay, I admit it. I had a tendency to graze once in a while and more often than not, the jar of malt became a dusty, yet sweet, midnight snack. When my older sister came home from a date one night, she was shocked to find me holed up in the sack with a jar of malt. I had been reading and she startled me while lifting the spoon to my lips.

"Wha...?" I yelped as my door opened. Malt went everywhere and I fumbled with the spoon, finally dropping it back in the jar with a distinctive "clink".

"Ooooh. I love that stuff. Here, gimme a bite." We sat on my bed eating malt by the mouthful, licking our lips and spitting malt dust into the air as we laughed.

A few nights later, our dad went to make a shake after dinner and we heard him bark from the pantry, "What the hell happened to all the malt?" Andrea and I exchanged a look and both played innocent when our dad stood there shaking the near empty malt jar in our faces.

Well, turns out good old Dad didn't like to be shortchanged either when it came to the malt. We got a stern lecture and promised not to eat it plain anymore. After that, the malt became somewhat of a joke in our home, a challenge to see who could eat it all first and irritate the one to find the jar. Andrea and I started getting crafty too, putting the empty jar strategically in each other's backpacks, closets, even in the underwear drawers. It was a hoot to find that empty jar when you least expected to. Andrea topped all the tricks by devouring the last of it one night then placing my school picture with a spoon in the jar. She positioned it at the front of the cupboard for my dad to find.

Then the game changed. The malt disappeared altogether. We could never locate it. Confused, Andrea and I refused to believe they had stopped buying the malt, we figured they had just started hiding it. This created two opposing camps in our home: malt hiders and malt seekers. Dad would whip up malted milk shakes for us at night, but we weren't allowed downstairs during the process. We spent hours scouring the house trying to find that jar, but we never did.

Then one night I brought a boy home and we sat kissing on the couch after the parents had gone to bed. A little uncomfortable shifting of the weight and... "Ouch," my date reached under one of the cushions and came up with a malt jar. Almost full. "Oh yes!" I screamed, "Whooo hoooo…I found their hiding place!"

Rather than eat it, I put it back in the couch, confident I'd have some power over my sister at a later time, when I planned to dangle the information in front of her. Unfortunately, I never got my opportunity; the next time I went seeking out the malt in the couch, it had disappeared.

The game continued through the years and we played it more out of the love of the routine, than the needing to eat malt during the wee hours of the night. Though we hadn't found their exact hiding place, we always enjoyed telling stories of "malt jar hide-and-seek."

A few years back my parents hosted a family barbeque and somehow the subject of the malt jar found its way into the conversation. Andrea and I sat laughing with an uncle, who had heard of the family tradition over time. He took a swig of his drink and shaking his head, asked, "So do your parents still hide the malt in their antique telephone?"

Mouths agape, we were silent. He saw the look pass between us sisters and then shifted nervously in his chair. "You never knew. Well look at that…I better refill my drink…" he excused himself.

As I sat there staring at my sister, it occurred to me; I never really wanted to find that malt jar. Knowing now where it had been all that time didn't make me feel better, it made me feel sad. One look at Andrea told me she felt the same way. Our game was officially over, even though we had both moved away from home years before.

"Do we tell them we know?" she asked me.

"It looks like we don't need to. Uncle Jerry is confessing at this very moment." We watched as our uncle profusely apologized to our parents, who just laughed and shrugged it off.

I like to think we would never have told them.

Liquid Fire Slathered on Open Wounds

Topical antiseptics sure have come a long way since I was a kid. These days, children don't have to contend with the sting of a scratch or scrape very long due to Bactine, Neosporin, and Cortaid. Check the first-aid aisle at any store and you'll see a wide variety of boo-boo ointments.

I know this because I live with two little boys that have no grasp on the concept of action/consequence.

Just yesterday—"Agghhhh!" One son's shrill scream rode the breeze through the screen of my back slider. I knew better than to react quickly, my eldest practices the art of melodrama on a daily basis. When the scream continued, then shifted slightly in key, I recognize this as a real cry for help, rather than an appeal at extra attention. Once I had the scene of the accident in my sights, I stifled a giggle. The 6-year-old, like every other kid his age, learns things the hard way. Never mind that I told him earlier not to stand on the table. He opted to disregard my instructions and have himself a king-sized tumble.

Though he lay on the ground in a heap, whimpering, with one knee tucked up to his chin, he had learned a valuable lesson. Or two. The first was that his old mom might know what she's talking about. The second was that even if you turn one round spool table on its side and stand on the middle, chances are it will roll out underneath you and drop you on your back. Which is where I came in.

When his abrasions were cleaned out and he was all doctored up, I sent him on his merry way and thought back to how dissimilar accident scenes looked when I was his age.

My folks practiced more of the "tough love" philosophy of parenting, rather than the more encouraged "nurture, respect, and openly show affection" types of today. For example, "What are you lying underneath your bicycle for?" might be what I'd hear rather than, "Oh honey, are you all right?" "Why is your leg wrapped around your head like that?" "Are those your teeth that you're standing there holding?" and "Don't drip all that blood on my living room carpet!" were all commonplace quotes. Nothing unusual about making the child pick up her own dismembered limbs, should that be the case.

Back then there was no Bactine. You could have looked all over the earth and not found anything close to the likes of Neosporin. In my day, parents were firm believers in the power of Mercurochrome and Merthiolate. I'd rather repeat the fall and land again and again on my open sore than have that liquid fire applied to my injuries. And my parents abused that stuff. They had it on hand for every occasion. I think my mother carried it around in her purse, just in case. Skinned knee, scratched elbow, chapped lips. Lost a tooth? No problem—Dad's eyes would glaze over while a slow smile spread across his face. "I'll get the merthilolate." (Cue sinister laugh). I think my parents rather enjoyed the reaction it invited. They swore that "If it didn't sting, it wouldn't work."

Both little bottles of red ink taught my sister and I early on to nurse ourselves back to wellbeing. I once miscalculated my steps while hopping from log to log during a summer daytrip to our cabin in Twain Harte. A neighbor child and I were singing and frolicking—on logs—and one false move found me with my bare leg wedged between two of them. I howled. Partly from the shock of it, but mostly because I knew I'd be sitting in agony with a red leg in a matter of minutes.

Even today, a bottle no bigger than the size of one's thumb sits perched in my parent's medicine cabinet, its label faded to a dull yellow and the price ($1.15) still boldly visible. It's a wonder they still use it.

"Hasn't this stuff been declared poisonous and highly toxic by the Board of Health yet?" I recently asked my father. "Are you aware that this is pure acid you apply to your open wounds?" I shook the jar to drive home my point. "Have you ever heard of Bactine, Dad? It's painless and does the same thing..."

He grinned and replied, "Well, you know what they say: if it doesn't sting..." I already knew the rest. I just wonder if he knows that he is "they."

The Real Reason I Hate Clowns

I had a flashback. The real reason I hate clowns came bubbling to the surface of my psyche when a kid with a squeaky horn rode past me on his bike. Never before had I been forced into a honk-induced realization, so this was obviously a profound moment.

Until the biker crossed my path, I had believed my abhorrence of the pasty-faced rogue was brought about by my parents forcing me to room with an oil painting of a sad hobo clown that silently tortured my conscious. When the painting fell from the wall and landed smack on my head in the middle of the night, the pandemonium that followed was—what I thought—the reasoning behind a lifelong paranoia of all falsely happy, suspiciously dressed freaks of nature. But that kid's "bleep" is what made me recall my first-ever encounter with one of those sketchy characters.

1979. The year I was in second grade at Monte Verde Elementary School. I loved school, and I adored this particular teacher. Miss Melvin was a young lady who fancied psychedelic colors and long, gauzy skirts. She wore boots with fringe and, on special occasions, leather sandals that laced up her calves. Ribbons and flowers adorned her hair, and she always smelled of something earthy and sweet. It wasn't until I hit the party scene in high school that I inhaled that earthy aroma once again and then figured out why my former teacher was always so relaxed.

There we were one day, our class working diligently on word jumbles, while Steppenwolf, the "Band of the Week," played softly on Miss Melvin's eight track. I sat humming along to "Magic Carpet Ride" when our classroom door opened. Granted, I had never been to a circus at this point, nor was I familiar with anything more unusual than H.R. PufnStuf. I stared wide-eyed at the intruder, my hand frozen in midair, gripping the pencil tighter by the second.

The clown bellowed, "Hello, boys and girls…I'm Fruity the Clown" and then went into a fit of smoker's cough. He bent at the waist, hacking and wheezing. With one hand on his knee, he waved the other around wildly, holding up one finger. His curly rainbow wig bounced limply against his head. I didn't trust the stripey jumpsuit and the exaggerated painted red mouth reminded me too much of Mrs. Johnson, an old lady who lived on my street. She'd stand out in her front yard wearing a housecoat and curlers, holding a martini glass and barking at neighborhood kids with a cigarette dangling from her lips. Always, her mouth caked in red lipstick.

Fear warmed my chest. I sat paralyzed and didn't relax even when Fruity cleared his phlegm and swallowed his hairball. I spied Miss Melvin at her desk. Her eyes were closed and she was rubbing her temples. Clearly, not a fan. I shot out of my desk and scurried in her direction.

Nothing like a frightened child to get the attention of a clown. "Ah—don't be skerred, little girlie! Fruity's friendly!" he forced a chuckle through his little, brown, corn nut teeth.

I cowered behind Miss Melvin and watched at a distance as he shaped balloons, juggled oranges, and stumbled in floppy red shoes. His passion for the squeaky horn was just wrong. I cringed each time it gasped for air. Get…you, get…you, it wheezed.

In an attempt at winning me over, or quite possibly at mocking me, Fruity tried to include me in his act. I swatted away his offering of a plastic flower, and practically relieved Miss Melvin of her gauzy skirt when shrieked and panicked, then made a move to crawl under it.

She wrestled me out and waved away Fruity, who was tossing scarves around to woo me. I kicked and thrashed, and don't recall what happened next.

Gee. Thank you, boy with squeaky horn. Now I remember why I hate clowns.

Bill Cookies

I dropped the blob of cookie dough onto the sheet and said to Josh, "We're making Bill Cookies…" He looked amazed and had that wide-eyed wonder gaze spread across his face. You've got to love kids—they are awed by the smallest of things.

"Bill Cookies…wow," he breathed. He's standing on a chair, looking hopefully into the bowl. Thinking perhaps, I may give him another taste of cookie dough. He's probably right—I'm a softie when it comes to limits on cookie dough. We're licking our fingers and I ask him, "Do you know why these cookies are called Bill Cookies?" He shakes his head and pops his finger out of his mouth. "Well, Bill Cookies are probably the BEST cookies in the whole world! Grandpa Bill taught me how to make them, and I'm going to teach you!" He looks at me like I have just handed him the moon.

Grandpa Bill is my dad. A big-time cookie lover and as a kid, I looked forward to his cookies more than anyone else's. He would break all of the cookie making rules and drop huge blobs of dough onto the sheet. Sometimes, he'd just make four big cookies out of an entire batch of dough.

This was before the time of Mrs. Fields and of Cookie Bouquet. This was when kids had to eat hard little rock cookies that their mommies made. Some mommies left the cookies in the oven too long and tried to tell their children that all cookies were black underneath. Maybe this was just my mom, I don't know. I do know that when Bill was in the kitchen, it was time for celebration. I knew we'd be eating good!

Over time, "Bill" became synonymous with "big", and we found ourselves eating Bill Omelets, Bill Pancakes, and Bill Burgers when Dad was at the helm of the kitchen. With Dad cooking, two things would be guaranteed: leftovers and kids slumped over at the dinner table, groaning and unbuttoning their pants at the waist.

"There is no reason these kids need to eat so much!" Mom would declare, adjusting herself so that we couldn't see her unbutton her jeans too. It was a regular feeding frenzy.

I haven't had a real Bill Cookie in years, I've had to make my own and they just don't taste the same. Licking a beater, I stand over the sink pondering the variance in cookie tastes. At that moment, Brad sauntered into the kitchen and seeing the big blobs of dough ready to be baked, exclaims, "Hey! You're making Bill Cookies!" That explains it.

We Did Not Raise You Like That

When Brad and I first bought our dining room furniture, we christened it by setting up a net, investing in some balls and paddles, and made it a game table, rather than something to eat on. My mom almost had a coronary when she saw it.

"Agh!" She threw her hands in the air, "We didn't raise you like that!" She had popped in for a visit during the middle of a heated ping-pong match and was totally unimpressed with our creativity.

"Well then, you'll really love this." I tossed my paddle onto the table, enjoying her wide-eyed shock at my nonchalance, and reached to remove a framed wall picture. Once down, it revealed our past and current scores hidden behind it. Written in pen. She nearly fainted. She stood shaking her head in disapproval. "I don't understand how you could be so careless with your belongings."

Careless? I disagree. I enjoy my home and everything it in, to the point that I refuse to own furniture people can't sit on, decorate rooms guests can't enter, and have knick-knacks that children can't touch. What's the point?

Growing up in a home where my mother would vacuum frantically after someone walked through the living room was painful. She owned couches that were off limits, ceramic cats that I could only observe from afar, and insisted on keeping the temperature set at a cool 65 degrees. Brrr…

The climate issue was the crux of a few inter-family debates. Dad, sister, and myself all claiming we could see out breath in the air while Mom insisting, we could all don sweaters rather than complain. As soon as I was tall enough to view the numbers on the thermostat, I was amazed that the prospect of running around in our shorts in the middle of winter loomed before us, and never had any adult seized the opportunity.

I shared what I knew with my older sister. "We do NOT have to freeze all the time," I told her. It was anarchy. We cranked the heat up to 85 one cool winter morning and put on our swimsuits. Dad came down for his cup of coffee and smiled at us, the realization that his two daughters were in their summer gear made no connection. It was short lived.

"Is the heat on?" We heard the shout from upstairs. The three of us exchanged knowing glances. Then my dad took a second look at me. I stood in my little bikini and swim fins. I peered out through neon green goggles at him and waved. Smiled with a snorkel between my teeth.

Mom flew into the kitchen, curlers popping out wildly, robe half opened. "Who turned on the…agh! What are you girls wearing?" Andrea's towel fell from her shoulders as she shrugged. "Swimsuits? In the middle of winter?" She threw her hands in the air, "I didn't raise you like that!" At 7 and 10, she sure had. We certainly hadn't been raised by anyone else.

As an adult homeowner, I vowed to never be uncomfortable in my own house. This knowledge has not escaped my mom, who remarks every time she visits how warm and cozy she is. Dad just grumbles, "Yeah, it's not the G-D icehouse you make us live in, that's for sure."

Some things will never change. I will happily paint over ink on my walls, keep paddles and balls rather than cloth napkins and placemats in the drawers of my table, and sit crossed-legged with my feet on the couch wearing my shorts and a tank-top while it rains outside. My kids can wear unseasonal clothing if they wish, jump on any bed in the house and be exactly the people I raise them to be.

19

The Best Things in Life are Free

Changing Times

"Hey," **my girlfriend** said to me as she passed me her son's sippy cup to rinse out at her sink, "Do you remember when it used to be frosty beer mugs and pool that brought us all together?"

I smiled. "Yeah…now it's more like Chuck E. Cheese and Hannah Montana."

"Chuck E. Cheese serves beer." She is totally serious. "And what do you know about Hannah Montana? You have sons…"

A group of us has gathered at her house to celebrate someone's birthday. Must be the kid with the hat—though I'm a little unsure who's kid he is. Between us, there must be about 43 rugrats racing around. Here's what happens when you grow older with the same people you were kids with. Conversations evolve from elusive plans to sneak out and cause trouble to reminiscing about elusive plans to sneak out and cause trouble. Only now there are small children milling about so the only thing that remains the same is that you still have to whisper.

I like change, but mostly when I generate it myself. Change is good when you're ready, confusing when you're not. The change in times is what I really find entertaining. Take for example my most recent visit to the doctor. I sat patiently in the waiting room perusing the bland variety of magazines. I shared space with a nice montage of people: a teenager who slumped over in her chair, rapidly text messaging, her mother who not so quietly chatted on her cell phone, and an elderly man. I was actually walking past this same gentleman on my way inside the building when he so kindly stopped me in the parking lot and pointed at his car.

"Yes?" I smiled.

"How'd you like to buy my pimp mobile?" He gestured at an ancient Lincoln Continental. I recognized this car because in high school my best friend's dad drove a yellow one and made us take it out on the nights we wanted to cruise around. Though the color wasn't that of a ripe banana, the model was exactly the same. I cringed and started to laugh. This guy was easily in his 70s and his remark caught me off guard. I began to apologize, but he waved me off with a huge grin, "Nah…I'm just kiddin ya. It's not for sale sweetheart." He opened the door for me and we entered together. Kindly, he allowed me to register first.

Once seated, I watched him rifle through the magazines, thinking that this kind of reading was probably right up his ally. I sat desperately craving some trash to catch up on when he suddenly whistled to the gals behind the reception desk. "What say you get some real reading material in here?" He waved around *TIME*. "I don't wanna read about what's happening in the war or who's campaign is good for what…I need to know what Britney's doing and if LiLo is goin' to the slammer."

I don't know which was funnier—that he voiced what was the consensus opinion regarding the offered magazine selection, or that he knew who Britney was and that Lindsey Lohan goes by 'LiLo' in the press. Hilarious, welcome, but mostly unexpected. Surely, a sign of the change in times.

I think growing older takes some getting used to. I once watched my mom examine her face for crow's feet and fine lines, check herself out from all angles in her bedroom mirror, and powder her face for 'all over coverage', none of it making any sense to me whatsoever. Now I study the age defying products in the cosmetic department, throw on a ball cap to fix my hair, and hope like hell my sweats and sneakers will pass for an athletic-yet-casual look while doing the birthday party circuit.

Retired Teacher Turns Preschool Mom

Once upon a time, I used to be a preschool teacher. This was before my eldest was born, and back in the days when I had no real concept of time management. I was clueless to how my life would go from 'slightly hectic' to 'full bore out of control' once I had my own children. (Spending a good portion of my day with kids who belonged to other people must have given me a false sense of security when it came to parenting.) I treasured my job though; the hustle and bustle of frolicking children partnered with my adoration of all things related to education, I was in a world all my own. And I loved it. The children never wore me down, usually it was their parents that had me reaching for my Excedrin Migraine. I vowed never to be one of *those* moms. I like to think I had a pretty good handle on being the exact opposite.

And then my son barfed on me at his preschool the other day. I had been holding him, while explaining to a teacher that yes, he was a little crabby, but not to worry—he wasn't sick. The next thing I knew I was wearing his breakfast and clearing a path for the two of us, trying to make a quick getaway. I apologized profusely. Horrified, I was. Because I knew, *I knew* how it appeared. Mom knows kid is sick, brings him anyway in the hopes of running off to get a pedicure or massage, while the staff is forced to deal with a child who is better being home in bed. Not to mention the exposure to and the contamination of the rest of the class. I'd seen it far too often when I was a teacher. And though this wasn't the case, it felt like it seemed so, at least for the moment.

I once taught a little chap who just wasn't ready for preschool. Though his Mommy insisted he was, he proved her wrong every day by vomiting upon arrival in my classroom, his nerves having gotten the best of him. But he wasn't a sickie-pie, just genuinely nervous. Unlike one little fellow who marched into my classroom one afternoon with his mouth hidden behind open, running sores. My shock must have been apparent to his mother who flicked her wrist at me and said, "Oh it's nothing. Just impetigo. See you at 3 p.m. after my pedicure!" Once I gathered my senses, I chased her into the parking lot to explain contagion and school policy, only to get a severe verbal lashing before she huffily escorted her charge off the campus. Either way, I'd rather clarify safety and health guidelines to an irritated parent than try to explain a classroom outbreak to 19 other families.

I taught for 12 years. I've seen everything from hand, foot, and mouth disease to slapped cheek and the common flu. The illnesses never surprised me. The insistence of their child's attendance in school by the parents sent me reeling every time. For example:

"Junior has a fever of 101, okay? He'll be fine if you just let him sleep in the book corner."
(Shall I let him snuggle up against the healthy kids and share their sippy cups too?)

"Little Sally has severe diarrhea. Please keep a close eye on her."
(As if I wouldn't?!)

"I know these red spots may look suspicious, but if they're still here after school, then I'll take her to the doctor..."
(Let's call the advice nurse now, shall we?)

And my all-time favorite,

"We did find quite a few nits in Johnny's hair this morning. But seriously, nothing was crawling around, so can't he just stay?"
(Well of course! And bring in his stuffed animals and blankey too!)

So, while I try not to be one of *those* moms, I do occasionally misjudge a situation. And when I do, I have two little boys who keep me walking the straight and narrow, especially around schools.

Sleeping Around?

I'm not sure if the ability to fall asleep anywhere at any time qualifies as a special talent, but if it does, then I should enter a contest. Lately I've been nodding off at the most inopportune times.

A sharp HONK jars me from my dream state, and I'm disappointed. In this midday vision I was winning a reward challenge during a Survivor episode. But suddenly here I am, in the kindergarten pickup loop, not on a deserted island with Boston Rob or Colby. The driver of the car behind me is frustrated at my inability to follow the procession of anxious parents, all waiting to acquire their child. Teachers escort children to their proper vehicles and where am I? Why, dozing inside an idling truck, my head propped up against a window, drool creeping out the left side of my mouth. Attractive. I'm sure everyone will trust me to pick up their children now for them.

"Sorry! Sorry!" Embarrassed, I wave out the window and try to look duly awake. I wipe the corner of my mouth and pinch my cheeks in an effort to snap back to reality.

Just the other day at the supermarket I felt my neck snap down as the weight of my head pulled it forward when I started to drift. I shook it, imagined the sound of a quarter in a can, and then did my best to be involved in the act of paying for my groceries. I've just been so tired.

So why is this? Dietary imbalance? Possibly. Overexertion of physical and emotional strength? Probably not—at least not for me. I'm tired all of the time because, truth be told, I stay up too late. It's a vicious circle I am caught up in and I am helpless to stop it.

In the morning I wake up to the sound of children needing me. I shuffle around shoveling food into open mouths and slapping new diapers on wet bottoms. I chauffer everyone off to school, then return home only to participate in my youngest son's in-home therapy session. I'm lucky to squeeze in a shower. Sometimes Brad will ask me, "Didn't you wear that to bed last night?" And my truthful reply, accompanied by a blank stare, "If it looks familiar, it's because I've been wearing it for more than a week now." What else can he say except "Oh."

If I am running early, I reward myself with a cup of coffee. If I am running late, I reward myself with a cup of coffee. If I am smiling, frowning, awake, asleep, goofy or serious—I reward myself with a cup of coffee. Chock full of sugar, caffeine, calories and fat, I make sure I reward myself with a cup of coffee, because I am a good mommy and I deserve it.

This too is part of the reason I fall asleep throughout the day. Either I haven't had any, or I'm coming off of a caffeine bender, it doesn't matter—I am constantly in a state of caffeination.

By the end of the day, when the children are all fed, bathed, and ready for the following morning—I have a moment of clarity. It's a thought that runs like ticker tape through my head. It says: Go to bed…go to bed… go to bed… Then the moment passes, and I find myself on the couch flipping through TiVo. The sound of canned laughter, catchy one liners, clever jingles, and sound bites from the news all keep me perched and eager for more.

The hours pass and then I walk, like a zombie, into my room and fall onto my bed vowing to never do this again. I continuously fall victim to the lure of late-night trashy TV. *Blind Date*, *Cheaters*, E! Channel anything—it's brain candy for someone who should be on a diet.

The End of an Era

"Well," **Josh sighed**, "It's the end of an era." He is six. His understanding of 'era' I'm sure, isn't what it could be.

"Do you know what an 'era' is?" I'm cautious when I ask because, as past experience would tell me, doubting Josh doesn't go over well.

"Yes," he glares. "It's an e-r-a."

Since that much is true, I say nothing. And at the same time realize that while we are having this conversation, an era is in all actuality, ending. His kindergarten era, and this makes me sad.

When Josh first started school, I was worried. I thought him too sensitive and unprepared for all he was about to confront. New kids, new rules, no familiarity with what lay ahead. Not that we hadn't prepared him—he did go to preschool, albeit his grandma's preschool where all his teachers were once co-workers of mine. I taught for years at the very school he attended, his teachers came to my wedding, and later his baby shower. They each anticipated his arrival at the school with open arms. He had visited their classrooms for a of couple years off and on and enjoyed being a "special guest" to all of them, before actually being a real student.

Having friends teach my son comforted me and I enjoyed participating in his preschool experience. But kindergarten was a different story. I was nervous and didn't know what to expect. I had, in truth, underestimated my child.

Josh flourished in kindergarten. He made friends easily and enjoyed the process of the transition. I was able to step back and allow him to be himself, whatever that meant. His teacher assured me he was apt and prepared, ready to work and happy to be there.

Though his understanding of discipline was somewhat skewed at times.

"Mom!" he gleefully told me one day when I arrived to work in the class, "Come look! I pulled a card!" Grinning, he pointed to where he had placed his green discipline card. I paused, "Is this a good thing?" I had questioned. "Aren't you supposed to be sad or something?"

"Well," he whispered in my ear, "I got it for talking too much—just like you! I'm just like you!" he nodded and smiled, reassured me he was okay. Put his shoulders back a bit, stood a little straighter.

"I'll review the rules with him," I later promised his teacher.

Throughout the course of the school year, I worked in his class a few times a month. From this vantage point, I gleaned a new perspective on his classmates, his instructors, and his learning process. I'm glad I did that too because if I had believed everything he told me without seeing what reality was for myself, I might have missed a few key components of his experience.

"Wow…Josh sure likes his teacher," his grandma told me around Valentine's Day. "We were shopping the other day and he found some stuffed teddy bear bigger than your house that he wanted to buy for her!" We had laughed about that, but in truth—I was thrilled that he had such positive feelings for someone he had to spend so much time with.

I think every parent wants to instill a love of learning in their child, as well as have them partnered with teachers throughout their academic career who do the same. My biggest concern was that Josh would focus on the frustration of a new task at hand and lose his knack for curiosity. I was worried his ability to problem solve and/or think creatively would be squelched. We've always encouraged Josh to think outside the box, to tap into resources to find answers, and trust his own instinct with uncertain circumstance. Fortunately, he had a teacher this year who appreciated his sense of self and nurtured it—didn't contain it for the sake of control.

Car Sold as Is

A sign caught my eye in the Albertson's parking lot the other day. Seems someone is trying to sell their Volkswagen Jetta. The sign read in big bold letters NO LEAKS! I laughed out loud.

Once upon a time I drove a VW Jetta. In fact, it was the first car I ever bought. I was 21 years old, straight out of college, and dying for a car that said independent, free and single. Instead, I unwillingly opted for a vehicle that lied. While I was enjoying my first taste of autonomy cruising around in my red Mercedes-Benz GLS, the previous owner was laughing all the way to the bank.

That car was nothing less than a money pit. Not more than a month after purchase, the timing belt came unattached and left me and Little Red stranded on the side of the freeway in Oakland. The $99 tow truck ride back to Pleasanton was a mere foreshadowing of what to expect in the months to come,16 bent valves and $3,000 in repairs later, I now had a car payment equal to that of a BMW. Quite possibly a new one.

After the first rain of the season, I began to notice a strange odor permeating from some unidentifiable place within the interior. Others noticed it too.

Friends would flop down into the passenger seat, then immediately look at me with disgust on their faces. "What is that smell?!" I heard all the time.

I started telling people I thought someone had died in the car because no matter how hard I tried I could never pinpoint the source of the stench.

Too often friends, and even friends of friends, would tear apart the seats and floorboards in attempt to locate some decaying carcass, but nobody ever succeeded at uncovering anything more than some loose change or a stale french fry.

Out of nowhere, the windows would fog up; cold weather, warm weather, you name it. I needed the defroster to be on emergency call.

The final decree of an exasperated mechanic, "You have a leak but we have no idea where it is." I was left with a car that looked great but smelled rancid and couldn't be relied upon to get me around the corner.

Once, I took extreme pride in my good judgment. Now, I felt a slight twinge of humiliation each time I started the engine. I was such a sucker.

Not wanting to take full responsibility for such a bad choice in a vehicle, I turned my irritation toward my folks. "You always have so much to say about every move I make," I spat, "Why not at least warn me about buying a car from a guy who was so anxious to negotiate the price?"

Although sympathetic with my plight, my parents were no more willing to sell this lemon to another kid than I was. That left me with the only option, invest in her refurbishment and have a dependable car.

One fine spring day, almost one year after her original purchase, she was driven off by another college grad, smiling and waving at me out the sunroof (also repaired). He was headed for Texas.

Though I had long finished her renovation, I felt content she was on her way out of state.

I mean, how could I ever live with the guilt of maybe driving past them on the side of some road? Clutching my copy of the bill of sale, the one which read, "Car sold as is," I waved back, hoping he'd get a good distance up the road before turning on the defrost.

The Practical Joke

The entire concept of a practical joke is an oxymoron, isn't it? "Practical" and "joke" being two opposing notions and all…if you think about it, when is a joke practical? When is it not?

Take for example something that happened on my friend's vacation last year. Her and her husband checked in to Caesar's Palace in Vegas and shortly after dropping their bags, made their way down to the pool. I should mention that they're in their 30s. Not a lot of other 30-year-olds were near the pool—it was much too crowded and over populated by the near naked hard bodies in their early 20s who had just hit the strip after finishing their finals and were embarking on their spring break.

Being the people watchers that they are, they enjoyed watching all the co-eds engage in their lively post-finals activity. Drinking, frolicking, laughing, swimming—all of it only made the happily married couple enjoy the show even more. A slight commotion in one of the cabanas made my friend, Donna, kneel on her chaise lounge and peer over the top of the back of it. She came eye to cheek with a young girl getting a massage who had stripped down to nothing, but the plaster cast wrapped around her calf. Gulp. Donna giggled and jabbed her husband, Chad, who turned to get a peek at the adult massage.

But the naked female laying face down didn't keep their attention long. The girl's boyfriend plopped into her wheelchair and began doing wheelies and spinning in circles, egged on by his friends on the deck and in the pool. Not satisfied with the cheers and hoots for more, the kid wheeled back to the gate, then—at full speed, took off in the chair right towards the pool. Much to the young crowd's delight, he careened off the ledge and into the water, wheelchair and all.

The howls and applause got the attention of the lifeguard who, at this point, wasn't in on the joke. Donna and Chad watched as the lifeguard ran, *Baywatch* style, across the deck and dove into the pool to rescue the helpless wheelchair victim. Of course, this got gales of laughter from the co-eds when the lifeguard emerged, understandably annoyed. The kids were asked to leave the pool area, which they didn't, insisting the entire thing was "just a practical joke." Donna said the highlight was watching the naked girl hobble around in her cast, trying to convince the authorities to "chill out."

"Have you ever seen a drunk naked girl try to appear coherent?" Donna had asked me. "It was hilarious! She was arguing and defending her boyfriend, but standing there butt-naked the entire time with one hand on her hip and the other shaking a beer stein!"

I had to consider—just which part of their joke was practical? I'm sure had I been present, I'd have been laughing too. As it was, I laughed at the story and it was secondhand. I imagine the lifeguard later probably chuckled too, but as far as a joke goes, was it practical, or impractical?

I like a funny joke as much as the next person. In fact, with the help of a few friends, I pulled a good one over on Brad back in the 90s. We invited The Johnsons to join us on our annual Disneyland trip; this being before we had kids, and before Disneyland guests actually did participate in the Light Parade. Brad schemed to lead them to believe we'd all enter a Disneyland Park contest, the reward being an invitation to participate in the Light Parade. On our computer we created registration forms. Brad wanted them to attempt to submit their forms at the park, only to be told no such contest existed. End of story. That was our joke. In reality I had told the Johnsons of our plan and they took it to the next level, which was to create bogus entry form receipts, as well as their winning tickets. At the park, we all went through our assigned motions, eventually surprising Brad when he learned not only was there a contest (there wasn't), but the Johnsons actually did win it! (Yeah, right.) The look on his face when they feigned their delight by hugging and screaming and high-fiving each other was priceless. Yet, it certainly wasn't a joke that held any amount of practicality. (But at least it didn't involve wheelchairs and beer.)

So, what really constitutes a *practical* joke? Something sensible and realistic? Boring. There's nothing funny in realism. Perhaps the entire *idea* is where the comedy of irony lies.

A Dose of Magic Balances the Day

"Oh, this adult life of mine..." a friend groans to me over coffee. "It's just not what I expected." She tucks a flyaway hair behind her ear and blows into her cup, shaking her head. "I used to think my problems were exclusive, but now it's like everybody has the same set of them, you know?"

I do. You think your own life is so challenging, so different from anyone else's, and then you discover there are about 12,000 books written precisely about how you feel. Sure, the names are different, and the specifics vary, but in the big picture—haven't all of us experienced the same thing, just differently?

I find comfort in the fact that I can feel unique and individual in my journey, and I am, but wherein lies the distinguishing characteristics when an entire populace exists to help each of us navigate through life?

Therapists, books, motivational speakers, support groups all subsist because of the need for them. Necessity creates demand.

There is some great truth in watching a group of children being read to. The way they lean forward to see the pictures, some on their knees, their interest genuine. They'll unconsciously rest their dimpled hands on the person in front of them to get a better look, their little mouths all shaping O's when something amazing is uncovered. It's pure and real and when I see their curiosity piqued, my heart thumps to be teaching again.

I miss the smell of sharp pencils, miss the daily experience of seeing information become understanding. Introduce children to a new concept and watch as they turn it into acquired knowledge. Even little miracles are magical; you just have to know where to look for them.

"Yes," I tell my friend, "I thought I owned my struggles, but it turns out a lot of people share them with me." It's true, too. Most days when I take Ben to speech therapy, he pitches a king sized fit out in the parking lot. SO big, in fact, that it requires a mother-son match and I wind up exhausted, slightly embarrassed and wanting to run shrieking in the opposite direction.

In truth, the kid's had me in tears on more than one occasion. Also in truth, his behavior has made me go a little postal on perfect strangers who pause to bear witness to my struggle before raising their eyebrows, their opinions rising like heat. "He is disabled!" I screamed one time. "I suppose you are an expert on Chromosome Duplication Abnormalities? No? Then stop f***ing staring at us!" No, not my proudest moment, but I don't claim to be perfect.

Turns out when we pulled into the parking lot this week, Ben was all fired up and ready to brawl. Bring it on, his little fists told me. You want a piece of this? Every swat and kick at me said the same thing. And then we saw a friend of mine with her son. They too were doing battle, only they had his therapist involved, too. I saw my future, as her son is a few years older than Ben.

My heart went out to her as she struggled and grabbed, ducked and dodged, then cajoled and tried to reason with him. I walked over to rub her back. "I know," is all I had to say. The look on her face is the very one

I wear many times each week. It's the "don't ask me if I'm okay because I will start bawling right here on the spot" face.

That type of connection is the meaningful type, the kind I'd like to experience daily. Finding relatability, finding truth in circumstance. For example, her son's tantrum stunned my own son silent. Totally shocked, Ben entered the building and his therapist's office without making a peep. Thank you, God. Thank you, Pam. A little dose of magic smack dab in the middle of an ordinary day. Maybe I'm looking too hard to find some, but so far, I haven't been disappointed.

"My adult life isn't always what I pictured, either." I sip my coffee and watch as a service dog leads its companion into the shop. But then again, whose is? If we all got what we wanted out of life, wouldn't we be robbing ourselves of the opportunity to learn and grow and improve? I'll take tantrums in parking lots any day, just don't deny me my storytime with children. Necessity might create demand, but balance is the key to enlightenment.

20

Live and Learn

What Lives Next Door, Part 1

When I saw the For Sale by Owner sign being hammered into the front lawn of my next-door neighbor, I whooped for joy. I threw my dishtowel across the kitchen and raced outside to make sure I wasn't dreaming. "Are you really selling?" I smiled broadly at Al, not willing to feign even a drop of sadness. I had however jogged over to the homeowner pumping my fist in the air yelling "YEAH!" much like Tom Cruise when asked of his romance with Katie Holmes. "This is fantastic! Good for you!" I had almost said, "Good for us." Oops.

Not a lot of love lost between him and me. And I like to think I can get along with just about anyone. Less than a year ago, a very dear friend of mine, Liz, lived in that house. For the eight years prior, we had shared one lawn, countless hours of childcare, thousands of gallons of Diet Coke, and a friendship that still remains unmatched.

Due to a quite necessary divorce, her home wound up going on the market, and we had to mentally gear up in losing the close proximity that enabled us to continue our chit chat late into the evenings while our children lay like fallen trees, sleeping all around us. With her husband moved out and mine away on business for long stretches of time, I grew to feel as if her home and mine were one, separated by a mere stretch of grass.

When offers started coming in on her home, she ran each of them by me. I was gunning for the families, couples with children who could play with mine. Women I could befriend, men my husband could talk with over lifted truck hoods, barbecues and poker tables. A few good-looking prospects were up for her selection. And then came Al. He and Liz had only one thing in common: the same real estate agent.

"An investor?" I was flabbergasted when she suggested it. "No way! Don't even consider it unless he'll let you be his renter and then you can stay." She called the agent, who assured us the thought was pure genius. So, she sold her home to Al, and to celebrate that night, I brought over my children, a pan of gooey chocolate brownies, and of course—a 12-pack of Diet Coke. We toasted the end of her marriage, the closing of escrow, and the continuation of a friendship that would not have to be tested by the miles.

Three days later Al informed her that he had a family willing to pay him one year's rent up front for the house and if she could match it, she could stay. Otherwise, she had 30 days to pack her stuff and be gone. Devastated, she found a small home to rent near her family about an hour away. Signed a contract, started packing, enrolled her children in a school close by, and coped with me—who was carrying around Kleenex and sporadically breaking into uncontrollable sobbing. The family that Al was planning on moving into the house saw the place and then decided to pass.

Which lead to the next phase for him: finding renters who would be willing to live in a house that he refused to put a penny into. Cleaning carpets and painting walls were out of the question. Of the seven people he did move into the house, one was a 5-year-old boy, "Sam" who showed up at our house some mornings before 8 o'clock, and had no one looking for him until after 7 in the evening. I made a point of introducing myself to his family, asking if he had any food allergies since I was feeding him all day long. "We don't know. Guess we'll find out..." chuckle, chuckle, and a long drag on a cigarette. They kept to themselves until early February when one of them emotionally snapped (perhaps seven people living in 1,200 sq feet took its toll) and emerged from his house one chilly morning wearing nothing more than his boxers and began howling at the open sky.

Fascinated, I stared out the kitchen window. When he began to shout profanities while shadow boxing an imaginary friend in his driveway, I slowly turned the blinds to get a better look. He ran up the street and around the corner. Didn't see him again until about an hour later when he came to a screeching halt in his driveway after stealing a car in the neighborhood. Hot on his trail, police cars surrounded our two houses and officers pulled their guns. It was at this time that I learned Brentwood has a SWAT Team. They evacuated my children, my daycare child, my son's in-home therapist, and me in an unmarked vehicle. Josh still speaks of the incident to this day, occasionally wants to show the newspaper article with a picture of our house in it to his friends.

And though the gentleman now sits in San Quentin, since he was wanted for numerous priors, his girlfriend had little problem asking me to babysit their infant so she could visit him in jail. I politely declined and tried to keep my distance. I'd already cut off Josh's play dates with Sam, who taught him one day how to raise his middle finger and what the meaning of the gesture was. Months passed and they decided to move out of town, due to the frequent requests by Al to date one of the tenants, or so I'm told.

Either way, they're gone, and the house sits vacant and dark. I'm concerned who will move in next door, since now the house is nine years old, and has never seen a Rug Doctor or a can of Glidden paint.

What Lives Next Door; The Saga Continues

The afternoon I saw Al, the owner/investor of the house next door, tapping a "For Sale by Owner" sign into his lawn buoyed my spirits. Perhaps he would find a buyer willing to give it some much needed tender loving care. Having lost his renters the month prior, he shut off the water and the once lush green front lawn was now a dull, dry patch of sand-colored weeds. Nice look if you live in a desert. For the first time in nine years, I contemplated planting a hedge and splitting the shared spread of grass.

With no bites after posting his flashy 25-cent "For Sale" sign, Al decided to go with a real estate agent, who eventually dropped him as a client since she couldn't show the house. Not only did the exterior beg vagabonds to come and find shelter, but the interior also sat within a haze of stale cigarette smoke.

I begged the next real estate agent to turn the water back on so the lawn could be salvaged and the rest of the neighborhood would be spared the eyesore. Then, someone would purchase the property and I could wave goodbye to Al once and for all. The real estate agent phoned me back:

> Real estate agent: (cheery salesman voice booming over the line) "Hi, Carolyn! Spoke with Al, but we know Al, don't we? (Heh, heh.) It's hard to get him to do anything, isn't it? (Chuckle, chuckle.)"
>
> Me: "Have you even seen the house? Real estate agent: (pause) Well, um...not yet."
>
> Me: "Hmm. Interesting. Call me after you see the joint and tell me then if you think the water should remain off.
>
> Real estate agent: "Here's what I'm thinking..."
>
> Me: "Oh goody, then I'll tell you what I'm thinking, Okay?"
>
> Real estate agent: (pause) "Um...sure. Anyway, I spoke with Al, and he agreed to turn the water back on with the following condition: that you agree to water his grass for him, as it was your original request that he's granting."

The nerve. At first, I am tempted to say, "No." Visions of myself holding a hose while standing in the heat of the day dance in my head. The next image has me collapsed on the vastness of weeds and brittle foliage; heat-stroked, sun-burnt, and parched from lack of hydration, since I have stumbled and fallen only inches from where I dropped the hose as I passed out.

Then I see the alternative. I am power washing my house and the machine is hooked up to Al's hose. Or the children are frolicking in the sprinklers—his, not mine. From that thought emerges an entire aquatic festival involving all the neighborhood children and their friends, courtesy of Al and his unknowing generosity. We'll have Slip-N-Slides, kiddy pools, twisty hose attachments. I imagine children pouring out into the street, all laughing and dripping wet, the smell of sunblock in the air. Agreeing to his stipulation might not be such a bad idea.

Me: "Done. I'll water Al's lawn." (I try not to laugh maniacally.)

When I next saw Al, he "thanked" me for doing him the favor. "Hey, yeah—uh…(head jerk, neck twitch) my lawn looks a little better." He grabs what looks like a surgical brush from his back pocket and begins combing his beard. The thought that he'll groom his microscopic accumulation of facial hair, but not his front lawn, intrigues me.

He snaps his gum and looks as if he'd rather be anywhere but on my porch having to show me a smidgen of appreciation. "Hey, I really appreciate it, Charlotte. Let me know if there's anything I can ever do for you." The offer is tossed out nonchalantly, a courtesy but with no feeling behind it. His real estate agent put him up to it, I'm sure. He trots off, not expecting a reply.

Charlotte? Oh please. "Just don't sell it to another investor!" I grin broadly and wave, waiting for him to drive away so I can hook up the Slip-N-Slide.

Is Comcast for Suckers?

I am in a huge quandary. I can't figure out if A) Comcast doesn't train their Customer Service Reps, or B) they train them to be evasive, unresponsive, and impolite. It's a mystery to me, one I've tried to solve on my own—Nancy Drew style, but I'm met with dead ends and closed doors every time. (Also, like Nancy Drew.) I seem to repeatedly get disconnected after being put on hold, and truly I just can't muster up the patience to redial and go through the same process more than four times over the course of a day. I draw my line at four, I'm silly like that.

"How in love with Comcast are you?" I sobbed to my husband via the telephone last week. "Can't we just cancel them?" I wiped my nose on the back of my hand.

"Are you crying?" he asked me, "Are you sniffling? What is that…Carolyn…what the…you're not a crier…" Instantly he was on alert. "What the hell happened?"

Which time? I wanted to ask. When we moved across town just a month ago, we continued to use Comcast for high-speed internet, then added our phones to their service. We weren't informed that a second account in my name had been created and that it would wipe out our already existing account, i.e., our email addresses would have to be destroyed. I discovered that little ditty on my own, and it cost me hours of confusion and frustration while I worked out the logistics of creating new email accounts and coping with the loss of everything, I had accumulated over the last two years from our pre-existing ones.

Anyone and everyone who spoke to me during that particular period of time was given a healthy dose of anti-Comcast. I got over it just in time for Brad to schedule them to come out and put in a second telephone line for his business. Given the four-hour service window, I knew better than to go anywhere, so I cancelled Ben's therapies, arranged for Josh and his buddies to have alternative carpools, and waited for the service techs to arrive. And waited. And waited. And waited. Then my phone rang.

Me: Hello?

Them: Hi this is Comcast. Our service technicians can't seem to find your house.

Me: Oh okay. Where are they and I'll give them directions.

Them: Um…they're in Concord.

Me: Are they looking for my house in Concord? Because I live in Brentwood. I can't imagine they'd find my house in Concord.

Them: Well, they haven't left yet.

They eventually got their directions and again, I waited two hours after their window had expired, I called Comcast.

After being disconnected and put on hold, repeatedly, I got my first live customer service rep (CSR#1). After reviewing my 'case' CSR#1 sighed, "Oh…oh yeah…it says here that they'll call you to reschedule. Okay ma'am?"

"Actually, no. I took a day off work and am not doing that again. Find your drivers and get them out here immediately."

We argued. I was disconnected. This went on nine separate times. Nine! I'm embarrassed to admit that not only did I break my "four dials a day" rule, but that I got so worked up I kept calling back. Certainly, my number got red flagged within their system.

I had no choice but to call everyone I know and tell them how pathetic I was for even using Comcast after this. And even after that, I still couldn't get a person on the phone at Comcast to disconnect my service. I got online and did a search on Comcast and found out that wow- Comcast isn't so Comcastic to anyone. I felt a little justified. But still idiotic. Mad, sweaty, snot-nosed and idiotic.

It does have a somewhat happy ending. After much ado, I did get a live person who sympathized with me and gave me a sweet credit for my inconvenience. I had ranted, "Someone better work pretty hard to keep me as a customer!" And they did. I felt generous and offered to talk to their higher ups—and show this helpful individual in a good light. They put me on hold. It's not my fault we were disconnected.

Nasty Fall (Unexpected Helping Hands)

When I was five years old, I took a nasty fall. Thinking my plan was foolproof, I had strategically placed a chair on my bed, then a stack of thick books on the seat of the chair. At the very top I placed a large cardboard box, the intention being to sit inside and observe (God only knows what, my room?) everything from a very high perch. It seemed flawless at the time, genius even. During construction my parents looked on concerned.

"Doesn't seem like a good idea," they remarked skeptically. "You might get hurt." Instinct told me their points may be valid. Intuition suggested I might want to rethink my plan. Yet, I shrugged off the warnings, tossed instinct to the curb, and merrily went about my business. As expected, I crashed and burned, and as expected I received a few well-earned raised eyebrows, a couple of "There you have it(s)," and more than one, "We tried to tell you..." It hurt the entire tumble downward and I wound up seeking comfort in the depths of my covers after crawling into bed to bawl. I felt betrayed by my guardian angel—where was she that day? On a break?

As adults, this too can happen. Thirty years after that fall, I took another, metaphorically speaking. And while my plan may have seemed a good one at the time, warnings still poured in. Intuition continued to suggest a huge error in judgment, and a few spectators will even say I crashed and burned. All I know is that I fell hard and again, it hurt the entire way down. Once more, I sought comfort under my covers, wanting to remain in bed and cry for days.

Right around the time I was beginning to begrudge the whereabouts of my guardian angel, she reappeared, only this time with reinforcements. In fact, so many people stepped in to pick me up, dust me off, check for injuries, hug me fiercely, rightfully reprimand me, then remind me that I am loved unconditionally, that I had trouble recognizing just who was my angel and who worked for her. It seemed that her post was an open position and everyone who believes in me stepped up at some point to lead the troops.

Looking within myself, I don't know where I failed most: in my actions, or my expectations. I completely underestimated the very people I respect and adore. Though I love being in a position to assist others, by not asking for help when I desperately needed it, I robbed everyone I knew of the same luxury. Helping wounded spirits is a privilege, one that should not be easily overlooked. Human nature thrives on the osmosis of positive energy between people and how this simple pleasure temporarily escaped me, is beyond my scope of understanding.

There's an old axiom that reads 'Don't wear your emotions on your sleeve,' and this was an adage I adopted as a child. It's amusing how over time, perspectives change, and each new generation of parents works to instill a different value set. As did countless other children of the 70s, I grew up believing in the preservation of image management; a nice smile, a sunny disposition, and a held tongue were all viewed in high regard. Higher than say—being honest with your feelings, asserting any concerns, and (gasp) speaking up when you are afraid, confused, ashamed, or otherwise offended. Too much of anything is more than enough, as I can humbly profess now that over concern for public opinion kept me in the midst of a juggling act that was destined to fail. Given time, each ball I had in my performance was eventually going to hit the deck, which they did. And while I felt as if I was standing there alone, holding nothing, feeling terror, I realize now that I was not.

Friends and family rallied around me and continued to, each time I stepped forward, stumbled, then tried again. I eventually found my footing and much to my surprise discovered not only was I standing, but I was being pulled up, held up, supported even, by the hands and hearts of the very same loved ones I had so shamefully tried to hide my fall from. By the ones I had so badly wounded on my way down. How eternally grateful I will always be to have been given the gifts of forgiveness and understanding, compassion and empathy, outreach and encouragement.

The question is now not what should I say, or who should I tell? Its which lesson outweighs the next and how can each one be applied daily in order to forgive myself and move forward. I've been humbly reminded that every action has a reaction and that with a little faith—in myself, in human nature, but most importantly in God, miracles do happen.

Groovin' to Many Beats

Either a certain radio station is over-playing one song in particular, or someone, somewhere, is trying to tell me something. It seems I'm on the "Highway to Hell," or at least I feel like I am. I've heard that song a minimum of seven times in the last two weeks. I didn't know had bad it had gotten until my 3-year-old started singing along. "I'm on the highway to hell, yeah, the highway to hell, sing Mommy," So I sang. Well, why not?

Music has always been a big part of my life and it appears as if this passion has been passed down to Josh. His taste in tunes is about as broad as my own. He requests everything from Limp Bizkit to Frank Sinatra. Lately though, he's on a big Partridge Family kick and wants to listen to

"I Think I Love You" from sunup to sundown. At first this wasn't a bad thing. Gradually though, it's evolved from cute to obnoxious. Even I, who thought Keith Partridge was pretty hot back in the day, am sick of listening to him whine and bleat his lyrics throughout my car.

It's been said that you can tell a lot about a person by (A) going through their medicine cabinet or (B) checking out the disc player in their vehicle. Interesting concept for some, frighteningly real for others. I perused my disc changer on a whim to see what a stranger may learn of me, if given only my choice of music to judge me by.

> Disc one: *Blondie.* Hmm, I like classic rock and enjoy a good female vocalist. (Or I have 10,000 memories of dressing like Debbie Harry and lip-syncing her songs while I spiked my bangs and got ready for school.)
>
> Disc two: *Mission Impossible 2.* Now that's just good music to wake up to on a long commute. Wait—I don't commute. I must just like alternative rock.
>
> Disc three: *John Denver's Greatest Hits* Volume I. (And yes, as any die-hard John Denver fan knows, there is more than one volume.) There's just something about that guy singing of his being a country boy that I really dig.
>
> Disc four: *Blind Melon.* Takes me back to a certain houseboat trip in 1995. Ahhh, the good old days.
>
> Disc five: *The B52s.* Not mine. Brad obviously snuck that one in there on me.
>
> Disc six: *Frank Sinatra.* The guy was a genius. Enough said.
>
> Disc seven: *Billboards Greatest Hits 1972.* My tribute to the year I was born. I once thought Chuck Berry's "My Ding a Ling" was about something other than his anatomy.
>
> Disc eight: *Leighla's Disco Mix.* A great compact disc ("CD") made especially for me by the parent of one of the kids I taught. This CD has everything on it from "Get Down To-night" to the original "Funky Town" and "Brick House." Also includes "Boogeyman," "Stayin' Alive," and "Play that Funky

Music White Boy." Always a favorite around here. Josh sings along to "Ring My Bell" and has no trouble remembering the words to "Hot Stuff" when cued.

Disc nine: *A Scorpions Mix,* including two renditions of "Rock You Like a Hurricane." As an added bonus, the friend who burned it for me added a Def Leppard favorite: "Rock of Ages."

I don't know how to explain this one. Is it justification enough to say I was a closet hard rock fan in the 80s? While I might have looked like a blonde Pat Benatar, I secretly played tapes of Ratt and Winger.

And disc ten: *Kids Sing Along to Your ABC's and MORE!* The one CD we never listen to. Josh has no interest in pretend rock when he can have the real thing.

There you have it. What kind of judgment call can anyone make on me by that ridiculous selection of music? Perhaps, that I am just ridiculous. That maybe it. But given what I keep hearing on the radio it may be something more. Like maybe I'm on the Highway to Hell or something! Time to turn off the radio.

Sneaking Out

"**...And then I** caught her coming back in the window from sneaking out. Carolyn, she was outside...at night...with God knows who!" My friend is near hysterics as she narrates the most recent incident she's had with her 15-year-old daughter. I have a pretty good idea of whom she was with, but I don't tell her this. I was fifteen once.

"Oh, come on," I scoff, "I snuck out all the time and look at me. I turned out just fine."

She's silent. Pauses a bit too long. "I SAID I am just FINE," I say loudly. "We never got into any real trouble. Haven't you ever snuck out?"

"Never."

"What kind of kid were you? Everyone snuck out! Even the complete nerds got out at night." I would know. I ran into almost everyone I went to high school with at some time or another between the hours of

11:00 p.m. and 3:00 a.m. Prime T-P-ing ("Toilet papering") hours. "Did she come in carrying toilet paper?" I ask my friend.

"No, but she was covered in shaving cream and eggs." I imagine the sight and start to laugh. "It's not funny! She stunk too and got the mess all over her carpet."

I'm laughing partly because I remember being driven home by the very understanding father of a classmate of mine around 2:00 am one morning. My friend Jan and I sat in the backseat of his car, embarrassed beyond belief and scared to death my parents would wake up and bust us.

After sneaking out with a pack of toilet paper and two cans of silly string, we bumped into the very boy whose house we were on our way to decorate. His arsenal was considerably stronger than ours. He was packing whipped cream and eggs. Not to mention, an older brother trolling along in a car packed with his friends not too far behind. We ran fast and hard, dropping our loot and screeching the entire time.

They caught up with us and attacked in the center of their parent's perfectly groomed front lawn. It didn't take long for us to beg for mercy. Covered in slime and goop, we stood panting and trying to gather our senses. Then the rain poured down. The boys took pity on us and lead us inside to wash up before trekking back across town to sneak in through my window.

Just as we were finishing up with the towel snapping and noogies, in walk the parents, home a tad earlier than expected. Party's over. "Just tell me where you live and I'll drive you girls home. No sense running around in the rain..." His dad was very sweet.

We rode in silence, but for my quiet directions from the backseat. "Well, here we are, BYE!" I practically hurled myself out of the car before it stopped in front of my house.

"Nonsense," he said kindly, "I'd like to make sure you girls get inside safely." Gulp. Okaaaay. We had no choice but to gain entry by way of our exit. I climbed up onto the hood of my dad's truck, which was backed into our driveway. Jan followed. We waved at him. He waved back. Then we jumped onto the cab and from there, onto the shell. Jan and I grabbed the iron railing of the balcony and pulled ourselves up, until we could swing our legs over the top and be finally at our starting point. Standing outside my window we waved again. His clue to get a move on before the idling of the car woke my folks. No need to worry. As he drove away, he smiled, then to our horror, laid on the horn. We each had a leg in the window when my mom found us.

"You are dead," she pointed to me, "And which jackass friend of yours honked the horn when he dropped you off? What—did he want to get you girls in trouble?" The gall of that man has never escaped me.

I am still chuckling as my friend describes her daughter's antics. "What should I do?" she asks me. "What did your parents do to you?"

Stocked up on toilet paper and didn't ask questions.

Younger by the Minute

"**So…I guess the** big news here is that I have a boyfriend. You know…*a real one.*"

I pull my cell phone away from my ear and look at it. Cue the cartoon confusion sound of a quarter being shook in a can as I clear my head. Nicki? In a committed relationship? Must learn more…

"As opposed to your last one," I ask, "…who was imaginary?" She laughs and says, "Seriously—this one is the real deal. I actually like him."

"Well dish the dirt Hot Pants and tell me what he's made of." Of course, I never talk like this in real life, I save all of my movie star lingo for conversations with friends like her.

She is oddly quiet for a second and then offers up the goods. "He's younger than we are," she says slowly, "…by a few years."

I consider this. "A few can be anywhere between three and seven."

"Oh. (pause) Okay. He's younger than we are by 'numerous' years. How many is 'numerous'?"

Since I can only imagine just how young this buck may be I say with certainty, "Twenty. Is he potty trained?" I get a laugh, yet no answer. "Oh no, does this one still have a curfew?" She scoffs. "Can he vote?"

"Um…," she says, "How old do you have to be to vote these days?"

"Good girl!" And I mean it. Why not? She's having fun and she's happy for the first time in ages. "What did your family say?" I assume by now that she's brought him home to her parents and I'm dying to learn about the splash Baby Hughy made.

Nicki has presented a few interesting characters in her time. To their credit, her family has always offered a safe place to bring even the lowest of the low and get, if nothing else, a pat on the back and a "Better luck with your next choice." Good people, they are.

One time I introduced them to a boy I was dating in college—much to his displeasure—and they graciously sat through his ignoring their curious inquiries of his future. They watched with raised eyebrows as he double dipped his chips, exchanged amused glances when he asked for a brew, but still delivered him one and then feigned interest when he proceeded to open the can with his teeth, hands behind his back. They waited until he farted and sprayed crumbs from his mouth while laughing before excusing themselves from the table. We left pretty much right after that. "It didn't go well, right?" I asked her mom at the front door. "He's kind of a loser, huh?" She squeezed my hand and said, "Your mother will hate him. Better hang onto this one for a while." She didn't even mention the mullet or armpit stains on his shirt either.

Nicki tells me that her family loved the little guy and that they didn't know he was all that much younger than her. "Isn't that cool?" she asks me. I'm not sure. Does that say something about her maturity level or his?

"Well did you ride off into the sunset on his handlebars or does he drive? Cause you don't want to be chauffeuring this kid around. Pretty soon he'll be asking you to take him to the park or drive him to swim lessons or something."

"I like him! He treats me nice." I'm tempted to tell her that he was probably raised to respect his elders, but I bite my tongue. Truthfully, I may tease her, but I am thrilled that she is enjoying some male companionship, having been burned a few times in recent history.

"Plus," she tells me, "I'm getting younger by the minute, being with him. Pretty soon we'll be the same age." I smile and try to figure out just what the hell that age could be.

You've Got FWDs

I just replied to an email my cousin sent me. "Are you living by this recommendation or are you the shining example of the exact opposite?"

She forwarded ("FWD") me an email with quite insightful article from *Good Housekeeping Monthly*, dated May 13, 1955. It was entitled, "The Good Wife's Guide." Intriguing.

Casey loves to FWD me emails and because of her thoughtfulness I am now privy to a few things. For example, if I were a cartoon character, I would be Sponge Bob Square Pants. I know this because I took the little survey. I also know about 100 different things I can do with a Bounce dryer sheet, and I have the secret recipe to the Nordstrom Chocolate Chip Cookie.

In all fairness, I love FWDs. Who wouldn't love to see the latest in a Redneck photo album as well as a nicely designed flowchart for sex? While some people delete FWDs without reading them, dismissing them as crap, I do the polar opposite. I don't know why, I mean—I do have a life. But when I log on and hear the chime letting me know I have mail, I spring up in my chair and prepare to see what I've been sent. Occasionally, I'll get the obligatory one liner personal note at the beginning of a FWD, but most of the time my Inbox gets loaded with jokes, cartoons, a random scandalous video clip, and that unexpected, arbitrary hair-raising news article that leaves me guessing why the sender thought I may relate.

But without FWDs how would any of us know "The 10 Things You'd Love to Say but Never Do?" ("I don't know what your problem is, but I bet it's hard to pronounce." Or, "I see you've set aside this special time to humiliate yourself in public.") And for me, it's not enough to just hear that beer and fireworks shouldn't be mixed—I appreciate a good color photo that proves why not.

I'm never too busy to learn new words (reintarnation: coming back to life as a hillbilly, girafitti: vandalism spray painted very, very high) or learn new definitions for familiar words (esplanade: to attempt an explanation while drunk, and flatulence: an emergency vehicle that picks you up after you've been run over by a steamroller). And truly, honestly, I often enjoy reading about someone else's incident with bikini waxing or the trials of giving their cat a pill. It just doesn't get old for me. But please don't make me scroll down through 4 million *m*s and *v*s that that make up an angel. And though I enjoy a good anecdote for anger management as much as the next person, I never send FWDs. Ever. I don't assume anyone appreciates them as I do.

This article that Casey sent me deserved an immediate response. According to *Good Housekeeping Monthly* circa 1955, I should prepare for my husband's arrival home from work by tidying up and putting a ribbon in my hair. Have a cool drink in hand when he comes through the door. I should "be a little gayer and more interesting to him." I smile at how this would be interpreted today. Well sure, my husband would most definitely find me more interesting if I were gayer…especially since it continues to read "his boring day may need a lift and one of your duties is to provide it for him." Um, okaaaay…I should never question his judgment or integrity. It also says that catering to his comfort will provide me with immense personal satisfaction. It reads, "A good wife always knows her place."

Oh, I know mine all right. It isn't in the kitchen. Brad would faint if I morphed into a "Good Wife." He's too used to the tarnished version, thereof. If I ever spoke in the low, soothing tone of voice as recommended by *Good Housekeeping Monthly*, he'd correctly assume I'd taken a sip or three from his cool drink, or that I'd be working on him for something. And not a new apron, either.

What choice did I have here? I FWD'd it to every girl I knew.

21

Good Things Come in Small Packages

Perspectives on Valentine's Day

"Valentine's Day sucks," Karen tells me, "And it always will at least for me—I'll be single for the rest of my life." She is pouting. I can tell. I can be on the phone with people and know if they are pouting or not. And with that attitude, she's probably right about being single for a while.

Deep breath. "Just do something nice for yourself. Buy a new sweater or something," I suggest. I know the idea is dumb, but so is the conversation.

"You're lucky," she sniffs, "You're married and have a romantic guy." I snort, reply dryly, "You know I'm still married to my *first* husband, right?" I glance at my guy who at the moment has one hand in the waistband of his sweats and the other fisting a remote. An empty beer bottle lays on its side on our coffee table—positioned and ready for a game of 'spin the bottle' that's not about to happen. He belches and then laughs at how it sounds. "Did you hear that?" he shouts at me. Yeah. Romantic.

"Well, ignore the holiday like everyone else does," I tell her, "It's really only for the kids anyway." I am surprised that I have said this, but once spoken, I realize my sincerity. Valentine's Day around here the last few years has been about making cookies, decorating cards, trials with glue and lace, plus the occasional gritty surprise of glitter in my sheets.

Just last week I sat with my 4-year-old watching him sign his name to all 26 Valentines for his classmates. Painstakingly he sorted through the stack, over and over, until exasperated, I asked him, "What is the problem?" Teary eyed, he answered, "I have to find the perfect one for Daniella…I love her." Such earnestness put a lump in my throat.

Josh has a girlfriend. The same one he had last year. They have had a long-term relationship and they are four. Daniella's mom and I have become good friends because of them, and what we once thought was pretty cute, we now think is the purest form of love we've ever seen. Their teachers tell us daily that the friendship is unique—Josh holds her hand on the playground. He saves her a seat at circle time, gets her a paper towel when she's done washing up, and offers her a bite of his snack. The first bite—every single time.

I once saw him pat her on the rump affectionately when she won a sack race. He was clapping and cheering her on, then as she crossed the finish line—smack!—right on the butt. I looked around quickly to see if I was alone in the witnessing of the gesture, but I wasn't. Mothers were laughing all around me. I have no idea where he learned such protocol but it hasn't gone unnoticed. Mommies of little girls in his class try to arrange marriages with me all the time.

Frustrated, he sat hunched over his stack of cards looking for the just-right one for his little lady. "This one?" I held up one with a bee. He shook his head. "How about this?" I showed him a card with flowers. "Girls love flowers…" He shut his eyes and put his head down on the table. His passion made me wonder if ever a boy had done anything remotely as sweet for me. I doubt it. After class parties, I used to lay across my bed sorting through my stash of crumpled cards. I liked to fantasize about certain boys picking out specific ones just for me, but in all actuality, their names were hurriedly scrawled across the backs and rarely was my name actually on an envelope. Dang. Mass Valentines were a big hit back in elementary school. Josh has years of this ahead of him. Girls, crushes, broken hearts. I only hope he doesn't get jaded to love and all the fun it can be when it's done right.

My friend Karen's present sulk is a great case in point. "Fine," I tell her. "Come spend the day with me…I'll be taping Valentines in my kitchen window and eating candy hearts with Josh all day."

"Is that what married people do on Valentine's Day?" She sounds unimpressed. Skeptic even.

"I'll probably go to the gym that night too," I add.

"Oh." Silence. "Um, no thanks. But you have fun, okay?" It's all a matter of perspective, because for me, hanging out with my boys then being freed up to go work out is a gift.

Of Valentine's Days Gone By

You are dog gone terrific… I sat gazing at the Valentine I was given by my love interest in school that day. Deep sigh, and then a tiny smile flickered on my lips again. It was 1980 and I was in second grade. John Eric Waugh was the love of my life, only he didn't have any idea. I sat on my gingham bedspread and traced the crooked pencil signature on the back of the card. He had touched this card, picked it out just for me. Ahh…love was in the air.

Okay, so in all actuality, he had probably been forced to sign his name to all 30 cards while in a rush to get out the door for school that day. I imagine his mother ushering children out of the kitchen and shouting at him over her shoulder to "Get a move on…" while she loaded up his siblings into the station wagon. Annoyed, he scribbled his signature on each card and threw the stack into his book bag. Come to think of it, my name hadn't been on the envelope. Dang.

Love sure has come a long way since 1980, thank goodness. There was the Valentine's Day I had thrown up on the most popular girl in school in 7th grade, and the one I had received an anonymous "Stay away from my boyfriend, B**ch!" Passion Gram in the 9th. My junior year of high school I worked in a flower shop and had assembled a dozen roses for myself, by special order, and then my personal favorite—the valentine I received tucked under a windshield wiper of my car a few years back that read, "I love you sweaty." I freaked out until I realized it was left by

Brad, and in his rush to not get caught, he has misspelled *sweetie*, and scrawled the message at a crooked angle.

Four years ago, on Valentine's Day I lay in the hospital, anxiously awaiting the arrival of our first son. Determined to give birth on the one day in the year that symbolized universal love and affection, I insisted I was in labor and refused to leave the hospital. My doctor sympathized with my plight, took a final glance at my monstrous figure and concluded an induction would be arranged. Even so, Josh came an entire day later. Now, not only do I wonder what his real birthday may have been, I wish I could have experienced an actual labor since my second son was induced as well.

In anticipation of this Valentine's Day, the boys and I are decorating handmade cards and planning on delivering them to their grandparents and friends. Various sizes of construction paper hearts, painted by sponges and little fingers hang in our front kitchen window, courtesy of Josh. Our little home looks as if it's been hit by a cyclone of red, pink, and white. Scraps of lace and ribbon has found their way around our houseplants, I'm positive glitter knows how to reproduce itself and I've been dreaming about small puffy balls of cotton chasing me in my sleep. But I think it may just be the best Valentine's Day yet!

Bunnies, and Hippies and Buzz Lightyears—Oh My!

As a kid, when I wasn't charting and grafting my post Halloween plunder, I was planning what the following holiday's costume would consist of. In elementary school, I didn't have much to choose from: while most children dressed in the mall's best, I donned whatever my mother could scrape together and sew up. We sometimes named our costumes post-completion. "What are you going to be this year?" "Gee, I don't know—my mom hasn't finished it yet." Good thing Mom wasn't a heavy drinker.

Walk down my hallway even today and see a framed picture of my sister and I, dolled up for trick or treating. "What are you guys doing?" friends point with curiosity when they see the print. "We're dressed up for Halloween…see? She's a gypsy and I'm a princess." Then they lean in for closer scrutiny. It happens all the time. Mostly, I was too young to be embarrassed, and thought too highly of my mother's efforts to really care whether or not I was made fun of.

In high school, Halloween meant wild parties and squeezing into skimpy costumes intended for adults. "You are *not* going to be a French Maid, I don't give a good G-D, what you say." I was told this after my mother overheard me giggling and plotting with a girlfriend on what I thought was a private phone extension in my room. "Fine!" I huffed. "I'll be something dumb and boring—like a…a…rabbit!"

"Perfect!" she shouted back. That was nothing compared to the shouting that began when I emerged and tried to leave the house dressed like a Playboy Bunny. That cotton tail was snatched off my rear quicker than I could say 'Hugh Hefner'. Dad twisted and wrangled the bunny ears, before breaking them in two and flinging them past me into the hallway. "Hop back into your room and find something else." Mom suggested dryly, "And next time, no white bras under a black leotard. I can see your Little Bunny Foo Foos."

College Halloweens saw me in Fairy and Genie costumes, until my last two years when I went into whole earth mode and didn't do up myself at all. Just returned home in Birkenstocks, tie-dyes, cut off shorts, and flowers in my hair. "Are you dressed as a hippy?" my dad asked me. I smiled serenely and answered, "No, I'm a college student protesting the use of animals for laboratory experiments, the ingestion of all preservatives and numbered dyes, I'm for personal expression through henna and the usage of hemp for natural, but not addictive purposes." Dad stared blankly at me and told Mom, "She's a hippy this year. I just don't know why she's got to live in her costume." I made them anxious, I'm sure. They uneasily raised peace signs to me during that entire visit home.

The next phase was marriage and children and the focal point shifted from us to them. The little people. What to parade the kids around in, not ourselves. I was lucky if I got so much as a pair of googly alien eyes bouncing off my head as I took the gang door to door. This being Josh's fifth Halloween, he chose his own costume. The first year I had him squashed into a fuzzy bumblebee suit, much to his, and his grandmother's, displeasure. ("Why do that to the poor child? Humiliate him for the sake of a few smiles?") Each year after he opted to be Buzz Lightyear. Which means we own three identical costumes in varying sizes, all that we tried to shove Ben into the following years. Our Halloween pictures through the years show variations of the same scene: two Buzz Lightyears; one grinning broadly with his arm draped in brotherly fashion over the shoulder of his howling Mini-Me.

This year though, things will be different. I'll be chaperoned by a Pirate and Elmo, while I'm dressed to thrill in sweats, a warm jacket, mittens, hat, scarf, and cup of coffee complete with travel mug. I can't decide if I'm calling it The Referee, The Cook, The Chauffer, The Housekeeper, The Jester, or just plain The Mother. Either way, I'm not wearing a cotton tail.

The Haunts Within My Home

I love a good ghost story. Always have. Which explains why, when recently asked where I live, I was shocked to see the response of the asker after I described my exact location in Brentwood.

"Oh my," she gasped. "Isn't that land haunted?"

I stared at her.

Women continued to kick-box all around us and I stared at her. Mouth agape, gloves slowly descending, I looked at this woman and let the rest of my classmates punch and kick their way around me. I trailed along as she exited the mat.

"What do you mean haunted?" I inquired. Hands on hips, eyes all squinty. "You mean as in ghosts?" I waited as she toyed with her sports bottle. She sprayed water into her mouth and after wiping her face with the back of her hand, shrugged, "I don't know of any other kind. Do you?"

Oddly enough, I do not. So, I asked what she knew and sat wide-eyed as she described a story of horror and fire, loss and death that all occurred on the very land my neighborhood now resides on. "And who told you this?"

"The glass guy who worked on our windows knows a mechanic whose daughter married this guy whose uncle goes way back in this town. He told us."

What I heard was the opening line of REO Speedwagon's "Keep On Lovin' You" ("I heard it from a friend who…heard it from a friend who…heard it from a friend that you've been messin' around…") The song played in my head as I tried to follow her…"What?"

"Doesn't matter," she shook her little ponytail. "All I know is that everybody who's ever lived in your neighborhood all have creepy stories to tell that back up what this window guy says."

I considered this. And then gave more thought to the last 10 years I've spent in a home which I adore, no matter what the oddities have been. Continuously hearing a radio, or a TV on, only to enter a room to find nothing. The animals being skittish and paranoid, their eyes following something that I don't see. Running and hiding from the inexplicable. Growling and hissing at what I thought was lint.

The inconsistent current of electricity that runs through my home—TVs, lights, radios, power in general going on and off. But what I hear most often are the footsteps. The sound of walking, pacing even—throughout the house is usual, even predictable at this point. Numerous times each week I wake up expecting to see one of the boys at the foot of my bed, only to open my eyes and see nothing. Nobody. Not even a cat.

Just recently, I was with my youngest on my bed one evening, trying to get him to sleep. As we lay with our eyes closed, I heard my door open and listened to the familiar sound of little footfalls—my older son as he crept up next to the bed. He leaned over me to see if I was sleeping. I felt him. Without opening my eyes, I whispered, "I'll be right out. Brother is almost asleep then we can read a story, okay?" No answer. "Okay, sweetie?" I tried again. His lack of reply made me open my eyes and realize he was never there. The hair stood up on the back of my neck as I called out, "Josh?" His reply came from the bathroom down the hall. The door had been closed.

Often, unusual things have occurred that now I've grown to anticipate. When the heater or AC turns on, what sounds like voices, or music—it depends on the night, comes out of both vents in my bedroom. In no other room in the house can you hear it. I love sitting on my bed late at night in anticipation of what I'll hear. What friends have called "bizarre," "strange" and "scary" I deem a comfortable part of interesting.

Even the rare occurrence of walking into a dark room and seeing what looks like a silhouette doesn't startle me the way it used to. In a rush to grab a towel for the sons in the bathtub the other night, I darted into my room, stepped over what looked like a person sitting on my floor at the foot of my bed and told it, "Whoops, 'scuse me!" before I realized I was talking to thin air.

Perhaps I should be concerned, but I'm not. Perhaps my land is haunted, but it probably isn't. I bet I just love a good ghost story.

That Holiday Competitive Edge

Looking over the guest list for this year's Thanksgiving attendance, I wonder…of the twelve of us planning on being present, who will storm off angrily during "Family Game Time?" As most families who have traditions of turkey and cranberries, mashed potatoes and glazed carrots—we too enjoy all that, and more. We play games. Every year our guests break out the *Trivial Pursuit, Cranium, Pictionary, Dictionary Dabble*, and one year—*Monopoly*. But only one year.

The holidays seem to bring out the competitive edge in the family. We can sit with full bellies around a game board and as questions fly, cards are passed out, clay structures are molded, or whatever is required for that particular round—the only real thing accomplished is the group rise in blood pressure and the all too predictable increased probability for Temporomandibular Joint Dysfunction ("TMJ") due to teeth grinding. Example: I have a brother-in-law who amazingly seems to know the answer to every question asked to someone else ("What? That is easy! Oh, come on!") yet continually draws a blank at his turn ("What? No one would know that! This game is impossible!"). This happens every year.

My father-in-law, Jim, doesn't play games, and doesn't like to participate in the family torment and charade of unity. While we all start out hoping for some type of quality genetic bonding, what happens is something exactly the opposite. Shouting, pouting, arguing, and inevitably, the storming away from the table. This is usually accompanied by a few snide remarks upon departure from he who retreated. Snickers and hoots from those left holding their cards complete the scene. I now understand that such behavior is an indication of how you know your family is close. When anyone from the 'adult table' can openly act like a child with no long-term repercussions, it's pretty certain you're in a safe place.

It's fodder for the instigators when someone behaves badly because of what can be expected the following holiday gathering. Two things are commonplace. First, everyone will have to rehash the previous holiday's episode of "boo hoo, sniff sniff, I'm not playing with you guys anymore." Secondly, the person responsible for that tantrum can cling to nothing but the hope that someone, anyone, will outdo him this year. He may even initiate a friendly debate, with the thought in mind that his contender might eventually breakdown. Thus, Jim politely passes and takes no part in what he would term the unnecessary family drama. But on this Thanksgiving…

"Brian might throw his cards at me again this year!" I try to lure him in for just one game. "You don't want to miss that!"

"And Paula might start cussing like a tourette syndrome child when she's losing!" Brad too attempts to set an enticing scene for consideration. That said, seeing my normally composed mother fall behind in a game is truly something no one should miss out on. Not missing a beat, my mom pipes up, "Not true! That's horse****!"

"Brian actually threw his cards at me," my sister-in-law, Laura says, "But his aim was so bad they hit Carolyn. And really, Dad, getting Brian all riled up like that can be fun." Still nothing. "You should try it." Heads bob in agreement.

"Bad aim?" Brian huffs in the background. "BAD aim? I meant to hit both of you!" He starts shuffling the cards with more vigor. He raises his eyebrows at me when I look over to him. "You want some of this?" he jerks his head. I start snickering.

"Ooohhh…tough guy…" I taunt him back.

"I don't know whether you guys like to play games or just piss one another off," Jim replies.

Well, neither do we. Which is why we do this every holiday. Both offer quality entertainment value, plus a little family bonding time.

It's Never too Early

"Oh no you didn't." My friend stands staring into my living room, shaking her head in awe and then turning to me with a look of bewilderment that has since gone unmatched. She gestures towards the tall tree positioned in the corner and says, "What in the hell is that?"

"Teacher says every time a bell rings, an angel gets her wings..." I give her a toothy grin.

"It's not even Thanksgiving yet; why on earth would you have your tree up this early?"

It's a fair question. I'm not sure I should confess to her that our tree has been up since before Halloween. Imagine the look on the faces of our little trick-or-treaters when we opened our door and the lights from our tree shone into the entryway. We stunned a few kids that night, shocked them even, just not in the traditional, talking-skeleton way.

Ordinarily, I would not be breaking out the stockings, making apple cider, and listening to holiday jingles just yet, but we saw a fake tree at Costco we couldn't pass up, and...well...how were we to get it in the house without our four-year old wanting to assemble it? In October. Before it actually started to get cold.

Brad and I are the "sounds good" kind of folk—the ones who leave their holiday lights up until July, stumble across rotten Easter eggs in May, decorate the walls with preschool art, and yes—even assemble a tree in October, much to the delight of their four-year-old son. The boy doesn't ask much of us: some food, a few stories, kisses good night and this year—a tree up before anyone else's. We weren't ones to say no to that; not when we love a good holiday season, too.

So, while our friends and neighbors were rifling through cartons searching for plastic pumpkins, cardboard Frankensteins, and spooky bats to hang in their windows, we too were on the hunt. For stockings, wreaths, gold and silver garland, and that piece of garbage tree skirt I swear at every year. "This year I vow to be unpredictable..." says my husband, who rummages in a nearby box, looking for our icicle lights. I am stunned by the very thought that he would have those lights up before the men from the neighborhood stood assembled on our porch, ladders in hand, forcing Brad to get onto the roof and decorate his house.

So far, it's been turning out to be a pretty festive month. Why, with the tree up so early, I've been inspired to do a little holiday purchasing before the crowds. This might the first Christmas for us where I'm not in a mad scramble to buy last-minute gifts, wrap in a frenzied convulsion of paper and ribbon, and decorate just in time for the New Year. Being so ahead of the game is foreign to me, but I think I might have found the perfect inspiration to relax during the holidays: tree up = stress down. I like it.

22

It's the Thought That Counts

The Hanging of the Lights

The grumbling. The loud footfalls on the roof. The husband stomping through the house, muttering and towing a football field length string of lights in his wake. Hmmm…it seems the hanging of the lights has begun in full. I just cannot understand what motivated him to start the process without all his buddies egging him on. That much will remain a mystery, the rest is pretty much predictable.

I jump when the door slams shut and look up to see Brad, lights in one hand, some fancy new gizmo in the other, come into the house. "These stupid…" he gripes, "Do you really need lights on the house this year?" I know better than to answer.

He marches past me, starts rifling through his tool drawer in the hall, then slams it shut and storms out to the garage. The door shuts behind him with a bang. I don't think of his not returning until I hear the home phone ring a few minutes later. I look at caller ID and seeing who it is, I glance out the kitchen window and see the caller's truck in our driveway.

"Hello?"

"Where is Brad?" asks Scott, who's been over all day helping Brad clean up the work side of our yard.

"Aren't you on our roof?" I ask.

"YES! And I'm waiting for him to get his butt back out here and help me with these lights. I got a strand caught under the bushes in front of your kitchen window."

I go out in front and peer up. Scott waves to me. I hang up the phone, free the bushes of the lights, and apologize for my husband who has now gone MIA. When I do find him, he is clustered in the office talking on his work phone. Laughing. Engaged in friendly conversation. Tilted back in his chair, feet up, exchanging pleasantries with God knows who.

Isn't that nice? I get to live with the irritable craftsman and his friend waits in the cold for his return. But someone gets the jolly Brad today, it just happens to be a client who is paying for his kindness. Hanging lights does not bring out the best in Brad. I take the youngest and leave for a few hours, leaving our four-year-old with Daddy and the project in process.

When I return, the house is bright with white lights strung carefully across the pillars, windows, and door. It is a festive scene that we come upon and exiting the truck I am met by Josh who excitedly tells me, "I went on the roof with Daddy!" I try to keep the smile on my face. I feel my teeth grinding somewhere in the rear of my mouth.

As we enter the house, Daddy is nowhere to be seen and I have heard far too many details of Josh's afternoon with his father. "And then once he slipped…and I screamed, 'Daddy don't fall! And he didn't fall, I mean not too far…it was cool."

I work hard to look unconcerned. "And where is Daddy? At the hospital?" Josh laughs at my question. "I even brought him up his beer when he asked me to," says Josh, pride thick in his voice.

My smile is beginning to twitch, then erode. I am struck with the memory of watching our neighbor hang his lights a few years back. He had climbed to the highest peak on the roof of his two-story house and with care, guided his seven-year-old daughter up next to him. "Brad!" I had called, "Come look at Jim!" Brad came running, video camera in hand. "Michelle is never going to believe this…" he laughed. We both laughed then, a little nervous perhaps, but still we stood watching father and daughter enjoying a moment together on their roof. Michelle told me later she wanted to kill Jim when she found out, which is about how I feel right now.

Brad enters the kitchen, grinning and smug—the lights are hung, no one is hurt, and we won't have to do this again for another year. Something we can all feel good about finally.

Christmas Letter to my Sons

Dear Boys,

Gift giving was a little different this year. I couldn't find what I wanted to give in any stores, on any shelves, under any discount racks, not even online. And though there were presents under the tree, my real gifts for you guys aren't things that can be packaged in fancy paper, made prettier with colorful bows.

More than a bicycle Josh, what I wanted to give you was time. Time for just you and I to look at books, work on stickers, talk about our family, laugh at jokes, and play in the mud. Time to color outside the lines, eat popcorn, jump in puddles, and watch the rain through an open window. Time for shadow puppets, real puppets, silly puddy, play dough, and finger painting. It seems this year I fell short on time. I don't know how it happened, but it won't happen again.

More than just a puzzle Josh, what I wanted to give you was understanding. I understand you are frustrated with being left at a friend's while I take Ben to therapy, I don't always show it, but I do. I understand you are sad when I have to stop reading to you so I can help your brother breathe, cry, and eat without vomiting. I understand you are upset when I promise to lay in bed with you and snuggle before sleep, but then have to get up and tend to Ben, who wakes unexpectedly and may have a seizure. I understand our time together will forever be interrupted, cut short, and haphazard. What I'd like to give you is the understanding of your role in life as a sibling of a special needs child. You are being shaped and molded to be more compassionate and nurturing, more patient and kind to everyone around you.

More than just a rain-stick Ben, what I wanted to give you was the use of my legs. The strength in my hips, the balance I have in my lower body.

I wanted you to have a feeling of confidence in your little frame, a feeling of pride to stand on your own. I wanted to give you steps without braces, strength to run miles, and legs you'd be proud to show at the beach.

More than just a T-shirt Ben, what I wanted to give you was the ability to speak—to communicate without frustration, to verbalize your wants, your needs, your fears. I wanted to give you laughter with Josh, jokes on your father, shouts at me to leave you alone. I wanted to give you a way to articulate your thoughts, to let us know who you are; to tell us you love us.

More than any toys, any clothes or any items to be wrapped, what I want you both to have is my patience, my strength and my dedication to my job of Mommy. I will always hold you when you want to be held, and let you go when the time is right. I will change your sheets, kiss your owies, converse with your stuffed animal friends, smile when I want to frown, and speak in low tones when I want to scream. I will drive you where you need to go, pick up your friends, pick up your towels, pick up your undies, pick up your toys, and drop everything when you need me. My time will be divided between you two, but more than an explanation of why, what I wanted to give you was a promise to always do my best.

Though I can't give you boys what I'd really like to, I'll give you all that I can.

Love,
Mom

Christmas Memories

"**Remember that one** Christmas when…?"

"YES! *Yes*, that was a riot!"

For me, this is the best part of the holidays—when memories get revisited, and everyone gets a good belly laugh over something from the days gone by.

One Christmas when I was a kid my sister didn't get the OP jacket she had asked for. She threw a fit and became the target for ridicule in the years to come. "Oh gee—I hope this is an *OP jacket*," and "All I wanted this year was an *OP jacket*," I'd mock her endlessly. Her standard reply,

"Knock it off you little alkie." Ouch. A jab at the time I got bombed on my uncle's homemade eggnog when I was eight. I had no idea it had been laced with brandy and I had made repeated trips into his kitchen to help myself. In the middle of all the gift opening, I staggered into the living room with my thumbs tucked behind my overall straps, did a poor rendition of "Deck the Halls" in my loudest voice, then proceeded to pop both buttons off my overalls as I fell to the floor and passed out. No one could figure me out. They all got their answer though when I later awoke with a splitting headache and started spewing eggnog everywhere. Now, we weren't a religious family, but I did hear a few cries of, "Holy ****" and "For the love of God!" when the nog started flying.

In recent years, there was a holiday party where my husband had a few too many Christmas Spirits and claimed to be a palm reader. And then there's Christmas Eve 2000. A night we recall with much amusement.

We attended a church service that evening with friends, Mark and Joanne, and their daughter, Jamie. While our baby slept peacefully in his car seat, Jamie squeaked and wriggled and was passed back and forth on laps. In an attempt to occupy her during a prayer, Joanne handed Jamie a bag of Cheerios. A struggle ensued between mother and daughter, which launched the bag into the air. Cheerios rained down on the four of us. Mark and Joanne were brown in their layer of cheerio dust. Mark raised his eyebrow at Joanne and was doing a pretty impressive impersonation of The Rock, when I started giggling. I couldn't stop. Then we all started laughing- you know the kind- where you try to keep silent then your body starts shaking and you unwillingly spit out little gasps and snorts. Brad plucked cereal from my hair, while Joanne brushed dust off herself, Mark, and the folks sitting directly in front of them.

We feasted that night on franks and beans, Capri Suns and stale goldfish crackers; all courtesy of the Baker family, whose cupboards we raided since they were in Colorado. (Incidentally, Caps, Pee-Wee's, and The Boardwalk all stay closed on Christmas Eve, no matter how many times you drive by.)

So, what is this year going to bring? I don't know- but we did get an invite to a holiday party. Says here they're serving eggnog...I better find my overalls.

Hounded into a Merry iChristmas

Well, the holidays have arrived at the Dodds' house, and I think now I've officially lost it. My sense, that is. My marbles, my brains, my whatever you want to call it—it's gone.

I know this because I recently bought clothes for an iDog. I'm 34 years old. I have no business buying clothing for something that is not an actual live member of this family, especially when I fail to buy clothing for myself when needed.

Oh sure, I'll hang around in pajamas and boots, oversized sweatshirts and hoodies, but my iDog, well, she's all gussied up for winter right now.

"Oh," said Brad when he saw it. "Isn't that…festive." He exited without further comment.

"That's cute!" said my six year old, then furrowed his brow and flashed me a look that suggested he thought I should be on medication.

"Dog," signed Ben. Then he paused and signed, "Dog?" Even my non-verbal child is questioning my sanity.

I suppose this isn't all too unexpected—me losing my mind and all. I mean, just last week I asked Brad, "Does Sammy Hagar have a Christmas album?" He stared blankly at me and then quietly offered to draw me a bath. "No, I'm serious," I said as he guided me down the hall. "I think his version of "O Holy Night" would be just lovely…"

I guess it's due to the fact that I'm cooped up inside with the kids, watching them ransack a house I'm trying to sell. I feel like Alice from the Brady Bunch—just following along picking up clothes and toys, making smart-aleck comments to no one in particular. Fake smile plastered in place, head bobbing side to side. Next thing you'll know I'll be dating someone named Sam the Butcher and bringing home gifts wrapped in white paper, tied pretty with twine.

I suppose the shopping and hoopla have gotten the best of me and it's not even Christmas yet. I keep getting the same "Getting to Know You Holiday Version" e-mail, where you answer questions like "Eggnog or Hot Chocolate? Best Christmas memory? Do you hang mistletoe?" And I've now found myself answering in the lewdest way possible just trying to mock people for fun. I imagine their gasps and slack jaws and start to laugh maniacally at my laptop. I do this by myself. Ho, ho, ho.

Life has become a colorful blur of wreaths and white lights, stockings and snowflakes, and yet—in the midst of all the tinsel and glitter, the ribbon and tape, I have found that above all, I've not lost my sense of appreciation. Oh sure, common sense and fashion sense have long since escaped me, but not a sense of belonging. I seem to have held a firm grasp on what's truly important this time of year—the people in my life. My phone rings off the hook, cards pile up in the mail, neighbors pop in nightly to chit-chat, and no one questions just why I have my jammies tucked into my boots whenever I open my front door.

So yes, I may be losing my mind, but no, I'm not losing myself. Or the innate knowledge that I am loved just because I am me. And on that note, I think I'll go buy my iDog another outfit.

A Very Naked Christmas

Rarely does nudity come into play when it's time to pose for the annual holiday photo. I would never assume that, when it came time to choose pictures to include in our yearly collage, we'd be considering a snapshot or two that left little to the imagination.

Take that Christmas a few years back when I was learning how to use my new camera. Anything and everything became my subject matter, and nobody was safe from my ever-ready flash. The camera actually came before the holidays, which was great because it allowed me to click-click-click, and capture, what I thought would be perfectly natural pictures.

I came across a splendid photo op one day while Brad showered with our infant son, Joshua. I was unable to catch them unawares, but no matter—Brad happily posed holding his new son, and I joyfully aimed and shot, over and over. A roll of 24 disappeared rather quickly, but I figured there had to be at least one good one in the batch. I was careful to snap photos of the waist up and had no worries of embarrassing my husband or myself when dropping the film off at the one-hour photo lab at Albertson's.

I've since learned a thing or two since goofing around with that camera. Most importantly, the view finder captures a lot more than what the photographer sees while setting up the shot. When I returned to the store to retrieve my roll of film, I was greeted by two blushing young ladies and one smirking teen-aged boy, all holding back their chuckles. Slightly amused by their on-duty antics, I thought nothing of their giggles and snorts until I got to my car and opened the package of film. I pulled out the first shot and horrified, I saw Brad in all his glory, holding up his baby boy while the shower streamed down on the two of them. Panicked, I rifled through the rest: 24 shots of full front and back, while Brad smiled all the while.

I laughed so hard I cried. I knew Brad would see the humor in it too, so I drove home and decided to surprise him with a little holiday hardy-har-har. I chose a grand frontal shot of the two boys wearing nothing but their broad smiles and shoved it into one of those picture ready holiday cards. Inside I wrote, *Happy Holidays Love, The Dodds,* and put it on his desk in the office. It was my intent for him, and only him to see it. My idea of a joke, see…

Well, time wore on and papers piled up and we soon forgot about the joke card after our initial laugh. For a short time, I couldn't even find it. No problem. My mom has a keen eye for lost items. She even comes across things she isn't even looking for. Say, for example, naked pictures of my husband in the shower.

So, after we calmed her down and explained that YES it was a joke, and that NO the cards would not go out, we did the only thing we could think of—asked her if she'd like to pose for a perfectly natural picture.

Ghost from Christmas Past

"Boots!" Nicki squeals into my ear, "What's it gonna be? Christmas isn't the same without you…"

I can hardly believe who is shouting at me: Nicki Mickels, my best friend from childhood. I adjust the telephone to make room for the smile that has crept across my face and settle back onto the sofa for some entertaining conversation.

"Please come this year," she implores, "No one has seen you in ages and we want to make sure you're wearing your boots."

What a joke. She's referring to the Christmas when we were 10 and I got a pair of black, high-heeled boots from my Uncle Elwood. They went up to my knees and were no doubt intended for an older, more developed young lady. I loved them. Put them on first thing under my nightie and had no interest in opening any other presents after that. My mother was mortified. She hissed at my father, "Those are *hooker boots* and she will NOT leave the house in them." On the contrary, I marched through the neighborhood straight to Nicki's house that very day. Upon arrival I held up a leg and announced loudly, "My mom calls these my hooker boots!" Silence.

"Well, that's dumb," says Nicki, "There aren't even hooks on them."

"I KNOW!" I nodded, reveling in my mother's foolishness. Her parents laughed and shared a look, though it was years before I fully understood why.

So, I tell Nicki now, "Oh I don't know...maybe I'll be there. Am I going to have to pull you off any strange boys in the laundry room?"

One year, when Nicki and I were in college, we spent the holiday at her parents' house and enjoyed a few cocktails throughout the evening. Sometime during the night, Nicki had disappeared with someone else's date and I went on a quick hunt to find the pair before the date did. Sure enough, she was lip locked with the boy beside the washing machine. Nothing much came of it until the following year when I learned that Nicki's mom had married the boy's dad and I got to rib her for kissing her stepbrother at a holiday party.

She sighs dramatically. "He wasn't my brother then. Anyway, what about you? Are you going to make out with any mysterious men under the mistletoe this year?"

"God, I hope so." We laugh long and hard. It's a standing joke between us—she loves to be single, has never been able to understand being married. I always call her my wicked half. In fact, in one of my wedding pictures, Nicki and I are standing together and for some unknown reason, when the print was developed, she is surrounded in a red aura, while I am in white. "Look, look!" I had told her, "I always knew I was pure and you were the daughter of Satan!"

She tries to tempt me into coming to her parent's house again with an offer to see her older brother, "Todd will be there..." she sings, "I know how much you always liked Toddles." The last time I saw "Toddles," he had shown up with an angry wife and a set of twins that sounded remarkably like howler monkeys.

"I'll come if Uncle Artie is there," I tell her. Nicki's Uncle Artie was actually her grandmother's brother. A relic of a guy, he thought no child was too young to drink out of martini glasses. And not just any glasses— he'd hand out the ones with naked ladies for stems to all the kids. One year Uncle Artie waltzed me around the living room singing Christmas carols in my ear. He was so wildly out of tune I thought he was kidding. Until I looked closely into his watery blue eyes and saw that he was not. It was at that moment I developed a profound respect for older people and a love so deep for the song "Oh Holy Night," that I buy a new Christmas compact disc every year with that song on it.

"Come on Boots, say you'll come." Nicki tells me now, "My grandma forgives you for trying to shut her head in the fridge so many years ago." More laughter.

"That was an accident! I didn't see her there." The same year I almost took out her granny, Nicki had a little too much brandy in her eggnog and showed everyone there her new boob job. I sat a tad envious at the table, my arms crossed protectively over my chest and tried not to be impressed with what my little boobs could aspire. She got the approval of the crowd, especially since the year before she had modeled her new nose for us and no one could really tell the difference.

I haven't been to Nicki's in years. I think of the last time I attended a Mickels' Christmas party; her sister's date was a self-absorbed fire-eater from a local carnival. The man stunk of lighter fluid all night and Nicki and I discussed the idea of dropping a match in his lap to see if he'd ignite and spare us all. Once I got married and Nicki moved out of state, events such as holiday parties seemed to stretch further and further apart.

While Nicki yaps in my ear, I remember that while Brad and I were at a Christmas party this year, we saw a girl who was wearing boots that laced all the way up her thighs and disappeared under her very short skirt. Brad had nudged me, "Why don't you wear boots like that?" I rolled my eyes. "I do. I wear them every day if you must know, I just make sure to have on those fuzzy slippers you like so much when you get home from work." Boots like that would be perfect for a Mickels' holiday party.

I interrupt her, "Yes! I'll be there. I know just the boots I'm going to wear too!"

New Year's Eve to Remember

Few people can recall what they did for New Year's Eve in 1998. I, on the other hand, will never forget what I did, where I was, and whom I was with. I can hardly look at a game of *Clue* the same.

"Yahoo! I can't believe I am coming to California for New Years!" my cousin Casey can hardly contain her excitement as she spills forth her plans for the holiday. "I have always dreamed of spending the New Year in sunny California!" she rambles on and on as the sinking feeling of panic begins to warm my chest.

"Um…" I try to intercede.

"And then we can go to Tahoe, and then San Francisco, and then Monterey, okay? I can't wait!" She is on a roll. Casey's sense of geography was a tad out of whack, but I hesitated to inform her of that just yet. I'd allow her to find out just how hard it would be to see all that in a mere four days.

"Well…" I make another attempt at a conversation diversion. No luck.

"And find me a date too!" Uh oh. Now that would be hard. I was married, my friends were married, their friends were married, even their pets were all hitched. Rounding up a date for New Year's Eve was no small task. Was I sweating? I wiped my brow, yes, indeed I was.

I jotted down her flight information and tried to fight off the feeling of dread that was slowly making a home in the pit of my stomach. I knew Brad wasn't going to like this.

Though Brad adores Casey now, back in 1998 he thought of her as a dangerous fireball. Too wild, too crazy, too out of control. Perhaps too tempting a lifestyle for his wife. She and I have a menagerie of memories involving each other, piercings, tattoos, boys, cars, and her trip out to see me at University of California, Davis, in 1993, a little one-week vacation we don't talk about in front of too many people.

370   *This Crazy Little Thing Called Life*

"Good news! You'll never guess…" I say cheerfully to Brad later that night, "It's the greatest thing…really. You're gonna love this…" I begin my presentation, making sure to smile widely the entire time.

"Here? She wants to come here for New Year? But why? We don't do anything fun…" What? We've been to Tahoe, we've been to Konocti Harbor, we've been to the City…all for New Year's. Apparently, this year, plans were set to be a tad lower key. He groaned. "I don't know what to do to show her a good time. She's used to huge parties and famous people."

I stare at him. Casey grew up in Otisville, Michigan. She called me once during her senior year of high school to tell me how excited she was—the town was getting a Taco Hut. "We're talking about my cousin, right?"

Brad decided—we'd take her to the family cabin in Twain Harte. She'd love it. I started taking antacids. When I pitched the idea to Casey, I was sure my voice cracked due to forced enthusiasm. It was a hard sell. Twain Harte versus San Francisco or the South Shore of Tahoe. No big cities, no bright lights. No parties carousing with strange good-looking young men. I didn't even mention finding her a date to Brad, I knew better than that.

Fast forward a few weeks. It is New Year's Eve and there we sat. The three of us at the cabin all engaged in our seventh hour of *Clue*. Casey was a great sport. I, sadly, was not. As the night wore on, my patience wore thin. I was young. I was hip. I wanted to show my cousin a good time, not be cloistered in some stuffy cabin playing board games to ring in the New Year. Around 11 p.m., Brad announced he was off to bed. My last straw.

After some colorful dialogue, the three of us were no longer sitting in the cabin, but sitting in some empty dive called The Old Doghouse in Sonora. Us and the bartender. He was kind—gave us all hats and whistles. I can't imagine what Casey thought. She was too polite to say anything. Just drank her weight in beer, since this was a bar that didn't serve hard alcohol. I later held her hair while she barfed in the parking lot. A possible sign of success, depending on your perspective.

Brad felt bad. So bad in fact, that the next day he took Casey and I to see *Titanic* at a local mountain theatre to make up for it. Not the best choice in viewing when one wants to lift another's spirits. I sobbed so hard on the drive home, Brad pulled over so I could go into Denny's and compose myself. Casey stood rubbing my back while I ordered a hot chocolate for the road. "Oh sweetheart," a kind, elderly waitress said to me, "Did you just see Titanic?" Weeping, I nodded and squeaked a pitiful 'yes' then accepted her hug like a cozy blanket around me. She patted my hair gently and whispered "Shh...there, there now dear," softly in my ear. Over her shoulder, I smiled at Casey and then we started to giggle.

She clutched my arm and dragged me from the restaurant. "Seeing you hug some strange lady was worth this whole trip." By the time we got back to the truck we were hooting and nudging one another. Brad just shook his head.

Ringing in 1998. I can't tell you what I did any other year, but seven hours of *Clue*, a bar that can't serve hard liquor, and bawling in the arms of a Denny's waitress are markers of one New Year's Eve I will never forget.

23
Hitting the Road

Preparing for the Family Vacation

"You can't tie the suitcases on top of the truck tonight," I tell Brad, "They'll get stolen." He is red faced and doing his best to maintain his composure.

This is probably the last piece of advice he is going to take from me. It's been a day of suggestions, corrections, questions, and lastly modifications. Packing for a family trip certainly hasn't brought us any closer together. His idea of trip preparation and mine obviously differ.

Where I see the importance of doing laundry the day before, he has no problem running the dryer and stuffing damp clothing into his bag as the children and I wait in the car.

While I neatly stack graham crackers, diluted juice, pretzels, and sugar free snacks into the cooler, Brad hovers about, his arms laden with licorice, soda, fruit bites, and Cheesy Poofs.

I like to tidy the house a bit before we leave so as to avoid coming home to more responsibility. At the last minute he'll remember the valuable tools on his work truck and pile them in the entryway to greet us when we return.

We seem to work against one another at times. This never really happened before the children came along.

Brad approaches me as I am pondering how many diapers to pack for our youngest. I stand gazing into a suitcase considering bringing an extra bag just for the bare essentials. He sees the question on my face and suggests, "We can buy diapers when we get there. Pack extra clothes for the boys—they'll need that more anyway."

"More than diapers?? Are you serious??"

He glares at me. "Who are you anyway? You used to be so much fun. You never used to care so much about organization. When did you become such a bossy boots?"

He does have a point. Back in the day I used to jump in his truck and be unconcerned about the destination. There was no such thing as bare essentials, orderliness and making good time. I opted for candy snacks and regular soda too. Did the births of my children thrust me headfirst into the semblance of every other mom I swore I'd not emulate?

I used to flit around and say, "Come on! Let's go! We'll grab what we need on the way..." while he stood rooted to his spot, one finger in the air, and touted his famous seven P's: Proper Prior Planning Prevents Piss Poor Performance. We were such opposites even back then.

And now look at us. He is the free spirit I once prided myself on being and I am...my mother. Oh my.

Upon realization of this ghastly truth, I stuff a few more pairs of jeans into the suitcase for the kids, shut the lid, throw a wicked grin in his direction and say, "Come on...let's go...we'll grab what we need on the way!"

Going on Holiday

I counted our bags: 7. Plus a double stroller and two car seats. Not to mention the twin set of carry-on backpacks for the boys, my two carry-on bags, Brad's briefcase and his mom's shoulder bag. Ah, the family vacation. We are all screaming and writhing, some sobbing and sniffling, a few scratching and pinching and we haven't even left for the airport yet. And so it goes.

We did pretty good, considering. I had begged our pediatrician for a sedative for our youngest (almost two) and figured I could slip one to the three year old if necessary. Heck, I could slip one to myself if I got desperate. He denied me this request and suggested Children's Benadryl. I packed the Adult Vicks instead. I wasn't taking any chances.

Two flights later we arrived in Omaha. Vacation in Nebraska? Why not the Caribbean or Jamaica? Well, we are simple folk. The family farm in Norfolk holds a lot of appeal to us, especially since it comes complete with one John Deere tractor, two loving family members, three friendly horses, and countless opportunities to laugh, cry, and take lots of pictures. I couldn't imagine going anywhere else.

With both Brad and I having deep roots in Nebraska, we go "back home" to see both sides of the family. This time it was for a wedding and then some much needed down time on the farm. Down time would ordinarily involve rest, but this trip—we brought the kids. Boys. Both under age four. Rest was not an ingredient in this recipe. I should have seen this coming. I thought I had. After all, I had begged and pleaded with Brad's mom to come with us. Spend a little time with her parents, visit with her sister and brother-in-law…you know, perhaps take a boy or two off our hands if someone started going a little ape on us. She happily complied but even with her help, I found myself wanting to stay tucked inside that warm fluffy bed covered in quilts more than once.

We took Josh out trick or treating in 30-degree weather. None of us were prepared for the cold. We frequented the local Walmart to make sporadic purchases of turtlenecks and hats. I stood in the frost to take pictures of the kids on the tractor, on the horses, in the dingy on the lake, and then trotting up driveways to get their holiday loot. Quite a change from our traditional end of October short sleeves and capris.

Josh was not ready to go home when the time came. I was itching to give him a dose of Vicks, but held off in case it knocked him out before we got to the airport. I knew I'd be forced to hear him drone on about needing his own tractor for two flights, plus have to explain why we didn't have horses in our backyard and then conclude by presenting the (now well-rehearsed) dissertation on the importance of seatbelts on airplanes. That said, I still didn't want to miss his excitement of the take-off. I was hoping he'd yell, "I'm flying! I'm REALLY, REALLY flying!" as he had en route to Nebraska just 10 days before.

He didn't fail me. Not only did he squeal with delight, he sang flying songs, cloud songs, airplane songs, and then waved at all the passengers who turned to stare at us. I was proud of my boy. Even when he announced his need to use the bathroom to go *big, huge tremendous potty*, I stayed proud. What mom wouldn't?

All in all, a good trip. Would I recommend air travel with two young kids? Of course. I'd also recommend Adult Vicks. And the occasional in-flight Bloody Mary.

Doing Las Vegas

I've been to hell in a handbasket. I went eye to eye with the Red Devil himself and came away a stronger woman.

Okay, okay, so I didn't actually go to hell, per se, and I didn't really stare down Satan, but I did go to Las Vegas and I'm pretty sure most of the folks I came in contact with were on parade in one of his evil fashion shows. Now I suppose it sounds as if l had a horrible time. On the contrary, it was a ball. Life in Las Vegas just happens to be the exact opposite of how I live now. So, one can imagine the culture shock this small-town farm girl underwent upon arrival in Sin City.

So how did all of this come about? Our good friends, Chris and Krisanne Jackson, wanted to help us celebrate our wedding anniversary. Dinner and dancing? Nope. A fruit basket perhaps? Uh-uh. Cookie bouquet? Not this time. They opted to treat us to Las Vegas instead.

V-day arrived and so did we…at the airport that is, with our free drink coupons in hand. I believe when Chris slurred, "I'll keep drinking triples till I'm seeing double and acting single!" that statement may have been the foreshadowing of what was to come for the next three days.

The bright lights of the big city had me draped across Krisanne's lap, gaping out the window in order to see The Strip from the air. As we deplaned, we were hit with gusts of 105-degree heat, quite a change from what we flew out of. Although it was well after 10 p.m., I was amazed to see how many people lined the streets and filed in and out of hotels.

Afraid to spoil anyone's fun, I didn't mention how exhausted I was, I concealed every yawn that managed to escape. I fell into step with all the high rollers just a short time later, and by 2 a.m. I was throwing money around like I was the banker for *Monopoly*. (I even called a waitress "Honey" while I tossed her a tip and then dismissed her with a swift flick of my wrist. I'm a quick learner.)

Each day just seemed to mimic the one before. As did each night, unfortunately. We did, however, get to squeeze in a show. I don't recommend anyone else put themselves through any "Free admission with purchase of a drink," shows in the middle of the afternoon. These must be the ones staffed by all the hopefuls who just arrived in Vegas and trying to make it big. And oh, did I mention it was topless? I mentally prepared the next week's grocery list while young starlets shook their money makers just inches from my face. I tried to look polite and encouraging in their choice of career while I smiled and nodded, but truthfully, I wanted to ask, "Why?" At one point I leaned over and whispered to Chris, "Do you think their moms know they do this?"

An incident worth mentioning would be the narcoleptic cab driver. Yep, one gentleman fell asleep while toting· us around. He dozed peacefully in traffic while Krisanne shouted, "SIR! SIR! Please wake up and GO!"

And then there was the sarcastic cab driver. He was the one who, when I innocently asked, "So have you ever won really big here?" answered dryly, "Yeah lady, that's why I drive a cab for a living."

I tried to cover my humiliation by saying, "Well for me, a couple of hundred bucks is really big." His reply was directed at the men in the cab, "Don't any of you let HER pay me tonight."

Aside from the entertainment we received out on the streets, we did eat well, drink well, sleep well and do some shopping. By Sunday we were more than ready to go home. We missed the kids and wanted to get that small town feeling back.

Did we win big? Nope. But we did learn why most folks refer to that particular strip of desert as "Lost Wages."

Nothing Like a Family Trip

There's nothing like a family vacation. "I can see your mom from here...check her out in her hot pink pants." We are pulling up to our cabin in Twain Harte where my parents have invited us to stay with them through the weekend. I peer over the steering wheel, since I am driving and sure enough, there's Paula donning some pretty intense pants, her ensemble made complete with a fantastically bright white T-shirt. I squint my eyes. Seeing us, she darts out into the street and dramatically waves us down. A little unnecessary since we are the only vehicle approaching, but that's her style.

She does the arm gesture for 'roll-down-your window' which starts me snickering right away. Brad rolls his down and tells her, "We have power windows now Paula, just do this…" he makes an inchworm gesture with his pointer finger. She ignores the sarcasm, and points to the cabin asking, "Well…what do you think?" Big grin of anticipation, eyebrows up, head bobbing. We are silent. Glance at one another and then, "Uh… it's a cabin?"

"See?" My dad yells at her from the porch, "I knew they wouldn't see it where you put it! Hidden, I tell you! It's G-D hidden from sight." He crumples his beer can. I feel a slight wave of hysteria coming on and try to control my smile.

They have obviously been arguing over where to place the welcome sign, which I now spy on the railing. She proceeds to have us stay idling in the middle of the street so she can reposition it time and again, looking to us for our approval. It's her grand ta-da motion at each placement that has Brad quietly groaning while he rubs his forehead. I continue nodding and smiling at her while I repeatedly sneak glances at my cell phone. Hasn't anyone sent me a text by now? Must I participate fully in this family event?

Since four people cannot decide where it looks best, the sign is moved to the table on the deck. Face down. "Well, come on in!" bellows my dad, "We got the kids some treats!" Treats? From the same people who thought Grape Nuts was a sugar cereal? Curious now, I tag along hoping for a treat too.

Packages of donuts, pastries, chips, cookies and candy line the countertop. I stop in my tracks and look to my mom for explanation. I am wondering if they realize we are only staying one night. I glance over to the fruit bowl. Empty. Who are these people? Surely not the same duo who insisted I eat fruit daily and considered a granola bar to be as hazardous as a Milky Way. We were lucky to get low-fat milk or real yogurt when I was a kid.

Since most of my afternoon was spent rationing Josh's sugar intake and thrusting a toothbrush at him whenever he sprung by me, the change in temperature from warm to cool by early evening caught me by surprise. By the time I tucked the kids into their beds, I was begging my mom to shut the windows and turn on a space heater. "Nonsense!" she sang out, "Put on a sweater!"

I was kind of hoping she'd realize I was already wearing *her* sweater as well as my dad's flannel. All night long I shivered and shuddered, finally getting up to grab the spare sleeping bag out of a closet. I draped it over Ben and myself while Brad snoozed on the sofa under a window in the living room. Throughout the night I heard him rustle and turn, bumping the blinds and then swearing. Ben slept soundly next to me on a mattress that was remarkably comparable to a slab of cement. As I lay there trembling, I could feel the bruises forming on my shoulder and hip.

At 6:45 a.m. my dad bounded up the stairs and woke us all, extending a joyful—yet deafening—invitation to go fishing. I declined but volunteered Brad for the trip. I had, after all, unloaded the truck by myself while he napped in a deck chair the day before.

When Josh inquired to Grandma's whereabouts, Grandpa told him she was downstairs painting her face. "Sears weather-beater," he chuckled. I had forgotten about some of his good one-liners.

I was still lying in bed with Ben when my mom emerged, all polished and spruced for a day in the mountains. She poked her head into the room and eyed the sleeping bag. "Oh Carolyn! Your bed didn't have any blankets on it! You should have said something!" She gave me a pouty lip. The scent of hairspray and Oil of Olay hung in the air between us.

I rubbed my eyes, "I might pick up a mattress for this box-spring you made me sleep on last night."

She doesn't appreciate sarcasm first thing in the morning, "That bed comes from a line of quality mattresses young lady, it's called something or another." I know enough to understand that the mattress doesn't have a name, but my mother will make one up just to prove her point.

"The Foundation?" I suggest, "The Slab? The Plank?" I start snorting. Brad enters the room, fanning the air and making a face. He does a mock imitation of Paula hair-spraying her hair, her armpits, the room in general.

"I slept like crap last night," he flops down onto the bed. "Ow—how did you get any sleep on this?"

"Tell me about it. I have abrasions from this thing. What time are we leaving?"

He shouts out to my mom, "Hey- it's plenty cool in here now. Can you turn off the AC?" We both start laughing out loud.

"You two are a riot," she shouts back, "And anyway…what time are you leaving?" Nothing like a family vacation.

Pre-boarding and The Puffer

"Is that our flight?" I am worried. "Did they just announce pre-boarding for our flight?" On my barstool, I lean over my friends to check the airport terminal, and sure enough, I see people lining up at our gate to board the plane. Hastily, I down the rest of my drink and start waving my finger around to encourage others to do the same. I don't know why, but I have this innate fear that I am going to miss my plane, no matter how early I'm at an airport. As soon as I step into a terminal, my internal distress signal kicks into high gear. All logic escapes me but for the known whereabouts of my boarding pass and picture ID. I continuously double check the size of my carry-on bags, and endlessly doubt that I've gotten the correct gate number. I'm a nervous flier, thus my current affair with a Bloody Mary.

"You know," my friend is in no hurry to leave the bar. "They aren't actually *pre-boarding* right now. They're *boarding*. Technically," he pauses for dramatic effect, "anything done before stepping onto the plane qualifies as *pre-boarding*." We stare at him. The logic is crystal. "That's true," my husband brightens considerably. "Right now, WE are pre-boarding." He holds up his glass to toast the profound realization of this thought. One more round of pre-boarding, then we got on our plane.

The redefining of the term came just in time. Earlier in the day I had gotten stuck in "The Puffer." I had never seen The Puffer anywhere before and to watch it in action was thrilling. The Puffer is a new addition to routine security checks. One at a time, will-be fliers enter what looks like a telephone booth. Air puffs out at the puffee in an amusing puffing sequence, then the person emerges to a smiling crowd of viewers, all hoping to be chosen for a turn in The Puffer too. The idea is that foreign particles will be puffed from your body, travel into a ventilation system and scanned for determination of anything dangerous. Our group lucked out. All of us were chosen for a random puffing experience.

"Hold your shirt down ma'am," I was instructed. I smiled and waved at the crowd then stepped into the booth. Puff, puff, puff, puff, puff… puff, puff. I tried to exit. My door remained locked. Inside, I was unaware that alarms were sounding outside the box all around me. Through the glass, I saw onlookers' smiles turn to looks of confusion. Suspicion. Hesitated alarm. The security guards quickly moved into huddle formation and planned my future. I raised my hand to knock on the window and instantly had a guard opposite the glass from me. He mouthed, "Ma'am— keep your hand OFF the door. OFF the door, please." He patted his baton in the holster on his hip.

I then got re-puffed. Ill-prepared for this round, I stood in shock as my shirt flew up around me. The previous looks of confusion were replaced by giggles and smirking. Funny. Ha, ha. When I did step out, Officer Pat-The-Baton said, "Hmm…maybe you wear too much perfume." Oh yes, of course. I have on no makeup and own Tom's All Natural everything. My shirt is crocheted, my hair has air-dried into ringlets, and I am bedecked in jewelry my children have made from beads they've plucked out of our sofa. It makes perfect sense that he assumes I marinate in Jean Nate. I intended to reply, "I wear no perfume," yet was too discombobulated to articulate myself well. Instead, I squeaked, "But I don't wear deodorant!" to which some wisenheimer in the crowd piped up, "There you go! Mystery solved!"

I stomped off, directly to the bar, where I sat anxiously keeping an eye on my gate. "Don't sweat it, you're the only one here who can say she was stuck in The Puffer during pre-boarding," Brad tells me. True.

Adventures in Travel, via the Airline

You want five bucks for a Bloody Mary?" I am astonished. Yet, not so insulted that I don't rifle through my wallet and pull out the dough. Sighing, I hand over the cash and then scan the airport for a place to sit. To say it's been one hell of a weekend would be putting it lightly; if anyone deserves this five-dollar beverage, it's me.

I'm heading home from Kansas after a four-day tour of duty spent with my out-of-town hubby. I'm looking forward to seeing my children again, but not anticipating another month without my main man. My emotions are in combat—eager to hug my boys but distressed at saying yet another goodbye to their father. That childhood feeling of airport adventures clashes with the awe and fascination of watching the crowds shuffle by.

As if by cue, I am jolted from thought by a woman on a cell phone, "You bastard!" she sobs. "You are an absolute son of a b***ch!" She is weeping as she runs by but stops short and carefully scrutinizes her reflection in the window of the restaurant I am looking through. It's like one-way security glass, because I am staring at her square in the eye and she has no clue. The absurdity of this alone makes me snicker. She adjusts her hair, checks her lip-gloss, and then continues to yell obscenities as she rushes off. I cackle and take another sip of my drink.

On my perch I look around and see the normal airport throng: a family in a mad dash for their gate, the father struggling with the bags as the mother struggles with the kids. And a dog. I had no idea that was legal. Interesting. A young exec trots by, his glances shared between his watch and his phone. A mass of airline personnel all wearing white shirts and badges. None of them carrying drinks, thankfully.

Seeing the time, I head for the gate and, once tossing my bags onto the conveyer, am pulled aside for that ever-delightful body search for weapons and chemicals. I don't understand how I was selected for this, but having no choice, I subject myself to careful scrutiny. Why the wand starts beeping near my crotch is a mystery, but the even bigger reason for concern is why the attendant finds it funny, repeatedly wands that general area and starts beeping out a tune. While I am wondering how to tell the attendant to knock it off, I spy my luggage being studied. It is turned, picked at, prodded, and then flipped around by a crew of gentlemen who look remarkably like a group of monkeys inspecting something for fleas. My low-rise pants have slipped so low that I am hoping they stay on my hips and don't embarrass me further by dropping to my ankles.

Once on board I settle in and ignore the happily chatting gal who flopped down next to me. I'm in no mood for conversation, but she fails to recognize this in between her giggles about her boyfriend, small complaints about airline food, and the anxiety she suffers while flying. I pray she doesn't pass out in my lap. She yaps. I practice medication techniques. She laughs. I shut my eyes. She nudges me. I flip out. She isn't talking to me anymore.

My stomach growls and I immediately regret not stuffing my bags full of snacks. I say nothing as Chatty Cathy pulls out a bag of Oreos and nibbles away. I want to scream and it's not because I hate flying, but because I see First Class is being served a meal and I think I can hear music coming from up there. Are they playing Charades? Economy seats suck.

After a few dips and swerves, I carefully watch the flight attendants to see if their panic matches mine. I am clenching the armrests and riding out the bumps and drops, praying and negotiating with God to spare me. My fear somewhat subsides when, after peeking out through one slit eyelid, I see the First Classers clinking wine glasses and laughing heartily. Is that a flight attendant on someone's lap?

In an effort to ease some tension, I shift my focus to what I am coming home to. Two boys who have stayed with grandparents for four days, one cat who will have shredded everything in sight, a stack of mail that needs serious attention, countless bills to pay, an insurance agent to meet with—courtesy of a small backyard fire that spontaneously ignited the day after I left, and numerous appointments I have avoided until this month. I shudder.

"That'll be five dollars, sweetie," the flight attendant takes my money and hands me a drink. I can't believe what they want for Bloody Mary's these days.

Defining Vacation

Here's the thing—if you go somewhere, and it can be anywhere at all, but you still engage in the exact same activities you do at home, is that considered to be a vacation?

For example, we just went to Yosemite. As a family. Packed the kids, packed the truck, packed everything we thought we needed to make this trip the best vacation ever. But after about three hours of whining, unpacking, locating specific toys, changing diapers, and filling sippy cups, I began to question just who was on vacation. Even my husband, who ordinarily can be found reclined somewhere once we reach our destination, was seen huffing and puffing as he maneuvered our luggage out from under the kayak. I heard him mutter a few swears, then spotted our bags arc through the air before landing with "whumps" onto the parking lot. My guess was he didn't feel relaxed either.

I juggled the youngest, a diaper bag, a few stray toys, and an older brother while we waited for Daddy. During Brad's struggle with the oars, I contemplated our situation. Doesn't vacation mean "relaxation", or have I been delusional all this time? When anticipating a vacation in the past, I have always thought of it as a switch from the norm, something to break up the monotony of everyday life. Maybe even take in a few sights…

Granted I did look around Yosemite, I'm not a complete dolt. I did see the wonder and beauty of where we were. I just saw it from behind a stroller, or over the shoulder of a child I was wrestling. I did look out my hotel window once—when I was putting the kids to bed at night. And I was able to see the valley floor, from a bus window, where I sat with my autistic child for hours one day as we cruised around once he discovered he liked the bus there, and nothing else.

When one of the children complained of a sore ear, while another climbed me like a jungle gym, I blew the stray hairs out of my eyes, tried to heave up one kid who had gone completely boneless on me and asked Brad, "Are we having fun yet?" I didn't hear his reply, just felt my ponytail yanked, and wet sticky hands slid down my cheek. I smelled like saliva. "Ow…ow…ow…my ear huuuuurts…" the oldest child began writhing at my feet. I stared at him and wondered if he was actually mine.

"Your eyes look glazed over," Brad told me later. "You look a little removed."

I said nothing. Just continued passing out snacks to the kids and tried to figure out what we paid for this experience. On the second day Brad and I took our oldest son kayaking. Beautiful views, stunning scenery, ice cold water. I know this because for the hour trek downstream, Josh felt compelled to splash me. Repeatedly. I held off splashing him back because I knew, in less than a second, I would have dunked him and then I'd have to live with the repercussions of that move the rest of the way downstream.

I was beginning to hear circus music in the depths of my mind.

"What were we thinking?' Brad whispered one night after the kids had fallen asleep. "We look like hell." It was true. We did look pretty bad, plus we hadn't eaten more than fruits snacks and granola bars for the last two days. "I need a real meal!" he hissed as he drop-kicked an empty juice box across the room.

"Do you want me to make you a drink?" I offered. I held up the Pedialyte. "Surely we can find a mixer for this…" He growled in reply.

"Let's just agree right now that this doesn't qualify as our vacation, okay? This is our *family outing*," I suggested. On cue, one of the sleeping kids passed gas.

"So, a vacation is anything minus the children?" Brad clarified; eyebrows raised. I nodded.

"I can be at a carwash, or a deli, or even at work and I can consider that a vacation, right?" he inquired.

I visualize my trips to any of these places with people I have given birth to. "Yes, if you are solo, then you are on vacation."

"Well then, I'll be out in a second." He stepped into the bathroom. "I'm going on vacation."

Update

Since 2011, I have divided my time between raising two boys, pursuing and obtaining multiple teaching credentials and delivering instruction to both General Education and Special Education students up through eighth grade.

Lessons in co-parenting commenced, the dating world opened its doors, and what was once a "Nuclear American Family" gradually evolved into an impressive and unique model of parenthood. A new definition of family was born, and as we grew in numbers to include new partners, each of us trudged ahead, hyper aware of the amount of patience, acceptance, trust and effort it takes to foster and nurture a safe place for the boys, free from drama or trauma that divorce may inspire. We put in the work, and the boys thrived in two homes.

Now in his 20s, Josh studies forestry at Oregon State University. He continues to add beauty, comedy and perspective to the world. Still an expert-level communicator, still a lover of the outdoors, still a kind and compassionate, easy-going old soul, Josh left California to spread his wings in pursuit of a higher education. Ben, also in his 20s, lives at home full time with a steady rotation of care providers who bless all of our lives immensely. His golden soul shines through a wide smile and his laughter is music to our ears. There are simply not enough words to adequately describe the privilege of raising a child with special needs. There are even less words to describe seeing that child into adulthood and trying to prepare the world for him, rather than him for the world. My silly, sweet, inquisitive sons have grown into kind, thoughtful, warm hearted young men who have entered adulthood with their adventurous spirits and profound appreciation of where they come from.

Since 2011, I have divided my time between raising the boys, pursuing and obtaining teaching credentials, standing in the front of student classrooms aged kindergarten through eighth grade, and delivering instruction. Committees needed members, clubs needed leaders, and meetings needed to be facilitated. Families needed to be advocated, resources needed to be shared, the world of special education needed a new voice. I took it all on. Still active with the Alisa Ann Ruch Burn Foundation, I've continued to counsel burn survivors ages 5 to17 each year.

In 2021 my first children's book, *Tessa's Tall Tales*, was published. It's an accomplishment I am humbled to have attained. In 2015, I met the man I am still with today. A real estate guru, Jim is the most ethical, honest and hard working person. I've been raising his daughter, now our daughter, since then. An entire new book of columns could be written just about the difference in raising a teenage daughter 15 years after raising two sons. Lauren keeps me on my toes in all ways and is the living example of an apple not falling far from a tree. My mom always hoped I'd raise a daughter exactly like myself. My children are fortunate to have both sets of grandparents alive and local, all active in their worlds. Blessings abound. Yes, since pen met paper in 2003 much has changed. My depth of gratitude has not. This new crazy life goes on.

Tessa's Tall Tales

by Carolyn Joyce Dodds as illustrated by June Gomez

San Francisco Bay Area native and author, Carolyn Joyce Dodds, creates *Tessa's Tall Tales*, a quick-witted, whimsical tale intended for school-age children. Tessa delights in telling tall tales but has she stopped telling the truth altogether? Tessa and her parents must navigate the waters between truth and falsehood without crushing creativity. It is a challenge for all imaginative children. Readers will delight in the adventures of wolf cub Tessa, her parents and friends as fancifully drawn by Academy of Art College graduate, June Gomez.

The author confesses to be an inveterate, storyteller herself. "Children are instinctive storytellers often unable or unwilling to distinguish between truths and untruths. The knowing parent encourages their young child's creative gifts while carefully guiding them away from deceit. Tessa and her parents navigate that journey as the little wolf explores space, seeks pirate treasure and awaits the tooth fairy."

ISBN: 978-0-578-76211-1

Available at area bookstores, independent retailers, online retailers, Amazon, Barnes & Noble and eBay.

Follow the adventures of Tessa, her parents, classmates and imaginary friends on her website: *http://TessasTallTales.com*, Instagram and Facebook.

CPSIA information can be obtained
at www.ICGtesting.com
Printed in the USA
BVHW080010180323
660664BV00006B/159